About the Underground Guide Series

Welcome to the underground!

Are you tired of all the fluff—books that tell you what you already know, ones that assume you're an idiot and treat you accordingly, or dwell on the trivial while completely ignoring the tough parts?

Good. You're in the right place.

Series Editor Woody Leonhard and Addison-Wesley bring you the Underground Guides—serious books that tackle the tough questions head-on but still manage to keep a sense of humor (not to mention a sense of perspective!). Every page is chock full of ideas you can put to use right away. We'll tell you what works and what doesn't—no bull, no pulled punches. We don't kowtow to the gods of the industry, we won't waste your time or your money, and we *will* treat you like the intelligent computer user we know you are.

Each Underground Guide is written by somebody who's been there—a working stiff who's suffered through the problems you're up against right now—and lived to tell about it. You're going to strike a rich vein of hard truth in these pages, and come away with a wealth of information you can put to use all day, every day.

So come along as we go spelunking where no book has gone before. Mind your head, and don't step in anything squishy. There will be lots of unexpected twists and turns... and maybe a laugh or two along the way.

The Underground Guide Series

Woody Leonhard, Series Editor

The Underground Guide to Word for Windows™:
Slightly Askew Advice from a WinWord Wizard

Woody Leonhard

The Underground Guide to Excel 5.0 for Windows™:
Slightly Askew Advice from Two Excel Wizards

Lee Hudspeth and Timothy-James Lee

The Underground Guide to UNIX®:
Slightly Askew Advice from a UNIX Guru

John Montgomery

The Underground Guide to Microsoft® Office, OLE, and VBA:
Slightly Askew Advice from Two Integration Wizards

Lee Hudspeth and Timothy-James Lee

The Underground Guide to
Microsoft® Office, OLE, and VBA

Slightly
    Askew
        Advice
            from
                Two
                    Integration
                        Wizards

Lee Hudspeth
and
Timothy-James Lee

ADDISON-WESLEY PUBLISHING COMPANY

Reading, Massachusetts • Menlo Park, California • New York • Don Mills, Ontario
Wokingham, England • Amsterdam • Bonn • Sydney • Singapore • Tokyo
Madrid • San Juan • Paris • Seoul • Milan • Mexico City • Taipei

Many of the designations used by manufacturers and sellers to distinguish their products are claimed as trademarks. Where those designations appear in this book, and Addison-Wesley was aware of a trademark claim, the designations have been printed in initial capital letters or all capital letters.

The authors and publishers have taken care in preparation of this book, but make no expressed or implied warranty of any kind and assume no responsibility for errors or omissions. No liability is assumed for incidental or consequential damages in connection with or arising out of the use of the information or programs contained herein.

Library of Congress Cataloging-in-Publication Data

ISBN 0-201-41035-4

Series Hack: Woody Leonhard
Sponsoring Editor: Kathleen Tibbetts
Project Manager: Eleanor McCarthy
Production Coordinator: Deborah McKenna
Cover design: Jean Seal
Text Design: Kenneth L. Wilson, Wilson Graphics & Design
Set in 10 point Palatino by Rob Mauhar and Mike Drummond

1 2 3 4 5 6 7 8 9 -MA- 9998979695
First printing, April, 1995

Addison-Wesley books are available for bulk purchases by corporations, institutions, and other organizations. For more information please contact the Corporate, Government and Special Sales Department at (800) 238-9682.

Contents

Foreword

One of the big advantages touted in the Windows suite marketing wars is Microsoft Office's ability to link various applications together: it's supposed to be easy to put an Excel spreadsheet in your WinWord document, for example, or to feed names for a mass mailing from an Access database into the WinWord mail merge.

Hey, it's a great theory. When all this interapplication stuff works, it's mighty cool. When it doesn't work, you can waste hours tearing your hair out trying to figure out what you did wrong, only to discover that you didn't do anything wrong at all—the applications themselves are all screwed up.

If you've ever tried to interconnect two MS Office applications, this is the book you need. Lots of books will show you how to paste an Excel spreadsheet in a WinWord document—how it's supposed to work, the official party line. But only the Underground Guide will show you how it really works: what's solid; what's goofy; how to avoid the parts that don't work right; how to use the parts that do work right to get your job done.

Even if you never do anything more complicated than paste a spreadsheet into a document, this book will pay for itself in the first few minutes. But wait! There's more! For those of you who go spelunking into the depths of the Office applications, this Underground Guide contains a gold mine of information on the ties between Office apps that lurk just beneath the surface, in the macro languages and the OLE Automation links. Can't get OLE Automation to work with WinWord? Are your Excel VBA apps eating Free System Resources like a Russian scarfing sticky raw fish eggs? Looking for the best way to make Visual Basic behave itself with an Office app server?

Yep. You need this book.

Lee Hudspeth and T.J. Lee spent months wallowing in the rank mire that is OLE Automation, Visual Basic for Applications, and Office app interconnection, and have returned to bring you this firsthand account. I hope you find their account enlightening—and entertaining. Because, if you're going to venture out in this wilderness, you're going to need all the technical insight you can get…and a sense of humor.

Here thar be tygers.

Woody Leonhard
Series Hack

Acknowledgments

This book is dedicated to you, the reader. You've shelled out big bucks for hardware, more bucks for software, and you'd like to get your money's worth. You're not a dummy, nor an idiot; *you're an Underground commando!* So take heart and keep Underground!

We couldn't have written this book without Woody Leonhard, our series editor, and Vince Chen, our incomparable technical editor. Thanks guys!

Many thanks and kudos to the following individuals: Dick Apcar, Chase Ashley, Chris Barlow, Steven Bretherick, Steve Bridgeland, Brad Brunell, Don Buchanan, Paul Cameron, Vince Chen, Bryan de Silva, Peter Deegan, John Donaldson, Malcolm Eaton, Stephen Edgington, Bill Edmett, Charlotte Empey, Michael Evans, Pilar Ferrera, Brant Freer, Guy Gallo, Steve Gerber, Brian Gray, Liz Harsch, Arthur Hixon, Ed Hoffman, Michael J. Holden, Michael Hyatt, David Jennings, Roger Jennings, Laurence Johansen, Joel Kanter, Jim Kauffman, Joseph Kelly, Charlie Kindel, Doug Klippert, John Kois, Scott Krueger, Todd Laney, Ray Lassiter, Woody Leonhard, Patrick Long, Tom Looker, Michael McDonnell, Dave Mitchell, Ken Mocabee, Dick Moffat, Ellen Nagler, Rich Ostrowski, Ken Paul, Rob Perelli-Minetti, Jim Powell, Terence Pritchard, Diane Reeves, Adam Rodman, Jonathan Sachs, J. Bradford Sears, Jim Shatz-Akin, Terry Sherb, Matthew Smith, Cees Smits, Paul Stokes, M. David Stone, Stephen Stuart, Karl Swensson, Peter Thompson, Tim Tow, Bill Walton, Brett Weiss, Eric Wells, Eileen Wharmby, JB Whitwell, Stu Wiley, John Winer, Bryan Woodruff, and Bob Yens.

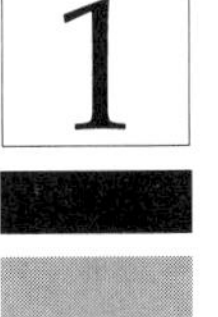# Read Me First, Please!

They're back ...

Heather O'Rourke
Poltergeist II

If you're new to the *Underground Guide* series, let us welcome you to the Underground! This is where we separate fact from fiction and get down and dirty in the innards of the software beast you're trying to goad into *letting you get some useful work done!*

As your hosts, we're going to provide you with as much information as we can and try to have some fun doing it. This won't be as easy as it sounds since some of this stuff is as much fun as sticking your head in a bucket of oatmeal, but we'll do our best. At the very least, we'll hand you a towel to wipe off the gruel.

We're going to try to give you the feeling you'd get if you were in the Old West, out on the prairie, surrounded by hostiles, down to your last cartridge, when, just as things looked hopeless, you hear galloping hooves and the stillness is split by a bugle sounding a cavalry charge. There just cresting the rise, it's the *Underground Guides* to the rescue! Good feeling that, eh?

NOW JUST WHY DID YOU BUY THIS BOOK?

What time is it, boys and girls?

Buffalo Bob
The Howdy Doody Show

Yep, it's time again for the Jim and Lee Show. Join us as we dispel the myths and mysteries surrounding application integration, OLE, DDE, ODBC, VBA, and a bunch of other scary acronyms that seem to pop up everywhere these days. We'll make you laugh, er, cry,—well, we'll *damn sure see to it that you get your money's worth!*

The Jim and
Lee Show ...

And that's what it's really all about, isn't it? Getting your money's worth. Not the cost of this book (although we'll get you that in the first chapter)—we're talking about the substantial investment you've made in the computer sitting on your desk, the software therein, and the time you spend trying to make it all work for you.

We're going to address some sticky issues in this tome so that you'll have a handle on things like drag-and-drop, what is meant by an "embedded link," and why you should care. We'll nail down how the pieces of software on your computer fit together and can actually be used in concert to do serious work. Utilization is what we're talking about. Integration. Making pieces of software come together and become a whole that is greater than the sum of their parts.

The big push in selling software these days is in sets of applications called suites. The idea is that you use the suite's applications as an integrated whole. And a good idea it is, too. The reality, however, sometimes falls a little short. There are some flies in the ointment as well as some nuggets of gold. The reality we're talking about is OLE 2.0 for the most part. That's short for Object Linking and Embedding and that's one of the main focal points of this book. We'll talk about what OLE is, what it does, what it doesn't do, and how you can use it.

Four-point-whatever   In this book we're going to use Microsoft Office Professional version 4.2, no, that's not right, 4.1? No. Isn't 4.2 the *Standard* version of office? Hmmm, seems it was 4.0 only yesterday. You know, come to think of it, it *was* yesterday. Alas, it's really hard to stay up with Office version numbers. Ah, 4.3, yeah, that's it, that's the Professional version. Still, it's early in the week and by Friday it may change again. We'll just call it *four-point-whatever* and that should cover it.

Anyway, we'll use this suite of applications as a base set and add other applications as necessary. More on that later. Right now, what say we define a few terms and get going!

SO WHAT'S IT ALL ABOUT?

Incomprehensible jargon is the hallmark of a profession.

Kingman Brewster
Speech, December 13, 1977

First, let's lay a very simple foundation for understanding some tricky concepts that aren't really all that tricky once you get used to them. And don't let the jargon get you down. With a little practice you'll be throwing terms like **protocol** (n. a set of rules governing the communication and the transfer of data) and **paradigm** (n. model or pattern) around like a pro. A big part of learning any subject involves getting comfortable with the vocabulary.

Defining the Problem to Be Solved

I never varied from the managerial rule that the worst possible thing we could do was to lie dead in the water of any problem.

Thomas J. Watson, Jr.
Fortune, 1977

Computers are used to manipulate information or data. The data may be contained in a letter, a spreadsheet, a database—in almost any application. You keep the data in the application best suited for manipulating it; you don't want to keep the same data in more than one place. So far so good.

The data in application A is needed occasionally in application B. And the data in application C needs to stay in application C but is best manipulated with application D. You need to share data between applications and you need to allow the use of one application's tools from within some other application.

For our purposes then, **integration** becomes the ability to share information and functionality between different software programs.

The Early Solutions

... nothing up my sleeves ...

Bullwinkle the Moose
Adventures of Rocky and Bullwinkle

If you have ever copied something in one application and pasted it in another application, you have used this concept of integration. The Windows Clipboard was the first stab at integrating applications. Copy the data here, paste it there. Rudimentary but practical.

Horse and buggy days

Next, the idea of letting applications actually communicate with each other was implemented using a communications protocol called **Dynamic Data Exchange** (DDE). DDE provided the ability to *link* the pasted data so that if the data changed in the application it was copied from (the **source application** or **server application**), that change was reflected in the application that it was paste-linked into (the **destination application** or **client application**).

More Ambitious Solutions

Ambition should be made of sterner stuff.

Shakespeare
Julius Caesar

Paste-links and DDE did not address the need to share functionality between applications very well. A new protocol was needed and along came **Object**

Linking and Embedding (OLE). If you've ever used Excel or Microsoft Graph to create a chart in another application, then you have used OLE.

Split personalities Both OLE and DDE have dual personalities. On the one hand, they allow you to use their abilities from an application's interface. Armed with nothing more than your trusty mouse, you can Edit / Copy, switch applications and Edit / Paste Special. Or you can Insert / Object / Microsoft Graph 5.0 and create a chart in your document. On the other hand, they provide a way to tap their power from within an application's macro language to build a user-customized integrated application.

Next comes **Open Database Connectivity** (ODBC). This protocol allows you to access and manipulate database records from within applications other than the database application that stores the data. Really cool stuff.

Okay, that gives us a smattering of concepts and new terms to use in talking about this technology. We'll come back to these acronyms and add some more as we progress. Oh, yes indeedy. But for now, let's jump on the back of this integration tiger and go for a ride.

THINGS YOU SHOULD BE DOING WITH OLE 2.0 AND OFFICE 4.(WHATEVER) TODAY

> Don't put off until tomorrow what you can do today.
>
> Old Saw

Trite but true. In this section you learn how to utilize some of the magic programmed into the Office applications by the wizards up in Redmond. If you aren't using these techniques, then you're working too hard!

The focus here is on what you can do with the technology, the big picture. The nuts and bolts come later.

OLE Automation and Visual Basic for Applications

> Ohhhhh! Scary stuff, boys and girls, scary stuff.
>
> Count Floyd
> *SCTV*

Macros from the black lagoon Most users get a bit skittish when suddenly confronted with the idea of having to write a macro. If this applies to you, well, as Douglas Adams so aptly put it, DON'T PANIC. Take a deep breath and you'll be fine.

If you've never written a macro, it's time to start. Sure, more and more features are being built into software applications, but we'll wager that there are several things on your personal "I just wish it would do ..." list. A macro may grant your wish. Or something that takes you eight or nine steps to do every day might be reduced to a single click with a macro.

Macros can up your utilization by orders of magnitude.

A Macro Ain't Really a Macro Anymore

"Macro" is really a misnomer. The original macro language add-ons and built-ins only recorded keystrokes, then allowed you to play back those keystrokes as if some invisible being were sitting at the keyboard.

What you're dealing with nowadays are nothing short of full-blown programming languages that are really quite accessible even if you have no formal training in programming. You can do some massively useful things with very little code. Honest.

Common Macro Language Is Spelled "V-B-A"

In the olden days every software developer that decided to add a macro language to an application did it from scratch. Every language was different in form and substance much like each application sported a different user interface. This made learning to write macros an uphill battle because every time you turned around, you had to deal with a different way of doing things, different commands, different everything. Microsoft to the rescue (now there's a scary thought, eh?).

Not long ago (in geological terms) Microsoft decreed its intention to create a common macro language to be used across all their applications. **Visual Basic for Applications** (VBA) is the first incarnation of this common language and has been newly implemented in Excel and Project. Eventually, all Microsoft applications will support VBA, so now's the time to learn the fundamentals of macro programming. In Chapters 5 and 6 we explore the world of this wunderkind VBA.

What Does OLE Automation Mean to Me?

OLE Automation. Sound a bit intimidating? A little background may make things less frightening. The idea of a common macro language is a good one, but it's tough in execution. You do different kinds of things in a spreadsheet than in a word processor, so there are naturally some differences in how the macro language is implemented in each application. But these differences have to be dealt with if you are going to use one application to control another application using one application's macro language.

For example, a spreadsheet needs a way to allow you to select a cell. A word processor doesn't know squat about cells. So if you're using Word to talk to and control Excel, for example, you need a way for an application to "speak" to a cell in Excel. Along comes OLE Automation.

Here's the official definition from the Microsoft TechNet CD (August 1994).

A sordid
exposé
> "OLE Automation is an industry standard that applications use to expose their OLE objects to development tools, macro languages, and other applications that support OLE Automation."

Huh? What? Well, Microsoft sure seems intent on making OLE Automation an industry standard. The "expose their OLE objects" part might sound a little sordid; it means that one application can, from within its macro language, issue commands to the other application thereby effectively controlling that application. Every command is "exposed" and thereby made available.

A programming language with the ability to control other applications is a pretty powerful combination, friend. Processes that you perform manually can be fully automated even if several applications are involved. You spend some time getting to know OLE Automation in Chapters 7 and 8.

Show and Tell

Ready for a sip of some delectable home-made OLE Automation stew? How about a ten-line teaser macro written in Excel VBA. This macro uses OLE Automation to tell Word to create a new file, insert some text, format it, then print it. Here 'tis. (Note: make sure Word is already running before you run ShowAndTell.)

```
Option Explicit
Sub ShowAndTell()
    Dim wordbas As Object
    Set wordbas = CreateObject("Word.Basic")
    wordbas.FileNewDefault
    wordbas.Insert "Hello Underground!"
    wordbas.StartOfDocument 1
    wordbas.FormatFont "36", _
        , , , , , , , , , , , , , , , 1, 1
    wordbas.FilePrint 1
End Sub
```

Even such a short macro exposes you to some of the important OLE Automation details we cover in Chapters 7 and 8. Issues like these ... "By golly, VBA code isn't as esoteric as I thought it might be!" (we agree). "Does Word have to be running before I use OLE Automation?" (no, but there are some coding gymnastics awaiting you). "What's that dangling underscore for?" (a line continuation character). "Why all those empty comma separators in the `FormatFont` statement?" (because this is an example of positional, not named, arguments). We'll explain all terms in coming chapters.

Links (Not of the OLE Variety) for Document Artwork

A little reciprocity goes a long way.

Malcolm Forbes

Do you paste graphics into your Word documents to jazz them up? You do? Well, stop it! The Insert / Picture command in Word and PowerPoint lets you link to any graphics file for which you have an import filter. See Figure 1.1. Word and PowerPoint provide a "link" to a graphics file sitting out there on your hard disk, but it's not an OLE link.

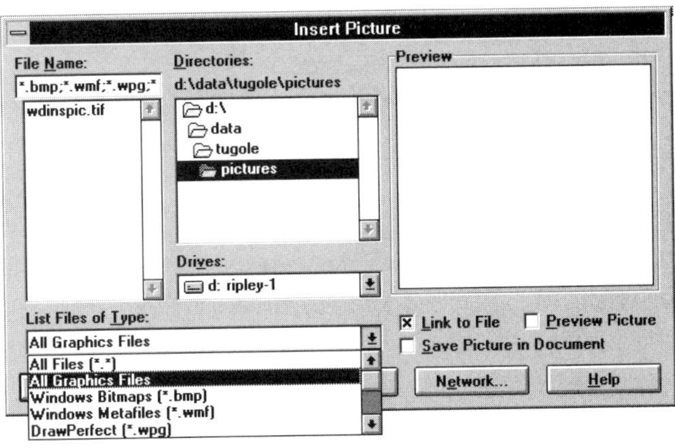

Figure 1.1 Word's Insert Picture Dialog Box

You can see what filters are installed by checking the drop-down list box under List Files of Type or by looking at the [MS Graphic Import Filters] section of your `WIN.INI` file.

Reduce Overall Document File Size

What does a link give you that plain old pasting does not? A greatly reduced file size for one. Consider an empty Word document which, when saved, has a file size of approximately 6,600 bytes. To display the graphic shown in Figure 1.1, you could snap a shot of the displayed dialog box (`ALT + PRINT SCREEN`) and paste the resultant graphic from the clipboard into the Word document. Save the document and the file size jumps to almost 180,000 bytes. Whew!

But if the dialog box is captured and saved as a `.TIF` file (91,442 bytes in our test) and is linked to the Word document using the IncludePicture field, the size of the document does not appreciably increase. So you can have a single file of almost 180,000 bytes or two files linked whose combined size is a mite over 98,000 bytes, a savings of over 80,000 bytes. See Figure 1.2.

One [linked] picture is worth about 90K.

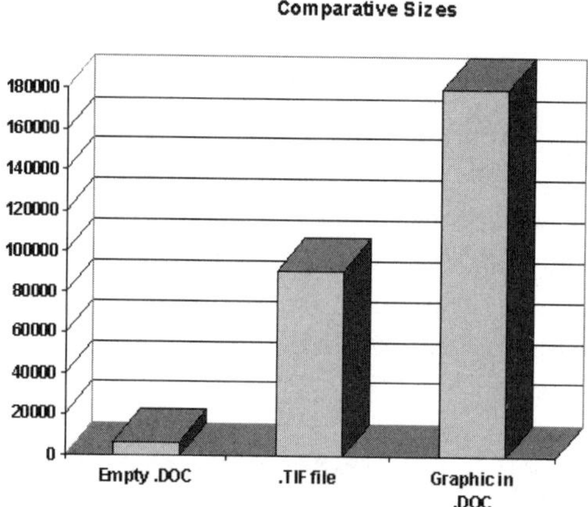

Figure 1.2 Linking and File Size Comparison

Improve Document Consistency and Currency

Here's another big incentive to use links to external files. Doing so ensures that everyone in a work group situation is using the same piece of artwork for the corporate logo, divisional logo, product logo, or latest product shot scanned from a video infomercial, for example. The link provides (guarantees!) consistency and currency for any document that needs to "represent" a given piece of information.

There are some caveats, to be sure. If you send the document to someone outside your environment (that is, someone who doesn't have access to the linked file), you must send the document and any files that are linked to it. Otherwise when the document is opened, the recipient sees only the last *presentation* of the linked data. The link is broken, but the last presentation remains intact.

Mail Merge with Query

> Neither rain nor sleet nor gloom of night ...
>
> U.S. Post Office motto

Mail merges have really driven home the need for integration. Say you want to send a form letter to everyone in a database that meets certain criteria. You do the letter in Word, but the names, addresses, and information upon which you'll filter your selections reside in a database application.

When in Word

No problem! One of the steps in performing a mail merge in Word is "get data." You can choose an existing data file or fire up Microsoft Query and go after the live data. See Figure 1.3.

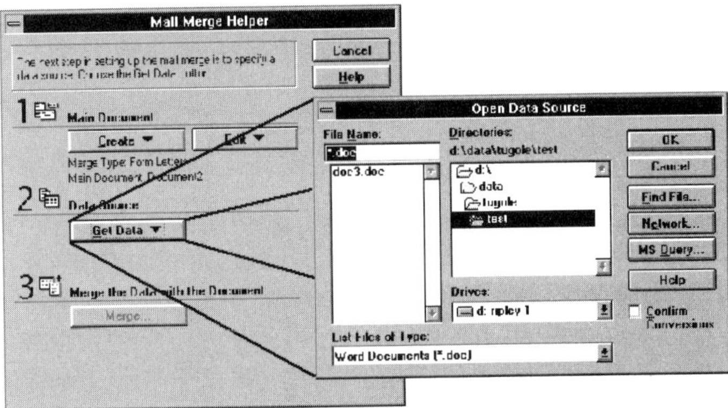

Figure 1.3 Mail Merge Data Open Source Dialog Box

From Word's Mail Merge Helper dialog box you can access (no pun intended) the Open Data Source dialog box. The fifth command button from the top fires up MS Query and allows you to search databases for which you have the appropriate ODBC drivers. If you have the Access driver, you can query Access `.MDB` files, for example. See Figure 1.4.

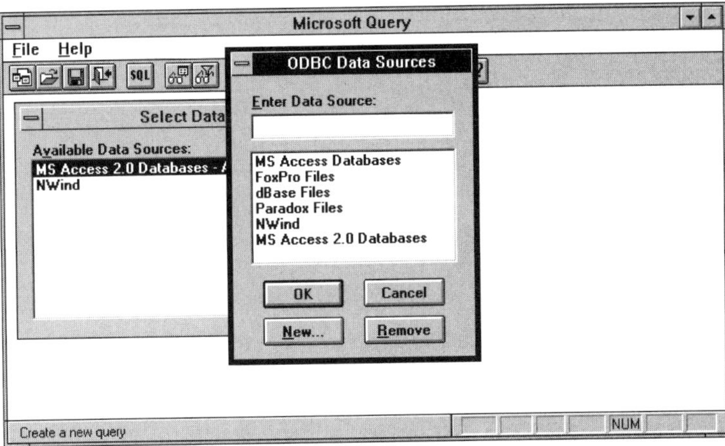

Figure 1.4　Microsoft Query

If you want to pull some data into Word from a database but are not doing a mail merge, try Insert / Database, which gets you to the same Open Data Source dialog box shown in Figure 1.3.

Once in Query, you can specify what type of database you want to go up against (ooh, mainframe talk; "go up against" refers to the process of getting data from a database). You can query the database and after reviewing the records you can "Return Data to Microsoft Word" from the File menu in Query.

Both Excel and Word (as standalone applications) and Office ship with Microsoft Query. You can invoke Query from within Excel via Data / Get External Data.

Starting From Access

The truth is that some people are word processing people, while others have more of a database bent. So if you spend most of your time in Access, you need not despair. You can search your database for the users you want for your mail merge and kick the whole thing off from within Access.

Merge It button

On the Access toolbar is a button with the Word flying *W* on it. The ToolTip label is Merge It. If you click on it, up pops the Microsoft Word Mail Merge Wizard. See Figure 1.5.

As you can see, application integration within the Office suite gets tighter and tighter as time passes.

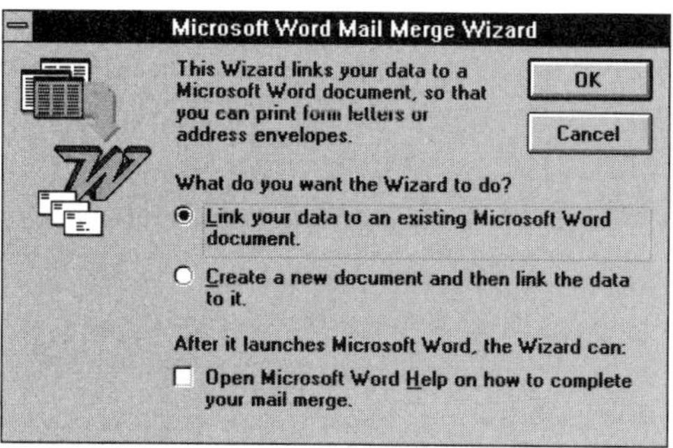

Figure 1.5 Mail Merge Wizard from within Access

Graphing Tabular Data for Better Presentation

> I want to reach that state of condensation of sensations which constitutes a picture.
>
> Henri Matisse
> *Notes d'un Peintre*, 1908

Here is a quick and easy way to jazz up a table of numbers in Word. Toss in some simple charts. Of course, it's only easy if you know how.

Say you have a table of data in a Word document like this:

	Godzilla	Mothra	Rodan
Damage (in billions)	500	90	250

This is a perfect place to drop in a chart. You can create the chart using either Excel or Graph. Let's use Graph for this example. In fact, you'll not only create a chart—you'll link the table from your document to the embedded chart so that if you have to change any of the figures in the table, the chart gets updated automatically. Here is how you do it.

1. Highlight the table in the Word document.

2. From the Edit menu choose Copy.

3. From the Insert menu choose Object. The chart object gets inserted below the table (if you leave it selected in step 2), or at the cursor position if you moved the cursor out of the table after step 2.

4. In the Object dialog box, make sure the Create New filecard is **active**.

5. Select Microsoft Graph 5.0 in the Object Type list box, then click on the OK button.

At this point you are editing a Graph **object** (the heavy discussion on vocabulary begins in Chapter 2; for now just roll with it.) The chart object normally has some default data in it, which you'll notice has been replaced with the data from your table. But since you want to link the data in the table to the chart so that any subsequent changes in the table appear in the chart, you're not done yet.

If you left the table selected (that is, you did *not* change the cursor location between steps 2 and 3), you now see Graph's ChartWizard dialog. When you have data selected in your Word document (either a table or a block of tab-delimited information), Graph uses your data instead of its own default data and chart type and runs the ChartWizard to help you create a custom chart. If this is the case, go to step 6. However, if you do not have any data selected when you insert the Graph object, Graph's default data appears in the Datasheet and the ChartWizard does not appear at this time. If this is the case, skip step 6 and go directly to step 7.

6. Complete the ChartWizard to create the type of chart you want (we went with the defaults for this example, accomplished simply by clicking the Finish button).

7. In Graph's Datasheet window, select the upper leftmost cell. (If you don't see Graph's Datasheet window at this point, from Graph's menu bar select View / Datasheet.) This is critical. Miss this step and your data barfs all over and around and among Graph's default data set.

8. From the Edit menu, choose the Paste Link option. A message box appears, warning you that the existing data will be overwritten. Click on the OK button.

9. ChartWizard appears; click OK to accept the defaults. While the chart is still active in-place, you can do a little cosmetic editing—add a chart title and

delete the chart legend and you're all set. (If you're new to Graph, select Help for information on how to make these cosmetic refinements.)

10. Click anywhere back in your document. You now see the chart embedded in your document. See Figure 1.6.

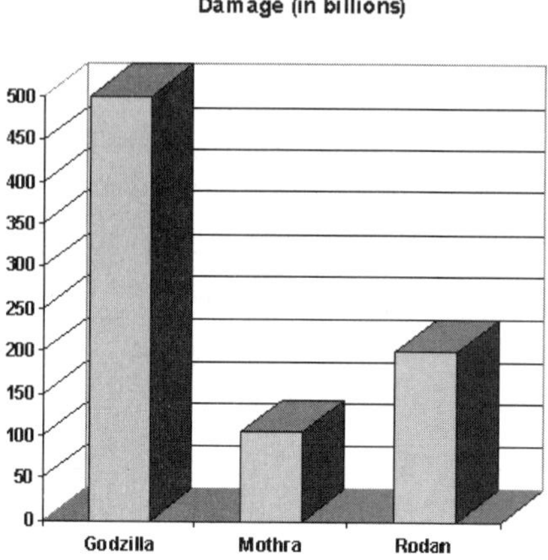

Figure 1.6   Better to be Attacked by Mothra

Make a change to a number in your table, and the chart reflects the new value. This is, as they say in Redmond, way cool, although you may have to wait a while for the update to take place depending on the speed of your computer. Remember, patience is a virtue.

It does work, but it's not all it could be. For one thing, there are far too many steps. More serious is that if you insert a new column into your table, you still only get three data points in your chart. Insert a new column between Godzilla and Mothra so that you can add Gammera to the table. When the chart updates, your new monster shows up but poor old Rodan out there on the end disappears. But if you add a row to the table, it is reflected in the chart.

Packaging Documents for Email Delivery and Routing

> Reach out and touch someone.
>
> AT&T

Email is really coming into its own. It's a most useful workhorse and its integration quotient in Office is very high. If Microsoft Mail is detected by Word, Excel, PowerPoint, Project, or Access, these applications magically add a Send command to their File menus.

Click on Send from within any of these applications, and you can embed a copy of the current document directly into an email message. This message, complete with the embedded file, can then be sent to a colleague.

Even Windows File Manager, once detecting Microsoft Mail, displays a Mail menu option and related toolbar button to facilitate selecting files and embedding them in an email message.

To utilize this Send feature from within an application, perform the following steps.

1. Open or create the document you wish to send. This could be an Access database, Word document, Excel workbook, PowerPoint presentation, or a project in Project.

2. From the File menu select Send.

   The following dialog box appears. See Figure 1.7.

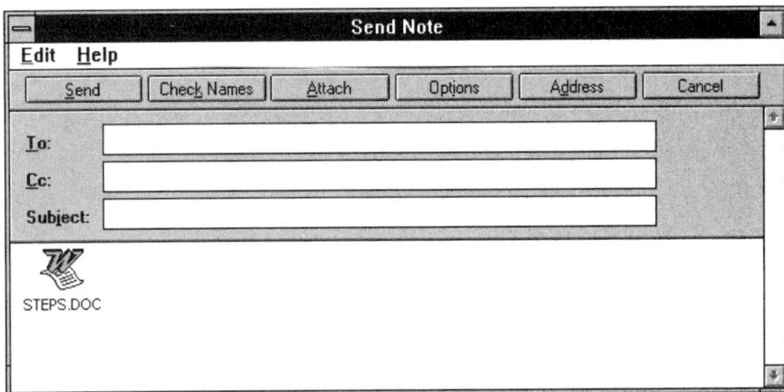

Figure 1.7 Integrated Email

3. Address as appropriate, type the message, and click the Send button.

The current document appears as an icon within the message space. The recipient can simply double-click this icon, and the file is loaded into the appropriate application (assuming that application is installed on the recipient's computer, of course). To work this magic, the file is temporarily saved to the TEMP directory on the recipient's computer upon activation .To keep the file, the recipient must save the attachment via File / Save Attachment in the Mail program.

What's missing from this whole process is a really good compression scheme to cut down on the size of the embedded file object. Embed some monster spreadsheets, a .WAV file or two, and (heaven forbid!) a video clip and you

have a rather substantial email message. Send that puppy to everyone on the network, and it's a good bet that you'll be chatting with the systems administrator real soon.

Specialized Server Applications

> Specialization has gotten out of hand.
>
> Jonathan Weiner
> *The Next One Hundred Years,* 1990

A bunch of specialized OLE server applications ship with Office. Things like Graph, Organizational Chart, and WordArt. To see a list of these applications, do an Insert / Object from almost any Office application and look at the Object Type list on the Create New filecard. We'll discuss most of them in some detail later in this chapter, as well as some you have to purchase separately.

Some of these applications are called "server only," which means they can create an object embedded within another application but that they cannot themselves create a standalone file. But the more interesting distinction is that some of them are programmable and some are not.

So what, you say? Stuff it, because you're not a programmer? Well, stick with us, pilgrim, and by the end of the book we'll see about that. But this is not to say that they are not all useful. As you've seen, you can do some pretty impressive things with Graph and no code is required.

Let's look at an example of each.

Non-programmable WordArt (Microsoft)

To use WordArt 2, you must do so using its provided interface (as you did with Graph in an earlier example). WordArt 2 is simply not programmable; you cannot control it programmatically from another application. Bummer. We suppose you could try to do it using a technique called `SendKeys` but, well, in a word, blecccch.

Hmmm, is that another "so what?" we just heard? Consider that WordArt is the *only* way you can rotate text in Word. What if you, as the automated integration expert for your firm, wanted to grab some text in Word and rotate it 270 degrees and stick it in a particular place. And you wanted to do it in a macro so that the user wouldn't have to deal with it. Better start looking up `SendKeys` in the WordBasic help file. Blecccch.

Programmable Visio (Shapeware)

Visio is a specialized drawing program that is not a part of Office. It's not even a Microsoft application. It has some really whizbang features like a collection of tools and pre-built shapes that are remarkably easy to use. What's more, it's a programmable OLE 2.0 application. This means that from another program that supports OLE Automation, you can completely control Visio and make it jump through hoops, roll over, lie down—oh, you get the idea.

For example, say you want to design a macro to create an organizational chart. You want the user to pick the names and positions from a displayed list and, with a single click of a button, build the chart. You could build such an application in Excel, Visual Basic, or Project since they all support OLE Automation.

What does that get you? For starters, your users need never spend any time learning about or dealing with native Visio. Zero learning curve. You, as the developer, can treat all the features of Visio as tools available to you, subject to your beck and call.

Conversely, you never have to write a single line of code to use Visio if you don't want to. It can be used as a standalone program in which you can create, save, and print your drawings, or as an OLE server to link or embed Visio objects in your other applications. Or you can embed other objects in Visio.

Visio is one of the niftiest programs we have seen in a long time. To check it out, call the folks at Shapeware at 800-446-3335 (outside the U.S. call 303-743-9533).

Some Tips for Dealing with OLE Server Applications

> Psssst. Hey Bud, wanna tip?
>
> Sheldon Leonard
> *The Burns and Allen Show*

Using OLE and OLE servers can increase your utilization of computer technology, no doubt about it. But getting up to speed with this stuff can be an uphill struggle. Here are some pointers to get you started. We're not going to get into finger pointing and blame (we'll do that later); right now, let's just focus on what *is*.

In Situ, Brute?

One of the new features in OLE 2.0 is called **in-situ editing** (or **in-place editing** or **visual editing**). It means that the menus and toolbars of the client application change and display the commands of the OLE server application when you activate the object for editing.

For example, double-click on a WordArt object in Excel and suddenly good old Excel looks mighty strange. Excel's menus have been aggregated (merged) with WordArt's. WordArt's toolbars replace Excel's toolbars. See Figure 1.8.

Users new to OLE 2.0 get freaked out by this all the time. One minute they're rockin' along in one application, they click on something, and suddenly they're in the digital Twilight Zone. A reasonable cause for alarm, we agree!

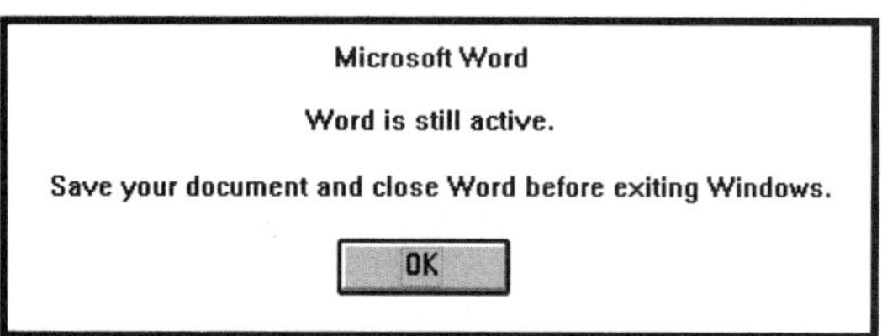

Figure 1.8 This is Excel?

The trick is to not lose track of the **container application**—this is the application that contains the OLE object. The title bar is your first clue; in this case, it displays "Microsoft Excel - WordArt 2.0," which means you're in Excel and that a WordArt 2.0 object is active for editing. The help menu is your next reference point. Help / About gives you the exact version of the OLE *server application* and Help / Contents takes you to the help file for the *server application*. Look at Figure 1.8 right now—the WordArt object is in "edit mode." Edit mode is synonymous with in-place editing.

It is not a good idea to leave OLE server objects active for longer than you have to. Consider this: You're working with several documents in Word and you activate an OLE object in one of the documents. In-place editing kicks in and there you are. You leave the object active and switch to another document. You get Word's native menus and toolbars. It's easy to forget that you have an active object in another document. Now, try to exit Windows. A system message appears. See Figure 1.9.

Microsoft Word

Word is still active.

Save your document and close Word before exiting Windows.

OK

Figure 1.9 Why Can't Windows Close It?

Windows can't deal with shutting down a container application with an active object. If the active object is in say, Excel, you get a slightly more cryptic message simply saying "Cannot quit Microsoft Excel." At no time are you given any hint as to what the problem may be.

So activate your OLE object, do whatever you're going to do with it, and *deactivate it!*

A Mouseless Escape

Once you are in an in-place editing situation you can edit the object, but what then? How do you deactivate the silly thing? Just click anywhere in the container document *outside* of the object and the container application's menus and toolbars reappear.

This technique, of course, requires having your handy dandy mouse at hand. If you find yourself mouseless, you can get out of in-place editing via the Escape key. Usually, you hit the Escape key once to close any server dialog box and then a second time to get the focus back in the container application.

For example, when you activate or insert a WordArt object, the focus is in the Enter Your Text Here dialog box. If you want to pull down the Format menu, you might think you can do an ALT + T from the keyboard. Think again. The focus stays firmly rooted in the dialog box. With a mouse, no problem—you click on the Format menu option. But from the keyboard, nada. But hit the Escape key one time and the dialog box is shut down and the menus are now accessible from the keyboard. (You can get the dialog box redisplayed via the Edit WordArt Text option on the Edit menu.) Hit the Escape key a second time and the WordArt object is deactivated, and you are back in the container application.

There's a problem with the Escape key technique, and it serves to illustrate the lack of consistency with which OLE has been implemented in various applications. You see, things don't always work the same way across applications (so what's new?). Oh, in WordArt the Escape key technique works great, but in Visio you'll get old and gray hitting the Escape key waiting for something to happen. Get this: In Visio, to mouselessly shut down an in-place editing session, you have to hit ALT + V to pop the View menu, hit O for Open in Visio to kick Visio into Open mode, and then you can ALT + F for the File menu and hit X for Exit & Return to Document. Whew. To shut down Graph while editing in-place, you have to first ALT + V to pull down the View menu, hit D to clear the Datasheet form, and only then does the Escape key get you out. Oy!

To Open or to Edit—That's a Question?

Okay, you've got a handle on in-place editing. But, you don't *have* to edit in-place if you'd rather not. No, no, no. You can *open* an OLE server application. In fact, some OLE server applications do not support in-place editing and can only be run in open mode.

So, like, what's the difference? Glad you asked. Figure 1.8 shows Excel with a WordArt object in edit mode. WordArt objects can also be edited in "open mode."

To do so you select the object and from the Edit menu select Objects. A flyout menu appears and you can choose either Edit or Open. Choose Open to edit the object in open mode. Here is the same Excel workbook with the WordArt object in open mode. See Figure 1.10.

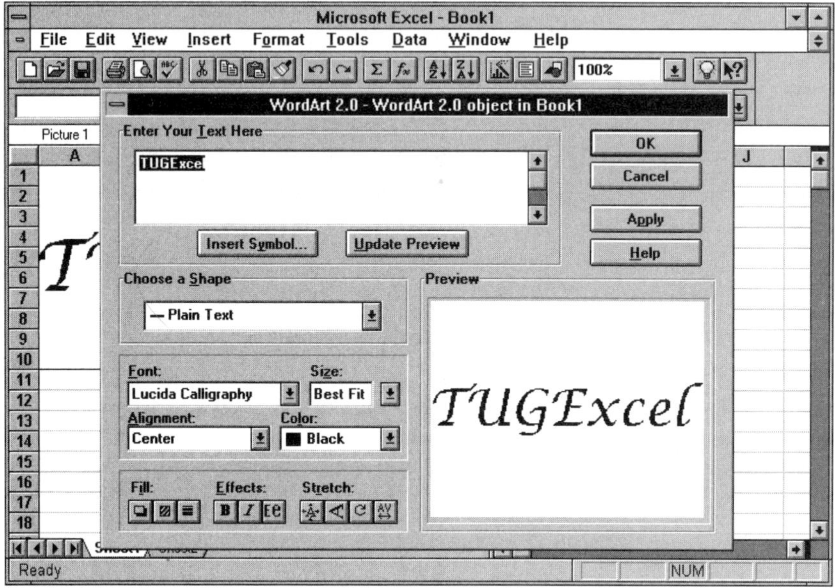

Figure 1.10 An Open WordArt Object

In open mode, WordArt pops up *over* the container application. Notice that the title bar does not have maximize or minimize buttons. If you were to pull down the control menu, you would also find these commands missing. The entire WordArt application consists of a single dialog box. You can make whatever changes you want, but you cannot simply click back in the container document to close the open OLE server. You must use the command buttons (in this case, the OK or Cancel buttons) in the OLE server dialog box to shut it down.

And because of the command buttons you had best avoid the Escape key, which triggers the Cancel button.

In this example, WordArt acts more like a modal dialog box than a separate application, meaning that you cannot do anything with the container application until you have closed the dialog box. You cannot save a piece of WordArt as a separate file. WordArt is strictly a *server only* type of OLE server.

Not all OLE server applications are like this. The major applications in the Office suite are, after all, OLE servers themselves, but some of the smaller OLE servers like Organizational Chart allow you to either embed their output as an object or save the output to a separate file. The Organization Chart application can only be run in open mode and does not support in-place editing. But it can be maximized or minimized; it appears in the Task List; and generally behaves like you'd expect a standalone application to behave.

Finding and Positioning Objects

This question crops up in Word now and again: How do you get an embedded object to be over *here* and not over *there*? The best methods for controlling object placement in Word are to place the object either inside a frame or within a table cell.

Another issue is how to find objects that are scattered throughout a document. In Excel it's easy: Edit / Go To / Special, select the Objects options button, and punch the OK button. All the objects in the current sheet are selected. Use the Tab key to cycle through them. (Warning: shameless plug coming!) This technique and many others are discussed in detail in that smash hit *The Underground Guide to Excel 5.0 for Windows*. Be sure to pick up twenty or thirty copies today!

In Word, you can turn on Picture Placeholders (Tools / Options / View / Picture Placeholders), and everywhere a big empty box appears you have an object. Hmmm, this forces you to scroll through the entire document searching for objects. Then if you find one, you can't see what it is. Alternately, use Word's Edit / Go To feature— select Edit / Go To / Go to What / Object, then select the type of object from the drop-down list and click Next repeatedly to scroll through them. A simple macro provides single-click searching for objects.

1. In Word, click on Tools / Macro, type in a macro name like FindNextObject, and click the Create button.

2. Between Sub MAIN and End Sub type in the following code:

```
Sub MAIN
    EditGoTo .Destination = "o+"
    CharRight 1, 1
End Sub
```

3. Switch to the document to be searched in Word.

4. Click on the macro toolbar's Start button. It's that right-pointing blue triangle gizmo.

Macro Start button

Each time you start the macro, Word selects the next object found until the last object in the document is found.

Finally, if you're looking at a document of any kind and it's just crawling with objects, here's a tip for finding out just what type of object each one is. Right click on that critter! Yeah, use the good old right-mouse button. The shortcut menu pops up, and somewhere around dead center you'll find a major clue as to what you're dealing with. See Figure 1.11.

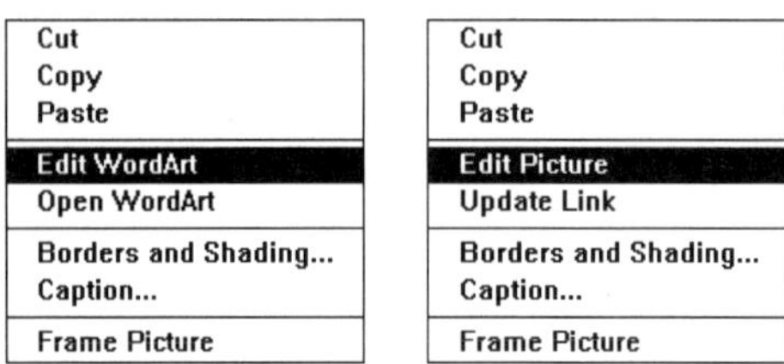

Figure 1.11 Object, Object, What Type of Object?

As you can see, a right-click on an object pops up the shortcut menu, and you can quickly discern what type of object you're looking at. The shortcut menus differ from application to application (Figure 1.11 was done in Word), but somewhere therein the type of object is shown.

MICROSOFT OFFICE 4.(WHATEVER)—THE SUITE SPOT?

That's it, baby. If you've got it, flaunt it.

Zero Mostel
The Producers, 1967

Why did we pick the Microsoft Office suite of applications to use in this book? Are we shilling for the Redmond Rangers? Have we sold out? (Hmmm, somebody, please, *make us an offer*.) Actually, the bottom line here is that Microsoft applications appear to implement integration technologies such as DDE, OLE, OLE Automation, ODBC, etc. almost as soon as these technologies are made available. And Microsoft's implementations seem to work a little (often a lot) better than other manufacturers' implementations.

In any event, in this section we'll discuss the applications found in Office and many of the integration features contained in that suite of programs. And here and there we'll toss in some non-Office applications. Like Project, which is the only other application outside of Excel that has been endowed with VBA. And Shapeware's Visio, to give you an example of a non-Microsoft programmable OLE server application.

Applications du Jour ... Where 2 + 3 + 4 + 5 + 6 = 4.3

Did you realize that most people's lives are governed by telephone numbers?

"Eddie" the shipboard computer
Douglas Adams, *Hitchhiker's Guide to the Galaxy*

Oh, for the good old days, when an application started with version 1.0 and progressed from there. Well, no sense living in the past. A version number is no longer determined by the programmers; it's now the decision of the marketing department. You could probably write a book just on the various jumps, hops, and skips in major software program version numbers and the reasons (both stated and actual) behind them.

Access 2

Included with the Office *Professional* version only. Programmable relational data-base software, pure and simple. Very powerful, very full featured, you can build some amazing database applications using this program. Microsoft stood Borland (and the rest of the software development community) on its ear by selling the initial release of Access for $99. Databases had until then been in the $495 to $695 range SRP (Suggested Retail Price). Prices for database software have never recovered.

Database

If you want to get into Access development you have to get the *Access 2 Developer's Guide* (Sams) by Roger Jennings. This book is the hot tip for developers. If you're new to databases, try *Using Access* (Que) again by Roger Jennings. Good stuff.

Mail 3

Mail is part of both the Standard and Professional versions of Office. You get one workstation license only and you must buy the Mail server license separately.

Communications

PowerPoint 4

PowerPoint is a dynamite presentation package and is included with both the Standard and Professional versions of Office.

Presentations

Excel 5

Both in Standard and Professional. Let us put it like this: the spreadsheet wars are over. Excel won. Okay, so we're a little prejudiced where Excel is concerned, but this is one *fine* spreadsheet program.

Spreadsheet

Word 6

Word processing crème de la crème found in both versions of Office. Microsoft really kicked off their whole BASIC-like built-into-the-application programming language idea with Word 1.0 and its revolutionary macro language WordBasic. For the first and last word on Word, get a copy of *The Underground Guide to Word for Windows* (Addison-Wesley) by Woody Leonhard and *Hacker's Guide to Word for Windows, Second Edition* by Leonhard, Chen, and Krueger (Addison-Wesley). Way cool.

Word processing

Project, Project, Where's My Project 4?

Project
management

Project is not a part of either the Standard or the Professional Office package. Why? Dunno. Microsoft stopped asking us for our ideas on marketing oh, must be, well, hmmm, actually they never asked us now that we come to think about it.

Anyway, Project is full-blown project-planning software. If you want to know the critical path, level some resources, or set up a baseline Gantt Chart, this is the software for you.

Project's place in this book is as the only other fully OLE Automation compliant application next to Excel—they both speak VBA and can play the role of OLE Automation client and server.

How Things Stack Up, OLE Automation-Wise

Table 1.1 reveals the three most important OLE Automation features possessed (or not) by each of the major applications under discussion. We'll occasionally abbreviate OLE Automation as "OLEAuto" from here on out.

Table 1.1 OLE Automation Support Across Applications

Application	Exposed Object Library	Controlling Language	Can It Be Controlled?
Access 2	No	Access Basic*	No
Excel 5	Yes	VBA	Yes
PowerPoint 4	No	None	No
Project 4	Yes	VBA	Yes
Word 6	No	None	Yes
Visio 3	No	None	Yes
Visual Basic 3	No	Visual Basic	No

Note the grade "None" for Word in the "Controlling Language" column. That's right. This means that Word doesn't speak VBA. *WordBasic can only control another application via DDE.* The upside is that Word can, via the monolithic Word.Basic **programmable object**, be controlled by an OLEAuto client like Access, Excel, Project, or Visual Basic.

Although Access can control other OLEAuto servers, it cannot *itself* be controlled via OLEAuto. However, it can be controlled via DDE. This is partly by design, since you can use ODBC or DAO to query and manipulate data in an Access database.

* Access Basic is not currently a dialect of VBA. However, Access Basic does possess the methods and functions necessary to access OLE Automation objects like Excel Worksheets, Charts, and PivotTables; Project Projects; or Word's Word.Basic object. For information on Data Access Object (DAO) technology, see the *Office Developer's Kit.*

Visio is OLE Automation compliant as a server but lacks a macro language of its own. So while another OLEAuto application can control Visio, Visio cannot control other OLEAuto applications.

Visual Basic 3 applications can control other OLEAuto servers, but cannot themselves be controlled via OLEAuto. Perhaps a future version of Visual Basic will include this latter capability.

But I Can Get It for You Wholesale!

> Follow the money.
>
> Deep Throat
> *All the President's Men*

Let's not lose track of the fact that we're talking about integration here. We've picked the Office suite as the base set of applications to use in discussing the technologies that allow you to integrate your applications. In turn, integrating your applications increases productivity. As noted earlier, suites are the primary way software is being marketed today by those software companies that have the resources to put a suite together, and integration is one of each suite's major selling features.

The software suite is analogous to an integrated package like yesterday's Symphony or Framework, or today's various "Works" packages. These packages provide a single program that does a lot of different things. The elder programs failed because they could not compete against the "best of breed" concept—where the idea was to provide the best standalone product in each class of software. The newer integrated packages have found niche markets on computers where resources like hard disk and memory are scarce.

The niche and the dead

The industry has come full circle back to the integrated package concept. Is it because the user community has demanded that software products work together flawlessly? Ha! The answer lies in the changing revenue model of the software industry.

The big bucks are in software upgrades these days. The battle is being fought to just get the products in the door. The more products in the door, the more money earned downstream when those applications are upgraded. Used to be you'd see a major upgrade every couple of years. Now you can almost set your watch to a twelve- to eighteen-month upgrade cycle.

If the goal is to get the boxes in the door, where does all this integration stuff come in? Ah, it's part hype and part genius. The hype is in convincing you that you can't live without some new wowie-pow-zowie feature like drag-and-drop. The genius is in providing common menus and toolbars across a set of applications and in providing a common macro language. The result? An approach that's extremely useful to the software buyer because it makes it easier to utilize a given set of software packages and also makes it *harder* to use software from another manufacturer.

Look and feel—not what you'd think.

Microsoft now licenses its "look and feel" to niche developers for products like Visio so that they can be plugged into Office and look like they were built right into Office all along. But it's unlikely that other vendors, like Lotus or Novell, will be able to do so. In response the other suite developers will standardize their toolbars and menus with their own look and feel. They'll develop their own common macro languages. It's every suite for itself. Ask yourself: if you had several applications that all looked and worked pretty much the same, would you relish adding one that was a glaring nonconformist? One that may not integrate quite as well as the others? The idea is to lock users into an entire product line. And the idea seems to be working.

Money makes it work (like the old marketing axiom "give away the razors and clean up selling blades"). Consider the economics of the Office suite (Professional version) taking into account everything but Mail. See Table 1.2.

Table 1.2 The Dollars Tell the Story

Application	Upgrade $	New Purchase $
Access 2	$119.00	$299.00
PowerPoint 4	119.00	329.00
Excel 5	119.00	299.00
Word 6	119.00	299.00
Sub Total	$476.00	$1,226.00
Office Professional	$279.00	$559.00

These numbers come from a typical mail order catalog and represent prices from a single vendor. Your mileage may vary slightly depending on where you like to shop, but the savings are pretty substantial if you go the suite route in any case. Other software manufacturers offer similar savings on their suites. It boggles the mind.

Get the Latest Version

> The path is not easy, the climbing is rugged and hard, but the glory at the end is worthwhile.
>
> Matt Henson
> Lecture notes, 1909

Whether or not to keep up with every revision of your software packages has always been a subject surrounded by controversy. Are the new features worth the upgrade price? Does the upgrade fix the bug that's been bugging you? When does the vendor pull the plug on supporting the old version?

The software companies, of course, want you to upgrade each and every piece of software you have as often as possible. Upgrade revenue is becoming their life's blood, so to them the issue is clear. What should you do?

Well, if you're trying to implement the integration technologies that we are discussing, you must adopt a policy of upgrading not only to major releases but to each and every maintenance release that comes along. Stuff like OLE Automation and ODBC represent a new science only slightly removed from magic and the developers are constantly working the kinks (and bugs) out. Stay current and more of this stuff will work right more often. 'Nuff said.

Consistency Advantages

> Seek simplicity and distrust it.
>
> Alfred North Whitehead

Ask any fighter pilot for a list of the most important considerations in the profession, and the number one response will be "the need for speed." For that, us lowly computer jocks must look to the likes of AMD, Cyrix, Intel, and Motorola for faster microprocessors. Also high on the aviator's list will undoubtedly be "a well-designed cockpit" or words to that effect. A pilot with ten bogies vectoring in from all sides, each one with an ear-splitting alarm-squealing hot radar-lock on his/her hindquarters, needs to get as much information as quickly as possible from the plane's brain. Consistent instrument clusters. Consistent instrumentation readouts. Small chunks of critical data on the HUD (heads-up display). Easy access to deeper levels of detail but only when needed. "Tight makes right." **Heads-up**

Sound familiar? It should. As Windows applications coming from all the major vendors begin to equal the complexity of a fighter plane's cockpit, they are also becoming more consistent, at least within their own respective suite families (God forbid there might be some industry-wide standard). Microsoft labored mightily to bring a much greater degree of consistency to the Office suite with version 4. Right on.

When you combine the foundation level of complexity that stems directly from an application's raw feature set with all the stuff you can do with OLE, a consistent application is going to save your bacon. Or at least reduce the inevitable waves of vertigo likely to strike when you're in the trenches "just trying to get things done, dammit." In the following sections we'll explore the key aspects of Office's consistent design, all in an effort to keep you safe as you explore the outer waters of OLE.

Menu Bars

Click and you're home.

Castle. Home. Safe haven. Call it what you will, but a time-and-motion study of what happens when a human being interacts with a Windows application reveals menu selections by the zillions. This makes the menu bar a good candidate for consistent design. By the way, what we're talking about here is the **user interface**. The *Microsoft Press Computer Dictionary, 2d ed.*, defines the term as "The portion of a program with which a user interacts." Geez, we could've said that! Oh well.

Every Microsoft sales representative worth his/her salt has demonstrated the following many times over, and we're gonna do it too because it's so important and really quite stunning—in the good sense of the word—when you see it for the first time. See Figure 1.12.

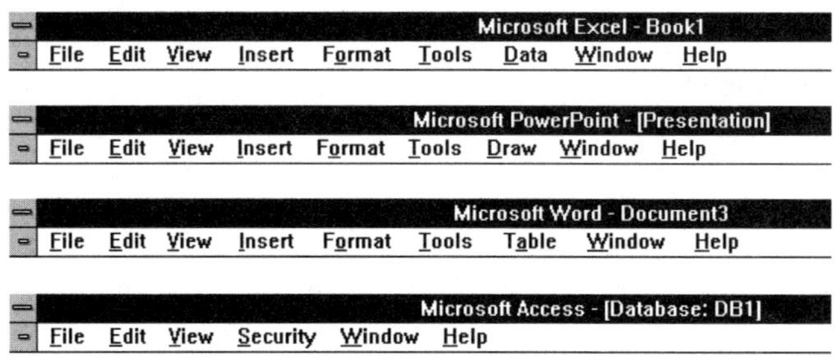

Figure 1.12 Menu Bar Consistency in Office

The left-to-right command order consistency is there, along with the customary Window-plus-Help pairing at the right margin, with special application-specific primary menus sandwiched nicely in between.

Pull-down and Shortcut Menus

Menu buoys

When you go down to the next level with the classic example of the heavily trafficked File pull-down, again notice the consistency of the command names, vertical order, groupings, accelerator keys, shortcuts, and so on. See Figure 1.13.

Other Office components that reveal varying degrees of consistency are ship-with toolbars, toolbar buttons, and common dialog boxes. We won't tour each component here. Suffice it to say that the current version of Office is vastly more consistent internally than its predecessor, and the trend toward greater consistency will continue well into the future. Yes, there are some glaring omissions and gaffes nestled in the soft underbelly of the Office user interface, and as we bump into 'em we'll point 'em out to you. Here's the main thing—Office's internal consistency provides a set of navigational markers. Now you can safely sail the outer waters of OLE in search of the Integrated Application Archipelago.

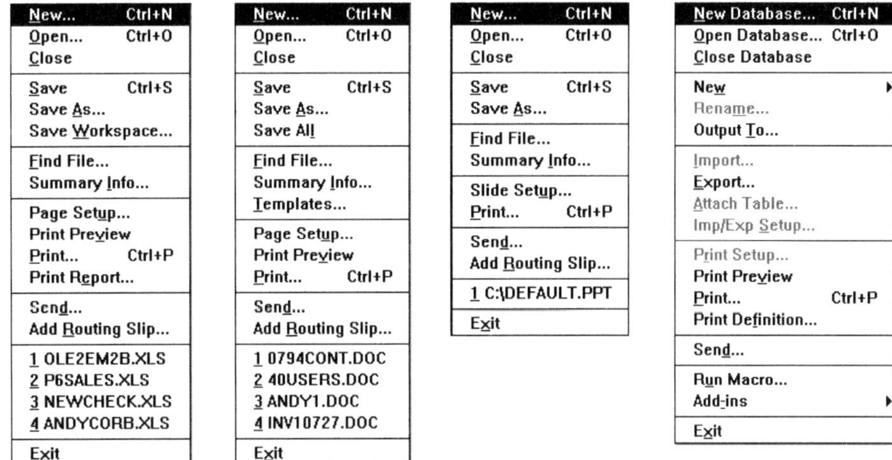

Figure 1.13 File Pull-down Consistency in Office

Shared Component Advantages

> Man is a tool-using animal … without tools he is nothing, with tools he is all.

> Thomas Carlyle

One hermetically sealed envelope and a mayonnaise jar. Two slightly askew but nevertheless wizardly pundits. One jointly echoed pronouncement (ring us up in, oh, say, mid-1996 and tell us how we did), "Microsoft Office applications designed specifically for the **Cairo** operating system will be very different animals from the Office 4 versions we use today." And we're not talking 16-bit versus 32-bit compilers, either. (If you've been away from the PC industry trades for a while, Cairo is the code word for Microsoft's next generation operating system—the generation *after* Windows 95.)

Imagine Word—WINWORD.EXE actually—as a relatively small nucleus of "managerial code" containing a user interface layer, a baseline word processing engine, plus the hooks necessary to interact with whatever OLE 3.0 (that's right, *OLE three-point-zero*, we're talkin' a whole new object game here sports fans) tools you, the user, want from one minute to the next. Likely CairoWord tool candidates? How about Find File (already a "core code" module in Office 4) as a full-featured document management system. OCR (optical character recognition). Electronic mailing and routing (the latter is already a core code module in Office 4). Spelling and grammar checking. Graphing. Special effects.

Lean, mean executable machines

A resounding "yes" to all these and more than we've yet to imagine! CairoWord will be a humble word-processing container application. You'll be able to run it lean-and-mean without any excess baggage (read "tools"), or plug-and-play these tools into your CairoWord configuration tailor-made just for you. Tools du jour!

Everybody wins (especially Microsoft). The container applications themselves get smaller and more fully optimized. The tools can be shared by all the container applications, thereby reaping the advantages of reusable code and dynamic, on-demand customization. Sound exciting? Initially chaotic? You bet! And everything you learn in this tome will benefit you in making the transition into the **document-centric**, er, Cairo, er, componentized, uhm, object-oriented—well, whatever buzz-word adjective sticks, *it'll be a whole new era in personal computing*. And we're here in the Underground to usher it in with you!

Let's briefly explore the various tools that come with Office. See Table 1.3.

Table 1.3 Office Shared Components Exposé

Component Name	MS-DOS Filename	Container Required?	Supports OLE?
ClipArt Gallery	ARTGALRY.EXE	Yes	Yes
Organization Chart	ORGCHART.EXE	No	Yes
Equation Editor	EQNEDIT.EXE	No*	Yes
Find File	Container's EXE	Yes	Yes[†]
Graphics and text filters	Various filters and DLLs	Yes	N/A[‡]
Graph	GRAPH5.EXE	Yes	Yes
Query	MSQUERY.EXE	No	N/A
Setup and uninstall	SETUP.EXE[§]	No	N/A
Spelling checker, grammar, and related	Container's EXE and proofing DLLs	Yes	No
WordArt	WORDART2.EXE	Yes	Yes
Drawing	MSDRAW.EXE	Yes	Yes
Electronic mail and routing	Container's EXE, MSMAIL.EXE, and mail-related DLLs[‖]	No	Yes

* Although Equation Editor doesn't require a container in order to run, it has neither a File Open nor a File Save dialog, so it's pointless to run it outside a container.

[†] Find File uses OLE in the sense that it uses OLE's structured storage technology to directly access a document's summary information without having the document's parent application (like Excel or Word) open at the time.

[‡] N/A = not applicable.

[§] The default location for Office's setup and uninstall application is C:\MSOFFICE\SETUP.

[‖] The following are all distinct entities: (1) the core code shared by each Office application's EXE file, (2) the standalone Microsoft Mail application MSMAIL.EXE, and (3) related supporting MAPI DLLs. However, taken together they functionally represent the "electronic mail and routing" features common to all Office applications. You can access these features either from within an Office container application or by starting Microsoft Mail stand-alone and embedding an Office application's document in the mail message. The latter point is why the table answers "No" to the question "Container required?" and "Yes" to the question "Supports OLE?"

As you can see from Table 1.3, Office tools meander in and out of several different categories—core code within the Office applications themselves, tools that can't run without a container, tools that can run without a container, and the various DLLs and other supporting files that sit quietly off-stage until called upon.

Interestingly, each of Office's container-required OLE tools provides a different message when you attempt to run them with a File / Run command or by double-clicking. Call us nitpickers if you like, but in our book, obfuscation is a dirty word. Particularly annoying is the missing tool name in Draw's message box title bar! See Figure 1.14 through Figure 1.17.

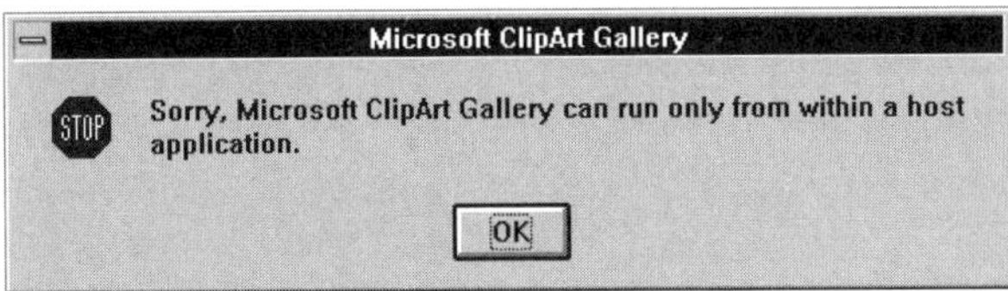

Figure 1.14 How to Say You're Sorry ...

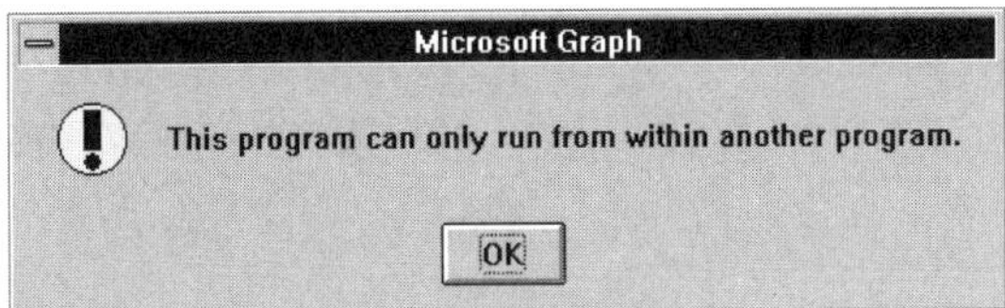

Figure 1.15 ... Four Different ...

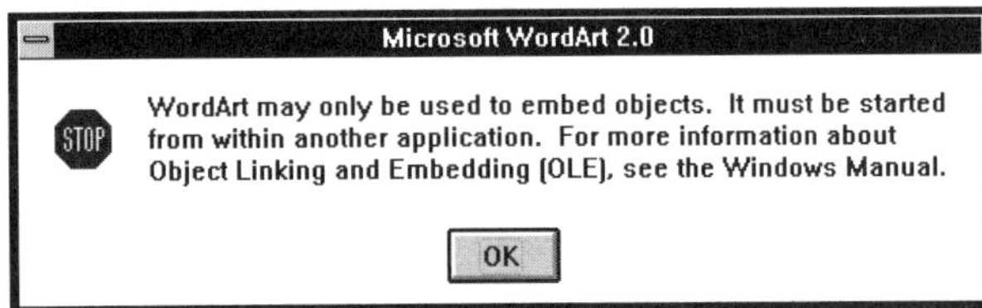

Figure 1.16 ... Ways from Sunday

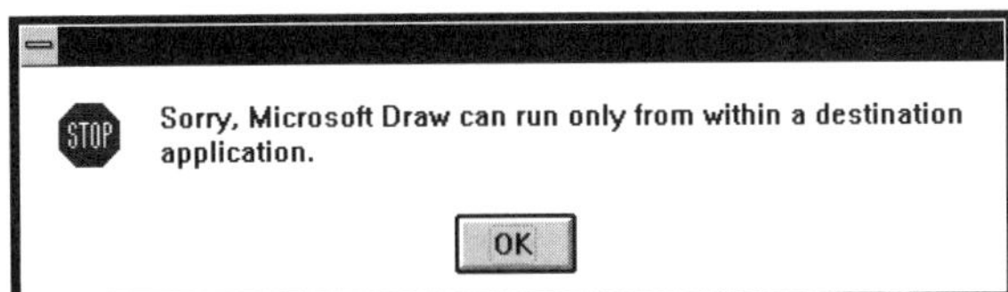

Figure 1.17 Some Common Message Box Text Would Be Nice

OfficeLinks

> If there were no internal propensity to unite, even at a prodigiously rudimentary level—indeed in the molecule itself—it would be physically impossible for love to appear higher up.
>
> Pierre Teilhard de Chardin
> *The Phenomenon of Man,* 1959

If you read enough Microsoft backgrounders, white papers, print media ad copy, and press releases (yawn), you'll eventually stumble onto the term OfficeLinks. It's a Madison Avenue expression that represents the following loose set of features, as of the time of this writing anyway. (Those that we've already mentioned earlier are listed with no discussion, just so you can see how these Redmondian umbrella terms overlap.)

In-place Editing

In our home town, when a cherry new 'Vette screams by on Main Street, we don't exclaim, "Wow, what a neat Hydrocarbon Transportation Device!" Us Real People simply say, "Wow, what a neat car." *In-place editing* is *visual editing* is *in situ editing* is an *OfficeLink* feature is … oh puh-leez, Microsoft, spare us the vernacular voodoo. Yes, it's a great feature, but isn't one appellation enough?

Inter-application Drag-and-Drop

Like in-place editing, this feature is straight out of the OLE 2.0 specifications. It's simply the act of dragging an object between two applications. Yes, it's a good thing but heck, as far as we're concerned this is plain vanilla OLE. That's Madison Avenue for ya.

Word and PowerPoint's Insert Excel Worksheet Feature

Insert Excel Worksheet button … voted Most Popular.

These buttons on Word and PowerPoint's standard toolbars call built-in code to embed an Excel worksheet object. These and other buttons streamline steps that you could perform manually or with a macro, depending on the application, thereby on the whole increasing each application's integration quotient. For example, the manual steps that parallel a single click on Word's Insert Excel Worksheet button are Insert / Object / "Microsoft Excel 5.0 Worksheet" from the Object Type list box / OK. The WordBasic command could be either `InsertExcelTable` or `InsertObject .Class = "Excel.Sheet.5"`. In the case of the programming language-less PowerPoint, your only option aside from the OfficeLinks button would be to insert the object manually.

There are other built-in object-insertion buttons that qualify for OfficeLinks status—a total of six in Word, nine in PowerPoint, and none in Excel.

Ka-boing. None in Excel? Yep, that's right. Excel, indubitably Office's corner-stone application, has no built-in object-insertion buttons. Go figure.

Anyway, the two buttons cited here—Word's Insert Excel Worksheet and PowerPoint's Insert Excel Worksheet—were voted Most Popular by the Redmond usability lab rats, er, participants.

PowerPoint's Insert Word Table Feature

Insert Word Table button

A button on PowerPoint's standard toolbar that invokes built-in code to embed a Word document object into the current slide.

PowerPoint's Report It Feature

Report It button

A button on PowerPoint's standard toolbar that converts a PowerPoint presentation into an outline in Word (as an RTF file).

Word's Present It Feature

Present It button

This button exports a Word outline to PowerPoint where it is converted into a presentation. The latest version of the PresentIt macro—an editable WordBasic macro—is located in the PRESENT.DOT template that comes with Office. To make it more challenging, Microsoft provides this same macro in a PRESENT.DOT file that comes with the Word 6.0a patch, and in the CONVERT.DOT file that comes with Word 6.0. (Watch out! The PresentIt macros in either PRESENT.DOT are identical, but CONVERT.DOT's version of PresentIt is outdated.)

There are, however, a couple of problems. (Kind of sad that one of the very few OfficeLinks features whose code you can actually muck around with is so downright unwilling to be easily installed. Oh well. Karma?) First, when you run the 6.0a "patch" upgrade, it doesn't automatically install PRESENT.DOT if PowerPoint wasn't installed by Office Setup. The workaround is to copy PRESENT.DOT manually from the patch source. Second, someone in Building 16 forgot to create and save the Present It custom toolbar with PRESENT.DOT, so the steps in Microsoft's Knowledge Base article Q112093* on the subject that refer to the Present It toolbar are useless, unless of course you want to create it for them. So much for Making It Easier™. Fortunately, the article's companion steps on how to install the macro as a Standard toolbar button are okay.

---

* See the Appendix to learn how to lay your hands on Knowledge Base articles.

If you have to install PRESENT.DOT manually, the simplest method is to copy it to Word's Startup directory (typically C:\WINWORD\STARTUP) and restart Word. Now, with PRESENT.DOT loaded as a global template, the Present It toolbar button automatically appears on Word's Microsoft toolbar and you don't have to think about it. If, however, you're already loading a bunch of global templates and want to avoid "global clutter," you can copy the PresentIt macro over to NORMAL.DOT.

Group Review and Editing Features

Just what they sound like, accomplished using Word's built-in features Revisions and Annotations in concert with e-mail routing (File / Send [Edit] Routing Slip), which is handled via **MAPI** (Messaging Application Program Interface). MAPI allows mail-enabled Windows applications to interact with a variety of electronic mail services. Not an example of OLE technology.

Import and Export Data Between Access and Its Office Siblings

From Excel's perspective this is the Get External Data feature. From Access' perspective this is the Export feature. Accomplished partly using OLE technology in the sense that Excel and Query communicate via DDE, and Query gets the data from Access via ODBC. Access, on the other hand, doesn't use OLE for this particular transaction, because it writes the data directly to disk in Excel's native file format (binary interchange file format or BIFF). Access' Merge It button, as you saw earlier, merges data with a Word mail merge main document via DDE, and a whole series of "Output To ..." buttons (like Output To MS Excel or Output To MS Word) that do just that via DDE.

Mail Merge Between Word and Its Office Siblings

Accomplished using OLE technology in the sense that Word gets the data from Access via DDE if you request this method, or Word can get the data from Access via ODBC. If Word gets the data from Excel, you have the choice of using a data conversion filter or DDE, but not ODBC (after all, Excel isn't a relational database management system).

Query

An application that can run standalone or serve as a middleman between the inquiring application and the source application. Many Office applications start Query for you automatically (see the previous section on data import/export). Uses DDE and ODBC to get its hands on the data.

Routing

Uses MAPI technology to circulate a document via email among your workgroup peers and let you watch its progress. Look for the File / Send [Edit] Routing Slip menu command available to any Office application that detects Mail installed on the current system. Not an example of OLE technology.

Send Mail

Classic MAPI technology. Not an example of OLE technology.

OfficeLinks Summary

To put this plethora of integration features in perspective, consider Table 1.4. (It's gloating time for your Underground tour guides. You won't easily find this information within any extant Microsoft documentation, and certainly not organized in such an easy to read fashion.)

The table presents each OfficeLinks feature in its order of appearance in this chapter. The implementation column summarizes the underlying technology and its manner of implementation. ("Built-in code" means the feature is compiled in the application's executable file.) Interestingly, note that only one OfficeLink feature is implemented as a user-accessible macro—Word's PresentIt macro.

Table 1.4 Summary of OfficeLinks Features by Application

Application	OfficeLinks Feature	Implementation
All (except Project)	In-place editing	Built-in code and OLE
All (except Access)	Inter-application drag-and-drop	Built-in code and OLE
PowerPoint	Nine object-insertion buttons	Built-in code and OLE
Word	Six object-insertion buttons	Built-in code and OLE
PowerPoint	Report It button	Built-in code
Word	Present It button	WordBasic macro
Excel & Word	Group review & edit	Built-in code
Excel	Get External Data	Built-in code, DDE, and ODBC
Access	Export	Built-in code and ODBC
Access	Merge It button	Built-in code and DDE
Access	Output To ... buttons	Built-in code and DDE
Word	Mail merge	Built-in code, DDE, and ODBC
Excel & Query	Query	Built-in code, DDE, and ODBC
All (except Access)	Routing	Built-in code and MAPI
All	Send Mail	Built-in code and MAPI

Cross-platform Support

> They say opportunity's only got one hair on its head and you got to grab it while it's going by.
>
> William Demarest
> American actor in Preston Sturges's 1944 motion picture *Hail the Conquering Hero*

Microsoft's goal is for all aspects of OLE to work similarly and transparently on all the following platforms—Windows 3.1, Windows NT, Windows 95, and Macintosh. A lofty and noble ambition, indeed. We're all for it. However, it's going to take someone with lots of payroll dollars sitting around idle in a working capital account to test all the permutations among these four platforms and applications running thereon. (Attention venture capitalists, you can contact us through our publisher.) Not to mention the different flavors of Office itself; for example, what about 16-bit Office running under NT or Windows 95, as opposed to 32-bit Office running under same? What about piecemeal applications installed outside the scope of Office (meaning, Word installed by itself as opposed to via Office's Setup), permuted again along the 16-bit or 32-bit dimension, and permuted again by platform? King Gordius himself would cringe.

What happens?   Or consider…if a 16-bit Word for Windows 3.1 flavor compound document with a couple of embedded objects ends up on a Macintosh, what happens? That simple two-word question—"What happens?"—could be answered for every permutation only with a federal grant commensurate with the L.A. Metro Rail project. Dear reader, could this be the conception of a new Underground tome née *The Underground Guide to Cross-Dressing, er, Cross-Platform*? Stay tuned.

Uh Oh, System Requirements

> Energy is beauty—a Ferrari with an empty tank doesn't run.
>
> Elsa Peretti

We found two different sources of information regarding how much disk real estate Office devours, er, requires. But both sources are from the same physical Microsoft CD case! *We're not kidding!* See Table 1.5.

The numbers provided in Table 1.5 come right out of the CD jewel case that ships with Microsoft Office Professional (version 4.3, to be precise). If you open up the jewel case insert (a 17-page document with a part number of 57413) and turn to page 3, you'll see the numbers shown in rows 1 and 3. Then, if you spin up the CD itself and run Office's Online Documentation, the help file reveals the numbers shown in rows 2 and 4 (the CD box has a part number of 55662). Why the differences? As the Shadow might say, "Who knows what evil, er, disk space Office requires?" Apparently, no one.

Table 1.5 Real Estate Is Booming!

Row	Version	Minimum	Typical	Maximum (Complete)
1	Office Standard	31 MB	50 MB	76 MB
2	Office Standard	21 MB	49 MB	68 MB
3	Office Professional	36 MB	68 MB	95 MB
4	Office Professional	29 MB	58 MB	82 MB

Whatever the cause of the requirement discrepancies, the fact remains that you'd better start saving your pennies now for a new one-gigabyte SCSI drive because the whole enchilada weighs in at 82–95 MB, *and that doesn't include Project 4!* Kick in this 13 MB wayward sibling, and you're staring bug-eyed at 95–108 MB. Cowabunga, dude, that's a lot of real estate.

We'll visit this issue of resources again in Chapter 3.

OLE'S BADDEST BUGS

> How would you like a job where, if you made a mistake, a big red light goes on and 18,000 people boo?
>
> Jacques Plante
> National Hockey League goalie

Call us wimps. Call us back-peddlers, turncoats, traitors. Call us wizards who speak with forked tongues. (It's okay, we thrive on rejection.) But before we plunge into the dark belly of the beast, we've got something nice to say. Seriously.

Despite the OLE ills we dissect for all to see herein, keep one thing in mind— *there ain't no competition.* No runners-up. No second place. OLE is the only compound document architecture in town. And you know what? Bottom-line it's a darned good one. Definitely still maturing, but a darned good one nonetheless. **Microsoft OLE is in first place …**

Some of you may have read about OpenDoc and Component Integration Laboratories (CI Labs) in the trades. CI Labs is an association between Apple, Borland, IBM, and Novell/WordPerfect with the goal of producing an object and compound document standard to compete with Microsoft's OLE. That standard is called OpenDoc. In August 1994, CI Labs began shipping an alpha version of OpenDoc for Windows. "Alpha" simply means "way premature." ("Alpha" is computerese for a testing phase prior to the "beta" testing phase. For a gizmo of this scale and complexity, beta typically represents a six to twelve month lag before public release, and alpha precedes beta by three to six months, so the Real Thing probably won't hit the streets for nine to eighteen months. And we're **… and there is no second place.**

betting more on the tail end of the eighteen-month spread.) So, OpenDoc is not running in any extant retail Windows (or other platform) applications. Since you can't put your Digital Extremities™ on a copy, 'nuff said. It's not a competitor. Just fodder for the trade journal pundits.

Now, on to the bug fête.

OLE's "One Page" Object Size Limitation

> If you don't find our canned corned beef to be all you hoped it would be, just leave word with the executor of your estate to return the unopened cans to us for refund.
>
> Bob and Ray

Several of Microsoft's white papers on OLE 2.0 use the term "logical object pagination." At one point in OLE 2.0's development, it was decided to improve on OLE 1.0's limitation whereby if a linked or embedded object spilled across a page break, the object's presentation in the container was truncated there. The underlying data "beyond" the page break was still there, but its truncated presentation made it appear that some data was missing. In spite of Microsoft's claims that OLE 2.0 supports logical object pagination, sadly, it ain't so.

Just because you can't see it doesn't mean it isn't there.

Create a new document in Word (assuming it's got a default Paper Size Height setting of 11 inches). Create a new workbook in Excel. Stuff some data into all the cells in the range A1 through D100 (far more than will fit on a single 11-inch vertical page in Word) and save the workbook. In Word do an Insert / Object / select "Microsoft Excel 5.0 Worksheet" / Create From File / select the saved workbook / click OK. With Word in Page Layout view, scroll to the bottom of the first page and you'll see the Excel worksheet object does not cross the page boundary. When you in-place edit the Excel object and scroll to row 100, you'll see that the underlying "across the border" data is safe and sound.

Excel provides scroll bars once you in-place edit an Excel worksheet object; this way you can easily get to the data that's just across the next page boundary. Not quite so when Word's the server. Embed a lengthy Word document in Excel, then activate it, and there's not a scroll bar in sight. Hitting the Page Down key can get mighty wearisome!

Try increasing the Word document object window beyond what Excel can show on one of its pages, and things can get pretty strange. You'll most likely see an odd horizontal pane separator bar that reacts in a bizarre manner if you try to interact with it. Overall we're of the mind that OLE 2.0 does not implement logical object pagination. Nosiree!

GPFs, Video Drivers, and the Endlessly Circular Finger-Pointing Exercise

> Nothing is ever accomplished by committee unless it consists of three members, one of whom happens to be sick and the other absent.
>
> Hendrik Van Loon

The overwhelming complaint about OLE up on CompuServe is "I did something to an object and all of a sudden ______ (fill in the Office application of your choice) caused a GPF (General Protection Fault)." The Microsoft Product Support Service rep's knee-jerk response is, "It must be your video driver. This won't happen if you run the Windows Standard VGA driver." Right, like we're all going to start commuting to work by horse and buggy. Both Microsoft and video card manufacturers en masse should be held accountable and fix this profusion of video driver–induced OLE GPFs.

Remember that with embedded and linked stuff, the container application has to be able to display the data from the source application. Drop an embedded Excel chart on another application and scale it. Chances are better than even money that the display goes gonzo and shows you a part of the underlying sheet at some huge size. Er, the problem seems to be your video driver.

For video problems, we don't have much better advice than take two aspirin and call the doctor in the morning. Best you can do is try to stay current with the latest driver available for your video board.

> **I got those "Latest video driver version 2.358" blues.**

A disconcerting note is that the cheaper SVGA boards seem to be much more well behaved than the super high-powered snakelike or fighter-plane–like cards. Just a pattern we've noticed. Take it with a grain of salt.

There's a Shortage of OLE Developers Out There

> I get satisfaction of three kinds. One is creating something, one is being paid for it, and one is the feeling that I haven't just been sitting on my ass all afternoon.
>
> William F. Buckley, Jr.

Developing OLE-compliant applications is an exceedingly daunting task. Even inside the Microsoft application family, you can see glimpses of inconsistent implementation. For example, Excel and Word have dramatically different dialog boxes governing broken-link management. The point is, if Microsoft's own application developers can fall victim to the overwhelming complexity of the OLE architecture, imagine the potential for inconsistency and confusion when non-Microsoft ISVs (independent software vendors) get on the OLE bandwagon and start delivering their own flavor of OLE-compliant applications. As the body of knowledge on this arcane subject grows and more OLE developers come on line, Windows applications in general will catch up to the standard being set today by Microsoft Office applications. But for right now, Microsoft and a small number of specialty tool developers are the entire line-up.

Cloaked Applications

> Something deeply hidden had to be behind things.
>
> Albert Einstein
> Autobiographical handwritten note

There are common, everyday scenarios in which a server application is started by some OLE editing session, OLE Automation macro call, or a DDE paste link, but is either started in a hidden window or never properly dismissed or both. We call these "cloaked applications." They're there in local memory sucking up resources but you can't easily tell they're there—well, not until you've read this book! We de-cloak these lurking resource hogs in Chapter 3.

No Network Awareness, Yet

> The mind, conscious of rectitude, laughed to scorn the falsehood of report.
>
> Ovid
> *Fasti*

OLE doesn't currently support distributed objects. Its benefits are limited to object interaction on the local workstation. Microsoft indicates it is hard at work on providing an extension to OLE whereby "users could easily integrate objects on different computers as if they were all local." It's called "Distributed OLE." Look for it in Cairo.

Inadequate Roving Link Management

> A young student, obviously enamored with the virtues of brevity, wrote the following essay on the life of Socrates: "Socrates was a philosopher. He went around pointing out errors in the way things were done. They fed him hemlock."
>
> Unknown

Imagine a Word compound document with a link to a range of cells in an Excel worksheet, where both documents are in the same directory. If you move only the container file, the link is maintained. No big surprise there. If you move both the container and the source files to another directory *and both are still together in the same directory*, the link is maintained. In fact, as long as the relative position of the container and the source files is maintained during a move, the link is maintained. Say you have a container file called

```
C:\TESTBED\MONDAY\HEATHER\CONTAINR.DOC
```

and a source file called

```
C:\TESTBED\MONDAY\SPRINGLI\SOURCE.XLS
```

If you move `C:\TESTBED` and all its children en masse to `D:\` or `D:\TARGET\KACHING` or ... (you get the idea), the link is maintained. This is all very good (and a new feature in OLE 2.0, by the way). However, any permutation that disrupts the relative position relationship will break the link.

Imagine a Word compound document with a link to an Excel object in an Excel worksheet, with each document in a different directory. If you move only the source file, *the link is broken and you get no automatic notification.* Alternately, if you move both of them somewhere else (thereby breaking their relative path relationship), even if that somewhere is the same directory, *the link is broken and you get no automatic notification.* You can (with some but not all the Office applications) tell the link management dialog to change the path to the source, thereby repairing the link, *but you have to figure out for yourself that the link is broken in the first place.* Bummer. What we'd *really* like to see (and admittedly this is no trivial programming task) is a robust link watchdog buried inside OLE and/or the operating system that transparently tracks all object links, without limitation. That'd be cool. Cairo, perhaps? In the meantime, read Table 1.6 and weep.

Table 1.6 Damage Control for Roving Links

Container and Source Location	Result
Origin irrelevant (move only the container file)	Link doesn't change so no link management feature involved
Same origin, same destination (move only the files themselves)	Link is updated (new in OLE 2.0)
Same origin, same destination (move the files and their relative paths)	Link is updated (new in OLE 2.0)
Relative paths change	Link is broken
Origin irrelevant (move only the source file)	Link is broken

Inner-to-Outer Embedded Object Rules

> If it moves, salute it.
>
> If it doesn't move, pick it up.
>
> If you can't pick it up, paint it.
>
> U.S. Army saying

It is possible to embed objects inside objects that are themselves embedded objects. You can go pretty deep, too, with this nested embedding stuff. However, hang on to your spelunking helmet and have plenty of Dramamine on hand. We explore the following Underground rules for navigating nested embeds in more detail in Chapter 4.

- Never quit an application that's behaving as an active server until all nested embeds have been individually updated.

- Always perform these updates in the proper order, that is, update from the innermost object back out to the outermost container.

Embedded Links Really Don't Work

> The doctor can bury his mistakes but an architect can only advise his client to plant vines.
>
> Frank Lloyd Wright

Question—can you nest links? Answer—yes, but you'd best be prepared to treat them all as manual links because even if they're Automatic, they're not. Sorry about that pilgrim, but it's the unadulterated truth. We dig into this issue in more detail in Chapter 3.

OLE Automation Is a Version 1.0 Technology

> A prudent question is one-half of wisdom.
>
> Francis Bacon

OLE itself is now up to version 2.0. But OLE Automation wasn't around in OLE version 1.0; it's new on the scene with OLE 2.0. The simple algebra is this—OLE Automation is in its very first release, so proceed with caution. In Chapters 7 and 8 we explore when OLE Automation is a prince and when it's a frog.

Woefully Inadequate Documentation

> By whom?
>
> Dorothy Parker, when told she was outspoken

There is no single, all-inclusive source of information about the user interface aspects of OLE object creation and manipulation. Office application *User Guide* documentation and help files typically contain a paragraph or two, at most, about this very complex and powerful feature set. In many cases, there is no documentation whatsoever. (We point these omissions out to you throughout this book where they are of consequence.)

Back to the point of "no single, all-inclusive source of information about the user interface aspects of OLE object creation and manipulation" in the previous paragraph. We stand corrected. There was no such source until now … and you're reading it! Let the Underground tour begin.

Oh, for the Love of Lexicon

All excellent things are as difficult as they are rare.

Benedict Spinoza
Ethics, 1677

This chapter is your first stepping stone in a series of hops, skips, and jumps along the trail to OLE nirvana.* Picture Chapter 1 as our introductory chat before embarking on this exciting journey. Now, as you plunge eagerly onto the trail itself, we'll hand out some new vocabulary terms, review the terms we explored briefly in Chapter 1, and begin to put the pieces of OLE's puzzle together into a meaningful context. Then in Chapter 3, with your burgeoning vocabulary slung over your shoulder like so many cartridges in your bandolier, you'll get down and dirty in the OLE trenches.

OLE nirvana

First, let's review where OLE's been these past few years.

OLE'S METEORIC HISTORY

Once you get into this great stream of history, you can't get out.

Richard M. Nixon

First there was DDE, provided as a service within Windows itself. Then there was OLE 1, born December 10, 1990, the formal specification's release date. And now there's OLE 2.

According to the historians, back in 1988 a couple of PC industry firms wanted to extend DDE. By the time the dust settled, the contributors to what was called the "extensible Compound Document Architecture" (eCDA) specification included folks from Aldus Corporation, Borland International, Iris Incorporated, Lotus Development Corporation, Metaphor Corporation, Micrografx, Microsoft's

OLE's Potsdam

* Kraig Brockschmidt has written "the book" on OLE 2 for C/C++ developers, aptly entitled *Inside OLE 2.* We first encountered (and fell in love with) the term "OLE nirvana" therein.

applications architecture group, Microsoft's PowerPoint product group, Samna Corporation, and WordPerfect Corporation. Microsoft announced the final eCDA specification at Comdex in November of 1990 and christened it Object Linking and Embedding, version 1.

The OLE avalanche of '91

In February 1991, Microsoft and Lotus shipped the first OLE 1-compliant applications—Microsoft Excel 3 and Lotus Notes 2. Many, many other ISVs followed in the OLE avalanche of '91.

According to Microsoft, the development of the OLE 2 specification began almost immediately after version 1 was a fait accompli. Also according to Microsoft, more than 150 ISVs were involved in something the Redmondians call the Open Process approach to the development of the OLE 2 specification. The following material is from the white paper *Microsoft's Open Process*.

"Open Process involves independent software vendors (ISVs) in operating system development at the earliest possible stage, during the time of the first technical proposal. This phase often occurs a full year or more before new technology is implemented to allow ample opportunity for ISVs to affect system development. At the developer-to-developer forums, senior designers and architects from Microsoft and from third-party vendors present their approaches and discuss operating system design challenges. This direct exchange leads to design modifications and finally results in new operating system features and functions.

Comments from ISVs have been instrumental in shaping APIs such as object linking and embedding (OLE), Messaging API (MAPI), Open Database Connectivity (ODBC), network interfacing, and Win32, the 32-bit Microsoft Windows API."

As the pages of the 1991 and 1992 calendars flew by, the specification took shape. It ultimately manifested itself in the host of Office 4, which was released in dribs and drabs in late 1993 and early 1994. Specifically, Word 6 and Excel 5 were the first commercial applications to incorporate OLE 2 technology. The rest of the Office family followed suite (pun intended) shortly thereafter. That was then, this is now, and OLE 2 is here to stay. Until OLE 3 gets here.

THE GESTALT OF OLE 2

> The principal mark of genius is not perfection but originality, the opening of new frontiers.
>
> Arthur Koestler

New frontiers. Yes indeed. OLE opens 'em wide up. A scintillating, breath-taking work of quintessential genius. But that begs the question, "What is it?" Let's take this from several different angles. We'll try a streamlined definition on for size (with apologies to the architects of OLE). Then we'll examine how big OLE is and what it's made of. Last we'll make a list of what it enables us—users, macro programmers, C/C++ programmers, system architects, the whole caboodle—to do, by golly.

Square One—A Streamlined Definition

> There is one thing stronger than all the armies in the world: and that is an idea whose time has come.
>
> Victor Hugo

Microsoft has this to say about its prodigy: "… object technology is useful only if there are commonly accepted methods of interaction among applications that use objects. A standard set of object services must be made available to applications through the operating system. The object linking and embedding (OLE) **application programming interface** (API), developed by Microsoft in cooperation with other independent software vendors (ISVs), provides this set of services." Pardon us for jumping in as we rearrange this a bit, "Object linking and embedding is an application programming interface that provides a standard set of object services." Fourteen words in all. Vastly, criminally oversimplified. (Hey, someone had to do it.)

How Big Is It?

> Windows version 1 had about 350 API functions. OLE 2 has over 100. So by measures of new functionality, OLE 2 is roughly one-third of an operating system.
>
> Kraig Brockschmidt
> *Inside OLE 2*

The files that comprise OLE total 1,114,080 bytes. A small footprint for an impressive object architecture. Table 2.1 lists the files that ship with OLE 2.

Table 2.1 OLE 2 Files, Sizes, and Descriptions

Filename	Size (bytes)	Description
COMPOBJ.DLL	102,400	A library of services that attach or bind objects to the application attempting to use those objects.
OLE2.DLL	313,344	A library of services used by OLE objects and containers.

continued

Table 2.1 OLE 2 Files, Sizes, and Descriptions (continued)

Filename	Size (bytes)	Description
OLE2.REG	24,606	Contains standard OLE 2 and OLE Automation registration information for use with the registration database REG.DAT.
OLE2CONV.DLL	57,328	Used to convert between object types.
OLE2DISP.DLL	98,336	A library of OLE Automation functions that allow the methods and properties of OLE Automation (programmable) objects to be invoked.
OLE2NLS.DLL*	147,440	A library of functions that support and resolve national language differences, primarily for OLE Automation applications. (Not needed if your application doesn't involve multiple languages.)
OLE2PROX.DLL	55,808	A library of services that acts as an ombudsman between container and server applications.
STDOLE.TLB	4,322	OLE type library.
STORAGE.DLL	157,184	A library of services that implements OLE's structured storage specification, which manifests itself in the form of compound files.
TYPELIB.DLL	153,312	Provides access to OLE Automation type libraries.

However, more relevant and compelling than the storage space required by OLE is its overall architecture.

What Treasures Lie Within?

> Settle back, mix your color-tinis, and relax as you watch the pictures fly through the air.
>
> Tom Snyder
> *Tom Snyder*

Table 2.2 is an overview of OLE's two-tier architecture and is adapted from the *OLE 2 Programmer's Reference, Volume 1* (Microsoft Press).

Table 2.2 OLE's Two-tier Architecture

Current Features		Future Features
Structured Storage	Data Transfer	Naming and Binding
Component Object Model		

* "NLS" stands for National Language Support.

The lower tier comprises OLE's infrastructure and the upper tier represents the features available to us, the users (both today and into the future). The Component Object Model is the cornerstone of OLE's infrastructure. According to the *OLE 2 Programmer's Reference*, "The Component Object Model specifies how objects interact within a single application or between applications." The Component Object Model has a specific set of services that it provides, namely, interface negotiation, memory management, error and status reporting, and interprocess communication. The three other elements (or service blocks) of the foundation tier—structured storage, data transfer, and naming and binding—provide additional basic services.

If you're interested in the extensive, gritty, fascinating details behind each and every one of these OLE components, then we have some recommended readings for you.*

Recall we said a moment ago that the upper tier is divided into current features and those made possible by OLE's architecture but which have yet to be implemented. The four extant feature categories are

OLE's current features

- compound document management

- in-place editing

- drag-and-drop

- programmability

As demonstrated early on in Chapter 1, behind those four simple phrases lies a tremendous amount of OLE firepower waiting to be unleashed through your Digital Extremities™. Let's take them one at a time.

Compound Document Management

> It's hard for me to get used to these changing times. I can remember when the air was clean and sex was dirty.
>
> George Burns

A **compound document** is a document maintained by a container application and contains one or more compound document objects. A compound document object (or, for our purposes, an object) is a piece of data created and maintained by a server application (also called an editor application[†]). So "compound document

---

* Kraig Brockschmidt's *Inside OLE 2* (Microsoft Press) and the *OLE 2 Programmer's Reference, Volume 1 and Volume 2* (Microsoft Press).

[†] Various OLE programming reference works use the term "object application" as a synonym for server application.

management" refers to the myriad OLE services that support compound documents and compound document objects.

From a user's perspective, an object can be either embedded or linked. An **embedded object** is physically stored entirely within the compound document. A **linked object** is a pointer to data that is physically stored outside the compound document. (With OLE 2 it is also possible for a linked object to point to data in a different location within the same compound document).

At the core of compound document technology is the idea that we, the users, are more productive when we interact with applications that help us focus our attention on the information at hand rather than on the application that houses that information. Idealistically and metaphorically speaking, in a human conversation you listen to what your partner is saying (the information) and pay little heed to her/his appearance (the "application"). An environment or architecture that focuses the user's attention on the information at hand is called document-centric (also, but less frequently, information-centric). This is in contrast to the waning computing model called application-centric, in which the user spent more energy relating to the application than the information at hand.

You'll see and use these concepts throughout Chapters 3 and 4.

In-place Editing

As described in Chapter 1, in-place editing is the ability to edit an embedded object directly from within the compound document. It means that the user interface of the container application changes and displays the commands of the server application.

As we pointed out in Chapter 1, but it bears repeating: *the following terms all mean exactly the same thing.*

- in-place editing
- in-place activation
- visual editing
- in situ editing

More on this concept in Chapters 3 and 4.

Drag-and-Drop

A seemingly innocuous user interface feature, once you start using it you're hooked and there's no going back. Drag-and-drop uses mouse/keyboard techniques plus informative, dynamic, and immediate mouse-cursor feedback to dramatically streamline the haggard old "copy/cut then switch to target then

paste" routine. Furthermore, drag-and-drop applies to whole files as well as objects. Drag-and-drop is as easy as it sounds. *Just do it.*

There is more to drag-and-drop than meets the eye, er, mouse as you'll see in Chapter 3.

Programmability

Programmability in this context is synonymous with OLE Automation. As defined in Chapter 1, OLE Automation is an industry standard that applications use to expose their OLE objects to development tools, macro languages, and other applications that support OLE Automation.

More on this in Chapters 7 and beyond.

THE RUNNING OF THE APPS

> Let Hercules himself do what he may,
> The cat will mew and dog will have his day.
>
> William Shakespeare
> *Hamlet*

Since we've been examining the infrastructure of the Office suite and the OLE model, it's only fair to see what type of cumulative drain Office puts on a traditional Windows workstation. Of course, there's no such thing as a "traditional workstation," so in the following list we define the test hardware and software configuration we used in our experiment.

1. 486DX2/66 CPU with 16 MB of RAM running MS-DOS 6.20, Windows for Workgroups 3.1, and Office Professional 4.3.

2. ATI Graphics Ultra Pro VLB mach32 video card running the ATI mach32 driver at 800x600x256.

3. Reasonably normal `AUTOEXEC.BAT` and `CONFIG.SYS` settings (no esoteric third-party memory managers or other such beasts loaded).

4. Clean load= and run= keys in `WIN.INI`.

5. Program Manager as the Windows shell.

6. Only the Microsoft Office Manager (MOM) in the StartUp program group, with MOM default buttons Word, Excel, PowerPoint, Access, Find File, Online Documentation, and Office.

7. Resource sharing disabled in Control Panel (Network / clear the Enable Sharing check box and allow Windows to reboot itself).

8. An average number of program groups and items within those groups.

9. All applications running as close as possible to stock, out-of-the-box, as delivered by Office Setup. For example, no Word add-ins loaded but some Access and Excel add-ins loaded (exactly as they were set up by Office Setup).

10. Each application allowed to create its traditional, empty startup document.

11. Use Microsoft System Info 1.00A (ships with Office) to check User and GDI percent available resources. (Close SysInfo after each examination.)

12. *Note that none of the results in Table 2.3 reflect what happens if Mail is running.*

Let's get experimental.   Table 2.3 and Table 2.4 present the experimental results as a pair of data points—User and GDI percent available per System Info 1.00A—in cumulative, load-order succession (User, GDI). We arbitrarily loaded the Office applications alphabetically (except for Project, which we loaded last in all tests because Project is not truly a part of the Office suite)

Table 2.3 Office Standard—Resource Stress Testing

	No Apps*	Access	Excel	PPT	Word	Project
With MOM	83, 78	—	61, 60	46, 49	34, 34	33, 21
Resources consumed	—	—	-22, -18	-15, -11	-12, -15	-1, -13

As a measure of the incremental drain on resources presented by each application in succession, see the "Resources consumed" row. These values represent the absolute percentage point change from the prior machine state (User, GDI).

Hmmm, seems okay. Excel and PowerPoint are the big drains, followed closely by Word. Project has the smallest User appetite. Resources are left a little thin, but all four applications—Excel, PowerPoint, Word, and Project—are up and running. Let's add Access to the mix. Office Professional, here we come! See Table 2.4.

Table 2.4 Office Professional—Resource Stress Testing

	No Apps	Access	Excel	PPT	Word	Project
With MOM	83, 78	78, 68	57, 52	41, 39	30, 26	28, 11
Without MOM	86, 85	80, 75	57, 59	41, 45	30, 31	28, 16
Without MOM (with test docs)	86, 85	78, 70	53, 45	38, 32[†]	26, 14	N/A

* Only Program Manager running on the Windows desktop.
† Slide view.

When we ran Project under the "Professional (w/ MOM)" scenario, Project started, then displayed a system-modal message box "Microsoft Project Out of memory or system resources." Clicking OK cleared the message box, Project's interface was fubar,* but we could still run System Info. We used ALT + F4 to exit Project. Under the same scenario without MOM running, Project started properly and presented its standard interface without incident. Don't get us wrong—we like MOM, but you might want to see if you can live without her.

As a final stress test, we loaded each application and opened one medium-sized document in each. (You, too, can perform this very same experiment from the comfort of your own PC! Each test document is one that ships with its parent application; the documents are listed in Table 2.5.) The results appear in the "Professional (without MOM with test docs)" row.[†] When we tried to run Project under this scenario, it started and then displayed the system-modal message box "Microsoft Project Out of memory or system resources" as before, at which point clicking OK cleared the message box but Project's interface was dysfunctional. For example, we selected Help / About and got the classic "An error has occurred in your application … WINPROJ4 [Close / Ignore]" message. The system refused to load System Info so we clicked the Close button and used ALT + F4 to get the hell out of Project.

Table 2.5 Sample In-the-box Documents We Used in the Underground Test Flight of Office

Application	Document Path And Filename	Size
Access	…\ACCESS\SAMPAPPS\ORDERS.MDB	229K
Excel	…\EXCEL\EXAMPLES\SAMPLES.XLS	139K
PowerPoint	…\POWERPNT\SAMPLES\TIMELINE.PPT	81K
Word	…\WINWORD\TEMPLATE\INVOICE.DOT	27K
Project	…\WINPROJ\LIBRARY\MKTPLAN.MPT	41K

Figure 2.1 graphically portrays the cumulative state of system resources in the "Professional (without MOM with test docs)" case.

The moral of the story is …

- To minimize Office's drain on your system resources, don't run MOM. You'll save 5% (absolute percentage points) in GDI resources.

- If you thought you'd be able to run all the Microsoft Office applications plus Project simultaneously, well, you can't (at least we couldn't). But it is possible

---

* Fouled up beyond all recognition.

[†] Only the sample document was open for any given application, that is, no other child windows were open.

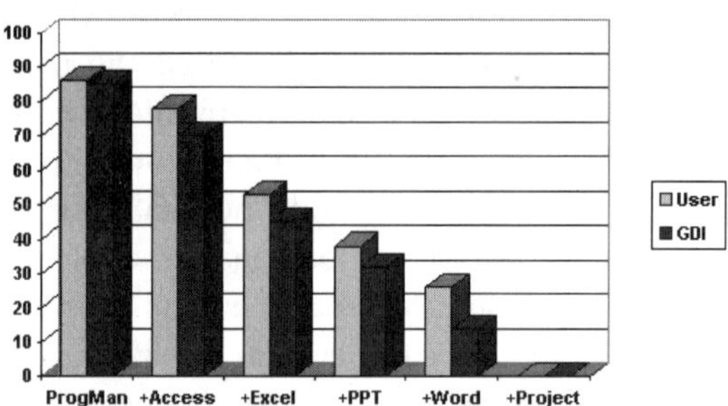

Figure 2.1 Changes in System Resource as Office Applications Load Cumulatively

to load up all of Office Professional (excluding Mail, see the gotcha below), including one medium-sized document per application. Remember, loading an application with a document is not the same as loading an application with a compound document which in turn is packed to the gills with links and embedded objects. This type of use taxes your resources even more, so beware.

If you run Mail, we have some news for you. And fer sure this ain't in the *User's Guide*. First, note that all the above experimental results were based on cases without Mail running. If you change the experimental steps by running Mail before any of the other Office applications are loaded, the end results are as follows. If you insist on running MOM and open our sample suite of documents, you'll do fine *until you try to load Word.* Then you'll be visited by Word's "There is not enough memory to complete the operation" message and spiral quickly into user interface hell. If you drop MOM like a hot potato and open our sample suite of documents, this time Word loads okay; Project won't load at all, but at least you get everyone in the immediate Office family together in the same room.

THERE'S A REGISTRATION DATABASE BEHIND THAT CURTAIN

> There is nothing so nice as doing good by stealth and being found out by accident.
>
> Charles Lamb

The registration database is a table of information about Windows applications. Most (but not all) of this information is related to OLE client and server applications and the services they are capable of providing. The registration database's filename is `REG.DAT`, which is typically located in your primary Windows directory (`C:\WINDOWS`). This file and the mechanics by which applications and Windows use the information stored in it are provided by Windows itself. When applications install themselves, they update the registration database as needed, all in a manner designed to be transparent to the user. You should rarely have cause to manually edit this file. *Warning—this is not a text file that can be edited by a text editor.*

You can use the Registration Editor either in plain vanilla mode (`REGEDIT.EXE`) or with the verbose switch (`REGEDIT.EXE /V`) to view the entries and settings therein. But a discussion of the database's structure and the techniques for editing, updating, merging, and restoring it are beyond the scope of this book. For clear and crafty instructions on when and how to probe your registration database, we highly recommend Woody Leonhard and Barry Simon's *The Mother of All Windows Books* (Addison-Wesley). (There really isn't much of anywhere else to go for helpful information on this topic, and besides, it's a hands-down must-have. And by all means get the CD-ROM version, affectionately nicknamed *CD-MOM*. Note: here our use of "MOM" is entirely different from the Microsoft Office "MOM" that's an acronym for "Microsoft Office Manager.")

But no matter what you do (or don't do) with your registration database, absolutely and without fail be sure to back up `REG.DAT` often. And if you ever do put on your latex gloves and go mucking about in the guts of this file, *please make a backup copy first*.

CD-MOM is recommended RegEdit reading.

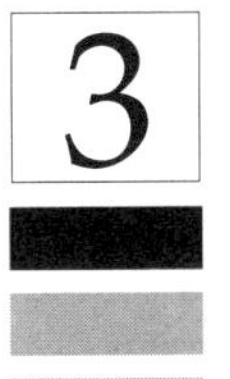 3   A Compound Document in Sheep's Clothing

Just as the move from MS-DOS-based applications to graphical applications resulted in new levels of usability and productivity, we believe the move from the current generation of applications to the new world of information-centric applications will result in tremendous increases in user productivity.

B. Gates
Microsoft press release (10/19/93)

"Information-centric." Now there's a mouthful for you. In Chapter 2 the hot buzz words like document-centric, compound document, and information-centric were discussed and brought down out of the marketing hype clouds. This information-centric concept is the linchpin of what we like to call the age of Information at Your Digital Extremities™. Catchy, huh?

Information at Your Digital Extremities™

"Objects" and the methods of linking and embedding them are supposed to usher in this new age. Eventually, the documents you create with your computer won't be the product of a single application at all. That's right. Instead of having a Word document or an Excel workbook, you'll have a data document that contains a word processing object and/or a spreadsheet object. These data documents will be created using a collection of OLE toolsets (*ka-ching!*). Did you hear something like a cash register ringing way up north just then? Hmmm, never mind. You'll plug different toolsets right into your operating system, a word processor toolset, a charting toolset, a spreadsheet toolset, and so on. Different companies will sell toolsets that plug into the operating system too, but it's quite likely that the operating system will come with an ample set to start with. *Ka-ching!*

Let's look at how OLE 2.0 measures up as the forerunner of this grand vision.

DOGGIN' THAT LINKING AND EMBEDDING DOGMA

Hey Red! Whatcha got in the basket?

B. B. Wolf

This is where we grab that Object Linking and Embedding tiger by the tail, throw it to the ground, muzzle it, look inside the beast and see how it works from the user's point of view.

OLE fundamentals   Fortunately, there is a common set of hoops that you jump through to utilize OLE technology in your documents, so once you grasp the fundamentals, you're 80% there for each OLE server or editor you might want to use. Sure there are gotchas, er, we mean, uhm, idiosyncrasies, yeah that's it! Some are situational, some are hardware dependent, but once you slog through all the ins and outs, it's like spiritual enlightenment—well worth the wait.

A lot of the terms used to describe different components of the typical compound document are used somewhat interchangeably as was discussed in Chapter 2. For the sake of clarity, even though the terms server and editor are synonymous, in this chapter we consistently use **server** to describe the application that provides updated information to the compound document versus **editor,** which describes an application used to edit an embedded data object.

The Compound Document

It is a melancholy of mine own, compounded of many simples, extracted from many objects ....

Shakespeare
As You Like It

We defined "compound document" in Chapter 2 as "a document maintained by a container application, and containing one or more compound document objects." Okay, but what the heck does that mean to us lowly users? Let's take a more empirical tack.

A document containing a link to another file is a compound document. Or a document with an embedded object is a compound document. For example, a Word document with a table of figures linked to Excel with maybe a Visio schematic thrown in is definitely a compound document.

If the figures in Excel are changed, the link in the compound Word document can be updated and so reflect the changes. To edit the schematic, a quick double-click on the Visio object and bam, Visio appears and you use its tools to make your changes.

In order for a compound document to be fully functional, you need to have installed the originating or server applications that were used to create:

- the file that your compound document is linked to

- the embedded objects

If you do not have access to the server program(s) or linked data files, only the last *presentation* of the linked data is displayed so you can view but not edit any of the linked objects. Oh, there's talk of someday passing compound documents around between dissimilar document-processing systems. Like taking a moderately complex Word compound document and opening it in AmiPro or WordPerfect using conversion utilities for converting from the format of one package to another. Don't hold your breath.

Links Across the Ether

> The silver link, the silken tie,
> Which heart to heart and mind to mind
> In body and in soul can bind.
>
> Sir Walter Scott
> *The Lay of the Last Minstrel*

Data (and you had best get in the habit of saying "data object" when referring to either data used in a link or data embedded as an object) can be *linked* to a compound document as opposed to *embedded* within it. This difference between object linking and object embedding all boils down to where the actual data resides. If you embed data from another application into say an Excel worksheet, *all* of that data is stuffed into the guts of the Excel binary file that us Mere Mortals call a workbook. The source data file could be deleted altogether with no effect on the embedded object. More on embedded objects coming up later.

If, on the other hand, data in another application's document is linked to an Excel worksheet, the data remains external to Excel. A representation, or perhaps more accurately, an echo of the data is displayed in the Excel worksheet. If the linked data in the external application is modified, the data in Excel is updated to reflect those changes.

Ask not for whom ... ask where the data tolls, er, resides.

The thing to remember when dealing with links is that the data isn't really in the container application at all, only its reflection is.

Edit Paste Special for Simple Links

One man's "simple" is another man's "huh?"

David Stone
Omni, May 1979

Let's look at an example. In Figure 3.1 you see a single paragraph linked from a Word document to an Excel worksheet. Here Word is the server, Excel is the container.

B2	↓	{=Word.Document.6|Document2!'DDE_LINK2'}				
A	**B**	**C**	**D**	**E**	**F**	**G**
1						
2	The quick green fox jumps over the lazy dog.					
3						

Figure 3.1 Data in Word Linked to Excel

Formulas, fields, and functions, oh my!

Note the strange looking stuff in Excel's formula bar. Links are accomplished using fields or functions since they are really just pointers to where the actual data resides. The field has to know where to find the data; in this case, it's an object of the class Word.Document.6, in a data file named Document2 (it has not yet been saved to disk or this would include a fully qualified path and filename), and the coordinates of the data within the data file being linked. In Word this is a **bookmark**, "DDE_LINK2." This array-entered formula can be created following these steps:

1. Select and copy some text in a Word document.

2. Switch to Excel and create a new workbook.

3. Select the destination (in Excel's case a cell).

4. Pull down the Edit menu and click Paste Special.

5. In the Paste Special dialog box, select Text in the As list box, click the Paste Link radio button, and then click on OK. See Figure 3.2.

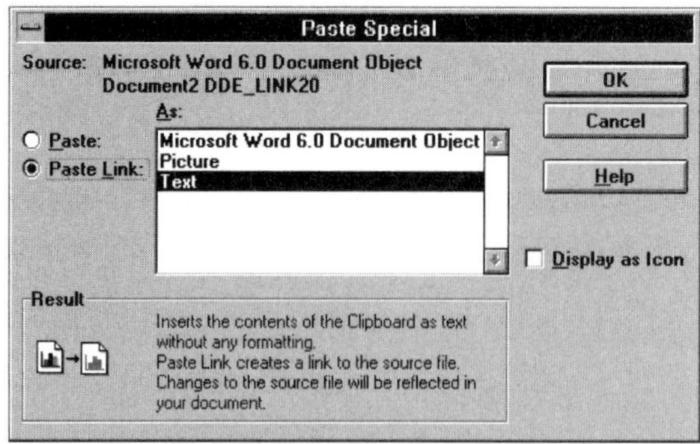

Figure 3.2 Paste Special Settings for Linked Text

Changes made to the text in Word are reflected in Excel. If both data files are open (both the Word document with the source data and the Excel worksheet that contains the link), changes are reflected almost instantaneously (give or take two to three seconds). Uhm, usually that is. There are, as we say in ConsultantSpeak, some "issues" here and we'll discuss them shortly.

Notice that Excel is willing to link the incoming data as Text, a Picture, or as a Document Object. Excel, being what it is, can only hold 255 characters in a cell. This severely limits the amount of Text you can link to. You can work around this limitation by linking the data as a Document Object, which displays the linked data as a graphic. This is like a text box or any of the other drawing objects you may be used to in Excel. It can be resized (once you know the tricks) or you can drag it over the graphical layer of the worksheet.

A link using the Text format creates an array formula in Excel (notice the curly brackets in Figure 3.1) whereas the Document Object and Picture formats do not. What is odd is that if you edit the Text link formula manually and fail to reenter it as an array, the link still works.

When you create a link from Excel to Word, the source data in Word is automatically marked with a bookmark (the DDE_LINK2 part of the formula shown in Figure 3.1). This provides a way for the link to find the specific data to be linked to in Word. A bookmark in Word is like a range name in Excel.

You can create multiple links from Excel to the same bookmark name where some links use the Document Object format and others use the Picture format. But you *can't* use either the Picture or Document Object formats *and* the Text format to the same bookmark name. If you copy some text in Word, switch to Excel, paste-link as a Document Object, select another cell in the same workbook, and do a paste-link using the Text format, the link formula returns a #VALUE error. If you assign a different bookmark name in Word (Edit / Bookmark / type in a name / click Add) to the same text and then edit the link formula in Excel to use the new bookmark name, the link won't work. Not that we can think why you'd ever want to do multiple links to the same data using different formats; but if you did, that's how you would do it.

Mechanics of Presentation in Edit Paste Special

If you were to link the same data residing in Word to Visio (either a Visio file or a Visio object embedded in another application), you would see almost the identical Paste Special dialog box in Visio. But Visio only supports linked data from Word as an object for presentation—remember, you have to select the Paste Link radio button to do a link as opposed to a plain paste. The link is simply a pointer in the compound document to where the data actually is; the data is not in the compound document.

The client application has to be able to *present* that data to the outside world from within the compound document. What format the presentation takes is controlled by the client application. Say you have a paragraph in Word and you want to include a key number from an Excel worksheet. Word can present the data linked in from Excel as an object, a picture, or as unformatted text. The best format would be unformatted text that lets the data *appear* to be a natural part of the text in Word.

The movement towards standardized dialog boxes is a great boon to software users. Within Microsoft applications, for example, the Paste Special dialog boxes are all nearly identical in form and function. Visio is a non-Microsoft application but its Paste Special dialog conforms to the Microsoft standard. Yea! One for the users!

Managing Links

The OLE specification allows for links to be *automatic* or *manual*. As you would think, automatic links update without any interaction required on your part. Manual links don't update until you update them. Pretty straightforward. Each container application provides a method to manage any links in the current compound document.

Rise up and break your chains, er, links. Figure 3.3 shows the current state of the art in links management dialog boxes with PowerPoint acting as our container application. If you're in a document that contains links, you'll usually find a Links option on the Edit menu.

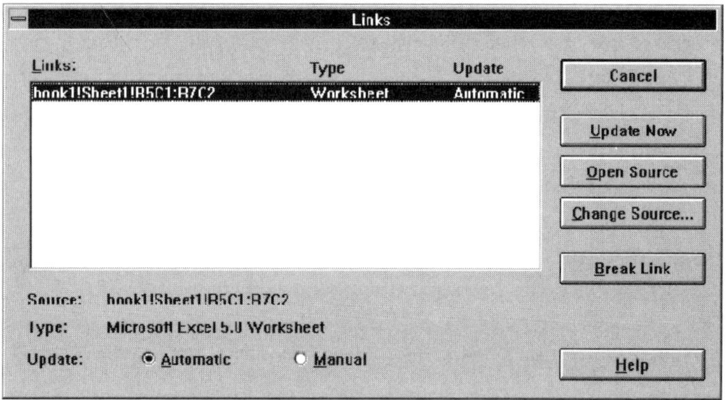

Figure 3.3 Edit Links Dialog Box in PowerPoint

You see a list of links (only one in this example), the Type (that is, what type of object the link is linked to), and the Update status of the link—in this case, Automatic. Using the command buttons, you can force a link to update, open the source document, change the link to a different source, and (drum roll, please) *break a link!*

We just mightily praised the Redmond Rangers for standardizing dialog boxes that perform the same function across applications. Well, the Underground Guide giveth, and the Underground Guide busteth in the chops. The standardization of the Links dialog boxes is still a work in progress. Word and Excel are marching to their own drummers at this point in time. Consider Figure 3.4.

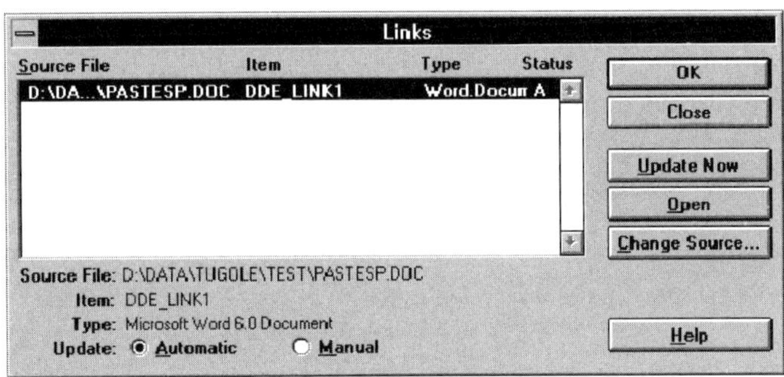

Figure 3.4 Excel's Links Dialog Box

Some differences in labels, hmmm, that's okay, although you have to guess that "A" in the status column means automatic. Still, not too long a stretch. But what's a real slap in the face with a wet fish is the lack of a Break Link command button.

Why is this a problem? The idea is to empower and encourage you to take this integration stuff seriously and use things like links in your documents. Let's say you link up a document (some kind of report or proposal) to several data files because the data is dynamic and you want the latest figures in your report. At some point this document goes golden, it's final, signed, sealed, and delivered. Right after you print the final copy you should break all the links. If you pull up this document later you don't want all the data changing. What if someone's been playing what-if with some of the data your report is linked to? You go back to print one more copy a week later and your numbers are fubar.

A link that you break using the Links dialog box in Visio or Word becomes static as though the data had been pasted (but not paste-linked) into your compound document. It is no longer just a presentation but becomes real data. Let's hope Excel catches up in this regard real soon.

When you have a linked object, you'll find link management tools right on the **Editing links** Edit menu. Select the linked object in the container document, and pull down the Edit menu. At the bottom of the Edit menu, you see both the Links option becoming available and a linked object command. See Figure 3.5.

We'll talk at length about selecting objects and the Edit, Open, and Convert commands later in this chapter.

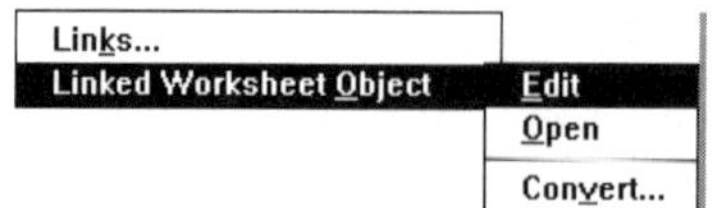

Figure 3.5 Editing a Linked
Object from the Edit Menu

To Update or Not to Update

Let's consider a link example and see how fast we can run into the "can't update them automatic links blues." Our link is from a Word document (SOURCE.DOC) to an Excel container workbook (CONTAINR.XLS). See Figure 3.6.

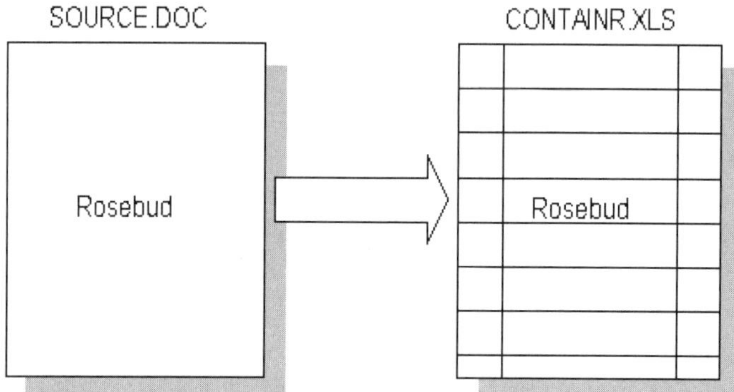

Figure 3.6 Our Link Example

No surprises here. Copy some text in SOURCE.DOC, activate Excel, and do a quick Edit / Paste Special / Text / Paste Link (the same steps used in the earlier example) in the CONTAINR.XLS. Then save both files.

Changes to the text in SOURCE.DOC are updated in Excel as you'd expect. Now we close SOURCE.DOC, then CONTAINR.XLS. So far pretty boring, but it gets more interesting.

If you open SOURCE.DOC (this is the data file, remember) and then open CONTAINR.XLS, it's no worries, mate. First Excel asks if you want the link updated assuming you have Tools / Options / General/ Ask to Update Automatic Links checked (more on this later). See Figure 3.7. Excel is very polite. Assume that you click on the Yes button. The link *is* updated. If any changes had been made to SOURCE.DOC's linked text after CONTAINR.XLS was closed, they are now reflected in the Excel document. If you click No, nothing is updated. Fair enough. Links are automatic and all is right in the world. If you reverse the order in which you open the two files, that is, open CONTAINR.XLS first and SOURCE.DOC second, the link again behaves itself quite nicely, thank you.

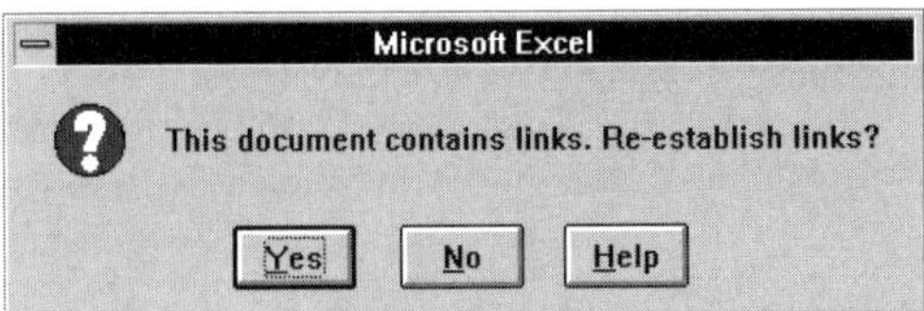

Figure 3.7 May I Update Your Links for You?

But if you dare set up this scenario with Excel as the source application and Word as the container application, gotcha! Here's the deal. Set up a link from an Excel document (`SOURCE.XLS`) to a Word container document (`CONTAINR.DOC`). Close both these files, saving any changes as you go. If you open `SOURCE.XLS` and then open `CONTAINR.DOC`, no problem. But open `CONTAINR.DOC` first and things are not so rosy.

Try it. First open `CONTAINR.DOC`, then open `SOURCE.XLS`. Change the linked text. Hmmm, nothing happens in `CONTAINR.DOC`. Maybe it needs some more time to update. Hmmm, how long has it been? Well, you can wait till the cows come home, that link is not going to update. If you check the Edit / Links in Word, the link shows "Auto" for automatic in the status column, but it's not automatic now. You have three choices to get the kinks out of the links: (1) close `CONTAINR.DOC` and reopen it, (2) from inside Word select Edit / Links / Update Now / Close, or (3) keyboard enthusiasts could press the F9 key with the cursor inside the link field in Word. Beware of this Word/Excel link scenario.

When Excel is the source application and Word is the container application, the source data file(s) *must be opened before* the container document(s) if you want the links to update automatically. When in doubt, you should manually update links to ensure that they get updated properly. Table 3.1 shows you the effect on inter-application links when the container file is opened before the source. Remember all the links are automatic to start with.

Oh, before we forget, you saw how Excel asked if you wanted to update the links? This assumes you've checked the Ask to Update Automatic Links check box (see Tools / Options / Edit filecard); otherwise, the update occurs without asking if you want it or not. Project has this identical functionality. Word also has an option related to link updates. *Hoo boy!* Does it ever. Read on.

In Word, if you do Tools / Options / General filecard, you'll see a check box labeled Update Automatic Links at Open. The difference between these two options in Word and Excel is staggering. In Excel if you uncheck the Ask to Update Automatic Links check box, the links *are always* updated; unchecking the Word Update Automatic Links at Open *prevents* Word from reestablishing the links as automatic. Confused? You should be.

Table 3.1 The Underground Table™ to Inter-Application Kinked Links

Server \ Container	Word	Excel	PPT	Access	Project
Word	N/A	Auto	Manual	Auto	Auto
Excel	Manual	N/A	Manual	Auto	Auto*
PPT	Manual	Manual	N/A	Manual	Manual†
Access	N/A	N/A	N/A	N/A	N/A
Project	Manual	Auto	Manual	Manual	N/A

Links and Cloaked Editors

Are you aware that those Microsoft Masters of the Universe have implemented a cloaking device in Windows? Sort of a "now you see it, now you don't" kind of thing. We'll explain using a worst case scenario.

Let's use the same example from the last section, namely, SOURCE.DOC has some data that has been linked into the Excel CONTAINR.XLS workbook. You've just fired up your computer, nothing running but Program Manager. Start Excel and load CONTAINR.XLS. The message box shown in Figure 3.7 appears and you click on Yes.

What happens behind the scenes is that Word is loaded *in a hidden window*. It's clear off the normal radar screens like the Task List. Ah, but let us check things out with the good ol' System Information utility that is standard equipment in Office. Since you can't live without this utility (you may not know that yet), the first thing to do is create a Program Manager icon for it.

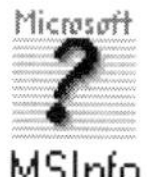

1. Open File Manager and switch to the C:\WINDOWS\MSAPPS\MSINFO directory.

2. Size the File Manager window so that it overlaps Program Manager leaving the program group you want to add the MSInfo icon to visible.

3. In File Manager locate the MSINFO.EXE file. Drag the MSINFO.EXE filename from File Manager to the Program Manager group and drop it.

   Hey, you can access this utility from practically any Microsoft application's Help menu. Just click on Help About and then on the System Info button in the Help dialog box. But, as you'll see, there are times when it's handy to run it standalone.

---

* For the reasons discussed in the next section, you can only open the source file via Edit / Links / Open Source in this case.

† Manual is all we could get out of Project linked to a PowerPoint presentation under any circumstances. Given the nature of the applications this is not a big deal.

4. Double-click on the MSInfo icon to start the System Information utility. Pull down the Choose a Category drop-down list and select Applications Running.

Remember, all you'd expect to see running at this point is Microsoft Office (MOM to her friends), Program Manager, and Excel. At least that's what the Task List reports, but System Info really lets you know what's going on. See Figure 3.8.

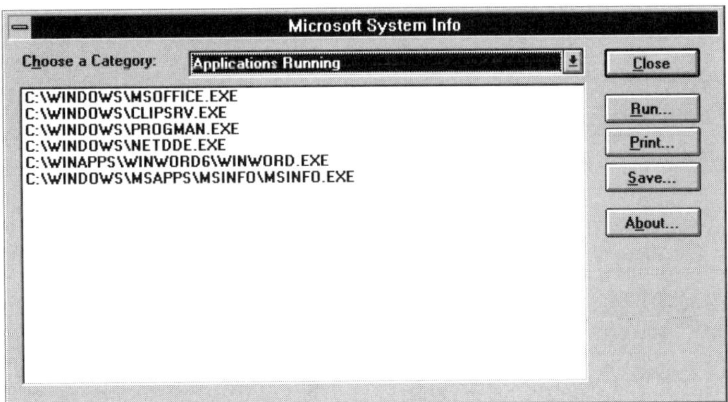

Figure 3.8 Microsoft System Info—Applications Running

What have we got here? `MSOFFICE.EXE`, `PROGMAN.EXE`, yeah that's expected. `CLIPSRV.EXE`, that's the ubiquitous clipboard lurking, ready to jump into action at the first sign of a Cut or Copy command. `NETDDE.EXE` means we're running a peer-to-peer network. Ah ha! `WINWORD.EXE`, lurking, as invisible as a Romulan Warbird. There it sits sucking up precious resources. It was loaded in order to open the `SOURCE.DOC` and thereby provide the latest data to `CONTAINR.XLS`.

But why is it still there, and can it be gotten rid of? If you try to start Word, you'll get a second instance; that is, Word will be running twice on your computer. If you try to open the `SOURCE.DOC` file, you'll be told that you can't because you already have it opened. Yikes! See Figure 3.9. 

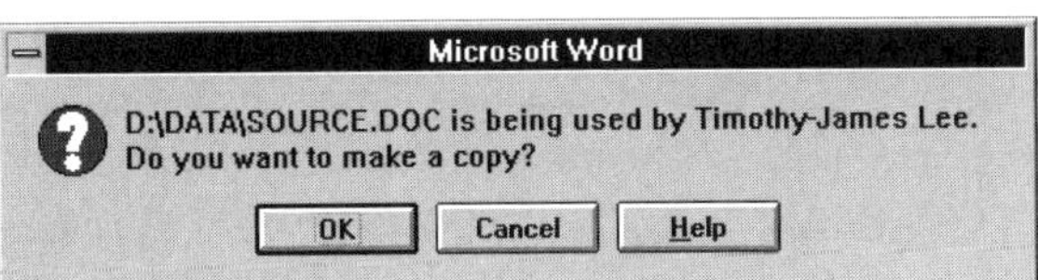

Figure 3.9 If That's Me, Who Am I?

Under certain circumstances, closing the `CONTAINR.XLS` in Excel won't have any effect on this situation. Closing Excel won't help either. To shut down the hidden instance of Word, you may be forced to close Windows (yuck!) or use the link in the Excel worksheet to open Word (in Excel select the link, then either double-click on it, or do an Edit / Links / Open [Source] and bang the cloaking device is turned off and Word appears).

Now the good news is that not all applications behave like this when acting as a server to some link. The bad news is that some applications are *almost* this bad. See Table 3.2.

Table 3.2 The Underground Table™ to Links and Cloaked Servers

Container / Server	Word	Excel	PPT	Access*	Project
Word	N/A	Icky/Barf	Okay/Barf	Okay/Barf	Okay[†]/Barf
Excel	Okay	N/A	Okay	Okay	Icky
PPT	So-so	So-so	N/A	So-so	So-so
Access[‡]	Okay	Okay[§]	N/A	N/A	N/A
Project	Okay	Icky	Okay	Okay	N/A

Word wins hands down as the most ill behaved server application where links are concerned *under certain circumstances*, hence its dual scores. If you do not have any global templates automatically loading via Word's STARTUP directory, then Word turns in an Okay score in our tests. However, it's most likely you have at least one global template being loaded. With *any* global templates Word gets a Barf score.

Barf   Runs hidden, keeps the source data file open, and stays that way until you exit Windows or use Edit / Links / Open to open its hidden instance which can then be closed and so removed from memory.

Icky   This is a little better. With an Icky server, closing the container file shuts down the hidden instance of the server application which is better than nothing. Keep in mind that Project does not support multiple instances either and so you can open the hidden server by starting Project from Program Manager or MOM.

* Objects paste-linked directly on a new Form.

[†] You get Okay with a linked object, but you get Icky if you link text into a Project cell.

[‡] With Word as the container, we used Insert / Database to grab records from an Access database; this in turn created a {Database} field in Word. With Excel as the container, we used Data / Get External Data to grab records from an Access database via Query. This created a link with `XLQUERY.XLA` as the Source File, a blank Item, a Worksheet Type, and an Automatic Update mode.

[§] Leaves Query running on the desktop (not cloaked).

So-so   Pilgrim, when PowerPoint's the server, you'd better gird your loins because anything can happen. At its worst, PowerPoint may run hidden and keep the source data file open. (If you use System Info to see what's what, notice that `POWERPPT.DLL`'s running but no `.EXE` file.) PowerPoint by design does not support multiple instances, so if you try to run it from Program Manager, the cloaked instance appears immediately. *The data file is still hidden and inaccessible even though PowerPoint is now displayed.* From here you can close PowerPoint and so free the data file. Sometimes, with no pattern that we could discern, PowerPoint behaves quite nicely, thank you, turning in a score of Okay. Go figure.

Okay   This is the way all server applications should behave when dealing with links. The server application opens, updates, and shuts down. You never see it and it does not hang about causing you resource grief.

These are all applications from a single vendor and they go from one extreme to the other in how they handle links when the server application is not initially running. Applications from other vendors may do even stranger things. Then again, maybe not. Visio, for example, is very well behaved in handling links when it is the unopened server. It came in Okay in our lab tests as a server with every application except Excel where it turned in an Icky score.

> **Barf to Icky and other scientific terms ...**

None of this appears to be a problem, however, if the server application is open *before* opening the container document. Nor will you trigger a hidden application if the container application asks you if it should update the links and you say no. Alas, not all applications ask before starting to update links.

Embed That Object!

> Once, before the start of a duel, I saw him embed a war axe in a tree with such force that the axe handle stuck out from the trunk like an old tree limb. The head of the axe was completely consumed, making it seem a natural part of the tree. His opponent, awed by such a show of force and skill, forfeited the duel and relinquished his claim on the ponies. Actually, Batu was quite drunk and had been aiming for his enemy's head.
>
> Amok Shing, Mongol
> *My Years in the Horde* (from the modern translation by K. Tibet, 1972)

Take a chunk of data (a spreadsheet, `.WAV` file, text document, or bitmap, etc.) from one application and dump it in the middle of another application and, by golly, you've got yourself an embedded object. In Chapter 1 you saw an example using Graph where a chart was embedded in Word and the embedded data was linked to a table in Word. Here we'll discuss some of the practical aspects of embedding objects in compound documents. In the next section we'll get into some of the more cerebral aspects of object technology.

Insert Object Gets You There

We've talked about the "server only" OLE applications that come with Office, like Graph and WordArt. These are often a user's first experience with embedded objects.

In Word, Excel, PowerPoint, and Project you can insert an object via Insert / Object. In Access you have to look on the Edit menu where it's called the Insert Object option. Other applications that support OLE 2.0 will have an Insert / Object selection or some equivalent. In any event you'll get the Insert Object dialog box. Unfortunately, this dialog box differs between applications in Office. See Figure 3.10.

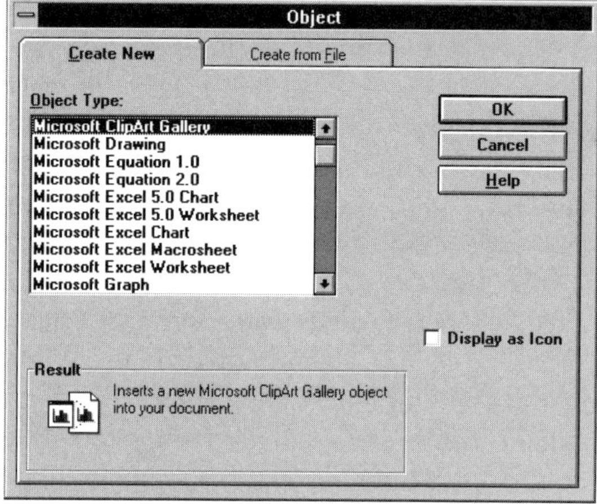

Figure 3.10 Insert Object Dialog Box as Found in Word and Excel

This is the dialog box format that you'll find in both Word and Excel. The same dialog box in Access, PowerPoint, and Project looks different but provides identical functionality.

Will the mystery server please sign in.   Any OLE-compliant application that has registered itself with the REG.DAT registration database appears in the Object Type list box—except for the exception, which in this case is Excel. Display this list from within Excel, and the Excel object types are conspicuous in their absence. As you'll see later, Excel is reluctant to insert an Excel object in an Excel compound document. Selecting one of these applications and clicking on the OK button fires up that application as an OLE editor using in-place editing mode (if the server and client applications support in-place editing) or open mode if one or the other of the applications don't support in-place editing. Let's build a compound document using this Insert Object method.

1. In Excel, pull down the Insert menu and choose Object.

2. In the Object dialog box, scroll the Object Type list box and select the Microsoft Word 6.0 Document option.

3. Click on the OK button. See Figure 3.11.

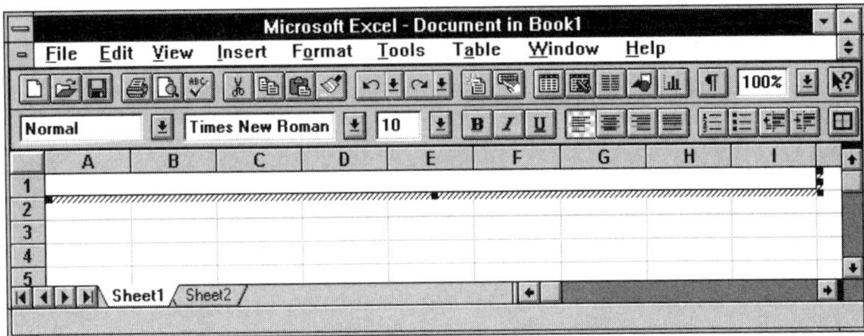

Figure 3.11 Excel as Container, Word as OLE Editor

Look carefully. The title bar is the main clue. The toolbars also provide a solid if more subtle hint that it may look like Excel, but what you have here is a Word document object that has been activated for in-place editing. The actual object has the **hatched border** showing you that this object is active. Start typing and you are really entering text in a Word document and all of Word's tools and features are available.

It doesn't look much like a Word document we'll grant you, but we can fix that. Since this is a graphic object it can be dragged and resized. A quick flick of the mouse to drag the object down and right a bit, resize a little, and Word's rulers appear. See Figure 3.12.

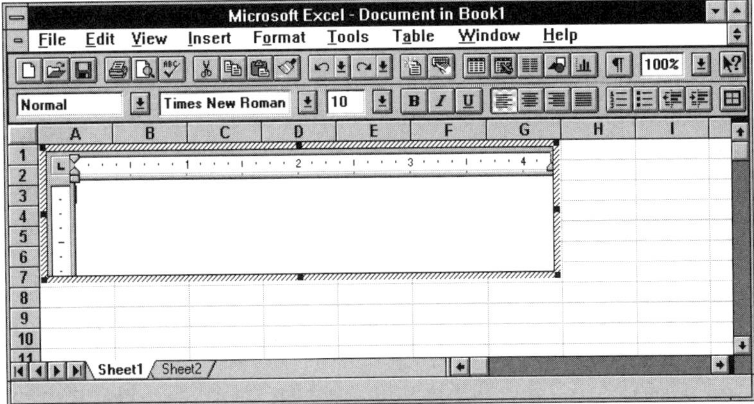

Figure 3.12 Word Object Moved and Resized

That's better. You enter and edit your text just as you would in Word because *you really are in Word!*

Mechanical Overview of Insert Object

An object can be inserted via Insert Object in its default presentation (that is, what it normally looks like), or you can display the object as an icon. This is useful when you want to provide some information in your container document that is unobtrusive but can be triggered for display (and editing) with a double-click. See Figure 3.13.

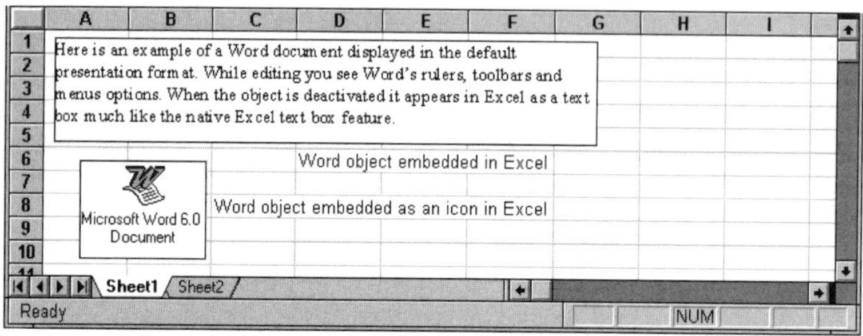

Figure 3.13 Word Objects Embedded

Display as icon To embed an object and display it as an icon, just check the Display as Icon check box in the Object dialog box. When you insert an object as an icon, subsequent edits are done in the open mode as opposed to in-place editing whether the applications involved support in-place editing or not.

In these examples the objects have been inserted using the Create New option in the Object dialog box. You can also create an embedded object from an existing file via the Create from File filecard (in Word and Excel) or the Create from File option button (in Access, PowerPoint, and Project). Don't you just *love* consistency? See Figure 3.14.

Excel is reluctant to embed Excel objects. Select the file you want to embed (check the Display as Icon check box if you want the embedded object to appear as an icon) and click on the OK button. Bam! Done deal. And the file can be linked instead of embedded by simply checking the Link to File check box. Ah, there's that exception again. Excel appears not to like embedding Excel data files in Excel workbooks. Oh, you can do it—just click on an **.XLS** file and it is embedded. It's just that the data file is actually opened and left opened in Excel as a hidden file. In Excel you can see hidden files via Windows / Unhide. Why Excel does this and to what purpose is lost on us.

Use the Create from File when you have already created the data file to be embedded. Use Create New when you want to create the data to be embedded from scratch. How hard can it get? Well, let's complicate things a bit.

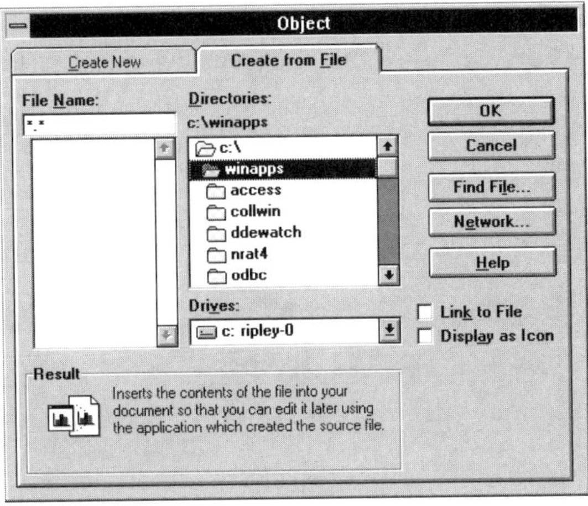

Figure 3.14 Objects Can Be Created from Existing Files

The trick is in what the Create from File routine decides the server application is or should be for a given data file. Let's say you like to usurp the three-character extension for your own dark and devious purposes. If you have a plain ASCII text file with a `.DOC` extension and you embedded it in another application, it would be treated as a Word document with the text translated into Word. Ah, but give this same file an extension of `.XLS` and embed it. You'll get an embedded Excel object with the text translated into an Excel workbook.

Actually, OLE does a great job of getting the server applications matched up with the data files. You can try to fool the system, for example, by renaming a Visio drawing data file with an `.XLS` extension, but OLE will have none of it and goes ahead and embeds the file using Visio as the server. The only gray area is when you embed a file that can be translated into different formats, like an ASCII file.

If you embed a data file that has no OLE server application in the registration database, the Object Packager application kicks in and you get an embedded object that contains the selected file. This embedded object displays the Object Packager generic icon. See Figure 3.15.

Here you see an object, `LEE1.ZIP`, embedded via Create from File. Since the program that created this file, `PKUNZIP.EXE`, is not a registered OLE server, the Object Packager program took over and embedded the file and displayed it as an icon using the generic Packager icon. The Object Packager program was whistled up by selecting the object in the Word document and doing an Edit / Package Object / Edit Package. Here you can tinker with the object's settings, change the icon, or assign a DOS command line string to be executed when you activate the icon. For example, if the `.ZIP` extension is associated with `PKUNZIP.EXE` in your `WIN.INI`, double-clicking on the object would unzip the file. If there is no associated executable, you could assign a command in Object Packager for this object like "`pkunzip.exe lee1.zip`" so that double-clicking unzips the embedded file.

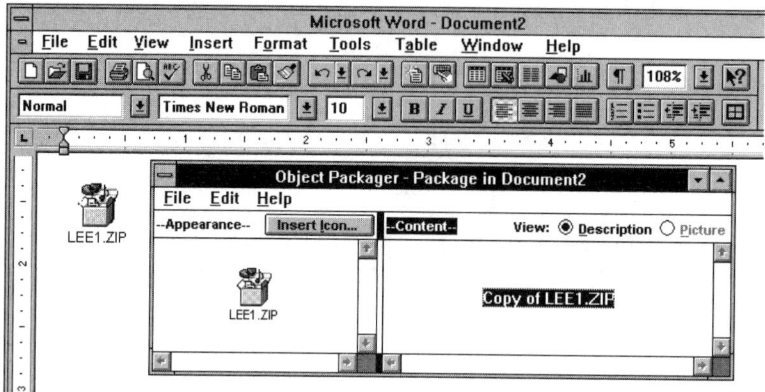

Figure 3.15 A ZIP File Embedded Via Object Packager

Objects Across the Page—Oops!

"A sophisticated object placement mechanism that allows large rectangular objects to span more than one page." Sounds impressive and it is, too. Or it will be when the OLE wizards up in the great Red north get it working. This feature, where an embedded object displays across page boundaries in the container application is killer, real whizbang stuff, but it missed the cut for OLE 2.0.

We only bring it up because it's in the 2.0 specification, so if you're staying up nights trying to figure out how to get it work, get some rest! Still, when it's available you'll want to use it. Here's what we mean. See Figure 3.16.

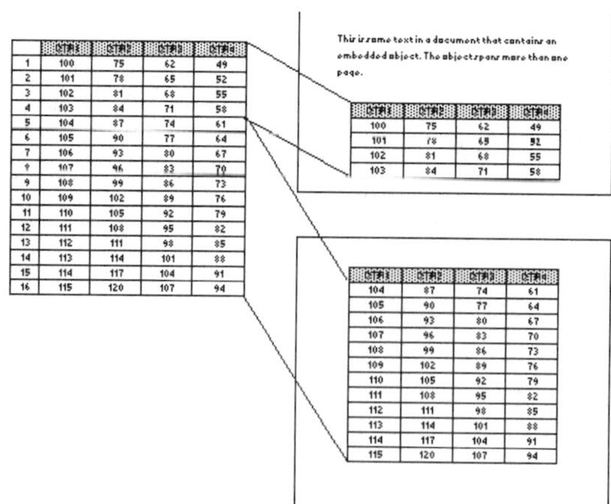

Figure 3.16 One Object Displayed Across Multiple Pages

Is this to die for or what? Figure 3.16 is an artist's conception of an Excel worksheet in a Word container document. Notice how the header is replicated on the second page. Cooooool. If they can make it work. We don't know, but that trick with headings ... looks like magic to us.

Alas, for now, if you embed a large object, you'll be unable to size it across more than one page. To see all of the data, view it in edit or open mode so you can scroll around.

Inheriting Properties—Oops Again!

Currently OLE 2.0 isolates certain properties within each server application. Embed a section of an Excel worksheet into a Word document, and that object displays the font and point size that it possessed in Excel. You can assign a Word style to the object, but the properties of the style are ignored by the object itself.

Another "missed the OLE 2.0 cut" feature should correct this. The specification (according to the "Microsoft Backgrounder Object Linking" article, which you can find on the TechNet CD-ROM) was supposed to enable OLE as follows.

> "To make embedded objects take on the look of their containing documents more closely, OLE allows containers to 'export' properties to an object. The object then inherits these properties and transforms its appearance to be more consistent with the object's container."

This feature is one we're looking forward to. It should go a long way to make compound documents appear even more seamless.

No Tunneling Across Objects—Yet

This is something you have to keep in mind when dealing with compound documents containing embedded objects (and linked objects in a graphical format). Some tools that you may have come to rely on inside the container application won't work on the embedded object.

For example, spell checking the container document with the container application's spell check utility won't check the text within an embedded object. And since the embedded object may not look like an embedded object, you may not notice that it's not being spell checked. Another utility that bypasses embedded objects is the search or find utility.

For now, the only way to deal with this issue is to invoke each server application and use the native spell checker and search commands in that application. Bummer. This capability, like splitting large objects across page boundaries, was supposed to be in the OLE 2.0 release but did not make the cut. Hopefully it'll make the next release.

REACH OUT AND TOUCH SOME OBJECTS

Work without Hope draws nectar in a sieve,
And Hope without an object cannot live.

Samuel Taylor Coleridge
Work Without Hope

At this point everyone should be comfortable with the term "object" as it relates to compound documents. Sure, you may not feel like doing your master's thesis on the term, but you're probably with us when we say things like, "drag this, drop it over there, voilà, an embedded *object*."

In this section we'll drill down on the care and feeding of embedded objects within your compound documents. By and large they are friendly, useful critters, and only occasionally do they bite the unwary. Chomp!

A Draggin' and A Droppin'

When I'm playful, I use the meridians of longitude and parallels of latitude for a seine, and drag the Atlantic Ocean for whales.

Mark Twain
Life on the Mississippi, 1883

OLE 2.0's drag-and-drop feature (not to be confused with drop and roll, which is what you should do if you catch on fire, or dragon drops, which is the preferred fertilizer in mythological locales) is a feature that the marketing types *love* big time. It shows really *well*. Flash, sizzle, and it is one of those features where you look past the sizzle and actually find a great steak.

Sizzle and substance!   Consider this. Select a paragraph in Word, point at the selection with your trusty mouse, click and hold down the mouse button, drag the mouse pointer to a new location in the same document, and release. This is classic drag-and-drop (assuming you have not disabled this feature). The text is *cut* from where it was and *pasted* to a new location.

Drag-and-drop can be disabled in Word and Excel (Tools / Options / Edit filecard and clear the Allow Cell Drag and Drop for Excel, and Drag and Drop Text Editing for Word). Obviously, if you're working along with the examples in the book, make sure you have these options checked.

Ah, but there is much more to this drag-and-drop stuff than meets the eye because as interesting as drag-and-drop is within an application, you can drag-and-drop *across applications!*

Embedding Can Be a Drag

With drag-and-drop you can embed an object with a simple flick of the mouse. Drag it from here and drop it on something over there. Sounds good, but is it boon to mankind or a boondoggle for computer users?

That sort of depends on what you want to drag from, and drop on, as well as how big a monitor you have sitting on your desk. A while back there was an ad for Microsoft Office that showed an Excel chart being dragged from Excel over to a Word document. We can illustrate the process with something a little simpler than that.

Big screen video is a plus.

1. Open Word and Excel. Close or minimize all other running applications.

2. Make Excel the active application, pop up the Task List (CTRL + ESC), and click on the Tile button to arrange both application windows side by side.

   If you're running MOM, you might find this doesn't work (the mysterious third empty window syndrome, don't you know). If you have any trouble, start Word and minimize everything else. Then before you click on the Excel button on MOM, hold down the Shift key. This should tile Word and Excel horizontally, with Word on the top and Excel on the bottom.

   If you go the Task List route, Excel should be on the left and Word on the right. The only reason that matters is we're trying to make the steps match the final figure shot. Hey, look at how small both application windows are—*now* you know why you need a 21-inch monitor.

3. Enter some data in Book1's worksheet and select same.

4. Place the Traditional Northwest Mouse Pointer™ on the edge of the selected cells in Excel.

5. Hold down the Control key, then click and drag the selection to the Word window and release the mouse button.

   If you click and drag the selection across the workbook in Excel, the sheet just scrolls. But if you drag the mouse *outside* the Excel application window, you can actually drag the selection into another application altogether.

Without holding down the Control key, clicking and dragging *from* Excel cuts the data out of the worksheet. You can drop the data into another application window but it is removed from Excel. To copy the data as we did in this example, you must first hold down the Control key while performing the drag operation. This *copies* the data from one application to the other. See Figure 3.17.

Notice in Figure 3.17 the odd mouse pointer? This is the Drag-and-Copy Pointer™, which is also new with OLE 2.0 drag-and-drop. The little plus sign tells you that you're *copying* the selection you're dragging as opposed to moving it. Before we embark on our drag-and-drop odyssey, let's look at some of the things

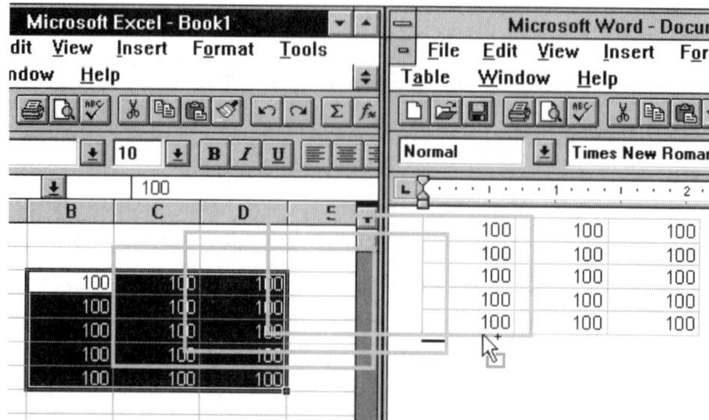

Figure 3.17 Drag-and-Drop to Create an Embedded Object

your mouse pointer is going to be morphing into. The mouse pointer gives you visual clues as to what's going on. In Table 3.3 we've listed some of the more common drag-and-drop pointers you're likely to encounter. And since it doesn't look like you-know-who has beat us to it, we'll just contact the Library of Congress and see about getting some trademarks. *Heh, heh, heh.*

Table 3.3 Drag-and-Drop Mouse Pointers

What It Looks Like	What We Call It
	The Drag-and-Drop Pointer™
	The Drag-and-Copy Pointer™
	The Drag-and-Link Pointer™
	The Slide Shot D and D Special™
	The No-Drop Zone Pointer™
	The File on Board Pointer™
	The Many Files on Board Pointer™
	The Drag-and-Scroll Pointer™

The Drag-and-Drop Pointer™ is most often found in Word and Excel (although in Excel it's lacking the rectangular baggage box on the arrow's tail that tells you that you're dragging something). Word and Excel both support the Drag-and-Copy Pointer™ (again, Excel lacks the baggage rectangle).

A plethora of pointers

The Drag-and-Link Pointer™ is very rare. You'll only see this pointer when dragging from Excel to either PowerPoint or Project *while holding down the Shift and Control keys.* When you do a drag-and-drop with the `Shift + Ctrl` down, you're performing a drag-and-link, which we'll discuss shortly.

PowerPoint is the odd man out with its own drag-and-drop pointer, the Slide Shot D and D Special™ (shown with the copy indicator). Very chic. 

If you drag something over a screen region that's not a valid "drop target," the pointer turns into the No-Drop Zone Pointer™. Drag over a scroll bar or trigger a "scroll event" (who makes up these terms?) and you should see the Drag-and-Scroll Pointer™. We say "should see" because this one is iffy as to when or if it's going to show up at all. We couldn't get it to display at all within Excel or Project and only sporadically in Word.

Dragging Around the Town

Let's look at what happens when you drop an object from one application on another program. Take a look at Table 3.4.

Table 3.4 The Underground Table™ to Drag-and-Drop

Drag from / Drop on	Word	Excel	PPT*	Access	Project
Word	Paste	Embed	Embed	N/A	Paste
Excel	Paste	Can't†	Embed	N/A	Paste
PPT	Embed	Embed	Paste	N/A	Paste
Access	N/A	N/A	N/A	N/A	N/A
Project	Both	Both	Embed	N/A	Paste

Access Characteristics

You cannot perform a drag from Access for the purpose of dropping on another application (hence the N/As in the Access column). This is by design given the

---

* PowerPoint must be in Slide Sorter view.

† "Can't" is such a strong word. You *can* run a second instance of Excel and drag from one instance to the other. Seems like a lot more trouble than it's worth since the best you get is a simple paste on the drop-zone.

nature of the information in Access. Oh sure, you can open a form in design mode and select a control and try to drag it over to Word or Excel, but it's no soap.

The only glitch is that the drag pointer for intra-application object drag-and-drop editing inside Access when in design mode (the little black hand) stays visible when you drag something from anywhere inside Access to a location outside the Access application window—even though no operation is performed if you try to drop an Access object outside Access. The pointer should revert to the No-Drop Zone Pointer™ as soon as you leave the Access window. If you try to drag a table or form from the database dialog box, you *do* get the No-Drop Zone Pointer™ if you drag outside Access.

The Office documentation does, however, state that you can drag from other applications (Word, Excel, PowerPoint) and drop on Access. The documentation does not elaborate exactly where you can drop in Access. A form? A field with an OLE Object data type? No matter—our test lab was unable to drop anything from anyone on anything in Access. It's No-Drop Zone all the way!

Access anomalies
Access does support embedded and linked objects, to be sure. In a table you can have a field with a data type of OLE Object and you can populate it via Edit / Insert Object. On a form you can have a Bound or Unbound Object Frame. A Bound Object Frame is linked to a table within Access, and an Unbound Object Frame can be linked to an external file. You just can't set them up via drag-and-drop from other applications.

Notice that the table rates dragging from Word to Word (that is, from one document window in Word to another document window) as Paste. That's because if a destination application can edit the incoming data directly within that application, the data is pasted and not embedded as a data object. To link or embed the data from one Word document to another you have to Copy and Paste Special. Drag-and-drop only does a plain ol' paste.

Paste or Embed with Word and Excel

Dragging from Word to Excel also triggers a "paste" since Excel just ups and translates the Word data into plain text which is pasted into Excel. No object, no embedding, no link. But oh boy, some paste! Each paragraph from the Word selection gets pasted into a separate cell and truncated at Excel's 255-cell character limit. Again, one workaround is to copy the data in Word and perform an Edit / Paste Special in Excel to do an embed or a link. Or if you want to embed the Word data into Excel, first select an existing object in Excel (a text box, embedded chart, whatever), then drag from Word to Excel and drop. The data from Word is *embedded* in Excel. Wild.

Intra-Application Issues

Word, PowerPoint, and Project support dragging "intra-application" in that you can drag stuff from one document window within the application to another document window within the same application. No real issues here.

> **The issues involved with dragging from one Excel worksheet to another Excel worksheet are simple—there aren't any! Can't do it. Not supported, period, end of story, that's it, put out the cat and turn out the light. Okay, okay, never say never. If you start multiple instances of Excel, you can drag from one instance to another. Not too effective though, as you can only do a simple paste on the drop zone. No embed, no drag-and-link. Just a simple paste that requires you to run multiple copies of Excel. No thanks.**

Powerful PowerPoint

It's no problem to tile presentations in PowerPoint (Window / Arrange All) and drag slides from one presentation to another (or rearrange the slides within an application) as long as you're in the Slide Sorter view (View / Slide Sorter).

While in Slide Sorter view you can tile PowerPoint and a destination application and drag the selected slide or slides over and drop them. Voilà, embedded slide show ready to go. If you want to embed an *entire* presentation, you'd be better off using Insert / Object / Create from File, but drag-and-drop works great if you only want some selected slides. To drag more than a single slide, do a multiple selection in the Slide Sorter. PowerPoint is non-standard in that to do a multiple selection you hold down the Shift key while clicking on the slides you want (not the Control key as you would expect). **Slipping amidst the slides**

The slide(s) dropped on the destination are embedded and the first slide (according to the slide order in PowerPoint) is displayed. Double-click on the embedded PowerPoint object; instead of slipping into edit mode, the object is played (or in the case of PowerPoint objects, shown). It's pretty cool. The first slide appears on-screen as though you were showing a slide presentation in PowerPoint, because actually that's just what you're doing. Cycle through the embedded presentation and after the last slide is shown you're back in the container application. Consider this: You're demonstrating an application in the big board room. At one point you want to run through some slides but instead of switching applications you just double-click on a graphic in your document and instant slide show! The audience is stunned and you get that big promotion. Way cool indeed. **Instant promotion**

To edit the embedded slides, you need to selected the object and do a Edit / Object in the container application, and from the flyout menu choose Edit.

The Many Places of Project

Dropping data from Word or Excel on Project may result in an embedded object or a plain old paste depending on just where you drop it in Project's Gantt view. The Gantt view is divided into the Gantt table and the Gantt bar chart area. Drops from Excel or Word on the Gantt table result in a simple paste (much like dropping Word data on an Excel workbook). But the Gantt bar chart is another story. Drop the data here and you get an embedded object. If the object you're dragging to Project is graphical in nature to begin with (like an Excel chart), you'll get the No-Drop Zone Pointer™ in the Gantt table.

Efforts to drop on Project in any other view than Gantt will be also be rewarded with the No-Drop Zone Pointer™.

Two-Step Undos

Whew! You've navigated the rocky shoals of drag-and-drop and finally have an embedded object. Ah, but what if you drop that Excel table on your Word document and are suddenly seized by fear's cold and clammy hand, terror running rampant in your mind as you scream, "Oopsie." Remorse sets in as you realize you didn't mean to embed the data after all. If only you could undo your actions—but wait, you can.

Mouse your way up to Word's Edit menu and click on Undo. The data disappears from Word. Wait for the data to reappear in Excel. Hmmm, still waiting. Gotcha! You have to Undo in both the container and editor applications. Quickly bop over to Excel and hit the Undo option on Excel's Edit menu. Remember that the drag-and-drop operation feels like a single fluid operation but in reality it's a two-step action. The data comes out of one application (step 1) and is embedded in another application (step 2).

Embedding Files with File Manager

The File on Board Pointer™

Here's a quickie way to embed an existing file into a container document. Just drag the filename from File Manager and drop it on the intended container document (like an Excel workbook running in Excel). Bing-bam-boom, one thoroughly embedded object. No fuss, no muss, no spare parts left over.

When you're dragging a file from File Manager to a container document, it's a good idea not to miss the exact point where you want to embed the file (the drop point, as it were). For example, drag a file to Word and as long as you hit a document Word tries to embed it. Ah, but miss and hit anything else, a scroll bar, a toolbar, or drop it on Word when Word is an icon on the desktop, and instead of embedding the file, Word tries to *open it, as in load this file into Word.*

If you drag a file over an iconized application running on the desktop, the mouse becomes the File on Board Pointer™ or the Many Files version (see Table 3.3). Drop it and the minimized application deals with the file in the manner of that application, meaning that if you drop a file on Excel, Excel opens the file (or tries to). Drop a file on Print Manager and Print Manager prints the file (using the server application's default print settings, the equivalent of File / Print / OK). If the application in question can't make heads or tails of the file type, the mouse stays the No-Drop Zone Pointer™. Plop a file on Mail and the file is embedded in an email message ready to send. Address it and off it goes out onto that information highway.

Mail drop

Dropping a Word file from File Manager on Excel (iconized or open) gets you nothing more than a flashing Excel icon on your desktop. Double-clicking on the flashing icon gets you a "format not valid" message. See Figure 3.18. Yet you can embed the same file via Insert / Object / Create from File. Go figure.

If you drop an Excel file on an Excel worksheet or anywhere in the program, Excel opens the document. There is no way to perform a drag-and-drop onto Excel and get an embedded object.

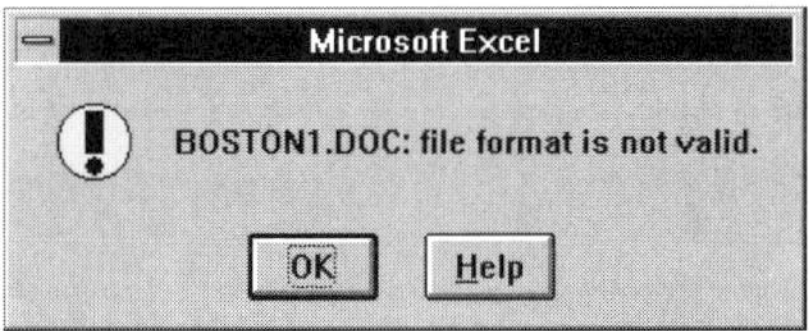

Figure 3.18 Excel Objects to Word Object, Huh?

If you drop a file on a container document and the editor application is not OLE 2.0-compliant, Object Packager kicks in and embeds the file in the container document and gives it the generic Packager icon.

PowerPoint tries real hard to utilize the data in a file dropped on it to make slides instead of just embedding it. For example, drop a Word file on PowerPoint and it uses the heading level styles found within (if any) to build a presentation where Heading 1 text is a slide title. Heading 2 becomes the first level of text, and so on. Any text not in a heading style is ignored. This lets you outline your presentation in Word and just drop the file on PowerPoint to generate the slides. Very slick, yea Microsoft!

Drop an Excel file, and PowerPoint tries to use Excel's outlining feature to create the slides. If you went to a lot of trouble to build your worksheets with

PowerPoint in mind, this might make sense, but the results with the Excel files we had laying about in our lab were less than satisfactory. Using Word makes more sense to us.

PowerPoint works this outline trick with a host of file types, like `.TXT`, `.RTF`, and `.WRI` files. But remember that the file in question really has to have been created with PowerPoint in mind for the experience to be a positive one. In files where PowerPoint cannot find heading level styles, it relies on paragraph indents to decide levels. In plain ASCII files, tabs are used. If neither indents nor tabs are found, each paragraph becomes a separate slide title.

Drag-and-Link

An OLE 2.0 feature that has not yet been implemented across all of Microsoft's applications is the drag-and-link feature. By holding down the Shift and Control keys before you drop the object you are dragging, you should be able to drop and have the resulting object be *linked instead of embedded!*

Drag-and-Link Pointer™

We say "should" because as of this writing it only works when you drag an Excel worksheet object and drop it on a PowerPoint slide or on a Project Gantt bar chart area. When you are over the drop zone in these applications, the mouse pointer changes to the rare Drag-and-Link Pointer™. With any other combination of inter-application drag-and-drop, you wind up with an embedded object or a normal paste (see Table 3.3).

Is it cool, is it wonderful? Well, like most shortcut key combinations, once you have them memorized they generally pay for themselves quickly in saved time so as a general rule we're for them. But the real bottom line is that until a majority of applications support this shortcut technique its usefulness is severely limited.

Keep it Clean

A side benefit of drag-and-drop is that, unlike the more traditional Cut, Copy, Paste Special, it completely bypasses the clipboard. Anything cut or copied to the clipboard stays on the clipboard even if you subsequently perform an inter- or intra-application drag-and-drop.

Arrrgghhhhhh! Except for the exception. Of course there's an exception. You were expecting an exception, weren't you? *There's always an exception!* Oh well. The exception is Excel. An Excel intra-application drag-and-drop not only dirties the clipboard—it purges it as well. Amazing, isn't it? We're not talking about dragging from one workbook and dropping on another workbook because Excel doesn't support that. Excel won't even let you drag from a sheet in one workbook to another sheet in the same workbook. Oh no, we're talking about from a location on the current sheet to a location on the *same sheet!* Bang, without so much as a "by your leave" or "excuuuuuuuse me" the

clipboard is dirtied then cleared. Emptied, dumped, purged, cleaned out. What makes this such a problem is you may come to rely on the clipboard remaining intact because every other Office application (and every non-Office application we can think of) leaves the clipboard alone when you drag-and-drop. You might cut something to the clipboard and bop over to Excel to paste it. You get there and decide to drag this one cell over to make room for the new incoming data. Guess what. There's no incoming data.

In-place Editing versus Open Editing

> He passed the flaming bounds of place and time...
>
> Thomas Gray
> *The Progress of Posey,* 1754

In-place editing is new in OLE 2.0. You saw an example of it back in Chapter 1, and all its various noms de plume like in-situ editing, visual editing, and in-place activation were discussed in Chapter 2. This is one of the most useful and yet jarring features of OLE 2.0, especially when contrasted with the open mode of editing objects where the server application runs in its own window. It really throws users the first time they run into it, but once you are acclimated to it the benefits are many.

Not all applications support OLE 2.0 and even those that do support OLE 2.0 don't all support in-place editing. In Table 3.5 some of more frequently used OLE applications are listed. This table shows which applications can create container documents and which support in-place editing when they are the editor or server application.

Table 3.5 In-Place versus Open Editing Support

Applications	Create Container Documents	When It's the Editor Program	When It's the Server Program
Access 2.0	Yes	—*	Open Only
ClipArt Gallery	No	Open Only	N/A
Drawing	No	Open Only	N/A
Equation Editor 2.0	No	In-Place	N/A
Excel 5.0 Chart	No	In-Place	N/A
Excel 5.0 Worksheet	Yes	In-Place	In-Place
Graph 5.0	No	In-Place	N/A
Organization Chart 1.0	No	Open Only	N/A

continued

* Access links to other applications via DDE and ODBC and does not support this aspect of OLE.

Table 3.5 In-Place versus Open Editing Support (continued)

Applications	Create Container Documents	When It's the Editor Program	When It's the Server Program
Paintbrush Picture	No	Open Only	N/A
PowerPoint 4.0 Presentation	Yes	Open Only	In-Place
PowerPoint 4.0 Slide	No	Open Only	N/A
Project 4.0 Project	Yes	Open Only	Open Only
Sound	No	Open Only	N/A
Word 6.0 Document	Yes	In-Place	In-Place
Word 6.0 Picture	No	In-Place	N/A
Visio 3.0 Drawing	Yes	In-Place	Open Only

State of the Object: Inactive, Selected, Active, and Open

An embedded object has four states of being (how New Age). Let's walk through an example and look at each state.

1. Tile Excel and PowerPoint.

2. Select a range of cells in Excel and drag-and-drop onto a blank presentation slide in PowerPoint.

3. Maximize PowerPoint and press the Escape key to *deselect* the embedded Excel object. See Figure 3.19.

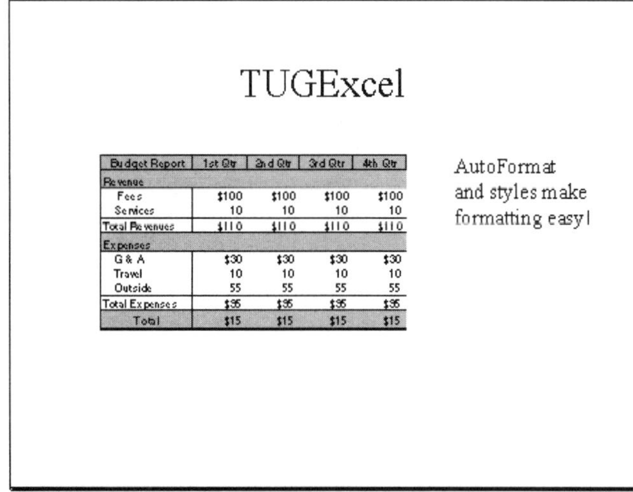

Figure 3.19 Inactive Excel Object in PowerPoint Slide

In Figure 3.19 you see the result of embedding an Excel object in a PowerPoint slide in all its glory. If you're working through the steps along with us, your slide looks pretty much like this. Okay, so we added a title and some text, but you get the idea.

Excel object within a PowerPoint slide

When you click *once* on the embedded object, the object is **selected**. It's now in the *selected state*. See Figure 3.20.

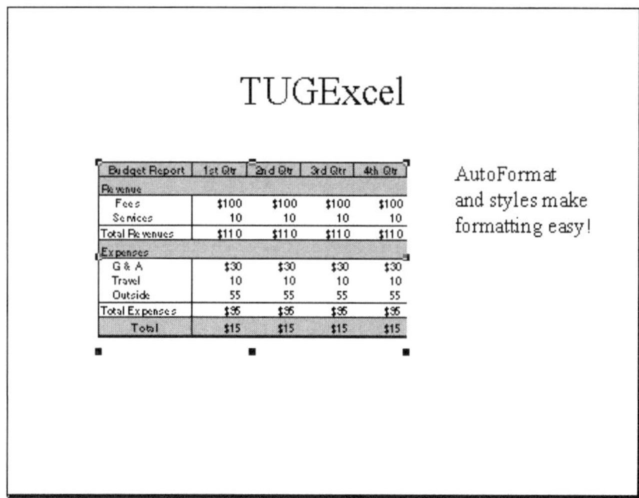

Figure 3.20 The Embedded Excel Object in the Selected State

When the object is selected you see the **sizing handles**, the black boxes outlining the object. By placing the tip of the mouse pointer on the line connecting any two of the boxes (but not touching any box itself), you can drag the object and reposition it on the slide or drop it on another container document. That's right, you can drag an object from one container document where it is embedded and drop it on another container document in a different application. You can also resize the object. We'll talk about resizing and scaling in a later section.

The next two modes both relate to manipulating the data within the embedded object. If the applications involved both support it, you can *activate* the object using the in-place editing mode. If one or both of the applications do not support in-place editing, you can activate the object using the *open* mode (that is, the editor is run as a separate application and the object data is opened in the editor as a pseudo-document). Open mode can be forced even if both applications support in-place editing.

Double-clicking on the embedded object activates the object using in-place editing if possible and open mode if in-place isn't supported.

Here's what our slide looks like when activated with in-place editing. See Figure 3.21.

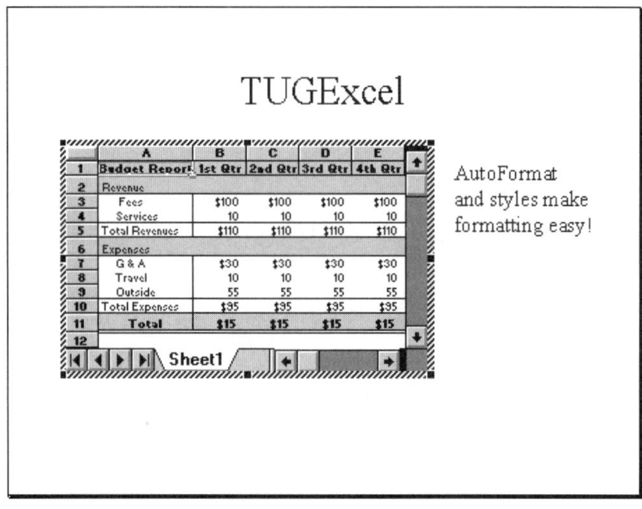

Figure 3.21 Embedded Excel Object in the Activated (In-place Editing) State

Excel, live and in person!

Hey, that looks like Excel. Yep, row and column headings, sheet tabs, scroll bars, by golly, it *is* Excel. When an object is activated with in-place editing, the editor application is loaded into memory and you actually use its tools to manipulate the embedded data. This is a live Excel workbook—you can add sheets, create a chart, or do anything you want. Whatever is displayed in the visible window is what's displayed in the object once you deactivate it. The toolbars and menus in the container application change when in-place editing kicks in and we'll talk about that shortly. The hatched border surrounding the object indicates that is has been activated and is being edited in-place.

Open mode is another story. Remember, OLE is about applications communicating with each other. When you activate an object and it is "opened," that's just what takes place. The editor application is loaded and the data stored in the embedded object is passed to the loaded application. See Figure 3.22.

Open mode

Here you edit the embedded object data in a more "traditional" environment. Notice the title bar "Worksheet in EMBED1.PPT." This shows that this is not a standard Excel worksheet but one that is populated with embedded data from the PowerPoint presentation file EMBED1.PPT. Sort of a pseudo-workbook. Now you can modify the data. When your edits are complete you can exit Excel, which updates the object data back in PowerPoint, or you can close the pseudo-workbook, which updates the object data and leaves Excel running.

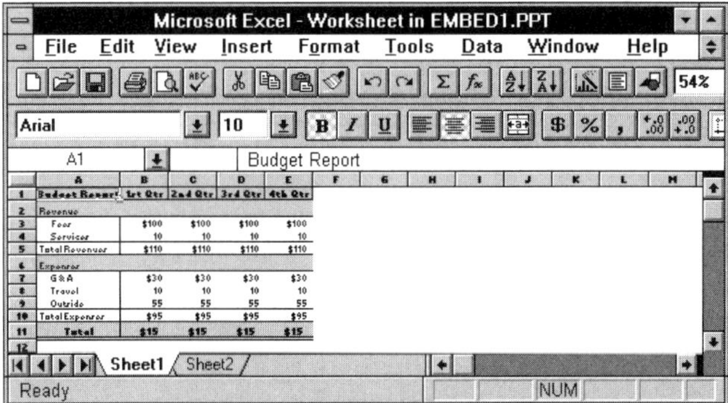

Figure 3.22 Editing an Object in Open Mode

In another glaring lack of consistency, some programs, when working as editor applications in open mode, make this "close and update" versus "exit and update" distinction clear as opposed to our Excel as editor example where you have only the standard Close and Exit commands on the menu.

Consider a PowerPoint presentation embedded in an Access table. Activating the object in Access pops up PowerPoint in open mode (the only mode available from within Access). Pull down PowerPoint's File menu. See Figure 3.23.

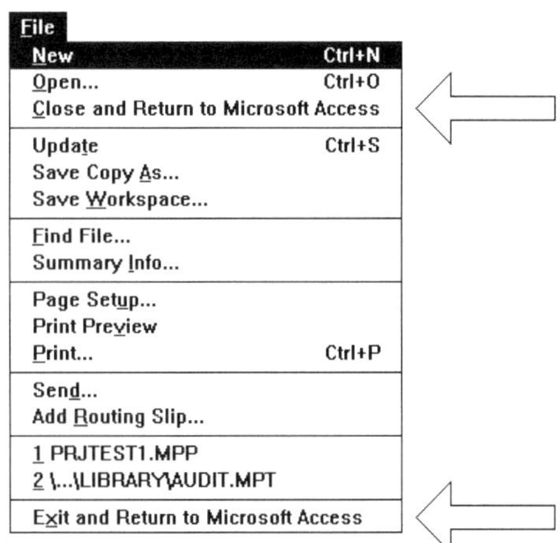

Figure 3.23 PowerPoint's File Menu When
Acting as Editor in Open Mode

If you want to shut down the editor application, you choose Exit and Return to *container application*, in this case Microsoft Access. If you want to leave the editor running on the desktop, choose Close and Return to *container application*.

Not all the Office applications display the same menu options (so what's new?). For example, when a PowerPoint slide is embedded in Excel and the slide is being edited in "open" mode in PowerPoint, the File menu only has "Close" and "Exit and Return to Microsoft Excel" items—no "Close and Return to Microsoft Excel" item.

Be warned, pilgrim, once you close the editor application or the pseudo-data file and the update takes place, there is no way to undo any changes made to the data. Since the container application did not edit the data, there is no way to undo it from there. And you can't undo the last action in the editor since either it's not running or the pseudo-data has been closed. We marked this gotcha as a bug in order to draw attention to it but it's debatable as to whether this is a bug or a design limitation. It seems unreasonable to ask every application to track everything that happens in other applications in order to unwind actions that occurred after the data file or application is closed. But that is exactly what a single-click "embedded object update undo" would entail.

Maybe when every application is part of the operating system this type of undo will be possible. *Ka-ching!*

While the editor application is open, the entire object in the container application is crosshatched to indicate that its underlying data is being edited in another program. See Figure 3.24.

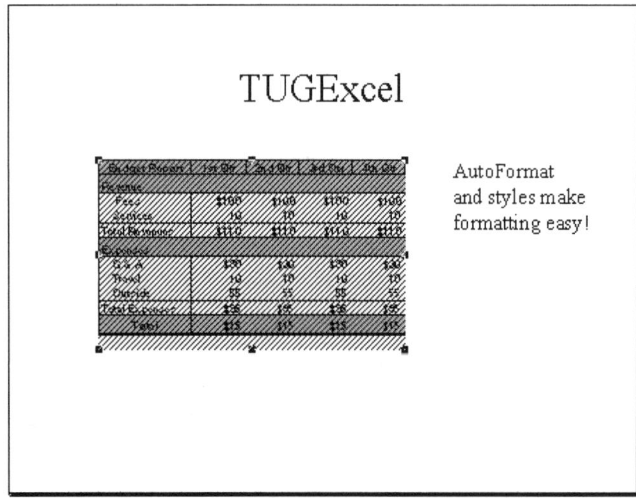

Figure 3.24 Object Being Edited in Another Application

When you see an object crosshatched like this, better check to see what editor application has it opened.

Embedded Objects and Cloaked Editor Application

When you activate an embedded object, you cause the editor application to be loaded into memory. Okey-dokey, but that opens the door for cloaked applications to run on your system, using up those precious system resources. Fortunately, things are more straightforward with embedded objects than they are with links. Again, we're only talking about the Office primary applications—Excel, Word, PowerPoint, Access, plus Project.

If you activate an object and both editor and container support in-place editing (Word or Excel in this case), the editor application loads *if it is not already running*. When you deactivate the embedded object, things get tricky. The editor application does not keep track of whether it was already running when you activated the object or if it had to be loaded. Consequently, it is not sure if it should shut itself down. You certainly *don't* want applications that you have opened on your Windows desktop to be shut down willy-nilly. But if an editor application was loaded and is running cloaked it should be shut down *but isn't!*

Cloaked applications to starboard, Captain.

Assume Excel is not running and you activate an embedded Excel object. Excel is loaded as a cloaked application and in-place editing kicks in within the container application. When you deactivate the Excel embedded object, *Excel is not unloaded*. It stays in memory. Verify this with the System Information utility. Word works the same way. To shut down the cloaked editor application, you have to force it open by selecting the object and going to the Edit menu in the container application. See Figure 3.25.

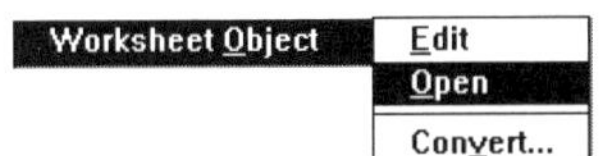

Figure 3.25 Force Object
Editing in Open Mode

Click on Open and the editor comes up in open mode with the object data loaded. The object in the container has the cross-hatching on it as shown in Figure 3.24. You can then Exit the editor application, which updates the object data for any changes made. This way nothing unwanted remains in memory.

Sizing and Scaling Issues—General

When you select an object its sizing handles appear (see Figure 3.20). By placing the mouse pointer on any of the black box sizing handles, you can resize and/or scale the object which is a very handy thing to do. And most of the time it works just fine. (If you drag on the sizing handles to scale the embedded object, does that make it a "dragon scale" operation? *<sorry, couldn't resist>*) WordArt objects, PowerPoint presentations, Excel worksheets, all scale without much problem.

Working for scale   When you think about all that is going on with the display of embedded data that is not native to the container application, it's pretty amazing that resizing and scaling works at all. Still there are times when changing the size or scale of an object causes trouble.

Consider Figure 3.26 which shows several Word objects embedded in an Excel worksheet. The top object in the figure appears as first embedded (100% × 100%).

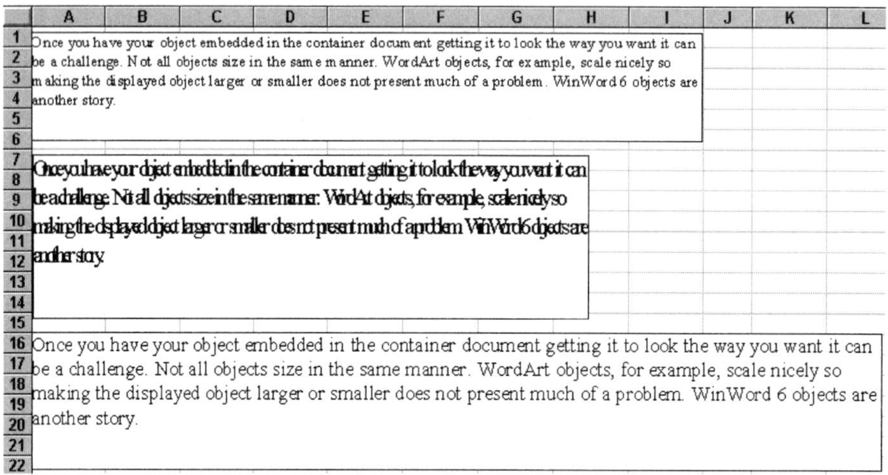

Figure 3.26 Scaling Can Be a Trick

The middle object was scaled by dragging the fill handles to 83% × 150%. Not so good, is it? The object does not behave like you might expect. The data does not wrap, so no matter what the size of the object, you get the same number of lines. The result is that the displayed text gets squished.

The bottom object was scaled to 124% × 124% and works a little better because it was dragged proportionally in the horizontal and vertical directions. When you encounter this type of problem (usually when working with Word-embedded objects), you can resize the object by editing the object in-place. In Figure 3.27 the Word object has been activated, in-place; when dragging the sizing handles, the Word document resizes and the text wraps properly.

The moral of this story is if you're having any problems with resizing an object, activate the object and resize it using the editor application.

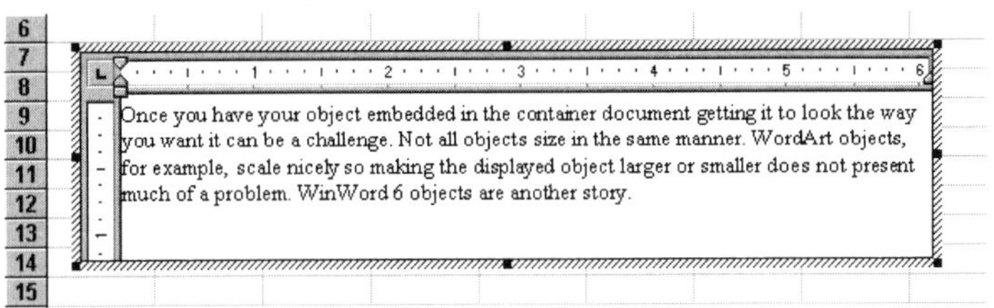

Figure 3.27 Use In-Place Editing for Resizing Problems

Scaling Issues—Excel Charts

This is probably the most common scaling problem we encounter. Say you have a chart in Excel. Embed said chart in a Word document. Try and tweak the size of the chart and the chart is fubar. Happens all the time.

There are two types of charts generated in Excel. Charts are either located in a chart sheet or they are (just to really confuse everyone) *embedded* on a worksheet. In keeping with Microsoft's shaky terminology we'll call them "chart sheet chart" and "worksheet chart." Either type can be embedded in a Word document.

An embedded Excel chart embedded as an object. Huh?

Here is an example of a worksheet chart embedded in a Word container document. See Figure 3.28.

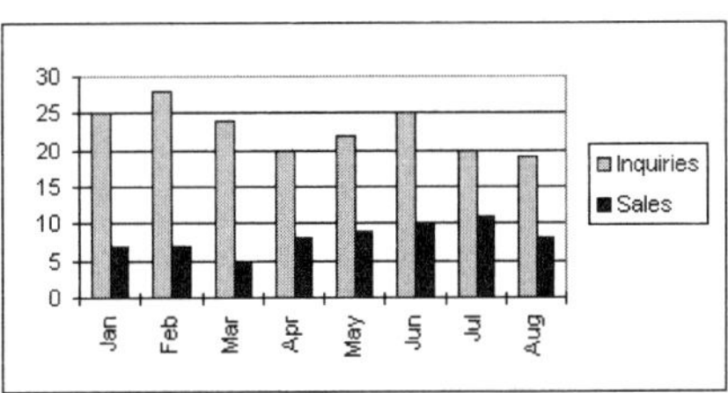

Figure 3.28 An Excel Worksheet Chart Embedded in Word

Select the chart and you can resize it via the sizing handles discussed earlier. But resize a chart like this at your peril. Here's what you get if you try to make it smaller. See Figure 3.29. Then again, given all the wacko problems caused by

	Jan	Feb
Inquiries	25	28
Sales	7	7

Figure 3.29 Same Chart Scaled Smaller

different video drivers, you might get this result or as Monty Python was fond of saying, "something completely different."

Visually fubar   Not so good, is it? What's that in the background? It's the worksheet that this chart is embedded in, in Excel, which is now embedded in Word along with everything else in the Excel workbook. The presentation has gone gonzo but is easily fixed in Word. When you embed a data object in Word, the Word program uses what is called an embed field to control the encapsulated data. If you turn on field codes (Tools / Options / View filecard / check the Field Codes check box), you'll see this field code in place of the displayed object.

```
{EMBED Excel.Chart.5 \s}
```

The trouble is that trailing backslash ess, "\s". Just delete it. Make it look like this:

```
{EMBED Excel.Chart.5}
```

Oh, and you have to remove it before it gets trashed or removing it won't help. An embedded chart sheet chart or an embedded worksheet chart with the offending \s removed can be resized by just selecting the object and dragging the sizing handles. Like so. See Figure 3.30.

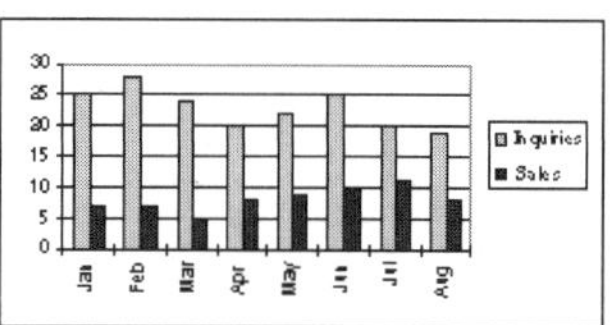

Figure 3.30 Rescaled Without Display Disaster

Major Merging

When an object supports in-place editing and you activate it, a very complex merging of the container and editor applications takes place. The editor application is loaded into memory (if not already running) and the toolbars of the editor application replace the toolbars in the container application.

For example, in Figure 3.31 you see PowerPoint's menu bar and toolbars before activating an embedded Excel object.

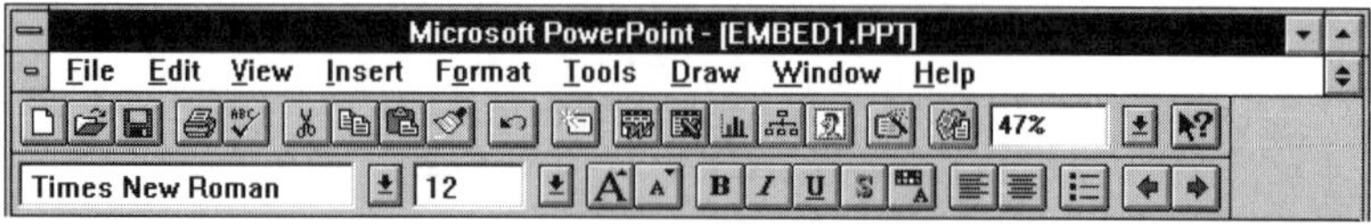

Figure 3.31 PowerPoint Menu and Toolbars

With a quick double-click of the mouse, activate the Excel embedded object from our earlier example (see Figure 3.19) and see that the PowerPoint menu and toolbars are replaced with Excel's. Excel is now running as the editor application and allows you to manipulate the object's data (see Figure 3.32).

A meeting of minds, er, applications

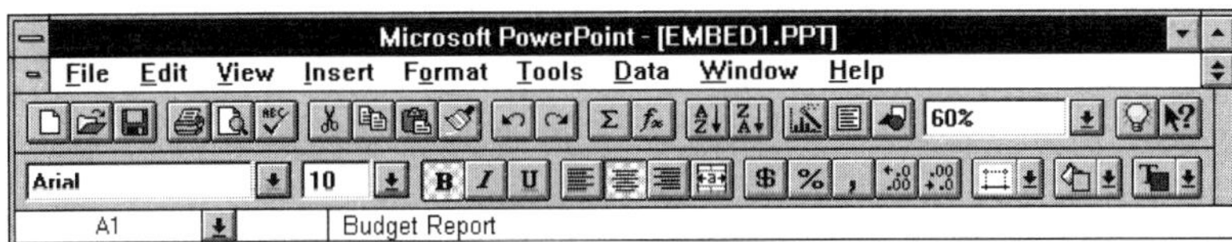

Figure 3.32 PowerPoint Sporting Excel's Toolbars and an Aggregated Menu Bar

It appears that the menus have been swapped but actually they have been aggregated, which means that some are from the container application and some from the editor. In this example, the File and Window menus and the options thereon are strictly PowerPoint's. The level of **aggregation** is negotiated between the two applications and is determined by how each program has implemented OLE 2.0.

New and Improved Menus

> 'Ban, 'Ban, Ca—Caliban,
> Has a new master—Get a new man.
>
> Shakespeare
> *The Tempest*

A container application is quite smart as regards the objects embedded within it. This is reflected in the menu options in the container application that allow you to interact with the object.

OLE 2.0's Improved Primary Menus

When an embedded object is selected (not activated) and you pull down the container application's Edit menu, you'll see something like this (see Figure 3.33) at the bottom of the menu.

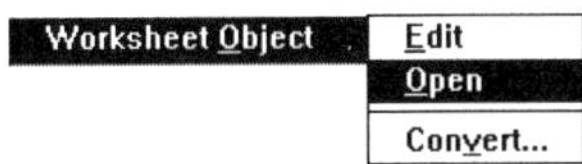

Figure 3.33 The Edit / Object Option

If there is no selected object in the container document, this option on the Edit menu just reads "Object" and is grayed out.

The menu option in this example says "Worksheet Object" since the object currently selected is just that—an embedded Excel worksheet. Activate the object from the flyout menu using Edit for in-place activation (if supported) or Open, which brings up the editor application in its own application window.

The Convert option lets you convert an object between the formats supported by the editor application. For example, say you have an embedded Excel object and you want to change the object's presentation so that it appears as an icon. Clicking on Convert presents you with the dialog box in Figure 3.34.

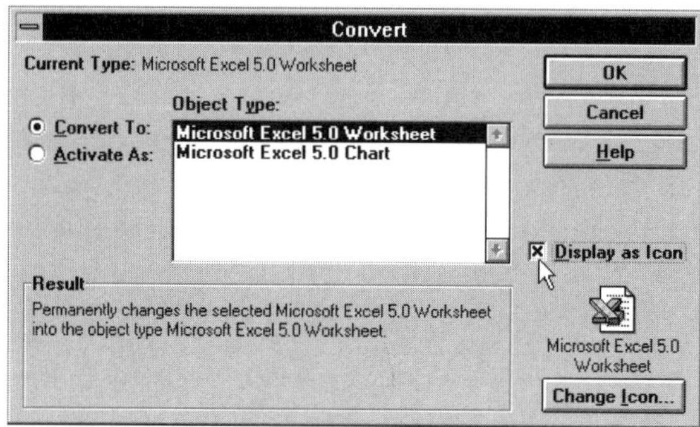

Figure 3.34 Object Convert Dialog Box

Icons to go   Excel supports object types of Worksheet and Chart. You can determine how the object is activated (as what object type), convert the object between types, and (as shown in this example) check the Display as Icon check box to have the object presented as an icon in the container application. You can also change the icon to any icon on your computer via the Change Icon command button. As Captain Planet says, "The Power is yours!"

OLE 2.0's Improved Shortcut Menus

As was mentioned back in Chapter 1, you can right-click on an object to pop up the container application's shortcut menu. The Container application peeks at the object type and lists it right on the edit portion of the shortcut menu, thereby letting you know what type of object it is and allowing you to activate it.

Container applications do not display the object choices on their shortcut menus consistently, however. This could be partially explained by the unproven rumor that the Word development team at Microsoft thought flyout menus were for sissies. Consider a ClipArt Gallery object embedded in both Word and Excel. In Word, if you right-click the object, you get the shortcut menu in Figure 3.35.

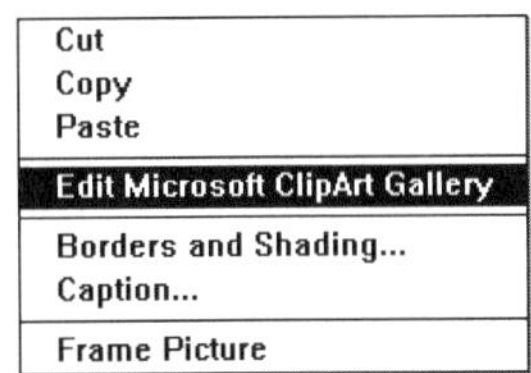

Figure 3.35 Shortcut Menu in
Word for ClipArt Gallery Object

The center option lets you activate the ClipArt Gallery object. ClipArt Gallery only supports editing in the open mode (see Table 3.5), so you don't need a choice between Edit and Open; you'll always get Open. (So why doesn't the menu option say "Open ..." instead of "Edit ..."? Dunno.) But you'll notice that there is no option for converting the object. It's true that ClipArt Gallery objects support only one object type, but if you wanted to convert the object to an icon you'd be out of luck with Word's shortcut menu. From Word's Edit menu, however, you have access to the Convert option via the flyout menu. *Sheesh.*

On the other hand, Excel's shortcut menu does have the Convert option. In Excel the shortcut menu gives you the same options you get on the Edit menu, which is what you'd expect. Right-click on a ClipArt Gallery object in Excel and here's what you get. See Figure 3.36.

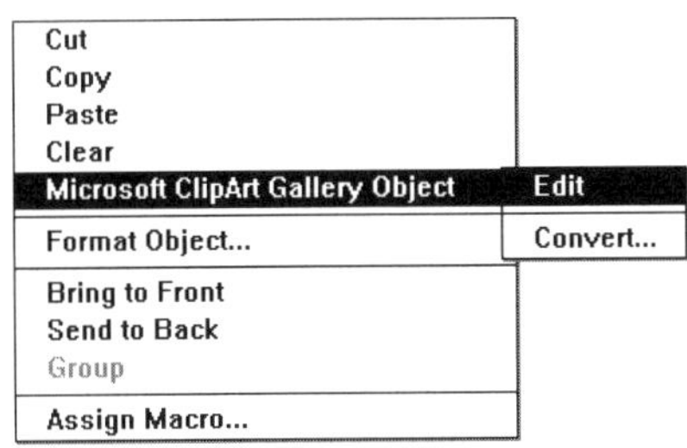

Figure 3.36 Shortcut Menu in Excel
for ClipArt Gallery Object

Sure, sure, we can't think of a reason you'd ever want to convert a ClipArt Gallery object to an icon but, by golly, *we want some consistency!* Sometimes a shortcut menu lists Open and Edit as menu options, sometimes they're on a flyout menu, sometimes they're not. Go figure.

There are other kinds of OLE actions besides just Edit and Open. If the object is, for example, an embedded `.WAV` sound file there will be a Play option on the menu.

Resource Requirements

> Oh, fudge! You realize that multi-tasking really requires buying several computers and arranging them in a circle around your desk.
>
> Arnold Shing, CPA
> Direct male-line descendant of Amok Shing

Captain, we just haven't *got* the power!

In Chapter 1 we talked about the amount of disk space that a suite of OLE applications (namely Office) consumes. Throw in a copy of Project and you're looking at 95–108 MB just for your applications. Er, "Would you like an operating system with that order, sir?" Yesiree, there's no respect for the disk, and not much else either when it comes to computer resources these days.

Ah, the good old days—when a standard PC came with a ridiculously small amount of RAM and a laughably tiny hard disk. Those were the days. And we're not talking about the old AT classic. We're waxing nostalgic about our last 386/33 with 8 megs RAM.

A base configuration

Listen up! Sixteen megabytes nowadays is *entry level. ENTRY LEVEL!!!* (To get the flavor of that statement, please imagine the late Sam Kinison screaming that in your face. Thanks.) And you'd better start planning on a new one-gigabyte SCSI drive or at the very least half a gigabyte. We'd yell it at you, but it is all so depressing. But that's the way it is. Better wrap all this stuff up in a 486DX2 running at 66 megahertz.

Oh, and don't get too carried away with yourself once you have this setup (or if you already have it). It's entry level for fooling around with OLE, embedded objects, drag-and-drop, and stuff like that. What a world.

Leggo My Resources!

In a perfect world you start an application and it uses up some system resources. Shut down the application and all those resources are released back to the system for the next application. Alas, it is *not* a perfect world. Open and close enough applications enough times and your precious supply of resources erodes until something croaks.

 **Applications just don't always release all the resources they use. In the current version of Graph at the time of this writing there is a known bug (Microsoft Knowledge Base Article Q114307) that prevents Graph from releasing resources when used to insert a graph object in either Word or Excel. The resources can only be recovered by closing the container application.**

During the creation of this book extensive testing was done in order to prepare the various tables you see scattered about showing you how applications behave under different circumstances. This object embedded here, that one embedded there, here a link, there a link, everywhere, oh, you get the idea. Now if we only had a dollar for every GPF we had, oh boy!

Best beef up that PC, then lock and load, pilgrim, lock and load.

The Case of the Missing Server

Dr. Watson: But Holmes, if it's not gone missing then why was Inspector LaStrade unable to locate it?

Holmes: Elementary my dear Watson! The server was there all along. The lack of system resources allowed Moriarty to manifest the error message and confound our old friend the Inspector.

And what error message is the king of deductive reasoning going on about? Well, if one cold, foggy evening, you're working in your Baker Street digs and try to do an Insert / Object in your container application and are suddenly confronted with the error message in Figure 3.37:

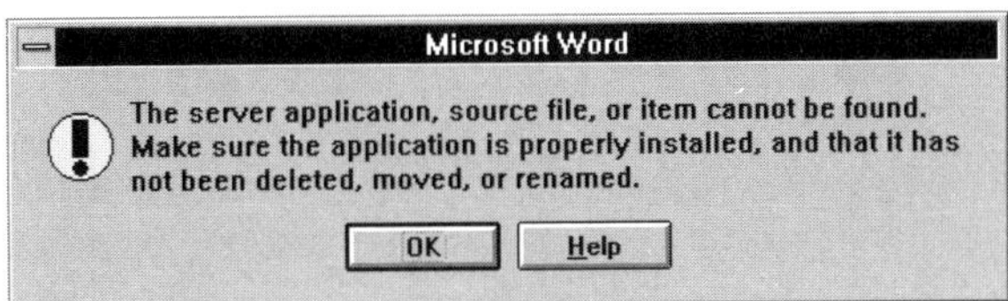

Figure 3.37 It's 10 O'clock. Do You Know Where Your Server Is?

either the editor (a.k.a. server) application is not where it should be, or the linked file has wandered off, or *you may just be below some critical threshold of system resources!*

That's right, low resources can trigger this error message, so before launching into full-scale panic, check the resource level (ProgMan Help About or run the System Information utility discussed earlier in this chapter). If you've got plenty of resources, then you can panic.

No, panicking may not help (although it would probably be amusing to any onlookers), so let's run down what might be wrong. Hmmm, did you rename any directories lately? Clean up your disk by moving a bunch of applications to that new E: drive? Remember when you could reorganize your hard disk without all your applications having conniptions? Well, in this day and age of applications talking to each other, you can forget casual disk reorgs.

Don't panic.

Think of it like this: For the applications to communicate effectively, they need to know each others' location or "address." When an application is installed, it registers its address with the `REG.DAT` database discussed in Chapter 2. If you drag one of your applications off in the middle of the night to some new place, all the other applications will be looking for it at the old address. No communication, ipso facto.

The correct procedure is to do an uninstall and reinstall of the application you want to move. This keeps the `REG.DAT` up to date. Doesn't reinstalling your applications sound like fun? No? Well, if you have a strong constitution and are quite comfortable editing INI files and the like you can opt for *updating* your `REG.DAT` file. We'll discuss this procedure later in this chapter.

Yes, We Have No Editor

Another situation that triggers a disconcerting error message occurs when you try to activate an object and the editor application is not installed on your computer at all. Hmmm, delete anything lately? Maybe you should panic after all.

Try to activate a WordArt object in an Excel compound document when WordArt is not to be found and you'll see the error message in Figure 3.38.

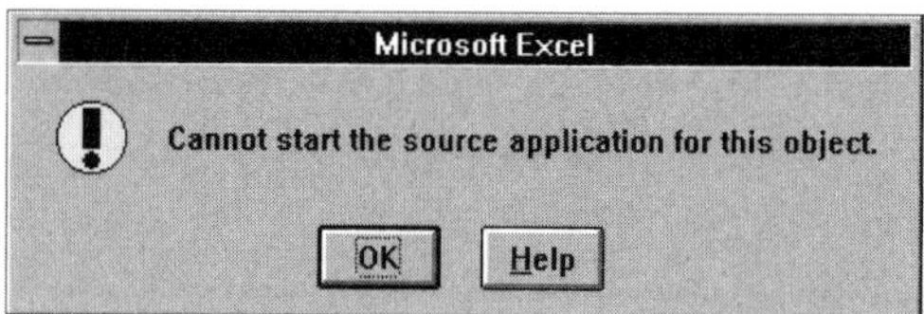

Figure 3.38 Excel's Cryptic Error Message

Not too helpful, is it? No idea as to what the problem is or even what the source application is.

Word is a little better. Word provides the name of the editor application at least. See Figure 3.39.

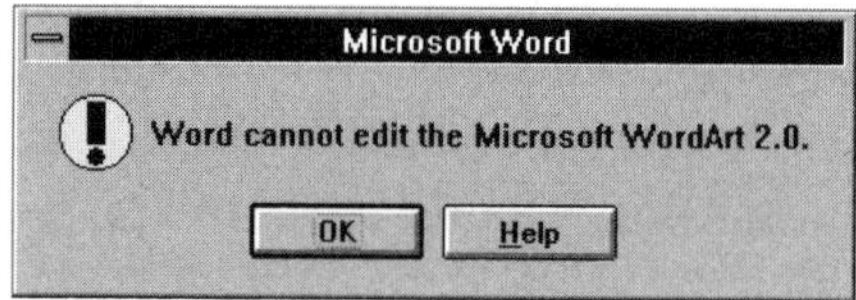

Figure 3.39 Word's "Cannot Edit"
Error Message

Ah, PowerPoint is the most verbose and provides the best list of what might be the problem, although as with Excel you have to figure out the name of the editor application on your own. PowerPoint displays the message in Figure 3.40.

Figure 3.40 PowerPoint's Missing Editor Message

All of these different messages are trying to tell you the same thing. Something is missing—moved, deleted, or renamed. Or you're lower on resources than you think.

WHAT WORKS AND WHAT DOESN'T

> In Italy for thirty years under the Borgias they had warfare, terror, murder, bloodshed—they produced Michelangelo, Leonardo da Vinci, and the Renaissance. In Switzerland they had brotherly love, five hundred years of democracy and peace, and what did that produce? The cuckoo clock.
>
> Harry Lime
> *The Third Man,* 1949

In this section we're going to recap those things to keep in mind when using and creating compound documents. Sure, there are some gotchas, resource issues, and the odd bug or two, but the incredible vision that has gone into the OLE 2.0 architecture and the promise of what's to come makes these minor issues pale to insignificance.   **Time for a quiz**

You've already seen this stuff in action earlier in the chapter, so this is mostly review. But everything in this chapter is fundamental to understanding the compound document, so a review is important. And just to keep it interesting we'll throw in some new application-specific gotchas that you'll want to know about.

Linking—A Recap

> A little neglect may breed great mischief ... for want of a nail the shoe was lost; for want of a shoe the horse was lost; and for want of the horse the rider was lost.
>
> Benjamin Franklin
> *Preface: Courteous Reader*

These are the basic points covered in the section on linking in this chapter. Links make for smaller file sizes and are the berries when you need to share data among several users.

What Works with Links

- Copy the data in the source application and Paste Special in the container document. Check the Paste Link radio button in the Paste Special dialog box.

- Highlight the object to be linked and drag it to the container document while holding down the Control and Shift keys. *This only works at present when dragging an Excel worksheet object to either a PowerPoint slide or a Project file's Gantt bar chart area.*

- Edit links via the Links option, usually found on the container application's Edit menu. Break links that you no longer want to update. You cannot break links via the Links dialog box in Excel. You have to copy the link *in Excel* to the clipboard and then perform a Paste Special *in Excel*. If the link format is text, use the Values option in the Paste Special dialog box. If the link format is an object (graphical), then choose the Paste option button from the Paste Special dialog box.

- A linked object can be edited from the Linked *type* Object menu option, usually found on the container application's Edit menu. The link *must* be selected in order for the menu option to become available.

- A link can usually be edited by double-clicking on the linked data in the container document.

- To link to a data file use Insert / Object / Create from File, select the data file, and check the Link to File check box.

What to Watch Out for with Links

- Open source files *before* container files or *links are manual without warning and do not automatically update!*

- If the container application asks you if you want to update the links in the document and you respond "No," the links are not updated and are now manual links. They still appear as automatic links in the Links dialog box.

- In Word you can uncheck the Tools / Options / General filecard / Update Automatic Links at Open option button and Word henceforward does not update automatic links. No message box, no nothing.

Embedding—A Recap

> Oh, what a tangled web we spread,
> When first we practice to embed!
>
> (with apologies to Sir Walter Scott)

Embedding is indeed a tricky business. Data objects encapsulated within documents yet foreign to the application that created the document, but editable with another program called an editor application .... Oy!

But not to worry, take it one step at a time and you too can make container documents jump through hoops.

What Works with Embedding

- To embed an object and create the data from scratch, you can use Insert / Objects / Create New filecard.

- To embed an entire data file that already exists, you can use Insert / Objects / Create from File filecard.

- To embed a data object, you can select the data in the editor (a.k.a. source or server) application and drag the data object to a valid drop zone in the container document. This is known as drag-and-drop.

- Holding down the Control key while doing the drag-and-drop causes the data object to be copied from the editor application instead of cut, which is the default.

- Filenames can be dragged from File Manager and dropped on applications. Dropping the file on different drop zones (that is, iconized application, container document, outside container document) within an application can cause other actions than embedding, like opening or printing a data file.

- Active objects being edited in-place have a hatched border.

- Active objects being edited in open mode are completely crosshatched.

- Double-clicking on an embedded object *activates* or *plays* the object.

- Right-clicking on an embedded object pops up the shortcut menu which *usually* allows you to open, edit in-place (if supported), play (if applicable), or convert the object.

What to Watch Out for with Embedded Objects

- Doing a drag-and-drop between some applications results in a paste instead of an embed under certain circumstances. Word to Word, Word to Excel, or Excel/ Word to Project's Gantt table drop zone all result in a paste, *not an embed!*

- Drag-and-drop within a single Excel worksheet clears the clipboard. (Okay, this does not really have anything to do with embedded objects but you should be aware of it.)

- When you embed an object there can be considerable overhead, more than meets the eye, as it were. For example, a small Excel table or an Excel chart dragged and dropped on a Word document embeds more than what is displayed. If the source workbook contains ten sheets jam-packed with data, *everything* in the Excel file is embedded in the compound document lock, stock, and barrel.

- Objects cannot span pages in the container application (even though the OLE 2.0 specification says they can).

- Objects do not inherit properties of the container application (even though the OLE 2.0 specification says they can).

- Container functions do not tunnel across objects (for example, running spell check in a Word container does not check the spelling of text within an embedded Excel object).

- To undo a drag-and-drop embed is a two-step process. Edit / Undo in the container application *and* in the source/editor application.

- Where both the container and editor applications support in-place editing, activate the embedded object using in-place editing to resize and scale the object. This avoids presentation problems within the container application.

- When editing an embedded object in open mode, you cannot undo any changes once the pseudo-document is closed and/or the editor application is shut down.

A Grab-bag of Tips, Tricks, and Gotchas

> Forewarned, forearmed.
>
> Miguel de Cervantes
> *Don Quixote de la Mancha*

One way to eliminate some potential problems when dealing with OLE objects is to keep all your applications in sync. Don't try to embed objects from server/ editor applications that only support OLE 1.0 into container applications that support OLE 2.0 and vice versa. It may work but the Microsoft Knowledge Base is full of articles that give us reason to believe that this practice is best shunned.

Excel unto Excel

Excel doesn't much like to embed Excel objects within Excel compound documents. You can make Excel do it, but as we've discussed it has some odd side effects. First, Excel tries to open any `.XLS` file you drop on it. If you try Insert / Object / Create New you find that all references to Excel are missing from the Object Type list. As a last resort you use Insert / Object / Create from File, only to wind up with the source file opened as a hidden worksheet. Curiouser and curiouser!

Keyboarding

The Escape key can be used to deactivate an embedded object. You may have to close some elements of the editor application (like the Datasheet window in Graph) before the Escape key trick can be used. This is a real life saver if you find yourself mouseless on some occasion.

If you find yourself in a situation where the accelerator keys for an editor application are not available when using in-place activation, try bringing up the editor program in open mode. Equation Editor suffers from this problem. In fact Microsoft has come up with a workaround to force Equation Editor to *always* come up in open mode. Add the line:

May the force be with you.

```
ForceOpen = 1
```

to the `EQNEDIT.INI` file (look for it in the C:\WINDOWS directory) in the [General] section. This disables in-place activation for Equation Editor.

This trick doesn't work in Word or Excel. Hmmm, might be nice to have the flexibility to turn off in-place activation on a program by program basis if you wanted, no? Well, write your congressman, er, Microsoft representative and request this feature.

Controlling Word's Templates

Speaking of cute INI tricks, how about this one: When you create a new Word object inside a container document, the template that Word uses is good old `NORMAL.DOT`. If you want Word to use another template, no problem. Add this line to the `WINWORD6.INI` file's [Microsoft Word] section:

```
OLEDot = template.ext
```

where *template.ext* is the name and extension of the template you want. This is very cool.

Regenerating the REG.DAT

Look, we don't want to talk about this. Not at all. We thought of referring you to Microsoft Product Support Services. We thought of just giving you the Knowledge

Base article number (Q107674). We thought about ignoring this issue and calling it a day. Messing with the `REG.DAT` is like oral surgery, only not as much fun. Besides, everyone has a good backup of `REG.DAT`, right? Let's see a show of hands.

But then that little voice started nagging us. Things like, "What if some poor reader has no backup, crashes the registration database late Friday night, and there's no tech support at Microsoft until Monday?" and "What if the reader is real desperate and promises to be real, real, careful?"

On your own ...   Okay, we're gonna tell you how to regenerate the `REG.DAT` file. This is the OLE Registration Database discussed in Chapter 2 that tracks all your OLE applications. It knows everything about everything. If your `REG.DAT` file gets fubar, you got troubles, my friend, right here in River City. But it's still not too late to just reinstall all your applications. Huh? Oh. Okay, here is how you regenerate the registration database, but we do not recommend doing this except as a last resort and we absolve ourselves from any liability. You're on your own with this one.

If you don't understand anything in the instructions shown here, STOP, take two ounces of the medicinal beverage of your choice, and call Microsoft in the morning. Oh, and if you've moved the MSAPPS directory or any of the contents therein, you will not be happy with the results of the merge for any of those applications.

1. Make a full backup of your system. (Just a precaution.) *Hell, make two backups!*

2. Clean out your Startup group in Program Manager. Make sure that the Load= and Run= lines in `WIN.INI` are remarked out.

3. Check the [embedding] section of the `WIN.INI` file and make sure each entry has the correct path. Make real sure.

4. Shut down Windows. In DOS rename the `REG.DAT` file to `REG.SOL`. (Just in case you want it back later.)

5. Start Windows and fire up File Manager. Only Program Manager and File Manager should be running at this point.

6. In File Manager do a search of the entire drive where your applications are installed for `*.REG` files.

7. Select the first `.REG` file in the Search Results window. Associate this file with the `REGEDIT.EXE` file (found in the Windows directory). If you've never associated a file, check out the *Windows User's Guide*.

8. Reconsider the whole thing. Are you sure you want to do this?

9. If you know which of your OLE programs are auto-registering, you can skip them. If you don't know which are which, just double-click on each `.REG` file shown in the search window.

That should do it at least for the applications installed on that drive. If you have programs installed elsewhere, run their `.REG` files as well. Hope you never need to do it, pilgrim.

Old Word for Windows 2 Baggage

If you have some Word 2.x embedded objects laying around in any compound documents, don't edit or open them in any of the Office applications. The phrase Microsoft uses is "may become irretrievably corrupt." And if you do get a Word 2.x object activated in Word 6, you'll have a strange looking object indeed because it will have a page size of the Word icon (little less than 3/4 inch).

Some Issues with Word

Word objects default to a fixed six-inch width. This plays hell with linked tables wider than six inches. The text in the right-side columns that extend beyond the six-inch mark are truncated in the linked display.

    A paragraph of text that extends beyond six inches is not a problem as the text is wrapped within the linked frame.

    This six-inch width problem crops up again (pun intended) when you embed Word objects. An embedded Word object defaults to a page size of about six inches by nine inches, or less, with zero inch margins. If the page width of the embedded data is more than six inches, the text appears truncated in the object display. But with an embedded Word *object* you can work around this problem by in-place activating the object and resizing it.

The six-inch limitation

Some Issues with Excel

Like Word, Excel objects may get truncated when large worksheet objects (over 20 columns by 75 rows) are embedded into a Word compound document. If this happens to you, just activate the object and in Excel reduce the column width, row height, and font size. Easy enough.

    More of a problem is for those of you that have customized the default templates in Excel by creating your own **SHEET.XLT** or **CHART.XLT**. Even though you have your own custom default templates, if you create a new worksheet or chart object in a container document you'll get the plain vanilla Excel template, *not your custom template.*

Issues with Server/Editor Applications that Support Auto-Macros

Auto-macros are macros that can be designed to run when an application is loaded. It is possible to create macros like this in Word, Excel, or Project. You must be aware that these routines *will be executed* whenever their host application is

Macro mayhem

loaded whether you load the application from Program Manager or the application is loaded because a data object was activated. Doesn't matter whether the application is loaded cloaked or in the "open." These puppies will run, so you had better be prepared for it.

Applications deal much better with other things that can be triggered just by loading the program. For example, the Tip of the Day routine is *not* executed when an application is loaded by activating an object.

We're not saying that this is necessarily a bad thing. Depends on what the macro does. Just be aware that this may happen. What is needed is a way to ensure that macros will run only when you want them to do so.

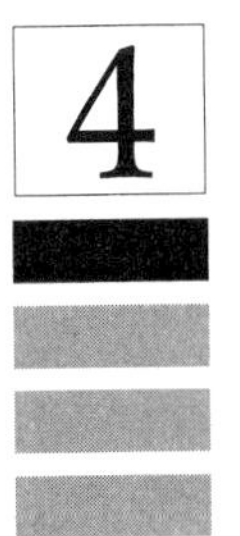# Object Kinks, OfficeLinks, and Things That Go Bump in the Night

Modern technology was made in America.

Thomas Hughes
American Genesis: A Century of Invention and Technological Enthusiasm

In this chapter you do final battle with the compound document dragon and look at some implementations of OLE 2.0 that the marketing folks may not have considered. Like what happens when object A is embedded in object B which is inside object C. Fun stuff, that.

As you've seen, a compound document is used to establish relationships. Relationships between the data object and the application that manipulates that object (the editor), and relationships between the data object and its presenter (the container). Let's explore the object relationship further.

Looking for
Mr. Goodobject

OBJECT ARCANA

One morning I shot an elephant in my pajamas. How he got into my pajamas I'll never know.

Captain Spaulding
Animal Crackers, 1929

In Chapter 3 you saw objects in action. Linking and embedding, where it works like you'd expect it to, where it works like, uhm, like it does whether you expect it to or not, and where the reality still falls short of the promise. Before we proceed further with our quest for object enlightenment, let's step back and talk about what's going on behind the whiz-bang technology found in OLE 2.0 as far as "objects" are concerned and how it affects what you can do with objects in a practical sense.

Incognito Objects

> Sometimes I sing and dance around my house in my underwear. That doesn't make me Madonna.
>
> Joan Cusack
> *Working Girl*, 1988

An OLE 1.0-enabled application, like Excel 4 or Word 2, did not possess the user interface (UI) hooks to allow you to save an embedded object outside the bounds of the compound document. For example, if a Word 2 container document contains an embedded Excel 4 worksheet and you edit that worksheet (it has a name like "Worksheet in COMPOUND.DOC"), there is absolutely no way you can take that one specific object and save it to disk as a separate, standalone file. No way, no ma'am, no sir, no how. Sure, you can copy it to the clipboard and paste it into a 100% true-blue Excel worksheet and save that worksheet to disk, but that's not the same as a direct, immediate, take-this-object-and-shove-er-save-it-to-disk-now option, is it? No. As they say in the consulting trade, that's TMT (too much trouble).

Saving objects to separate files   So, in grand style, OLE 2.0 provides both a programmatic specification and a UI specification for allowing us, the humble users (bothersome creatures, aren't we?) to save the object to a file. No clipboard juggling required.

The steps to save an OLE 2.0 embedded object, in its current state, out to a run-of-the-mill 8.3 DOS filename on your hard disk follow. (Not all OLE 2.0-compliant applications support this feature; for example, Equation Editor does not support saving its objects to files.)

1. Assuming you've got a Word document embedded in an Excel container worksheet, Open the Word document object. (You *do not* in-place edit it because when the server's and container's menus are aggregated during in-place editing, the File menu system always remains exclusively that of the container.) When you open the object, its owner application completely takes over the application display space so that the server's File menu system becomes available. Feeling vertiginous yet?

2. Select File from the primary menu bar, choose Save Copy As, and then enter a legitimate filename as appropriate (see Figure 4.1). This saves the embedded object, *in its current state*, to a free-standing file. Of course, from this point forward there's absolutely no relationship between the new file and the embedded object. They are forever two separate, distinct entities spawned from the moment in time when you clicked on OK in the Save As dialog box. This is as it should be because this is an embedded object, not a linked object.

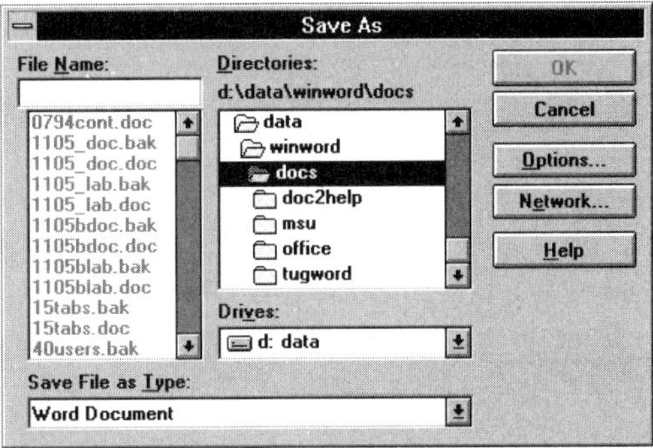

Figure 4.1 File Save Copy As Dialog for a
Word OLE 2.0 Object

As you saw earlier, OLE 2.0 allows you to spawn an embedded object based on the data in a free-standing file (again, not all OLE 2.0-compliant applications support this feature). When you use Insert Object to embed an OLE 2.0 object in the container document, you can select the Create from File filecard (as seen in Chapter 3) and create the embedded object using an extant file.

For those of you interested in some of the technical arcana of OLE 2.0, dig this. The syntax for object class names has changed a bit from the OLE 1.0 days. Table 4.1 shows some application and OLE object **class name** changes from version 1.0 to 2.0. Note the use of the period (dot) separator. In Chapter 5 you'll see a lot of this object expression syntax. (An object expression looks like object.method, object.property, object.object.method, and so on.)

Spawning objects from extant files

Table 4.1 Object Class Names In OLE 1.0 Versus OLE 2.0

"Human" Form	OLE 1 Object Class Name	OLE 2 Object Class Name
Microsoft Excel Worksheet	ExcelWorksheet	Excel.Sheet.5
Microsoft Excel Chart	ExcelChart	Excel.Chart.5
Microsoft Word Document	WordDocument	Word.Document.6

Post-mortem on Roving Links

> A reasonable amount o' fleas is good fer a dog—keeps him from broodin' over bein' a dog, mebbe.

> Edward Noyes Westcott

As discussed in Chapter 1, OLE 2.0 as implemented in Office provides only a partial mechanism for tracking a source file's movements. For example, assume that the Excel compound document `CONTAINR.XLS` contains a link to some source data in the Word document `SOURCE.DOC`. If you close `CONTAINR.XLS`, move `SOURCE.DOC` to a different subdirectory or volume, and reopen `CONTAINR.XLS`, you'll most likely be stuck looking at a #NAME error in Excel (it can't resolve the invalid path name or file name reference if the link is anything other than an object, in which case you get the last data that was updated displayed.). But if you reverse this scenario, Word handles this broken link situation far more gracefully—the container displays not an error, but instead the very last value of the linked source data even if the link format is just text. However, in Word as with Excel, updating the link at this point is impossible.

The way it might have been...
Furthermore, neither the applications Word and Excel, nor the object itself provide a visual clue that the link is "broken" or "out-of-date," a feature that was hinted at in Microsoft's *OLE 2.0 Design Specification* document. The document sketched one possible implementation—a linked object's border (a one-pixel wide *dotted* border to distinguish from an embedded object's *solid* border) would be presented in the Windows "disabled text" color if either the link was automatic and the update had failed or the link was manual. In our opinion, they're all good ideas that should have, but didn't, make the cut.

...and the way it is
Back to link management. Both OLE 1.0 and 2.0 lack a complete dynamic link management feature. Strictly speaking, this is true from a native user interface point of view, but not from a programmatic point of view. We've been preaching in our seminars since 1991 that you can write DDE macros to overcome many of these OLE user interface limitations. (Here "user interface" refers primarily to Edit Paste Link.) This is because your macro manages the dependent-source (a.k.a. client-server) data relationship. A macro can be far more robust and situation-specific than OLE's broad-band user interface feature set. But we digress.

Trying to fix broken links can drive you to distraction since each application in Office handles things differently. Let's take each Office application in turn.

Missing Links—Word

In Word, when you edit a broken OLE 2.0 link, the Links dialog's Update column reads "N/A" (not available). Remember, this is more than OLE 1.0 did, which, by the way, was nothing. Once an OLE 1.0 link was broken, you got no notification or indication anywhere. Nada, amigo. See Figure 4.2.

Busted links
The "N/A" may not seem like much, but it's all you get. The Open Source button is grayed out, which is another clue that the link is busted. Clicking on Update Now gets you nowhere, not even a message box that the source file cannot be found.

On the upside, Word provides a very nice interface to change the link. If the source file was moved or renamed, you can reestablish the link. The Change

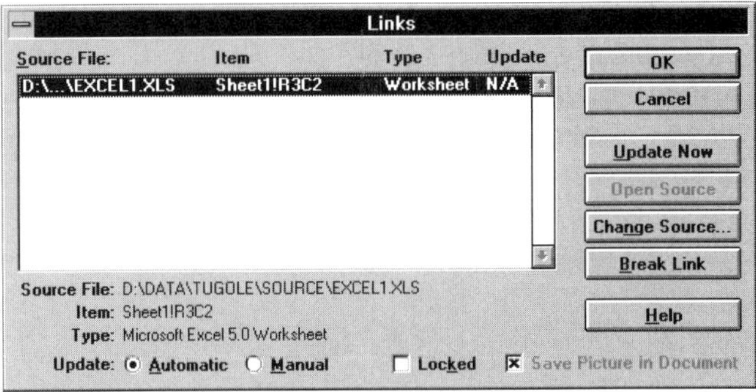

Figure 4.2 Word's Links Dialog Box with a Broken Link

Source button fires up a dialog that looks much like the common File Open, with the notable addition of an Item text box containing the item description, so you can go out and find the wayward source file (see Figure 4.3). It kindly points to the source file's last known directory and filename. Slick. Another nicety is that once you find the directory (using the Directories list box) that contains the source file, the dialog automatically selects the source's filename in the File Name list. There were no such features under OLE 1.0. Still, it's a bummer that you have to *manually* (ugh) invoke this OLE 2.0 feature.

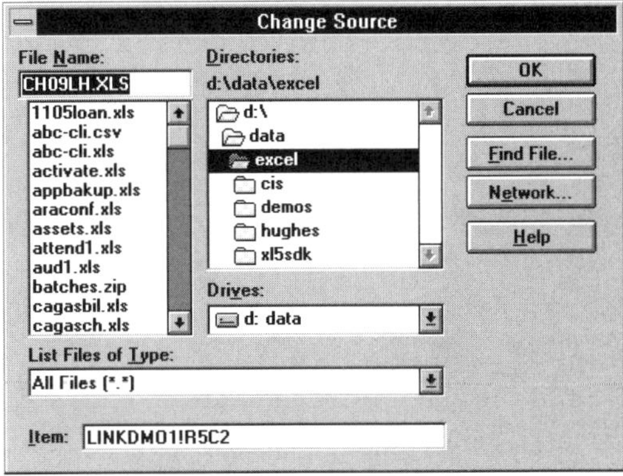

Figure 4.3 Word's Change Source Dialog Box

Missing Links—Excel

Excel is another can of worms altogether and is by far the most troublesome when it comes to maintaining links with other applications. Open a workbook that contains links and *you will not be notified if the update was unsuccessful.* You get no clue whatsoever.

In Excel, when you edit a broken OLE 2.0 link, there's still no functionality for representing the state of the link. First, the Links dialog incorrectly reports the broken link's status as "A" (Automatic). Second, the Change Source button invokes a minimalist dialog box that's missing several controls (the help topic for Change Links describes controls that simply aren't there). See Figure 4.4.

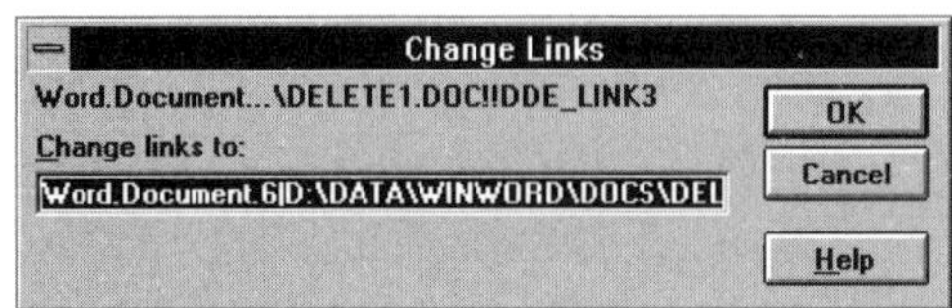

Figure 4.4 Excel's Minimalist Change Links Dialog

There is no way to easily change drives, browse for files, or "walk" the directory tree. You have to type in a fully-qualified path/filename and you have to get it right, no excuses, Katie bar the door. What's more, you may edit the link correctly here but be greeted with a "Name is not defined" error back in Excel. But if you edit the reference in the formula bar (or just pretend to by hitting F2 then Enter), the link does update properly. Go figure.

Missing Links—Access

Common dialog boxes, NOT! Access is only slightly better behaved than Excel (and that's not saying much). Like Excel, Access does not overtly warn you that a link cannot be updated automatically. If you check out the Links dialog box, the broken link still shows "Automatic." Trying to force an update gets you this message box. See Figure 4.5.

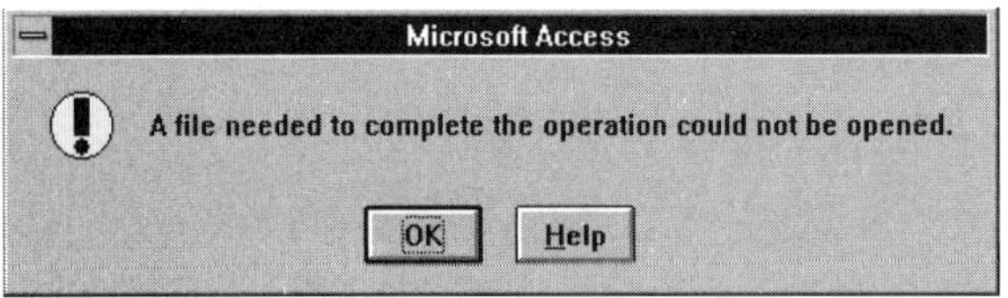

Figure 4.5 Access Warns You Something's Amiss, Sort Of

Cryptic, but better than nothing. However …

Check out the help text displayed when you click Help in Figure 4.5's message box. The help topic lists three possible causes of the error message but omits one of the most obvious possibilities—*that the file exists but has been relocated*. Go figure.

Head and shoulders above Excel is the Change Source dialog box in Access, which is a near match to Word's (shown back in Figure 4.3). You get the same functionality in a slightly different dialog box. Unfortunately, Access' Change Source dialog, unlike Word's, does not automatically select the source filename once you find its new directory. Sheesh, where are common dialog boxes when you need them?

Missing Links—PowerPoint

PowerPoint, on the other hand, is a joy where links are concerned. Open a presentation with a broken link and you are immediately notified. See Figure 4.6.

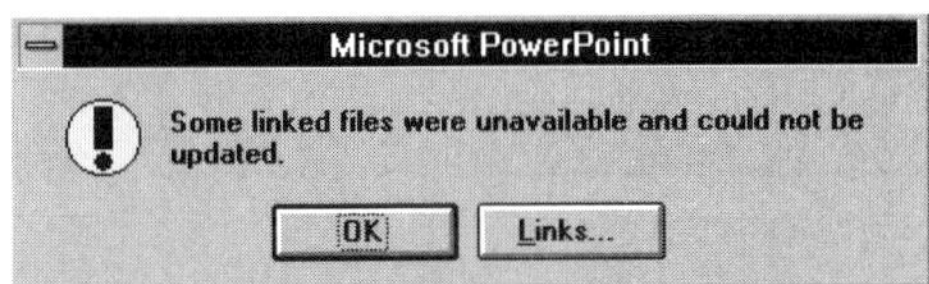

Figure 4.6 PowerPoint's Link Update
Failure Message Box

What's more, if you go into the Edit / Links dialog box *you are actually notified that the link source is unavailable. What a concept!* See Figure 4.7.

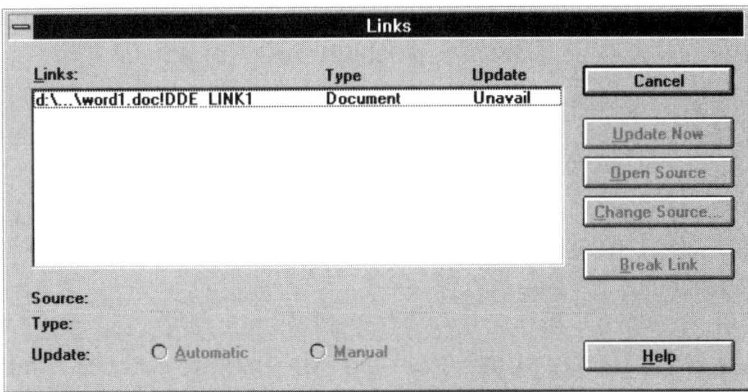

Figure 4.7 PowerPoint's Links Dialog Box with a Broken Link

Right there in the Update column the broken link shows "Unavail." Wow, are we easy to please or what? Try to update it or open the source file, and PowerPoint informs you that the linked file is unavailable and could not be updated.

Okay, wait a minute! We've been saying OLE 2.0 is new and improved, so why all these glitches in its implementation? It's true, the specifications are new **Only human, after all** and improved, but guess what? The human beings who programmed the various applications in Office the suite are, well, different human beings. This isn't a judgmental stance we're taking, mind you, we're simply pointing out that they're not the same people. The different development teams programmed the treatment of broken links differently, that's all. But with each application upgrade, you'll see a move to a common method of handling things like links. Have faith, pilgrim! Just click your heels together three times and say "there's nothing like commonality" over and over.

Links on the Loose

In Chapter 1 we touched on broken link management and what happens when you move and rename files that are linked. Under the right circumstances, however, you *can* move the source and container files and not break the links.

Let's say you have the following directory setup on your computer. See Figure 4.8.

Figure 4.8 A Monstrous Directory Structure

In the CONTAINR directory you have some files with links to files in the SOURCE directory. If you move the files in the SOURCE directory, the links in the container files break. That's logical since the links in the container files can't find the source files. Move the SOURCE directory *by itself* to some new location and again, the links are bust.

Ah, but move the MOTHRA directory and its subdirectories to a new location and the links are okay. For example, drag MOTHRA over and drop it on GODZILLA and everything is peachy (see Figure 4.9). Move MOTHRA to another drive altogether and still the links survive. This feature is what the Madison Avenue suits call "Adaptable Links." To us it's a big step in the right direction and Big BillG should buy the Redmond Ranger responsible for this a tall cold one. Or a villa in France, or whatever billionaires do to show gratitude (hey, Elvis gave away Cadillacs, didn't he?).

What makes this work is the use of "relative paths" versus "absolute paths." When establishing the links, the stored link uses "relative" information that says something like, "The source is one directory up, go across to the SOURCE directory and grab the source file (..\source\source.doc)."

Figure 4.9 Move Entire
Structure and Links Survive

Burrowing Objects

> Behold! human beings living in an underground den....Like ourselves...
> they see only their own shadows, or the shadows of one another, which
> the fire throws on the opposite wall of the cave.
>
> Plato
> *The Republic*

OLE 2.0 supports nested embedded objects and embedded links. Sure, you're thinking. More vocabulary terms. Well, you're right! A **nested embedded object** is an object inside an object, which is in turn inside the outermost container or compound document. A **nested linked object** is a link to an object that's inside the container instead of outside of it (therefore, the link points to an object with no file name). Reads a bit stiff, eh? Well, the verbiage required to describe these cool features does get a bit convoluted, but the features are worth their weight in gold, so hang tough.

Circles within circles

Objects Can Be Nested

Imagine a scenario where an Excel worksheet serves as the compound document. Inside the sheet is an embedded Word document object. Inside the Word document object is an embedded WordArt object. See Figure 4.10. To set up this scenario, follow these steps.

1. Maximize Excel.

2. Open a new Excel 5 workbook and save it as `OLE2EM1.XLS`.

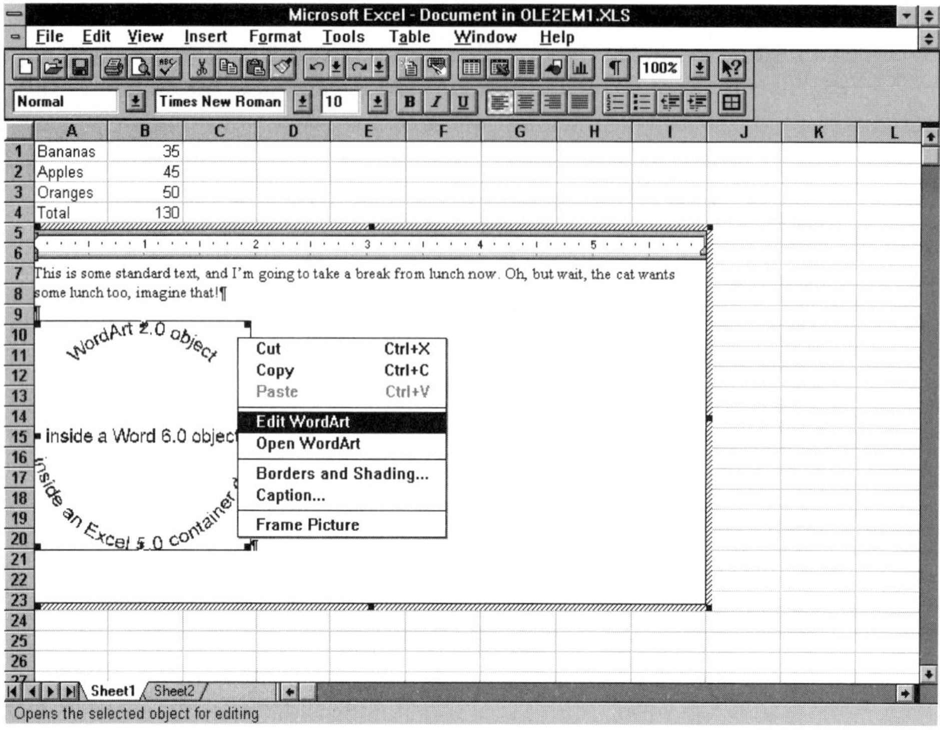

Figure 4.10 A Nested Embed Example

3. Select Insert Object, activate the Create New filecard, then choose Microsoft Word 6.0 Document and click on OK. The Word object is now embedded *and being edited in-place.*

4. Type in "Hello world." and press the Enter key.

5. Select Insert Object (remember, you're working with Word's menu system aggregated with Excel's), activate the Create New filecard, select Insert Object, then choose Microsoft WordArt 2.0, and click on OK.

6. WordArt opens with its default text "Your Text Here," which will do for this little experiment, only let's make it blue for sport. Click on OK. At this point *if* you only see the WordArt object's border but not its true contents, that's because you have Picture Placeholders turned on in Word—*and there's nothing you can do about it right now!* Lord knows, we tried. Pulled every rabbit out of every hat in our corporate HQ. The rule is: if the last time Windows "saw" Word and Word's Tools Options View Picture Placeholders check box was selected, meaning "show picture object borders but not the pictures themselves," you're not gonna see the WordArt object. *And you can't access Word's Tools Options menu when it's aggregated.* Catch-22.

7. The WordArt object is now embedded in another embedded object. This is called a nested embed. (BTW, if you're feeling dizzy and want to pinch yourself to prove that you're looking at a Word-aggregated-with-Excel menu system, select Help and notice that the About drop-down command reads "About Microsoft Word...")

8. Click anywhere outside the Word object and you're back into the standard Excel display space. *Thank goodness.*

9. Save `OLE2EM1.XLS` (or discard it, at your discretion).

OLE 1.0 had no equivalent of in-place editing. Under OLE 1.0 you could access the WordArt object once you had opened the Word server application, *but Word then took the screen over from Excel.* At that point you could open the WordArt server application and it would "float" above the Word screen. *You could no longer "see" the true container application (Excel).* OLE 2.0 to the rescue.

OLE 2.0 has in-place editing and it's a very, very, extraordinarily good thing. So you can now access the WordArt object *while the container application's screen persists.* Try this.

Assuming you're exactly where we left you in the last step,

1. Right-click inside the Word object, select Document Object, and then choose Edit. You're back into in-place edit mode.

2. Right-click inside the WordArt object and choose Edit WordArt.

> **Keep your helmet lamp handy.**

With your very own eyes you can see that the server application (WordArt) is running inside the first embedded object's server's menu system (that's Word). Now pay attention, pilgrim, because this is a bit labyrinthine. Notice that the WordArt server is not full-screen, rather it's floating in what WindowsSpeak calls "windowed" or "restored" mode. *Hey, wait a minute!* Edit is supposed to aggregate the server's menus into the container's menus, right? So why is WordArt running windowed? Presumably because aggregation ends after the first embed; that is, for any nested embeds (no matter how deep into the dark cave you go spelunking—more on this later), you don't get the benefits of aggregated menus when you select in-place editing. Click Cancel to dismiss WordArt.

If you're keeping up with our steps on your PC, the Word object is still being edited in-place. Therefore, to return to Excel's standard display space, click anywhere outside the Word object. Now let's see what happens when you Open the Word object and then fiddle with the nested embedded WordArt object.

Take these steps.

1. Right-click on the Word object, select Document Object, and choose Open. Be sure that Tools Options View's filecard check box called Picture Placeholders is *cleared.*

2. Right-click on the WordArt object, and choose Edit WordArt. Take note, pilgrim—*WordArt's menus aggregate with Word's menus.*

3. Select File from the primary menu bar, and choose Close and Return to `OLE2EM1.XLS` to dismiss WordArt and Word.

4. Right-click on the Word object, select Document Object, and choose Open.

5. Right-click on the WordArt object, and choose Open WordArt. WordArt appears windowed and its own menus are not aggregated with Word's, as you'd expect.

6. Click Cancel to dismiss WordArt.

7. From within Word, select File Close, and Return to `OLE2EM1.XLS`.

The moral of the story is…well, the story's not over. We want to take you on a journey deep into the caverns of OLE 2.0 nested embedding. (After all, this is the *Underground Guide*, eh?) When we emerge back at the cavern entrance, all smiling triumphantly, we'll divulge the moral.

How Low Can You Go?

> A man of genius makes no mistakes. His errors are volitional and are the portals of discovery.
>
> James Joyce
> *Ulysses*, 1922

We're really not crazy. Really. We're just very curious and very exacting. So, before you delve into this section, scratching your head mightily as to why we might even conceive of such an experiment, we'll tell you!

Playing chicken on the OLE highway

The point of the experiment lies in the discovery of how OLE 2.0 responds to stressful situations. Does it behave gracefully? Or leave your PC locked up in some brake-squealing, stomach-churning, torso-wrenching fishtail like a souped-up Chevy playing chicken with a timber-loaded 18-wheeler on some rain-slicked back-country road with no hospital within several hundred miles of your present location? Yeah, that's a feeling you'd better learn to live with if you decide to step so much as one angstrom beyond the boundary of what Microsoft considers "typical business application usage." Now about those usability lab rats and their due diligence…Oh, to hell with them. Remember, they may be calling it "OLE 2.0" (emphasis on the "2.0" part), but in-place editing and everything that goes with it is really a first-time-out-the-door feature. A commendable feature, yes indeedy. But we don't subscribe to the "three is six" school of thought, so how about "OLE 2.0 InPlace 1.0?" Read on.

It is not all that unreasonable to ask to exit an application, is it? *Well, in the course of testing this phenomenon, we saw Windows do stuff we had never ever seen before.* And we live for these kinds of out-of-bounds conditions.

First, we started a completely new session of Windows to guarantee a clean environment. Then we created a PowerPoint slide that had embedded within it an Excel object and a WordArt object. The slide was then embedded in a Word document that was in turn embedded in an Excel workbook. Are we gluttons for punishment or what? See Figure 4.11.

And we thought Tinkers to Evers to Chance was complicated....

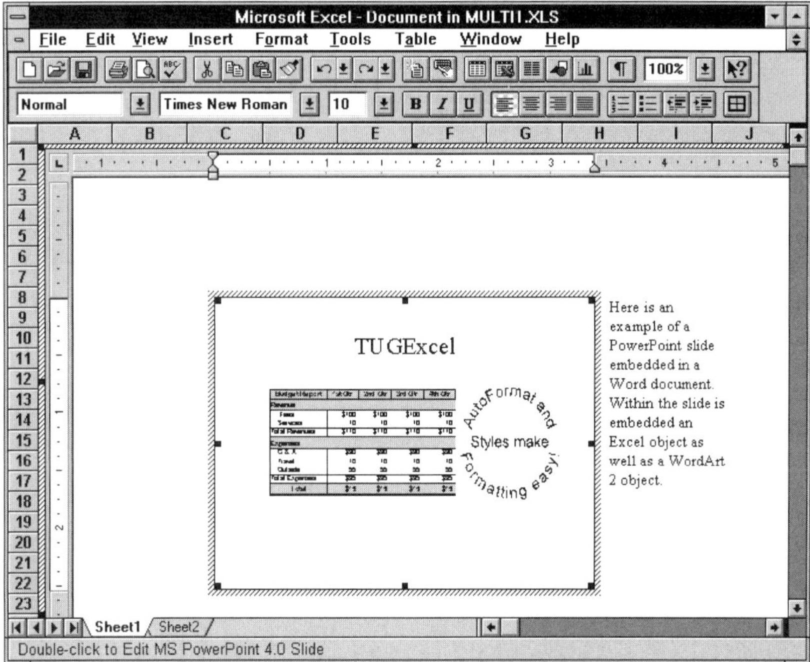

Figure 4.11 An Embedded Nightmare

Here you see the Word object activated within Excel (the container application). A quick right-click / Edit and PowerPoint is activated (in open mode). Another double-click and Excel is activated, in-place, in PowerPoint, in Word, in Excel. Oy! Talk about having your head pushed through a bucket of mush. As you can see, if you do much of this nested embedded object shtick, you had best have enough memory and resources to run several applications simultaneously.

At this point everything will probably work fine as you update objects *as long as you back out in the proper innermost-to-outermost object order*. If, however, you are editing the Excel object embedded in the PowerPoint slide and you switch to Excel (the outside container application) and Exit Excel (accidentally or masochistically), *oh,*

Always exit innie to outie.

brother. Sometimes everything shuts down in order, but in several of our tests, after about thirty seconds of hard disk activity, `EXCEL.EXE` GPFs. Once we dismiss that uplifting message box, `WINWORD.EXE` GPFs. Gaak. *Two GPFs for the price of one!* Not really that funny, is it? One test PC produces GPFs 100% of the time during this experiment, the other less than 25% of the time. Go figure. *But when we update and close each object in the proper innermost-to-outermost order, we never experience any problems!*

The steps to reproduce this nightmare are as follows. Let's make the Excel container document's name `NITEMARE.XLS`.

1. Start this little experiment from the point where Excel is activated in-place, in PowerPoint, in Word, in Excel. Also assume that you made an easy-to-notice change to the PowerPoint slide upstream in this session.

2. Switch to Excel (the outside container application) using either Task Manager or `ALT + TAB`.

3. Select File / Exit.

4. When Excel prompts to save changes, you'll be OK if you answer No. However, let's answer Yes.

5. Excel ruminates and churns momentarily then GPFs (`EXCEL.EXE` at 0014:2D15). Click the Close button.

6. Bam, faster than a breached warp core, Word immediately GPFs (`WINWORD.EXE` at 00DE:4137). Click the Close button.

7. After an interminable period of hard-disk thrashing, you're left in a whacked-out PowerPoint. Even though Help About points to Excel, System Info reports `POWERPNT.DLL` is running but not even a cloaked `EXCEL.EXE` is on the desktop.

8. Select File / Exit & Return to NITEMARE.XLS.

9. PowerPoint prompts you "Update Presentation in NITEMARE.XLS?" If you click Yes, although the application vanishes from your desktop almost immediately, the upstream change made to the PowerPoint slide survives (prove this by reopening the compound document and editing down deep enough to see the change). GPFs notwithstanding, *at least the change to the PowerPoint slide object was written to disk.*

Put your sadist's hat on once more and make a change in the embedded Excel object. Run through the experiment again. Even though the GPFs ensue, the change to the Excel object does get written to disk. Whew.

So what's the reason? Ah, the problem is your video drivers. No really, it *is* related to your video driver. If you're running the standard Windows SVGA driver, you probably won't experience the GPFs. Probably. We figure it's a timing problem in the shut-down and clean-up routines buried deep in an OLE 2.0 DLL. Regardless, watch for it. *The moral of the story is...*

- Empirically find the embedding level where you begin to experience resource-constraint problems, make note of that level, and from then on *stay above that threshold*.

- Never quit an application that's behaving as an active server until all nested embeds have been individually updated.

- Always perform these updates in the proper order—that is, update from the innermost object back out to the outermost container.

This is important, so we'll repeat it. *Always update embedded objects from the innermost object back out to the outermost container*. To do otherwise is to tempt system suicide.

Exploring the Embedded Link

Question—can you embed links? Answer—yes, but you'd best be prepared to treat them all as manual links because even if they're Automatic, they ain't. Sorry about that, but it's the unadulterated truth. **Sometimes even Automatic links aren't.**

We conducted a simple experiment. We started with a traditional Excel container worksheet. We embedded a Word 6.0 Document object. In this document we entered a lead-in paragraph, created a small table of sales data, and then in the Word object we embedded an Excel 5.0 Chart object, selected the Chart object's Sheet1, and replaced the default data with data as paste linked text. Next we closed the Chart object, closed the Word object, and stood back to admire our work. See Figure 4.12. At this point we had an Excel container with an embedded Word document that in turn had embedded in it an Excel chart linked to the text in the Word document. Whew, this is a lot like trying to discuss time travel, isn't it?

We tightened up our hiking boots, climbed back down into the cavern, and discovered that when we changed the data in the Word object's table, *the Chart object did not update*. (Remember, *this is an automatic link*.) We had to physically open the Chart object, select the sheet containing the link, run the Links dialog, and press the Update Now button. Then the chart changed to reflect the new data. This is "making it easier"? *Oh, brother*. Remember, if the link that points to Word is inside a traditional Excel worksheet with no embedding (a straight link), changes in Word's source data immediately cause the Excel-dependent chart to change. So we know the linking technology works in that respect. Introduce just one level of nesting, and you have to grab the link by the throat and throttle it to get it to respond. Go figure. **Nested links aren't automatic.**

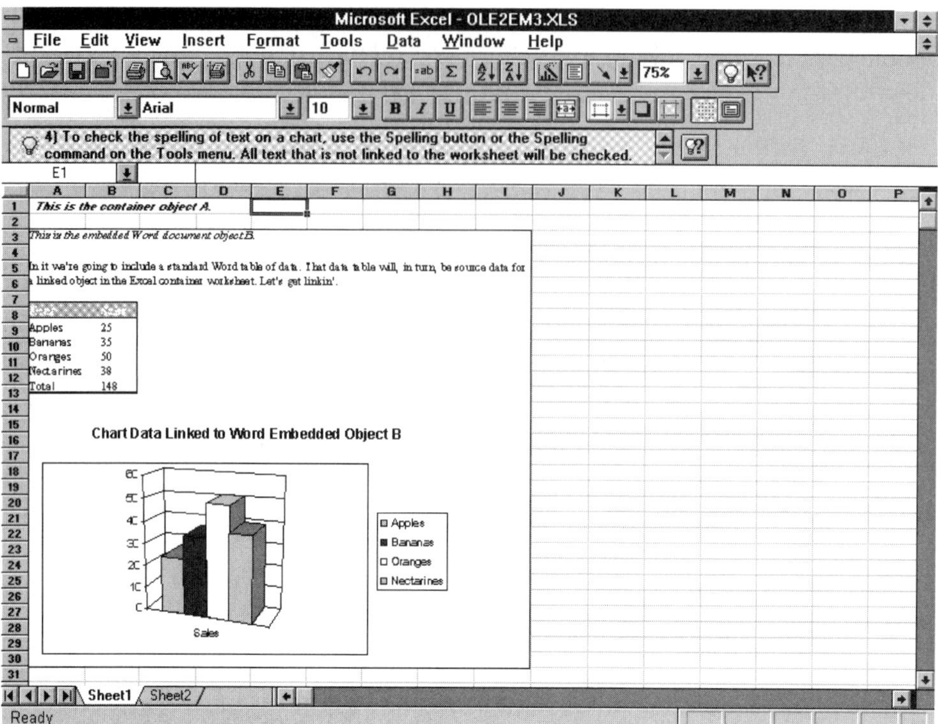

Figure 4.12 A Nested Link Scenario

CONTAINER AS KING

> Home is where the computer is.
>
> Poindexter
> *The Adventures of Felix the Cat*, 1960s

As you have seen, the container holds the objects, be they links to external data or the actual data itself embedded within the container file. The container controls updates to the linked data and you access editor applications from the container application.

Whew! The container does yeoman's duty in controlling all this inter-application communication. In this section we'll further explore containers and an OLE server/editor application that has not been seen as yet and look at some more examples of embedded and linked objects.

Hello Central? Link Update Calling...

> Roar, Boys, Roar
> It tastes like more
> What a flavor
> Zippity-zow – it's grand – and HOW.
>
> Advertisement for Grape-Nuts Flakes

One of the benefits of linking information from where it resides (the source) to where you want the data shown (the container) is that you can link a single source to many containers. This facilitates the sharing of data between container documents and between members of a workgroup where the shared data is stored in a source file in a central location accessible by each member of the group. **The benefits of linking**

Not only can information be updated by activating the editor application, but the server file could be swapped out entirely for a file of the same name containing modified information.

For example, a team leader might copy a source file down from the network server, modify the data therein, and then simply replace the old file with the updated one. Great care would, of course, have to be exercised so that range names or bookmarks that the links referenced in the source file are not damaged when the file is edited. As each container file that is linked to the source file is opened and updated on various network workstations, the source file is also opened on the workstation (in a cloaked application as discussed in Chapter 3) as part of the update process, and the container then presents the updated data. Then, assuming the server is well behaved, the server application and source file are closed automatically and the data is available when the next linked container file is opened.

A Trail of Bread Crumbs ...

If you need some Excel spreadsheet data in multiple reports in Word, links to the rescue. Change the data in Excel and then update the various reports. Very slick. Please do exercise some restraint and think things through before you start linking hither and yond, okay?

- Try to avoid making a single document both a container and a server. This quickly becomes confusing and makes later maintenance and editing difficult. Keeping all documents involved current can also become a problem.

- Keep notes detailing what the links for a given container accomplish. At some point you may forget that a given document contains links.

- Consider using a file naming convention or the Summary Information section for recording information about linked documents.

You might, for example, begin filenames with the letter ell (l) if the file contains links, and the letter ess (s) if the file is a source file. The Comments field in Summary Info might be used to store link data. See Figure 4.13.

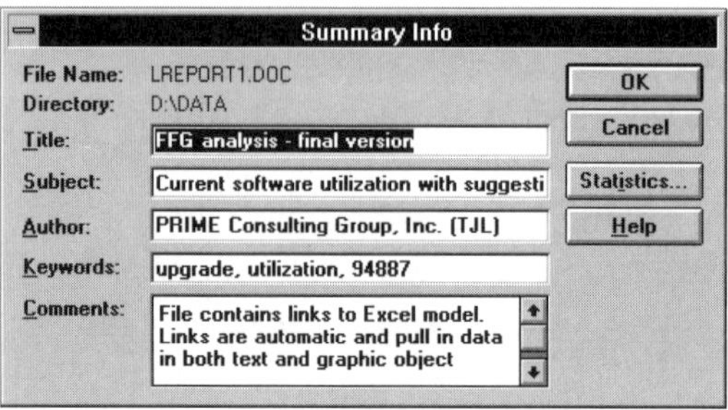

Figure 4.13 Use Summary Info to Record Link Information

A Picture Puzzle

Reducing container file size

Linking also lets you store the source data outside of the container application thereby cutting down on the physical space required for the container file as mentioned waaaaaay back in Chapter 1. For example, this book was first drafted in Word (amazement!) and every screen shot is a separate `.TIF` file that is linked to the Word container document.

Word makes it simple to insert a link to an external graphic file. A quick Insert / Picture and there you are. See Figure 4.14.

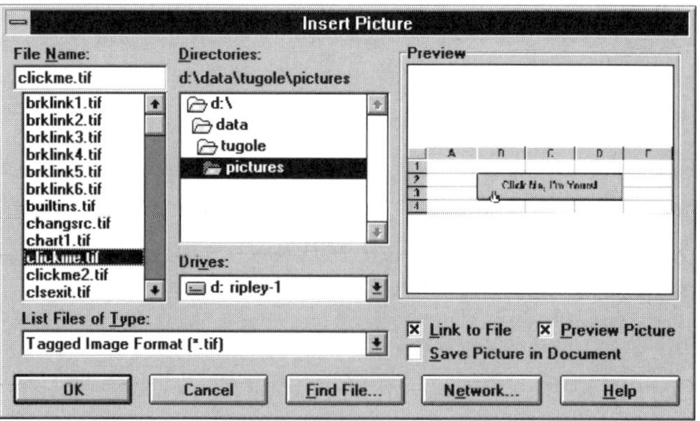

Figure 4.14 Word's Insert Picture Dialog Box

Excel and the linked picture

Note the check boxes in the lower-right corner of the dialog box. Check the Link to File check box and uncheck the Save Picture in Document check box, select a file, click the OK button, and bang you've got an INCLUDEPICTURE field in your Word document linked to an external graphic file. PowerPoint also lets you insert a link to a picture (of course the Link to File checkbox is in the lower-left corner.) But try to get a picture linked into Excel. Hang on to your hat. First the good news. Excel also has an Insert / Picture dialog box. See Figure 4.15.

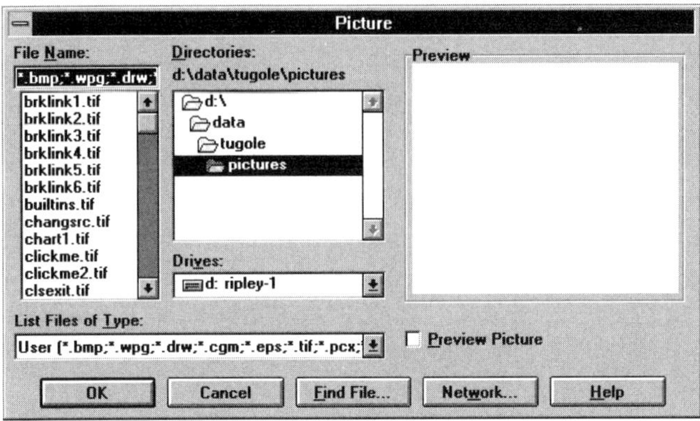

Figure 4.15 Excel's Insert Picture Dialog Box

Notice anything missing from the lower-right corner of the dialog box? Bingo, no Link to Picture check box. Why, you ask? Good question.

The answer is that while linking pictures in Word or PowerPoint looks like OLE linking, the links show up in the Edit / Links dialog box like OLE links, and generally the links act like OLE links. *It apparently has nothing to do with OLE objects at all!* Nada, zip, no relation. Looks like applications that allow you to link to picture files (Word, Visio, PowerPoint) do so because their programmers built the feature into those applications. If you link a Word document to a picture file and then turn loose some of the analysis tools we talk about shortly, the result is "OLE's not home, man."

Ahhhh, you say. *That's* why Insert / Picture is a separate menu item as opposed to going to Insert / Object to link to the picture file. The picture is *not* an OLE object. It looks like Excel's development team did not add the ability to link to pictures.

Of course, all this flies in the face of the Word *User's Guide* which says, "By default, when you create a link to another file, Word stores in the Word document a "picture," or complete representation, of the *linked object*" [emphasis ours]. Looks like someone in Redmond is playing fast and loose with the terminology.

Okay, so you scratch your chin and with a gleam in your eye you decide to link the picture to a Word document, and then link the Word document into Excel. That's logical thinking, and the only problem is it won't work. The data can be linked from Word but the picture won't display in the worksheet's graphic layer through the link. You wind up with an empty white space where the picture should be. Bummer.

Let's regroup and try again. How about inserting a Word object in Excel and then inserting a *linked* picture in the Word object in the Excel container. Resize the Word object in Excel to the exact size of the picture. A mite convoluted, true—but does it work? Nope, everything's peachy until you deactivate the Word object, and then it's oops—no picture city again. Excel just can't deal with the presentation of a Word INCLUDEPICTURE field.

Don't know about you, but we're running out of ideas. And it's not for lack of trying either. We even tried opening a .BMP file in Paintbrush, copying it to the clipboard, and paste-linking it into Excel. The first problem with this method is Paintbrush, while supporting OLE, doesn't support many graphic formats. Second, when you open the Excel container file and have the links updated, Paintbrush winds up running on the desktop. Not as a cloaked application mind you, but as an accessible application. But on our lab machines the contents of Paintbrush were cloaked. That's right, Paintbrush was there but if you opened it up nothing was visible below the menu bar. A bit odd, eh?

Anyway, we did the only thing a smart cookie can do in a situation like this. We gave up. Can't link pictures into an Excel container document. Oy!

Org! A Different Kind of Chart

> Bureaucracy is nothing more than a hardening of an organization's arteries.
>
> William P. Anthony
> *Managing Incompetence,* 1981

To link or embed—that's a question?

To link or to embed, that is the question. Okay, so it's a question that the melancholy Dane never had to wrestle with, but it's one that confronts every modern desktop warrior.

You've already seen a couple of OLE 2.0 server-only applications in action—notably Graph and WordArt. These are "server-only" in that they cannot be used to create standalone data files, but rather, can only create embedded objects within container files. Other OLE 2.0 applications can be used to create embedded objects *or* standalone files. An embedded object stores the data in the container application, and a link connects the container to the data which is stored in a source file *external* to the container. Okay, we're stating the obvious but bear with us.

The method you should use, embed or link, to show data in the container is determined by where the data is to be stored. In the case where several users are going to connect to a given piece of data, linking is the way to go. This is how we'll do this next example where you want to include the Sales Department organizational chart in an Excel container document. To create the org chart, you'll use the nifty new Microsoft Organizational Chart 1.0 program included in the Office suite.

Org Chart can be fired up from the Insert / Object dialog box, but it also can run standalone. To create an icon for Org Chart in Program Manager, tile Program Manager and File Manager and drag the `ORGCHART.EXE` executable file from the `C:\WINDOWS\MSAPPS\ORGCHART\` directory over to the Program Group of your choice. Great, here you go.

1. Start the Microsoft Organizational Chart 1.0 program (see Figure 4.16). If this is the first time you've ever run the application, first you'll see the Open Chart dialog. Click the New button and what you see next will match Figure 4.16.

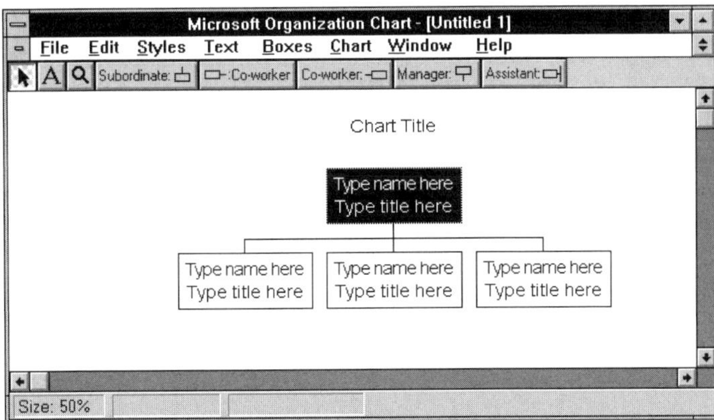

Figure 4.16 The Microsoft Organizational Chart 1.0 Program

2. Modify the default chart to match the sales organization of the Northwind Traders company (a V P Sales, Sales Manager, Inside Sales Coordinator, and five Sales Reps).

   If you have never used the Org Chart application you can use the default chart shown in Figure 4.16.

3. From the File menu in Org Chart, choose the Save option to save the chart as a separate source data file. Name it, oh, how about `ORGCHT1.OPX` for originality?

4. Exit the Org Chart program.

   So far so good. Next up is to create a container document in Excel and link in the organizational chart you just created. You'll link to the org chart because in our mythical scenario the chart is maintained by the personnel department and might be used in other container documents. Fire up Excel, that mighty king of spreadsheets, and create a new workbook. **Linking to a central file**

5. In Sheet1 of a new workbook, select cell A1.

6. Save the workbook as `CONTAIN1.XLS`.

7. Insert / Object / Create from File, and select the `ORGCHT1.OPX` you created.

8. Make sure you check the Link to File check box in the lower-right corner, and click on the OK button. See Figure 4.17.

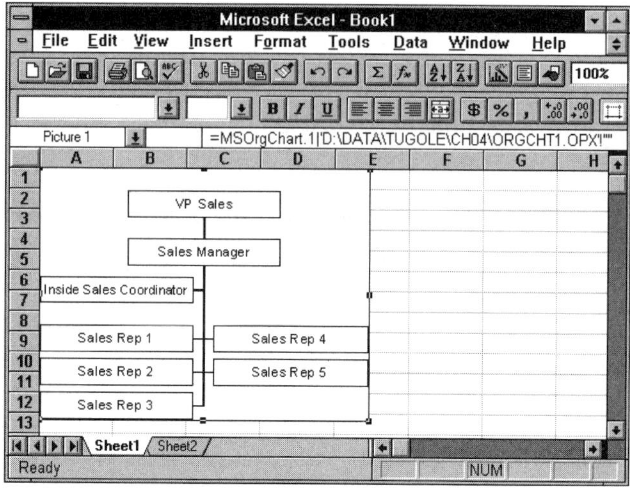

Figure 4.17 Excel Container Linked to Org Chart

Figure 4.17 shows how your container document in Excel will look. Well, more or less, depending on how you designed and formatted your org chart. If the Personnel Department updates the Sales Organizational Chart, `CONTAIN1.XLS` gets the latest data when the link updates as would any other container document linked to the Org Chart.

Get Some Data from the Outermost Reaches

> He, to get the cold side outside,
> Put the warm side fur side inside.
> That's why he put the fur side inside,
> Why he put the skin side outside,
> Why he turned them inside outside.
>
> Anonymous
> *The Modern Hiawatha*

A database is like a living breathing thing. It grows, it shrinks, *it changes*. It's dynamic. In this section you'll learn how to grab some data from an external data source (somewhere outside Excel itself), present it in a simple yet powerful way inside an Excel pivot table, refresh the pivot table at will, and link a graphic display of the pivot table to reflect changes there as well. We'll be using ODBC (which stands for Open Database Connectivity) in this example. When Excel launches Query to initially get data outside Excel, it uses DDE commands to get Query to jump through the required hoops. Once the pivot table is established, any data updating is done using low-level calls to ODBC, in such a way that avoids launching Query or any other application; rather, ODBC takes care of opening the table and refreshing the transaction without any user or other intervention.

Pivot Table Basics

The question that you ask yourself month in and month out ad nauseum, in exactly the same way each month, is this, "What are the life-to-date order amounts by employee?" *It's integration time!* The simplest and most expedient way to integrate this query process into a compound document is with an Excel feature called the pivot table.

It's integration time!

According to Excel's help file, "A pivot table is an interactive worksheet table you use to summarize and analyze data from an existing list or table. You can update a pivot table whenever changes occur in the original source data. The original data remains intact, and the pivot table stays on the worksheet you created it on." All these aspects of a pivot table will prove to be extraordinarily useful to you as the author of this model compound document. The following steps show you exactly how to perform this query on an external data source. We'll be using the Orders sample dBase-format database that ships with Query (which in turn ships with Excel and/or Office) as the external data source.

First you'll create a pivot table on a new, empty worksheet. Then in the next section you'll perform the query again, this time setting the pivot table up in the compound document.

1. Create a new workbook, and select cell A1 in Sheet1.

2. Select Tools / Add-Ins. If MS Query Add-In is listed and checked in the Add-Ins Available list box, click Cancel and proceed to step 3. If MS Query is listed but not checked, select the check box, and click on the OK button. If it does not appear in the list at all, refer to the *User's Guide* for installation instructions.

3. Select Data / PivotTable. This produces the Step 1 of 4 panel of Excel's PivotTable Wizard as shown in Figure 4.18.

4. Select the External Data Source radio button, and click Next. This produces the Step 2 of 4 panel as shown in Figure 4.19.

5. Click the Get Data button. This starts Microsoft Query and the Select Data Source dialog box appears.

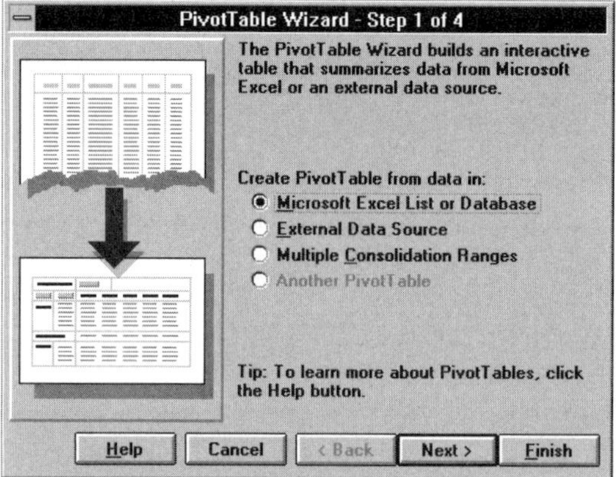

Figure 4.18 PivotTable Wizard to the Rescue

Figure 4.19 Me User, You PivotTable,
Get Data

6. If "dBase Files" appears in the list, select it, then press the Use button. See
   Figure 4.20. If it's not in the list, try clicking on the Other button, then select
   "dBase Files," click on OK, then select it and press the Use button. If "dBase
   Files" does not appear in the Others list, the dBase driver is not installed and
   you should refer to the *User's Guide* for installation instructions.

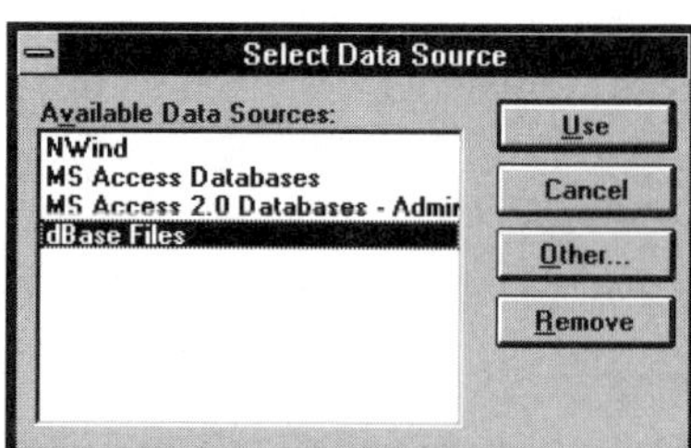

Figure 4.20 A dBase Format
Ombudsman

7. Scroll to locate the ORDERS.DBF file. Once this file is selected, click on Add.
   (The file's default location is C:\WINDOWS\MSAPPS\MSQUERY.)

8. Close the Add Tables dialog by clicking on the Close button.

9. Double-click the asterisk at the top of the Orders table frame (immediately above the CUSTMR_ID field name). This selects all fields and all records and places them in the data pane as shown in Figure 4.21.

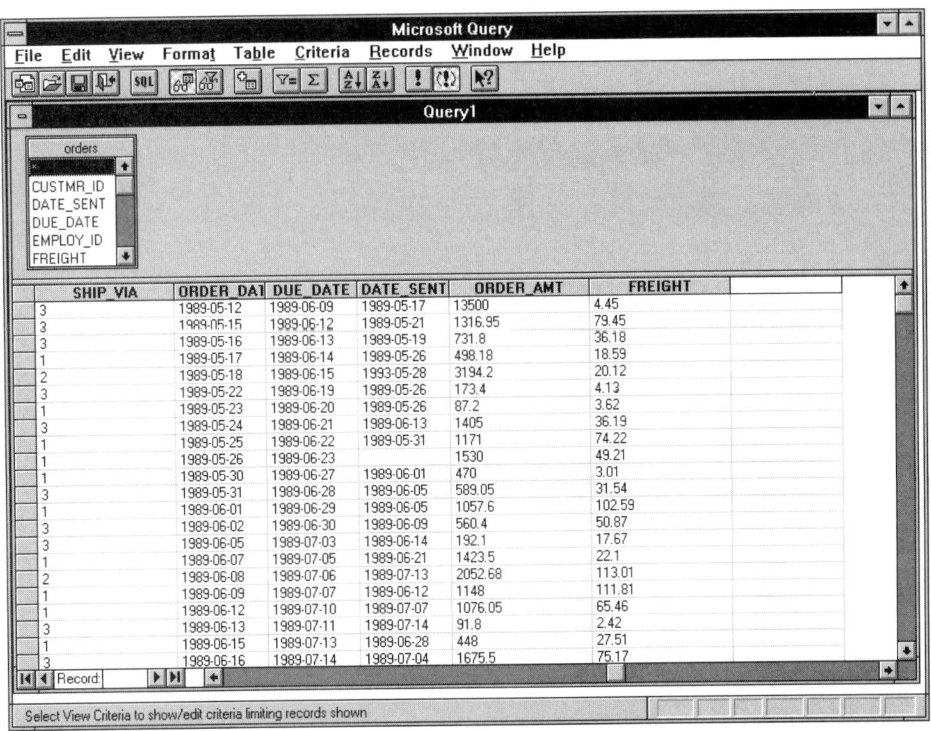

Figure 4.21 A Table of Fields

10. Select File / Return Data to Microsoft Excel. Query automatically returns focus to Excel. You should see the PivotTable Wizard's Step 2 of 4 panel again, which now displays "Data Retrieved" immediately to the right of the Get Data button. Click the Next button. It takes a second or two for Excel to retrieve all thirty-nine records from the table.

11. Drag the EMPLOY_ID field button, and drop it in the Row Area.

12. Drag the ORDER_AMT field button, and drop it in the Data area. Excel defaults to a Sum function. See Figure 4.22.

13. Click the Next button.

14. In the Step 4 of 4 panel, clear the Save Data With Table Layout check box; this prevents Excel from maintaining a hidden copy of the data along with the

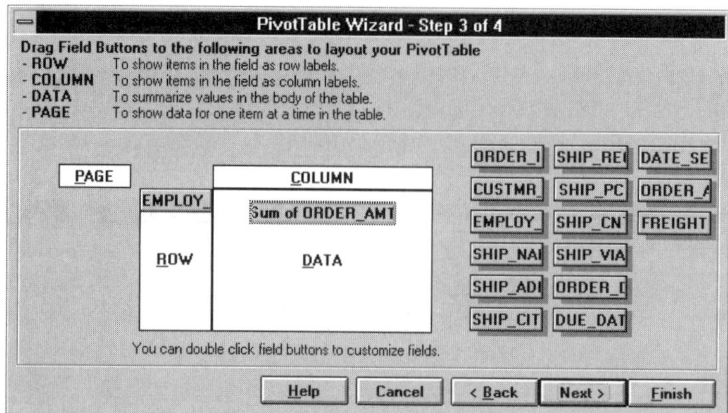

Figure 4.22 Drag-and-Drop, It's So Fine

pivot table layout. Excel creates the pivot table on the current sheet. Click the Finish button.

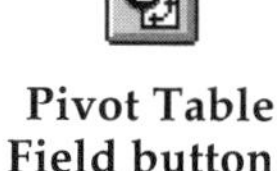

Pivot Table Field button

15. For cosmetic reasons, let's format the Total column data as currency. Select the first detail cell in the Total column (it should be cell B3, and B3 should contain the value 5271.7 representing employee 111's total order dollars). Click the Pivot Table Field button on the Query and Pivot toolbar. Click the Number button. Select the format code #,##0.00 and click OK. Click OK to clear the PivotTable Field dialog. See Figure 4.23.

	A	B	C
1	Sum of ORDER_AMT		
2	EMPLOY_ID	Total	
3	111	5,271.70	
4	222	1,991.43	
5	333	9,028.88	
6	444	6,977.45	
7	555	1,614.30	
8	666	1,646.65	
9	777	3,437.70	
10	888	5,672.71	
11	999	351.00	
12	Grand Total	35,991.82	
13			

Figure 4.23 A Pivot Table Is Born

16. Finally, save and close the current workbook as CONTAIN2.XLS.

Refreshing a Pivot Table

Let's see what happens when information in the database behind the pivot table changes.

1. If CONTAIN2.XLS is still open, save and close it.

2. Make backup copies of ORDERS.DBF and ORDERS.MDX. This way, when this exercise is over, you can easily return to the database's original state.

3. Use Excel (or Access if you prefer) to open ORDERS.DBF.

4. Change the value in order number 10000's ORDER_AMT field from 135.00 to 13500.00.

5. Save and close ORDERS.DBF, *making sure not to convert it from its native dBase format.* For example, in Excel select File / Close. When Excel prompts you "Save changes in 'ORDERS.DBF'? Note: the current file format is not Microsoft Excel Workbook", click Yes. The Save As dialog box appears with a File Name of ORDERS.DBF and a Save File As Type of DBF 4 (dBASE IV). Click OK to accept these defaults. When Excel prompts you "Replace existing 'ORDERS.DBF'?", click Yes.

6. Open the workbook CONTAIN2.XLS.

7. Note that employee 222's total order dollars stands at 1991.43. Uh oh. That's what it was before, but we just finished upping employee 222's ante by a significant amount.

   Guess what? Using the user interface side of Excel's pivot table feature set, there's no way to have a pivot table automatically refresh itself. (Don't despair, we'll show you how with a simple VBA macro in a moment.) This is a case where we all might scratch our heads and mull "is this a bug or a feature?" Well, keep in mind that the mechanism behind refreshing the pivot table based on ORDERS.DBF is ODBC, not OLE. We repeat, *this exercise is not an OLE link.* It is a stored query being handled by some middlemen ODBC drivers, and the assumption by the designers of the pivot table technology was that when you want to refresh the data, you'll click the Refresh Data button. Hey, no problem, since you can write a short macro to automatically refresh the data every time the workbook is opened. But before we put on our VBA hats, let's click that Refresh Data button to make sure the user interface stuff works as advertised.

   > Where there's an *Underground Guide*, there's a way.

8. Click the Refresh Data button on the Query and Pivot toolbar. If the button refuses to be clicked (you'll hear a beep and the button won't "depress"), make sure the active cell is inside the pivot table range (select any cell within the range A1:B12). The value updates to 15356.43. This value is 13365 greater than before based on the change you made to ORDERS.DBF (revised orders of 13500 minus original orders of 135 represents a net increase of 13365).

Refresh Data button

9. Save and close CONTAIN2.XLS.

Some Refreshing Automation

Abracadabra
Auto_Open

Here's that simple macro we promised you. The macro runs every time the CONTAIN2.XLS workbook opens. In VBA parlance, discussed in more detail in Chapters 5 and 6, this is an Auto_Open macro, a cool feature of VBA whereby a specific macro runs, well, whenever the workbook opens. Just what we need to solve our Refresh Data dilemma!

As you study this three-liner you'll get a feel for how readable VBA is. The first statement guarantees that Sheet1 is activated when the workbook is opened. The second statement ensures that the active cell is within the pivot table by selecting the A1 cell. The third refreshes the table (RefreshTable) called PivotTable1 (PivotTables("PivotTable1")) located in the sheet called Sheet1 (Sheets("Sheet1")). Don't be concerned about the syntax and order of the expressions in this code. That comes later in Chapters 5 and 6. Trust us. After all, we're your Underground guides!

```
Sub Auto_Open()
    Sheets("Sheet1").Activate
    Range("A1").Select
    Sheets("Sheet1").PivotTables("PivotTable1").RefreshTable
End Sub
```

Follow these steps to set up this macro in your CONTAIN2.XLS workbook.

1. Open CONTAIN2.XLS if it isn't already open.

2. Select Insert / Macro / Module. This creates a VBA module named Module1.

3. Type in the Auto_Open macro code exactly as shown at the beginning of this section.

4. Save and close CONTAIN2.XLS.

5. To test the new Auto_Open macro, change order 10000's order amount to 135 from 13500, then save and close ORDERS.DBF as before.

6. Open CONTAIN2.XLS. You'll see the refreshed data based on the behind-the-scenes operation of the Auto_Open macro.

7. Save and close CONTAIN2.XLS.

And a Picture Is Wowie-Pow-Zowie

To set up a graph that updates in unison with the pivot table, follow these steps.

1. Open CONTAIN2.XLS.

2. In Sheet1 select the entire pivot table except for the Grand Total cells. (The range you should select is A1:B11.)

3. Select Insert / Chart / On This Sheet.

4. Drag the drawing pointer to create the boundary of the chart.

5. Click Next in the Step 1 of 5 panel.

6. Select the 3-D Column format, then click Next in the Step 2 panel.

7. Click Next in the Step 3 panel (this accepts the default format number 4).

8. Click Next in the Step 4 panel (this accepts the defaults).

9. To suppress a legend, when you get to Step 5 of 5's panel, select the Add a Legend? section's No radio button, then click Finish. See Figure 4.24.

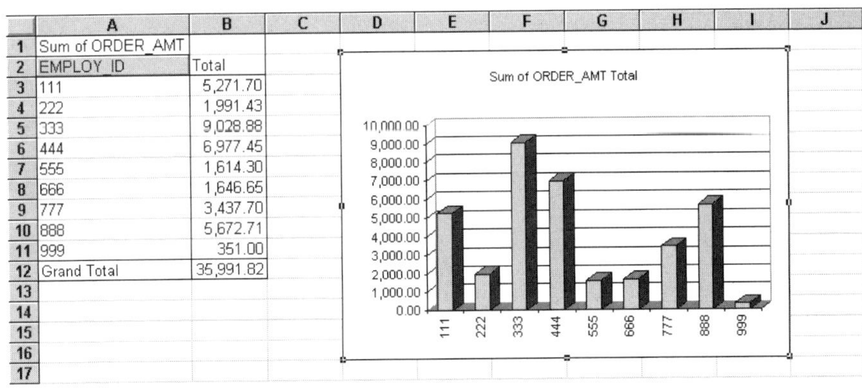

Figure 4.24 Pivot Table and a Side-kick Chart to Boot

10. Save `CONTAIN2.XLS`.

If you want to see how the chart reacts to a manual Refresh Data request, follow these steps.

1. With `CONTAIN2.XLS` still open, use Excel (or Access if you prefer) to change good ol' order 10000's order amount to 13500 from 135, then save and close `ORDERS.DBF` as before.

2. Select `CONTAIN2.XLS`'s Sheet1, make sure that the active cell is within the pivot table range, click the Refresh Data button, and the chart updates before your very eyes. Righteous, friend.

Now You Can Hear What You See

> Why, sometimes I've believed as many as six impossible things before breakfast.
>
> Lewis Carroll
> *Alice's Adventures in Wonderland*

Curiouser and curiouser...   Documents that read themselves, spreadsheets that can really "talk" numbers, presentations that speak to your audience while you drink a glass of water. Can this be true or have we fallen through the looking glass?

It's true, you betcha. Sound (or should we say "multimedia" and burn another industry buzzword?) is the hot thing these days, along with video and animation. Ever think you'd have to become the next Tim Burton in order to use your word processor? It's "lights, camera, action" now that you can link and/or embed sound and video objects in your compound documents.

What? Speak Up!

Sound is nothing really new to the industry. Personal computers have included a 79-cent speaker ever since the original IBM PC. Windows even lets you associate a given sound file (which you'll just have to start calling a "wave file" or people won't think you're hip) with an event like starting or exiting Windows, or getting an error message. Start Control Panel and run the Sound utility to access the Sound dialog box. See Figure 4.25.

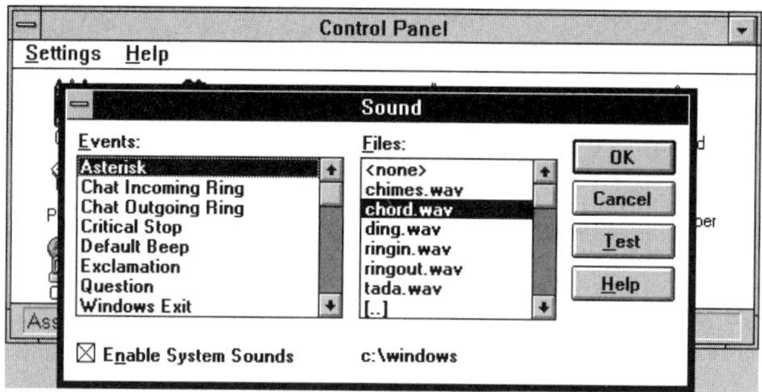

Figure 4.25 Make Windows a Cavalcade of Sounds

That's right, campers, now you too can make your computer go "Ta Daaaa." All you need is `SPEAKER.DRV`, which for some reason does not come with vanilla Windows 3.1, but which you can get from CompuServe or in some Microsoft products like the Windows Printing System. But with the cheapie standard speaker, sound is not very impressive on your average PC.

Ah, but add a hundred bucks worth of sound card, some powered speakers, and you can get some *sound* out of your computer. Oh, most important of all, you need some AC outlets to plug the speakers into. We don't know about you, but our lab draws about as much power as a nuclear sub. It's gotten to the point that every time we have to plug something in we have to unplug something else. Ever happen to you? But we digress.

Before we get into embedding these auditory gems in your documents, you need to know how to create and edit them. We'll assume that you have added a sound card and, if you plan on recording your own dulcet tones, that you have a microphone hooked up to it. The sound board you installed probably came with a bunch of software for doing recording and editing of sound files, but we'll stick to the software provided with Windows and Office.

The first utility to be aware of is the sound recorder SOUNDREC.EXE. You'll most likely find it in your Windows directory and you can use it to record your own wave files and to edit existing files by deleting parts of a file, mixing, or joining files together. See Figure 4.26.

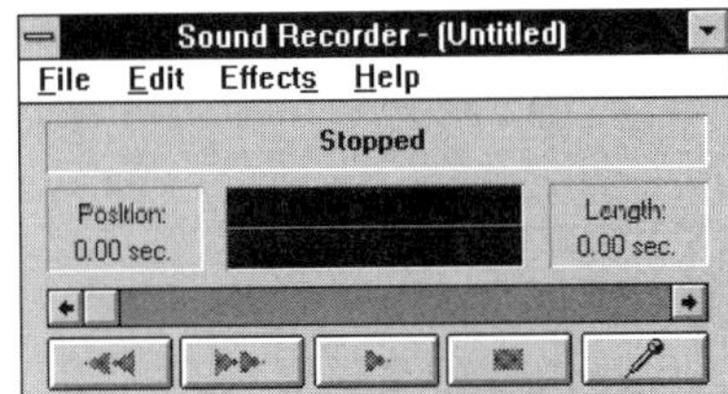

Figure 4.26 Windows Sound Recorder Application

Play it Again, Sam

Once you have created and edited your vocal masterpiece, hmmm, how many "takes" do you think you'll need to record "Lee, take a look at this spreadsheet and tell me what you think?" Be honest. Oh, only one you say. Sure, you say that now, but when you stare at that microphone and realize that the person receiving the file will play it for the entire office if you hiccup or your voice breaks, you'll be amazed how much time you'll spend fussing around with a simple sound byte (pun intended). "Amazed" also describes how you'll feel when you realize how much disk space sound uses up because sound goes through disk space like Grant took Richmond. Add maybe 25K to the size of the container file for that simple one sentence "Lee, take a look..." example.

Anyway, once you've got the wave file, what do you do with it? Embedding it in your container document is a piece of cake. To embed in Word, just drag the .WAV file from File Manager to your Word container document and bang, one embedded object. If you want to embed a .WAV file in most anything else, open the file in Sound Recorder and copy it, then paste the object into your container. Excel is the pits for the drag-and-drop embedding of files because it likes to open the file instead of embedding it. Drag CHIMES.WAV into an empty sheet and Excel opens the wave file. You get what you see in Figure 4.27. PowerPoint just complains in a message box.

Of all the containers in all the world, she has to walk into mine.

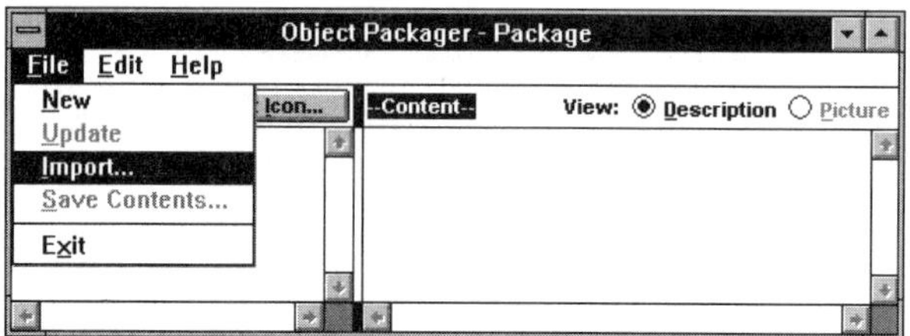

Figure 4.27 Wave Cleverly Disguised as Spreadsheet

You can even get fancy and import the file into Object Packager and change the caption and icon that represents the sound object if you like. See Figure 4.28.

Figure 4.28 Object Packager Application

A linked or embedded wave file appears as a little microphone icon unless you change the icon using Object Packager. Double-click on the object and it plays. If you want to load the sound object into the sound recorder application, you need to edit it instead of playing it. Easiest way to accomplish this is to right-click on the object and choose the Edit option. See Figure 4.29.

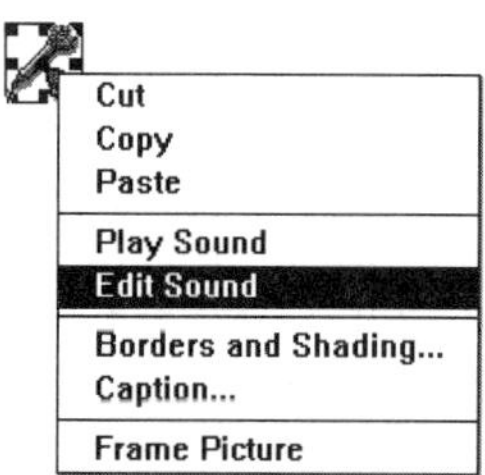

Figure 4.29 Edit or Play
from the Shortcut Menu

Run Silent, Run Deep

When it comes to auditory and visual assaults, we should mention that all this talking-document stuff, while very big on whiz-bang flash and sizzle, may be a bit short on productive substance. It's great for the executive who can't type, but do you really want to bloat your documents with these huge objects and then send them out across the network?

It also assumes that everyone you share your container documents with (you aren't really going to record voice notes to yourself, are you?) has the necessary hardware to hear your recorded wisdom. You are not going to hear Hendrix playing the *Star Spangled Banner* on your PC without some add-on sound hardware.

Media Player

The overhead that sound objects add to your container documents is nothing compared to video. If you have some video clip files laying about, you can run them (sound files too, for that matter) using the Media Player application that ships with Office. Just run `MPLAYER.EXE`. See Figure 4.30.

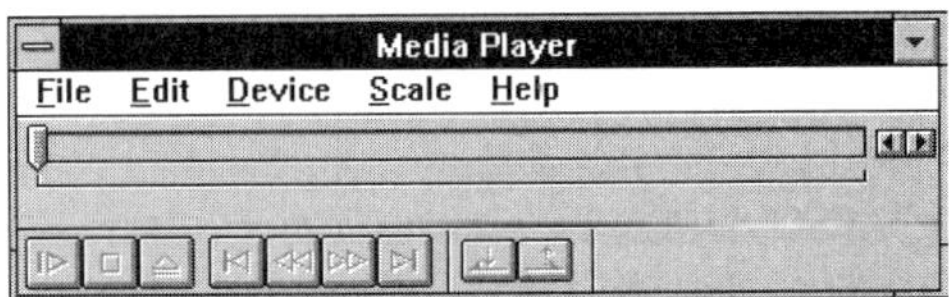

Figure 4.30 The Mighty Morphin' Media Player

Media Player plays things like QuickTime or Video for Windows video files, MIDI audio files, `.WAV` files—pretty much the whole multimedia shtick. You open the file to be embedded in Media Player. If the file is a video clip, you can use the slider to select the frame to use as the icon for the media-clip object. A quick Edit / Copy Object and you can paste the Media Player into your document.

We point out Media Player to you because, like the Matterhorn, it's there. Embedding sound and video makes for great demonstrations, but we are dubious of its practical value in a business environment due to the tremendous overhead added to the container document and the amount of time you can fiddle away playing with the technology.

Because it's there.

If You Really Must Embed Video...

Okay, you've listened to our arguments against it, but you remain unswayed and have just *got* to embed some multimedia stuff in your documents. Anyway, warnings aside, it's actually simple, right? Open the file in Sound Recorder or Object Packager, copy it, and paste it in your container document. The same rules must apply to video, right? Wrong.

You know that you can use Media Player to open a video file, that you can Edit / Copy Object, and paste into your compound document. You might assume that this procedure embeds not only Media Player but the video file as well. No, no, no. Media Player gets embedded but you wind up with a link to the actual video data file. No warning, no "whoa, this is a link, pilgrim," no nothing. You're just supposed to know that the steps that embed a sound bite only link a video file. Be a bit awkward if you give the boss a compound document thinking that video is going along with it and he gets up in front of the annual stockholders meeting and double-clicks on the object only to be told the data can't be found. Oh, you can be sure he'll remember your name from then on.

Okay, okay, is it a bug or a feature? More a limitation of the infrastructure itself, we would say. Consider that copying and pasting moves all the data through the clipboard, which is limited to available memory. Think of the terrible size considerations involved with video. We have a `.AVI` video file showing 37 seconds of the Space Shuttle launch that takes up $5^1/_2$ MB. A rock-climbing video taking a minute and twelve seconds eats up over 10 MB. Is it any wonder that the player gets embedded but the data to be played gets linked?

You can embed the actual video data under certain circumstances. Open it up in Object Packager (if you have enough memory available), copy the object to the clipboard using Edit / Copy Object (and hope you don't exceed the remaining available memory), and paste the whole shebang into your container document. Now that was easy, wasn't it? Save your document and look at it in File Manager. My, how your document has grown.

WORKING OUT THE KINKS

> Oh, the deuce you say.
>
> Buckaroo Banzai
> *Adventures Across the Eighth Dimension*

OfficeLinks is a set of features representing Microsoft's efforts to take the various standalone applications packaged in Office and make them behave as though they were a single integrated application. It's a pretty good idea, too, and those rollicking Redmond Rangers have done a fair job of implementation. As we discussed back in Chapter 1, OfficeLinks roughly encompasses the OLE, DDE, ODBC, and MAPI alphabet soup as well as some cool processes that are part and parcel of the application code for several programs in Office.

Insert Microsoft Excel Worksheet button

For example, on Word's default standard toolbar you'll find the Insert Microsoft Excel Worksheet button. This button works very much like Word's own Insert Table button in that it allows you to specify a table size, in rows and columns, using only your trusty mouse. Only instead of a Word table you get an Excel spreadsheet object sized to the specified number of rows and columns.

Hmmm, that sounds okay; it kind of soups up the Insert / Object / Microsoft Excel 5.0 Worksheet method of embedding an Excel object that you've learned. Ah, but there is a fly in the ointment of some OfficeLinks, and we fondly refer to these special features as OfficeKinks™.

If you have customized your default Excel template by creating your own BOOK.XLT, you'll be sorely disappointed if you expect to embed an Excel object based on your template. When you use Insert / Object or the Insert Worksheet button, your custom BOOK.XLT is ignored and you get an ultra plain-vanilla default Excel workbook embedded in your container. To solve this problem, you would have to create a new book in Excel using the template of your choice and then use the drag-and-drop method discussed in Chapter 3 to embed that book in your container document.

OfficeLinks—Word to PowerPoint

> I never did anything worth doing by accident, nor did any of my inventions come by accident; they came by work.
>
> Attributed to Thomas A. Edison

If you create a lot of presentations using PowerPoint, you'll love this OfficeLink feature. Create an outline in Word. Use all of Word's formidable features to polish each heading level. Click a single button and have the outline automagically turned into a PowerPoint presentation. Have we got your attention?

In Word, display the Microsoft toolbar, View / Toolbars / check the Microsoft option / click the OK button. On this toolbar you'll find the PresentIt button. This button starts the amazing Word outline to PowerPoint presentation process.

Present It

Before we proceed, however, we need some full disclosure on what you may perceive as smoke and mirrors. What makes this trick work from the Word side is a macro written by some anonymous 'Softie up in Redmond (partly anonymous; for what it's worth, Pete Morcos is listed as the last human being to save changes to PRESENT.DOT). We don't mean to demean the coolness of what Present It does because it's really a neat trick, but it does not involve OLE 2.0. Just hard work and some clever thinking.

You see, PowerPoint can take a file in a format called Rich Text Format, or RTF for short, and turn it into a presentation. And Word just so happens to be able to save a file in RTF format. All that was missing was a way of automating the process of saving the file in Word in the proper format and then firing up PowerPoint and loading the saved file. The PresentIt macro to the answer!

The PresentIt macro resides in a template file called PRESENT.DOT and this template is copied into Word's \STARTUP directory when you install Office. This loads PRESENT.DOT as a **global template** and makes the PresentIt macro available should you click on the Present It button. If you'd like to do this without loading the global template, copy the Present It macro contained therein to your NORMAL.DOT template.

Magic in a macro

The macro's function is really simple. If PowerPoint is installed on the computer, the macro saves the current Word document as a RTF file. Then the macro starts PowerPoint and opens the RTF file. Simple and elegant. Once PowerPoint loads the RTF, a presentation is built from the heading levels in the file. Let's try it.

1. Create a new Word document.

2. Switch to Outline view via View / Outline.

3. Type in a simple presentation using heading levels 1 and 2. See Figure 4.31.

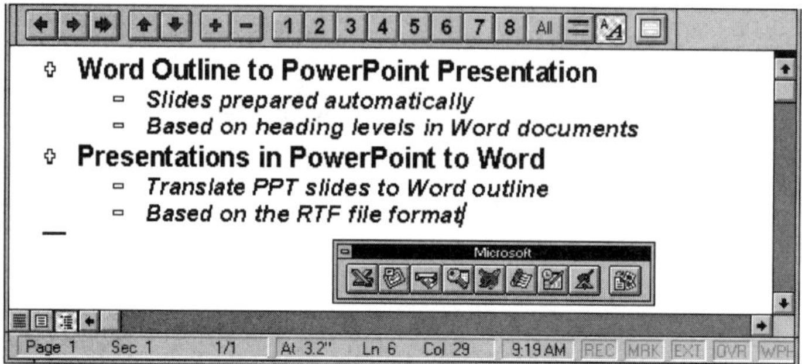

Figure 4.31 A Sample Outline in Word

4. Click on the Present It button on the Microsoft toolbar. See Figure 4.32.

Figure 4.32 PowerPoint Slide Based on Word Outline

Once in PowerPoint, each heading level 1 becomes the title of a new slide and subheadings become bulleted items. This process leaves the focus in PowerPoint where you can modify the presentation that has been built from the Word outline.

This whole process can be reversed in that PowerPoint can save a presentation in RTF format with all the titles and bulleted items as heading levels, start Word, and load the RTF file. PowerPoint provides a button on its standard toolbar called Report It that automates the process. Unlike Word, the procedure in PowerPoint is not stored in a macro (PowerPoint has no macro language at present) and cannot be modified by the user.

Report It button

One thing you need to be aware of before you do much of this back and forth between Word and PowerPoint is how styles are handled when zapped from one application to another. Take a Word document with three headings in it using default formatting like the ones shown in Figure 4.33.

Heading1 – Arial 14, Bold

Heading 2 – Arial 12, Italic

Heading 3 – Times New Roman 12

Figure 4.33 Default Heading Formats in Word

Use the Present It button in Word to automatically create a PowerPoint presentation. Once in PowerPoint use the Report It button to immediately send the presentation back to Word as an outline. The results appear in Figure 4.34.

Heading1 – Times New Roman 15, Centered

- Heading 2 – Times New Roman 11, Bulleted
  - Heading 3 – Times New Roman 9, Bulleted

Figure 4.34 Heading Formats Returned from PowerPoint

Notice the changes to font, point size, alignment, and paragraph spacing. What's going on? Even stranger is that in the PowerPoint presentation the point sizes are 48, 32, and 28 for headings 1, 2, and 3 respectively. Is it a bug? Is it by design? No telling, but whether you're dismayed or pleased by this, it's worth noting.

OfficeKinks™—Excel to Word to PowerPoint

We have met the enemy and he is us.

Pogo (Walt Kelly)
Pogo, ca. 1950

Things get sticky when you try to use Word just *as* Word when it is an embedded object.

Limits when in-place editing

Until Microsoft works out all the kinks with OfficeLinks, there will be problems when you try to use certain features in combination. When an application is running from within another application via in-place editing, there are limitations you have to work around given the context of the situation.

A Problem with In-Place Editing

Say you have an Excel container document, part of which is an embedded Word document. You are so jazzed by the results of using pivot tables in Excel that you decide to do a PowerPoint presentation that you can show to your entire department about the sheer wonderfulness of it all. So you knock out some text using the proper heading level styles. See Figure 4.35.

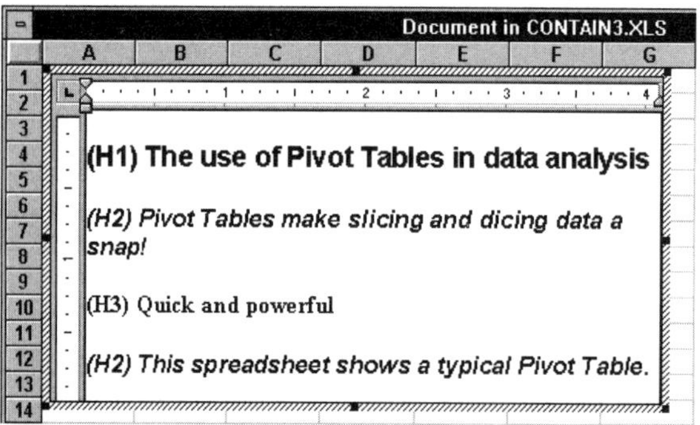

Figure 4.35 Word Document in Excel

Word doesn't support its own Outline view when it's doing in-place editing.

In this example we repositioned the Word document so that the rulers are visible, and typed in the heading levels for each line. So far, so good, but avast! There be rocky shoals ahead! For one thing, Word doesn't support its own Outline view when activated in-place within an Excel container. That's why Figure 4.35 doesn't display the Word document as an outline. Now click on the Present It button. Instead of a nice presentation in PowerPoint, quick as a rat you get an error message. See Figure 4.36.

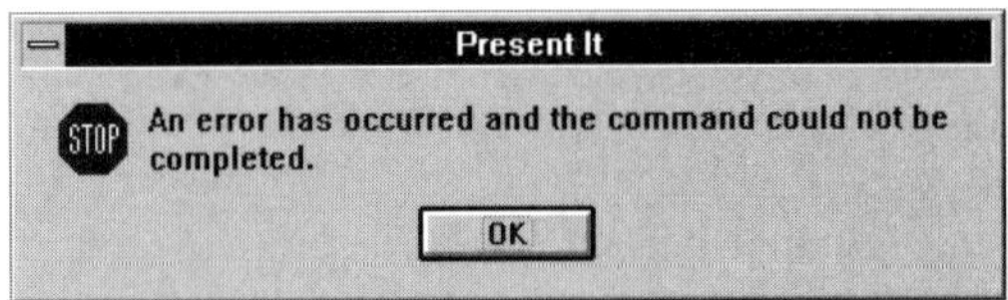

Figure 4.36 The PresentIt Macro Generic
Error Message

This is not the real error message because the PresentIt macro is trapping errors (as it should) and shielding you from cryptic WordBasic error messages.

In-Place Editing Workaround

The workaround to this particular problem is to open Word instead of trying to use in-place editing. This is quick and painless—clear the error message (click on the OK button) and right-click on the embedded Word object. Choose Document Object from the shortcut menu, and click on Open on the flyout menu. With Word running in open mode, you can click the Present It button and there is no problem with automatically creating the presentation.

If you're curious as to why you can't run the PresentIt macro from Word when using in-place editing, read on! First you have to know what is really causing the macro to fail.

Nailing down the problem

1. Fire up Word and unload the `PRESENT.DOT` as a global template via File / Templates / uncheck the `PRESENT.DOT` template / click OK.

2. Open the `PRESENT.DOT` template, click on Tools / Macro / PresentIt / then click on the Edit button.

3. Place the cursor at the beginning of the second line of the macro and type an apostrophe. The line now looks like this.

```
' On Error Goto Trouble
```

   This turns off the macro's internal error checking.

4. Close the macro and save the changes. Enable the global `PRESENT.DOT` template via File / Templates / check the `PRESENT.DOT` template / click OK.

5. Exit Word, and switch to Excel.

6. Activate the Word object in the Excel container by double-clicking on it.

7. Click on the Present It button.

Now we're getting somewhere! A real WordBasic error tells us what failed. See Figure 4.37.

The FileNewDefault command is not available because this document is being edited in another application.

OK   Help

WordBasic Err=509

Figure 4.37 Will the Real Problem Please Stand Up

Huh, what? How can the FileNewDefault command not be available? Ohhhh sure, you're in an Excel container and you can't start spawning new Word documents *from within Excel*. If you click on Word's FileNew button (first button on Word's standard toolbar), nothing happens and you see a message in Excel's status bar very similar to the one in this message box.

The macro needs to copy the current document's contents to a new document so that it can be saved as an RTF file. Hey, not only can't you create a new Word document when editing in-place from within the Excel container, you can't save a Word document object out as a separate file in RTF or any other format for that matter.

I SPY

Q: How many C++ programmers does it take to change a light bulb?

A: You're still thinking procedurally. A properly designed light bulb object would inherit a change method from a generic light bulb class, so all you'd have to do is send a light bulb change message.

Unknown

Even if you're not a C++ developer, there are some neat spy and viewer tools that ship with Microsoft's OLE 2.01 SDK. The fastest way to get hold of these tools is to subscribe to the Microsoft Developer Network (MSDN) CD program and the Microsoft Technical Information Network (TechNet) CD program.* Here's a sampling of the tools that can be useful to you, followed by the more esoteric tools intended primarily for folks writing OLE-compliant applications in C/C++.

Development
Library - CD 8
(July 1994)

The OLE2View Tool

For many years I was self-appointed inspector of snowstorms and rainstorms, and did my duty faithfully, though I never received one cent for it.

Henry David Thoreau
Journal, February 22

---

* For information on the Microsoft Developer Network or the Microsoft Technical Information Network (TechNet), check out the Appendix.

If you're interested in the low-level aspects of OLE 2.0 and you have access to the Microsoft TechNet CD, check out OLE2View (`OLE2VIEW.EXE`) written by Charlie Kindel at Microsoft. It can report on a wide variety of OLE 2.0 issues as shown in the following figures.

Figure 4.38 shows the OLE 2.0 version information display.

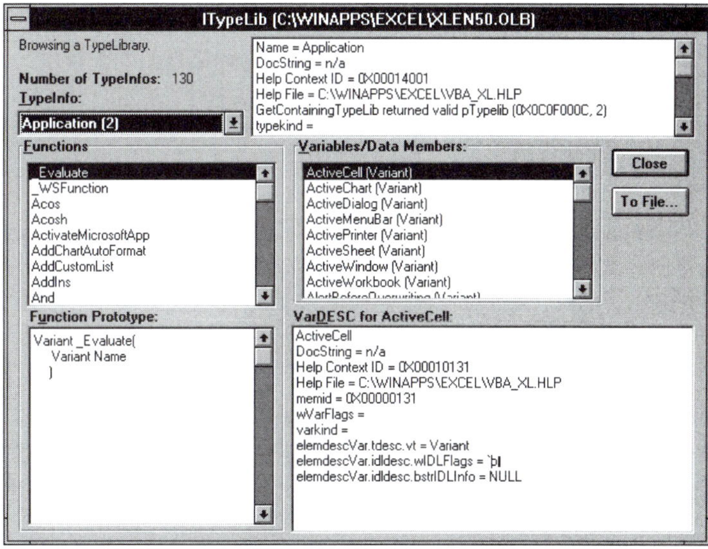

Figure 4.38 OLE2View's Display of OLE Version Information

Figure 4.39 shows a view of Excel 5's type library `XLEN50.OLB`, exploring the Application object.

Figure 4.39 OLE2VIEW's Perspective on Excel 5's Type Library

DocFile Viewer

> I shut my eyes in order to see.
>
> Paul Gauguin
> French painter

You'll find DocFile Viewer (`DFVIEW.EXE`) on the MSDN CD Disc 1 (Setup, SDKs, and DDKs) in the \WIN31\OLE201\BIN directory. It displays the contents of compound documents, but has a 64K file size limitation.

In Figure 4.40 DocFile Viewer exposes a smallish compound document's structured storage contents. Here `CONTAINR.DOC` contains one compound document object, a simple link to a range of cells in Excel.

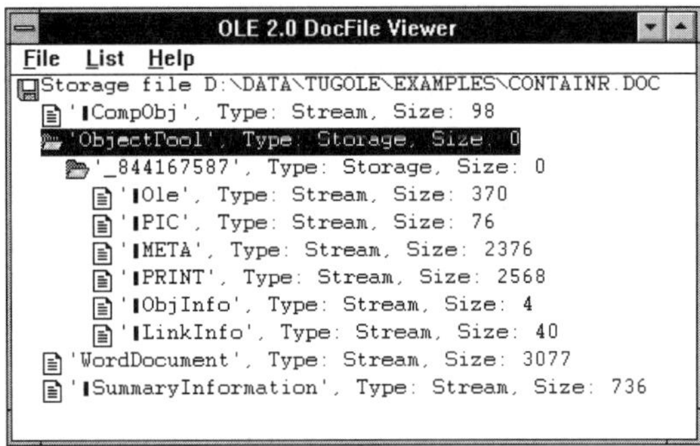

Figure 4.40 DocFile Viewer Peeks at a Word 6 Compound Document

DocFile Explorer

> An optimist is a fellow who believes a housefly is looking for a way to get out.
>
> George Jean Nathan

DocFile Explorer, written by Dave Mitchell and Joseph Kelly at Microsoft, can be found in the WINOBJ CompuServe forum's library 1—look for `DFEXPL.ZIP`. This utility overcomes DocFile Viewer's 64K limitation. (BTW, these guys are both witty and clever. If you leave their About box up for a few seconds, you'll notice their names animate and reverse themselves. Nice touch, guys!)

Figure 4.41 shows DocFile Explorer wading through the Word compound document `CONTAINR.DOC`. Note the additional information in the data area, for example, the item name—D:\DATA\TUGOLE\EXAMPLES\SOURCE.XLS Sheet1!R1C1.

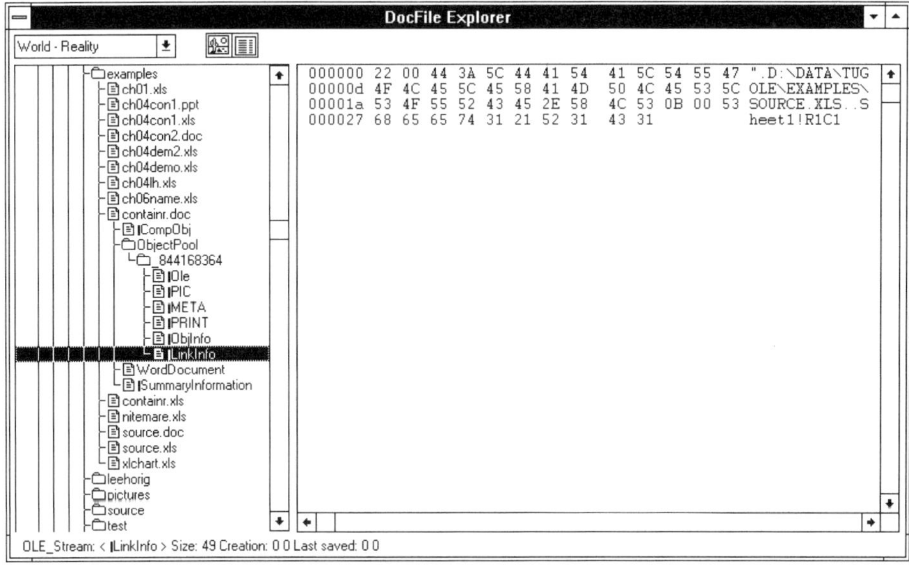

Figure 4.41 DocFile Explorer Digs a Tad Deeper

The Unsupported Windows Process Status Tool

The nifty windows process status monitoring program called WPS (`WPS.EXE`) is on the MSDN CD in the \UNTOOLS\WPS directory and reveals tasks, open files, and loaded modules. WPS was written by Todd Laney, Charlie Kindel, and Brian Woodruff at Microsoft. *Be careful when using WPS (or any module unloader) as you might unintentionally free a module still in use.* Figure 4.42 shows WPS in action.

Figure 4.42 WPS in Action

Other OLE Erotica, Er, Esoterica

> Whoever named it necking was a poor judge of anatomy.
>
> Groucho Marx

The following OLE viewer and spy programs provide a variety of services. All descriptions are quoted directly from the *Debugging OLE Applications: Tools* article.

- DOBJVIEW (*IDataObject* Viewer)—displays the list of data formats offered by OLE data objects created by the Clipboard or drag-and-drop operations.

- IROTVIEW (Running Object Table Viewer)—displays information about OLE 2 objects currently existing in memory.

- LRPCSPY (LRPC* Spy)—displays messages passed between two applications. You can view the messages in the window and store them in a file.

- OLE2FREE (OLE 2.0 Free Module)—frees OLE 2.0 DLLs and the modules that loaded them.

* LRPC = Lightweight Remote Procedure Call. For more information see Brockschmidt's *Inside OLE 2* or the *OLE 2 Programmer's Reference*. Per the latter source, "OLE uses a lightweight remote procedure call (LRPC) communication mechanism based on posting messages or events to window handles to transfer data between processes. The communication mechanism is referred to as 'lightweight' because, at present, it only handles communication between processes on one machine. In the future, communication will be across machines."

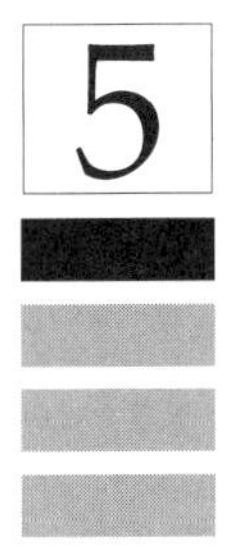 5   Visual Basic for Applications— Orienteering 101

> One of the greatest pains to human nature is the pain of a new idea.
>
> Walter Bagehot
> *Physics and Politics,* 1869

Question: Is Visual Basic for Applications the first common macro language? Answer: In a word, yes. Never mind that it was at one time called ObjectBasic, or, if you're a Woody Leonhard fan, Monster BASIC from Hell.*

Visual Basic for Applications (in some circles referred to as "Visual Basic, Applications Edition"), or simply VBA, is available as of this writing inside Excel 5, Project 4, and will hopefully show up in the next version of Visual Basic. No doubt it's destined to become part of additional Office applications—Access and Word—when they undergo their next major architectural upgrade. When might that be, you say? *Heh, heh, heh.* Honestly, that's anyone's guess. But mark our words that maximum portability and equality of language dialects is very, very high on the Redmondians' Office development wish list. You betcha.

We use Excel's implementation of VBA for all of the examples in this chapter. In later chapters we take you on a tour of Project's VBA coding environment and show you how to port your code from one VBA application to another.

INSTANT GRATIFICATION

> Instant gratification is not soon enough.
>
> from the 1990 movie *Postcards from the Edge*

In this first half of the chapter, you get a jump-start right into VBA, Excel's object model, procedures, the Object Browser, constants, assigning macros to various gizmos, and so on. In other words, you get to wallow around in the VBA kitchen sink and come out sloppin' wet. No toe-testing approach here. Head-first all the

Don't panic!

* Leonhard, Woody. *Windows 3.1 Programming for Mere Mortals.* Addison-Wesley, 1992.

way. In the second half of the chapter, we use actual code to demonstrate how to answer practical, everyday questions. Theory and practice aplenty, and don't panic if you've never written a macro before. We'll let you in on a little secret—it's only easy *after you know how*. Let's ride.

Put the Right Foot Forward with Tools Options Module Settings

It's what you learn after you know it all that counts.

John Wooden
American college basketball coach

Optimal module settings

Before you write a single line of VBA code, tweak your Module Settings in Excel as follows. See Figure 5.1.

1. Select Tools / Options.

2. Click the Module General filecard. Four check boxes are displayed therein.

3. Check Auto Indent, check Display Syntax Errors, clear Break on All Errors, and check Require Variable Declaration (details in the paragraphs following this list).

4. Click the Module Format filecard.

5. Module Format parameters control cosmetics only, so these are completely up to you. Probably easy enough to stick with the defaults (since that's the way code appears in Excel's own `SAMPLES.XLS`) for now and customize it downstream. Click on OK.

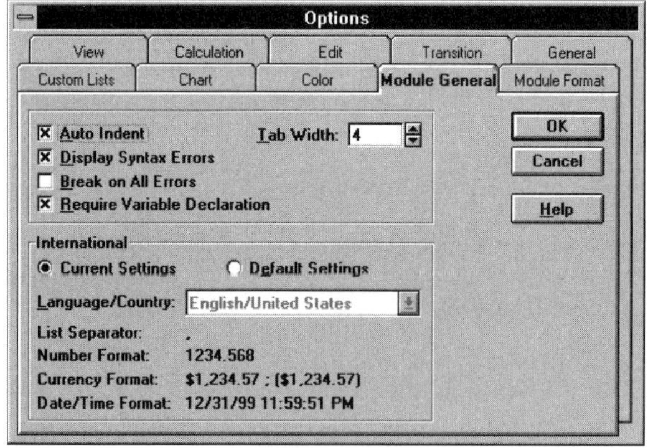

Figure 5.1 Recommended Module General Settings

When Auto Indent is active, the VBA module watches your keystrokes and does a fairly good job of indenting your code when appropriate. If you don't want an indentation level provided for a particular statement, place the cursor at the beginning of the line and press the Backspace key to un-indent one level.

When Display Syntax Errors is active, the VBA module monitors each statement. When you press the Enter key, VBA reports any syntax errors it sees. For VBA neophytes, this is a good thing. As you become more experienced, you may opt to clear this setting because as you cut-copy-and-paste code snippets around, the module monitor nags you relentlessly. No problem. Clear the check box to disable this feature.

When Break on All Errors is cleared, standard On Error trapping statements in your code work normally. When this setting is checked, VBA ignores your On Error statements and breaks on any error. This can be handy during gnarly debugging sessions, but typically this setting is cleared (off).

We saved the best, and most important setting, for last. Require Variable Declaration should be on, on, on. Without stepping up on Ye Olde Soapbox and lecturing evangelically about the virtues of strong data typing like a bunch of feral Computer Science 301 professors, let's just say that we encourage you to explicitly declare variables. The benefits are as follows.

> **Variable Declaration should be on, on, on!**

- Anyone who comes along later to maintain your code will kiss your feet for adhering to the convention of strong data typing. (Hell, come back to your own code after a one-week hiatus and if everything's neatly declared you'll kiss your own feet! Hmmm, on second thought maybe you should just treat yourself to a movie.)

- Your code will be more compact and efficient since without explicit declaration, Excel has no choice but to allocate excess memory to many variables that could be stored more compactly. (Without explicit declaration, everything is a Variant data type by default. Blecccch. See Figure 5.7 for details on the storage requirements for each VBA data type.)

Welcome to Your New Home, the VBA Module

> My mind is important to me. It's where I spend most of my time.
>
> Unknown

Hello, we're the Neighborhood Module Welcoming Committee. Care for some cookies and milk? Seriously, you'll be racking up some hours here, so take time to poke around. See Figure 5.2. The differences between the module environments in Excel and Project (at least in this first implementation of VBA) can be annoying. See Chapter 8 for details.

The Visual Basic toolbar and the module sheet's transmogrified menu pull-downs give you access to the components and features you need to get the job done. Keep in mind that you develop your Excel custom dialog boxes in a completely different sheet type—a dialog sheet (more on this later).

Insert Module button

To create a VBA module, start with an open workbook. Then select Insert / Macro / Module. VBA gives the new module the name Module1 if it's the first module in this workbook. Otherwise it uses the naming format "Module*n*" where *n* increments by one. If you're a button-o-phile, there's a button you can add to any toolbar that will insert a module. Select View / Toolbars / select a toolbar / Customize / File / drag-and-drop the Insert Module button (fifth from the left in the second row) / Close.

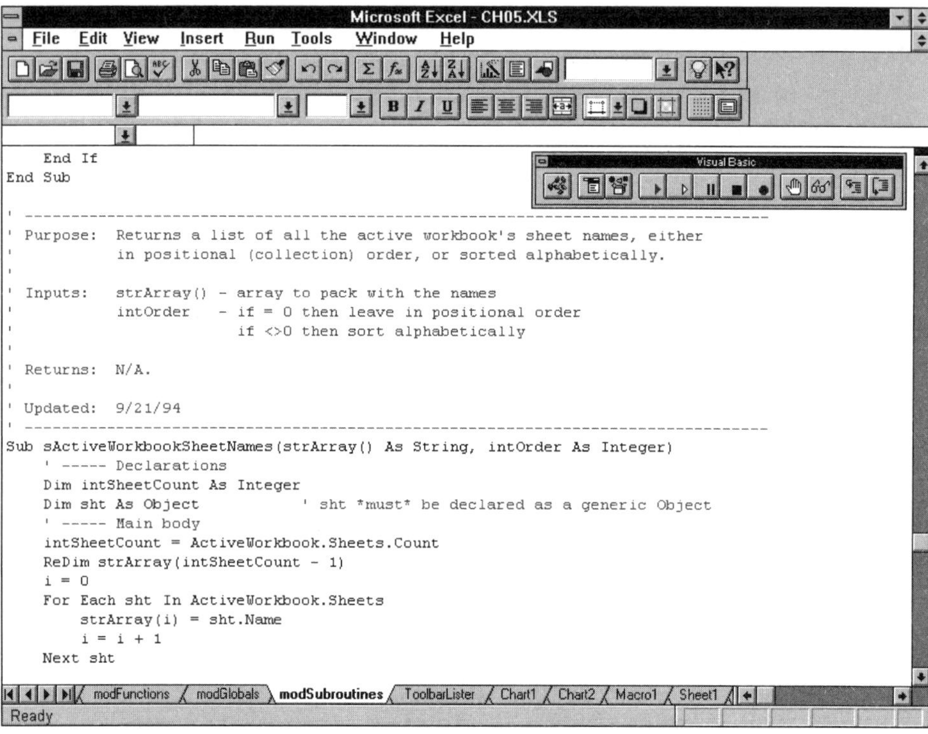

Figure 5.2 Full-on VBA Module

Recording a Macro

> There are three ways to get something done—do it yourself, hire someone to do it, or ask your kids not to do it.
>
> Malcolm Kushner

Recording a macro is as easy as falling off a log. In the first example you build (coming up shortly), we walk you through the steps. The best feature of the VBA recorder is that you can tell the recorder, before you turn it on, exactly where you want the recorder to dump the recorded actions.

In this example you'll record a simple macro that mimics the actions you go through when inserting a worksheet in Excel and renaming it something other than the default.

1. Activate a worksheet in a new workbook with no modules present.

2. Select Tools / Record Macro / Record New Macro / click the Options button / accept the default name of Macro1 and its description text / select the option button labeled This Workbook / OK. The Stop Recording toolbar should appear.

3. Select Insert / Worksheet.

4. Right-click on the newly inserted worksheet / Rename / type in SnaggleFritz / click on the OK button.

5. Click the Stop Recording button.

6. Select Module1 and you should see code similar to the following. Note that the precise name of the inserted sheet (Sheet2, Sheet3, Sheet17, or whatever) will depend on how many worksheets are in the workbook when you record the macro. In this example we started in a workbook with two extant worksheets.

Stop Recording button

```
'
' Macro1 Macro
' Macro recorded 10/6/94 by T. U. Greader
'
'
Sub Macro1()
    Sheets.Add
    Sheets("Sheet3").Select
    Sheets("Sheet3").Name = "SnaggleFritz"
End Sub
```

Throughout the rest of the chapter you'll explore various aspects of VBA. What you've learned from this brief example is that user actions can be readily recorded, and that often the very process of studying the recorded code can accelerate the development process by revealing which objects, methods, and properties are involved in a particular activity or feature.

Editing a Macro

Whether you recorded a macro or typed it in by hand, editing a macro is straight-forward. Dig the color-coding scheme. Balk at the lack of drag-and-drop within a module. That's right, you have to use old-fashioned cut-copy-and-paste techniques to copy or move statements around.

Need help with a particular object, method, or function in your source code? Place the insertion point next to (or anywhere inside) the name of the object, method, property, function, or statement and press F1. If you want help right now on the Option Explicit statement, simply click in that statement and press F1. See Figure 5.3 for the resulting help topic.

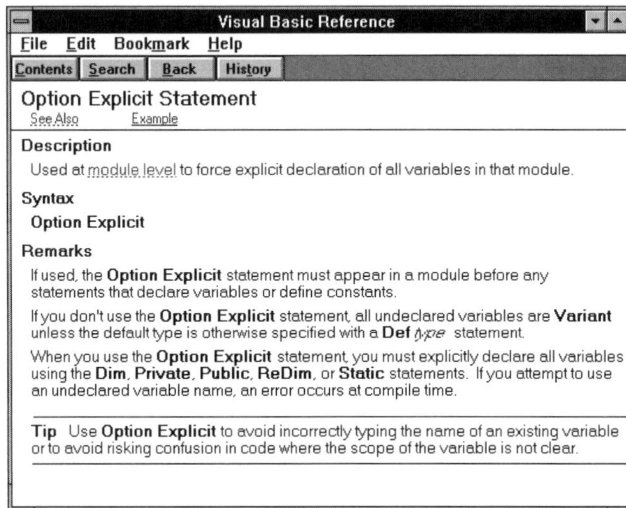

Figure 5.3 Just an F1 Away

The pain of splitting panes

Splitting panes so that you can see your VBA code and a target worksheet is probably the most painful aspect of working in an Excel module. Here's the trick. Let's start by assuming you've got one worksheet named Sheet1 and one module named Module1.

1. Select Module1.

2. Select Window / New Window.

3. Select Window / Arrange / Horizontal / select the Windows of Active Workbook check box / OK. Uh huh, that's right, your screen ain't quite there yet. One more step.

4. If you want your module on the top bunk and the sheet on the bottom bunk, activate the bottom window and click the Sheet1 tab. To flip things around, activate the appropriate window and then click the desired tab.

When you're in a hurry to move around among child windows, don't forget these handy keyboard shortcut keys. However, we don't recommend using the Tab key-based shortcuts because outside of Excel (for example, in Word) they produce a literal tab instead of the desired window-switching action, whereas the F6-based shortcuts work the same in all Office applications.

- **Go to the next window**—CTRL + F6 or CTRL + TAB

- **Go to the previous window**—CTRL + SHIFT + F6 or CTRL + SHIFT + TAB

Excel's Object Model

> Something hidden. Go and find it. Go and look behind the Ranges—
> Something lost behind the Ranges. Lost and waiting for you. Go!
>
> Rudyard Kipling
> *The Explorer*, 1903

Absolutely without question the best piece of advice we can offer you regarding the various Office application object models is this—get the *Microsoft Office Developer's Kit* (for pricing and order information see the Appendix). It includes the single-sheet, 13.5" by 8.5" document called the *Microsoft Object Model Reference Chart* (document no. DB57224-0294) which shows a graphic representation of the Excel, Data Access (Access 2.0), Access 1.1, and Project object models. (Word is omitted because Word has a monolithic or unitary object model. It'd be a real boring graphic. One object called "Word.Basic." More on this later.)

First off, are we still talking about the same kind of objects you read about in previous chapters? Yeah … sorta kinda. From a programming standpoint, a programmable object is something you can manipulate using VBA. A programmable object is an entity inside an application—maybe even the application itself!—that you and your sidekick VBA can grab by the throat and press into service for World Peace (or whatever crusade your client's paying you for this time around). If you want to make an Excel workbook jump through some hoops, you and VBA talk to an Excel Workbook object. Different applications possess different objects that they expose (make available). VBA remains constant throughout all this open-minded object nudity, er, exposure, and only the objects change depending on the individual application being controlled at any particular time.

An **object model** is a definition of each type of object and a description of how a particular object fits into the hierarchy of all an application's objects. An object model also includes the properties that describe these objects, along with the methods that each object supports. (We explain the terms method and property in detail later in this chapter.)

Figure 5.4 shows a graphic representation of Excel's highest-level object—Application—and its subordinate objects.

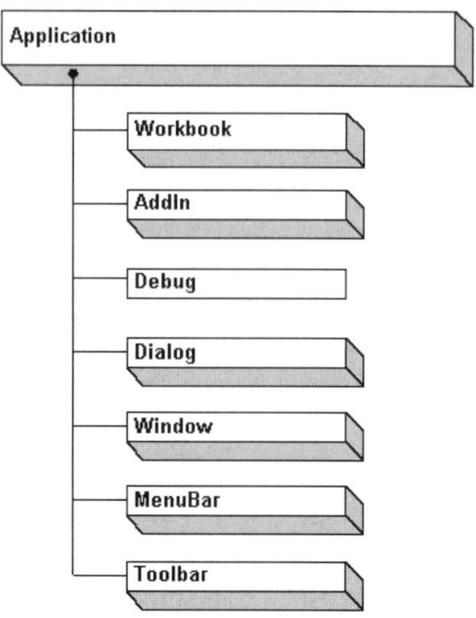

Figure 5.4 Excel's Application Object

In other similar figures throughout this book, we display objects that can also serve as collections in the form of 3-D boxes. We display those objects that cannot serve as collections as 2-D boxes, for example, Debug in Figure 5.4. The help file defines a *collection* as a "group of objects. An object's position in the collection can change whenever a change occurs in the collection. Therefore, the position of any specific object in the collection is unpredictable. This unpredictability distinguishes a collection from an array." The last sentence may sound a bit scary at first blush. Let's elaborate.

Here the term "unpredictability" means that the objects in a collection can be in any order at any time. For example, when you shake a bag of loose coins the individual coins move around unpredictably. In contrast, an array's contents don't move around by themselves—*you have to reorder them explicitly yourself.* By analogy, if you have a nicely wrapped roll of quarters in your hand, the first quarter isn't going anywhere unless you unwrap the roll and swap that quarter with one of its peers.

Next in Figure 5.5 is a graphic representation of one of the most commonly used portions of Excel's object model, the objects that belong to the Workbook category.

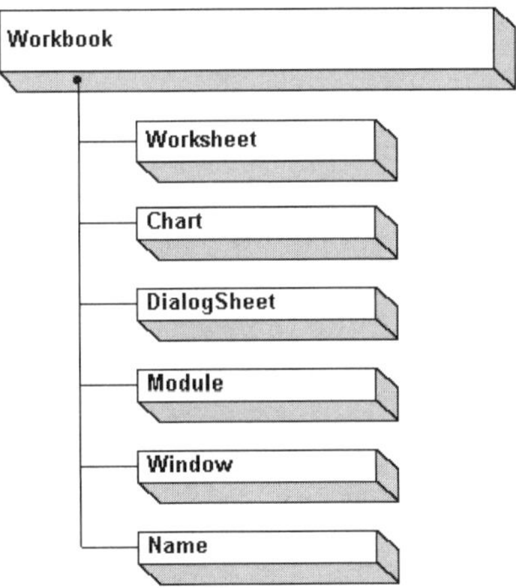

Figure 5.5 Excel's Workbook Object

OLE Automation and VBA

> The factory of the future will have only two employees, a man and a dog.
> The man will be there to feed the dog. The dog will be there to keep the
> man from touching the equipment.
>
> Warren Bennis

OLE Automation essentially involves exposing programmable objects to the outside world. Since Project speaks VBA, it can access any Excel programmable object (like those shown in Figure 5.5). This is made possible by the underlying architecture of OLE 2 and OLE Automation. So, Excel and Project can reach out and touch, query, and otherwise interact with each other's programmable objects. Ditto for other combinations like Access caressing Project objects, Visual Basic 3 massaging Excel objects, Excel fondling Visio objects, and so on. It's so simple it's almost unbelievable. (And if you think this is unbelievable, wait 'til Cairo, or Win 96, or whatever-the-heck they call it, when you'll be able to access programmable objects not just locally on your own workstation, but on any machine—and any OS platform that supports OLE—on any local or even wide-area or planetary or inter-galactic network you have privileges to!)

However, before we venture into the fascinating world of OLE Automation, we need to walk you through a tour of VBA's coding environment, syntax, and generally how you "get around" inside a VBA project and the other core components of Excel—the mighty Application and Workbook objects. So tighten up the laces on your Gore-Tex® hiking boots and let's get hacking!

You Say "Macro," VBA Says "Modules and Procedures Go Hand in Hand"

If my boss calls, get his name.

Anonymous

**A named block
of source code**   In layman's terms, **macro** and **procedure** essentially describe the same thing—*a distinct, named block of source code that runs when you press the Run button.* A **module** is a place where procedures live. But there's a subtle distinction that bears discussion. What happens when you create a new module? VBA kicks in its coding environment, tosses in the `Option Explicit` statement, and the cursor sits there staring at you. Blink. Blink. Blink.

If you press the Run button (assuming you have no `PERSONAL.XLS` loaded, hidden or otherwise), VBA displays an empty Macro dialog box. See Figure 5.6.

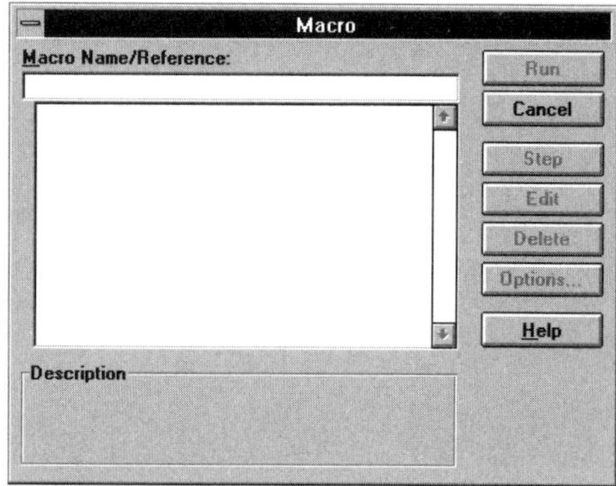

Figure 5.6 Nobody Home at the Module

The module exists, but there are no procedures inside it. To create a procedure, you have to tell VBA what kind of procedure you need. They come in three flavors.

- **Subroutine procedure**—a distinct, named block of source code
- **Function procedure**—a distinct, named block of source code that returns a value to whoever called it
- **Property procedure**—a distinct, named block of source code that behaves like a property value

Throughout this book we'll commonly refer to these three different procedure types as "subroutine," "function," and "property procedure" respectively. (We say "property procedure" to avoid confusion between a property—as in an object's property—and a property procedure). That's the shorthand we prefer and it is consistent within the VBA development community at large.

Subroutine Procedures

The code inside a subroutine is bounded by two required statements, the `Sub` statement (followed by a name and some optional arguments) and the simple `End Sub` statement that, you guessed it, marks the terminus of the subroutine. From there, the sky's the limit. You can write a novella's worth of statements, or just one single statement. Heck, you can even write an empty subroutine! (What, Ma, no source code!? You bet.) But you must provide a name along with the `Sub` statement. The logic's all up to you. Kind of like staring at a blank canvas, isn't it? A simple example follows.

```
Sub HelloDownThere()
    MsgBox "I'm from the Underground!"
End Sub
```

When you run this subroutine, up pops a message box declaring "I'm from the Underground!" Another procedure somewhere else in the current module, or even a module in another project (workbook) can call `HelloDownThere` too. More on that a bit later.

Function Procedures

As with a subroutine, a function is bounded by two required statements, the `Function` statement (followed by a name, some optional arguments, and an optional type declaration) and the simple `End Function` statement. The difference is, a function's raison d'être is to return a value. This means you can use it inside an expression or a statement. First we'll show you the function, then how it might get put to use.

```
Function WhereAreYouFrom() As String
    WhereAreYouFrom = "I'm from the Underground!"
End Function

Sub IAmCallingYou()
    Dim TheMessage As String
    ' put the function call in an expression
    TheMessage = WhereAreYouFrom
    MsgBox TheMessage
    ' or put the function call inside the stmt...
    MsgBox WhereAreYouFrom
End Sub
```

If you explicitly run the `WhereAreYouFrom` function, you don't see anything happen on the screen. This is as it should be, since this particular function's job is to assign itself a string value and give that back to whomever called it, in this case the subroutine `IAmCallingYou`. This way, any procedure that calls the `WhereAreYouFrom` function knows it will get back a value, but has the intoxicating freedom to decide for itself what to do with that return value.

Strong Data Typing and Coding Conventions

> The meek shall inherit the earth ... but the strong shall retain the mineral rights.
>
> Anonymous

According to the VBA help file, **data type** is defined as "the characteristic of a variable that determines what kind of data it can hold." VBA supports, in fact promotes, strong **data typing**; that is, limiting a variable to a given kind of data throughout the code's execution. That's why we had you select Tools Module General's Require Variable Declaration check box. VBA supports eleven data types, including user-defined. See Figure 5.7.

		Visual Basic Reference	

File   Edit   Bookmark   Help

Contents	Search	Back	History	

Data Type Summary
See Also

The following table shows the supported data types, including their storage sizes and ranges.

Data type	Storage size	Range
Boolean	2 bytes	**True** or **False**.
Integer	2 bytes	-32,768 to 32,767.
Long (long integer)	4 bytes	-2,147,483,648 to 2,147,483,647.
Single (single-precision floating-point)	4 bytes	-3.402823E38 to -1.401298E-45 for negative values; 1.401298E-45 to 3.402823E38 for positive values.
Double (double-precision floating-point)	8 bytes	-1.79769313486232E308 to -4.94065645841247E-324 for negative values; 4.94065645841247E-324 to 1.79769313486232E308 for positive values.
Currency (scaled integer)	8 bytes	-922,337,203,685,477.5808 to 922,337,203,685,477.5807.
Date	8 bytes	January 1, 100 to December 31, 9999.
Object	4 bytes	Any **Object** reference.
String	1 byte per character	0 to approximately 2 billion (approximately 65,535 for Microsoft Windows version 3.1 and earlier).
Variant	16 bytes + 1 byte for each character	Any numeric value up to the range of a **Double** or any character text.
User-defined (using Type)	Number required by elements	The range of each element is the same as the range of its data type.

Figure 5.7 Summary of VBA Data Types

To maintain order and improve readability as projects reach a certain critical "confusion mass," we strongly recommend you follow the naming and other coding conventions* outlined in the *Microsoft Office Developer's Kit* (ODK). The first step to take on the path to consistent use of conventions is in naming variables and functions. The conventions shown in Table 5.1 are straight out of the ODK.

Table 5.1 Recommended Variable & Function Name Prefixes

Data Type	Prefix	Example
Boolean	bln	blnFound
Currency	cur	curRevenue
Date (Time)	dat	datStart
Double	dbl	dblTolerance
Error	err	errOrderNum
Integer	int	intQuantity
Long	lng	lngDistance
Object	obj	objCurrent
Single	sng	sngAverage
String	str	strFName
User-defined type	udt	udtEmployee
Variant	vnt	vntCheckSum

Note that you should use these data type prefixes for *both* variables and functions. Remember that a function returns a value and that the return value must be *typed* (the default is Variant). No data type prefix is required for a subroutine because it doesn't itself return a value.

We prefer an additional convention whereby the single-letter "f" prefix is placed at the beginning of a function's name, and the single-letter "s" prefix for a subroutine's name. When you add all this together, the `HelloDownThere` subroutine and `WhereAreYouFrom` function you built most recently should instead look like this.

Use prefixes with both variables and functions.

```
Sub sHelloDownThere()
    MsgBox "I'm from the Underground!"
End Sub
```

* Historical note—A small part of these conventions can be found in the *Microsoft Visual Basic 3.0 Programmer's Reference.* For what it's worth, as best as our moles can determine these conventions started out somewhere deep in the labyrinths of Microsoft Consulting Services, Microsoft's mysto consulting division. They then found their way into Microsoft Education Services' Visual Basic 3 courseware and a Knowledge Base article, and now have come home to roost in the ODK for all the world to see. They are a Real Good Thing. Really.

```
Function fstrWhereAreYouFrom() As String
    fstrWhereAreYouFrom = "I'm from the Underground!"
End Function
```

Variant functions deserve special mention. You can get away with dropping the `As [type]` component of the opening `Function` statement, in which case VBA internally declares it to be a Variant function. However, we suggest you not get lazy! In the interest of clarity if you want to use the Variant type, you should explicitly include `As Variant` and be sure to name the function with the "f" and "vnt" prefixes like this.

```
Function fvntIAmVariant() As Variant
    fvntIAmVariant = Array("Underground Guide to Excel", _
        "Underground Guide to Microsoft Office, OLE 2, & VBA", _
        "Underground Guide to Unix", _
        "Underground Guide to Word")
End Function
```

The `Array()` function is one of VBA's many built-in functions. We discuss built-in functions in more detail shortly. `Array()` returns a Variant that contains an array. This is a convenient way to initialize an array without using a loop.

Methods and Properties Belong to Objects

> Whatever is not nailed down is mine. Whatever I can pry loose is not nailed down.
>
> ascribed to Collis P. Huntington, American railroad magnate

Excel's help file defines a **method** as "a procedure that applies to a specific object." A bit too academic for our taste. How about this: A method is a capability to act or the result of that act, as performed by a particular object using some underlying code procedure.

Excel's help file says a **property** is "a named attribute of an object. Properties define object characteristics (such as size, color, and screen location) or object behaviors (for example, whether it is enabled)." That's fine. A bit more terminology and we're set. A property can be either read-only or read-write. A read-only property can be looked at and returned but cannot be changed. A read-write property can be examined and returned and can also be changed. The help file topic for any given property will mention in the Description section whether the property is read-only or read-write.

Perhaps the best way to grok what methods and properties are all about is to spend about forty-eight uninterrupted hours tied to a chair while taking in an undiluted I.V. of Jolt Cola, scrolling through every single object in the Visual Basic Reference help file, alternately examining each Properties topic and each Methods topic. Bing. Bong. Bing. Bong. It's like the old adage—when you're learning a foreign language, you know you've got it when you start dreaming it.

Methods versus Functions

> Let schoolmasters puzzle their brain,
> With grammar, and nonsense, and learning;
> Good liquor, I stoutly maintain,
> Gives genius a better discerning.
>
> Oliver Goldsmith
> *She Stoops to Conquer*, 1773

The Excel help file tells us that a method is a procedure that applies to a specific object. So what's the difference between a method and a function? Well, this is an exercise in semantic hair-splitting, but method is a special term for a procedure that an object owns. Think of it this way—a procedure that converts between Celsius and Fahrenheit is a function but isn't a method, because there's no object involved. Say you're an application. You have no idea how to add menus, but you know that Excel knows how. You grab the Excel object and tell it, "Hey Excel! Add a menu to yourself." You've just used a method. A key aspect of OLE objects is that they know precisely what methods they have access to. *So do others outside the object*. The interface works both ways. A caller (user) of an object, even at a very fundamental level, can never associate a bogus method with the object. It can't be done.

For example, Toolbars("Standard") is a legitimate Excel object. Help is a legitimate Excel method. But a Toolbar object cannot under any circumstances ever ever ever call the Help method. No way. Prove it to yourself by looking at the help topics for the Toolbar object and the Toolbars object collection, click the Methods jump topics for each, and you won't see the Help method listed. Test it in reverse by looking up the Help method's help topic, and you'll see that the only object this method applies to is Application. Final proof is to run the following procedure. You'll immediately see the error message shown in Figure 5.8.

```
Sub sYouAreNoHelp()
    Toolbars("Standard").Help
End Sub
```

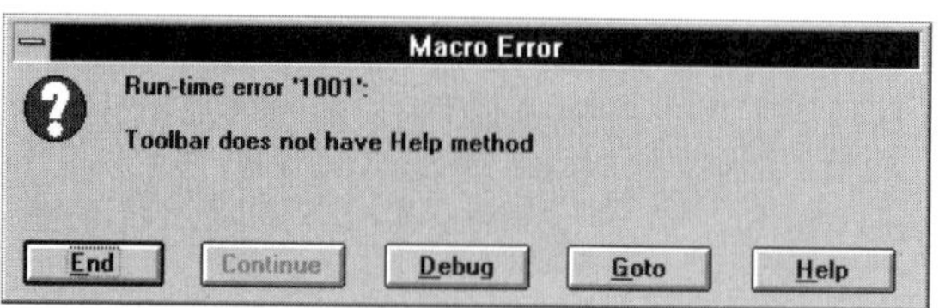

Figure 5.8 Toolbar Object and Help Method Don't Mix

Capturing a method's return value   Want more proof that method is—as far as the object involved is concerned—just a synonym for function? Let's see what happens if you do something legitimate like call the `Help` method on the `Application` object and display the return value in a message box. Here's how.

```
Sub sYouAreNoHelp()
    Dim vntReturn As Variant
    vntReturn = Application.Help
    MsgBox "Application.Help returns " & vntReturn
End Sub
```

When you run this procedure Excel displays its main help file's table of contents, returns the Boolean value True, assigns it to `vntReturn`, then displays this value in a message box. The Application object and the Help method are joined together with the dot operator "." in the expression `Application.Help`. The dot operator can also be used to associate an object with a property, or to join several objects in a parent.child kind of relationship. Various examples of the dot operator occur throughout the rest of this chapter.

Note that since this is a very simple procedure, once it invokes the Windows Help application, Excel's title bar starts flashing to indicate it wants focus back so that it can show you the waiting message box. At this point you should ALT + TAB back to Excel where you'll see the waiting message box that reads "Application.Help returns True." You don't have to explicitly assign a method's return value to a variable in order for the method to work, but it is certainly possible to do so and you'll find this technique to be useful in certain circumstances.

There's another important distinction between types of functions—built-in versus user-defined (also called custom). A **built-in function** comes with VBA. An example is the built-in function called `Now`. See Figure 5.9.

To see a list of all Excel/VBA's built-in functions from inside a module press F1, select the Functions topic and Excel displays the alphabetized buttons and list shown in Figure 5.10.

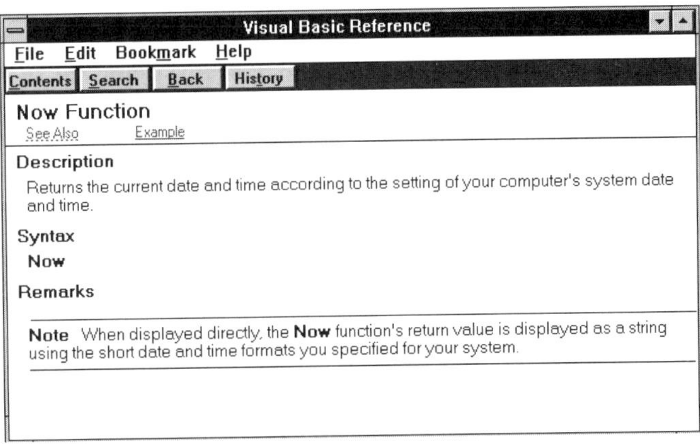

Figure 5.9 Now Is the Time … Is a Built-in Function

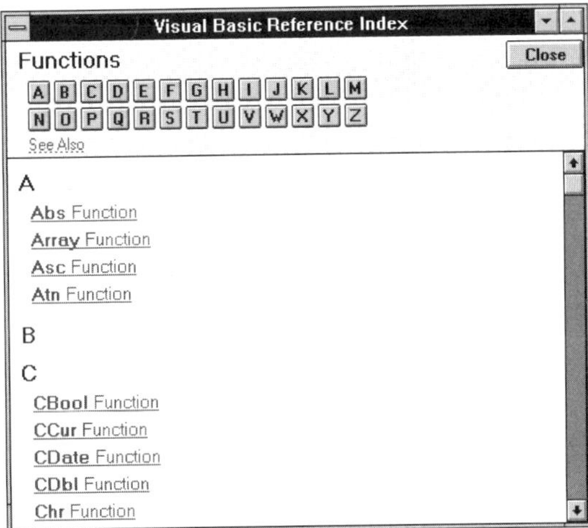

Figure 5.10 Built-in Functions Are Free of Charge

You can also browse VBA's built-in functions with the Object Browser (and even paste them into the current module; more on this later) in which case the Object Browser list box is labeled "Methods/Properties"—but don't panic! This is just more semantic hair-splitting. If you select VBA in the Libraries/Workbooks drop-down list box and select the DateTime category in the Objects/Modules list box, you'll see Now listed along with the other built-in date and time-related methods (functions) as in Figure 5.11. Confusing? Initially. Say, how's that Jolt Cola I.V. doing? Time for a refill?

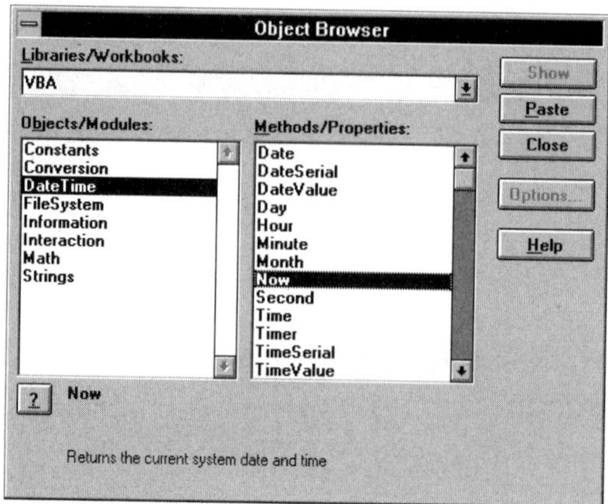

Figure 5.11 More Than One Way to Be Here Now

Now the free ride's over, in the sense that you know what an Excel method is, and a VBA built-in function, but what about rolling your own? No problem. In fact, you already rolled one when you keyed in the source code for the custom function `fstrWhereAreYouFrom()`. You can use a custom function inside a worksheet and include a custom function in the list of functions displayed by Excel's Function Wizard. For more information on these operations, see the *Excel User's Guide* and the *Excel Visual Basic User's Guide*.

Dialing for Objects

> What song the Sirens sang, or what name Achilles assumed when he hid himself among women, though puzzling questions, are not beyond all conjecture.
>
> Sir Thomas Browne
> *Urn-Burial; or, Hydriotaphia,* 1658

There are two ways to navigate through the multilayered, object-oriented infrastructure of Excel objects while inside a VBA module.

1. Use the F1 key help technique with the cursor on an object, function, method, property, or statement name, and examine the associated help jump topics for the entity of interest.

2. Use Object Browser to get help on the entity and, where appropriate, look at it. And in some cases, insert VBA code based on the selected entity.

Object Browser gives you quick access to all procedures in all loaded workbooks (including the typically hidden `PERSONAL.XLS` and any other hidden workbooks), and to all objects and modules in both VBA and Excel (see Figure 5.11 and Figure 5.12). Simply click on the Libraries/Workbooks drop-down to see the list of available entities. The dialog's two list boxes provide drill-down style access to deeper and deeper layers of the OLE Automation object model lurking within Excel and its sidekick VBA.

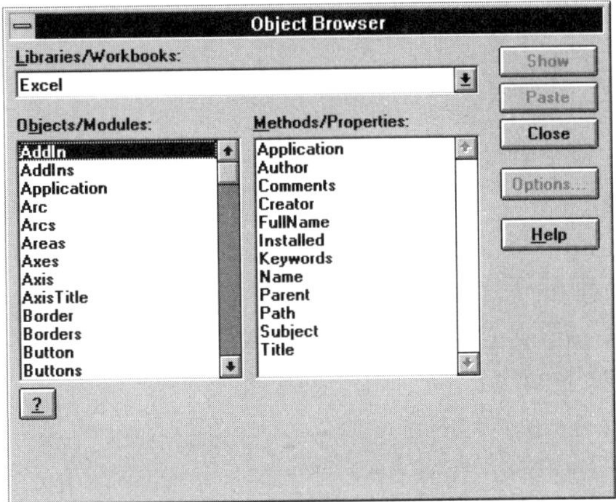

Figure 5.12 Object Browser Sniffing Excel

Excel's Object Browser is only available within a VBA module. If the entity is a procedure, you can edit it by clicking Show, or change its settings by clicking Options. These are the optional settings you can change via the Options button.

- description

- menu assignment

- shortcut key

- four help-related characteristics—function category, status bar text, help context ID, and help file name

If the entity is a method (this includes built-in methods, built-in functions, and custom procedures) or a property, you can insert partial statement code into the module—wherever the cursor is—by clicking Paste. If the entity is anything other than a custom procedure, the Help button (below the Objects/Modules list box) is enabled. Click it to see the associated help.

Another Object Browser nicety is that no matter how disorganized (not alphabetically arranged) individual procedures are in a specific module, it automatically presents them by name in alphabetical order in the Methods/Properties list box.

Object Browser Paste to reduce typing and syntax errors

Here's an example of how to use Paste to insert the syntax of the MsgBox command into a procedure.

1. Locate the `sHelloDownThere` procedure. You're going to add a second message box to this procedure, formatted differently from the first.

2. Click the cursor once at the end of the `MsgBox "I'm from the Underground!"` statement.

3. Press the Enter key to start a new line.

4. Select View / Object Browser / select VBA in the Libraries/Workbooks list / select Interaction from the Objects/Modules list / select MsgBox from the Methods/Properties list / Paste.

5. The statement `MsgBox(Prompt:=, Buttons:=, Title:=, HelpFile:=, Context:=)` is inserted.

6. After each `:=` operator (called the "named argument" operator), insert values so that your procedure looks like this. Also, remove the MsgBox's original parentheses because you're using MsgBox here in its command as opposed to its function form. The underscore character at the end of some of the lines is VBA's line continuation character; you type an underscore and then press the Enter key to start a new line. Use it along with tab indenting to make your code more readable.

```
Sub sHelloDownThere()
    MsgBox "I'm from the Underground!"
    MsgBox Prompt:="Are you talking to me?", _
        Buttons:=vbYesNoCancel + vbQuestion, _
        Title:="Way Down in The Underground"
End Sub
```

We'll revisit the Object Browser in Chapter 7.

Constants

In the space age, man will be able to go around the world in two hours—one for flying and the other to get to the airport.

Neil McElroy
chairman, Procter & Gamble; U.S. secretary of defense

VBA and Excel provide a comprehensive set of built-in constants that you can insert on demand right into your source code. A constant is a named item the value of which remains, well, constant, while your source code is running. A built-in constant is one that comes with the language at hand. A user-defined constant is one you create in your source code. You can search for VBA constants (those constants unique to VBA) using the Object Browser—View / Object Browser / select VBA in the Libraries/Workbooks drop-down list box / select Constants in the Objects/Modules list box / select the constant of interest in the Methods/Properties list box. To paste the constant into the module, click the Paste button. These constants all have the prefix "vb." Note that before you click Paste, while the focus is on the target constant in the Methods/Properties list, the Object Browser dialog displays a brief description of the constant in the lower-left corner of the dialog. If you need help on a constant, click the ? button located directly beneath the Objects/Modules list box. To find Excel constants (those constants unique to the Excel application) using the Object Browser—View / Object Browser / select Excel in the Libraries/ Workbooks list / select Constants in the Objects/Modules list / select the constant of interest in the Methods/Properties list. To paste the constant into the module, click the Paste button. These constants all have the prefix "xl."

If you instead want to use the help file to scan VBA's constants, make sure you're in the Visual Basic Reference help file, search on "Visual Basic constants," click on Show Topics, click on Go To, and you'll be able to choose from four categories.

- Dir, GetAttr, and SetAttr Constants

- MsgBox Constants

- StrConv Constants

- VarType Constants

Note that although you can view an alphabetical list of Excel constants using the Object Browser technique described earlier in this section, *there are no help topics dedicated exclusively to Excel constants.* Instead, look at the help topic for the Excel object method or property that a particular constant belongs to. For example, if you want to find out about xl3DArea, you won't be able to work backwards given just the constant name. You'll have to hunt around for a method or property that accepts xl3DArea; in this case, one such property is Type when associated with a Chart object.

As of mid-March 1994, Microsoft made available an Excel workbook XLCONST.XLS that provides bi-directional searching for built-in constants. This very slick workbook exposes constants in both alphabetical and numerical order, *along with complete cross-references to the associated object and*

statement combinations. **Hip hip hooray! To get your hands on this invaluable tool, well, there's a veritable plethora of choices—CompuServe (GO MSL), GEnie, Microsoft Online, Microsoft Download Service (MSDL), the Internet, and PSS. Whatever source you pick, look for and download the self-extracting file `WE0993.EXE`. Dig it! (For detailed information on WE0993, read the Microsoft Knowledge Base article Q112671.)**

Hey Man, Where's the Start Button on This Thing?

> It's nice to be here in Iowa.
>
> Gerald Ford in Ohio, 1976

There are many ways to run a macro. It all depends on whether the focus is in a VBA module or not. You can assign macros to objects like toolbar buttons and graphic objects in sheets, assign macros to controls in custom dialog boxes, and have macros jump through hoops when triggered by various events.

Inside a VBA Module

If you're inside a VBA module, you can start a macro in one of three ways.

1. Select Run / Start (or press F5). If the cursor is inside a macro, bingo, that's the one it runs. If the cursor is outside a macro, VBA tries to figure out which macro to run. If it can't decide, it shows you the Macro dialog with a list of all the macros currently available to you. There is one special case—if the current macro is a function procedure and it has arguments, then you can't run it directly no matter what. You have to call it from a separate subroutine. Makes sense, right? After all, what use is a function with an argument if we don't call the function in such a way that the argument has a value?

2. Select Tools / Macro / then locate the macro of choice and click Run.

Run Macro button

3. Pressing the Run Macro button on the Visual Basic toolbar has the same effect as the above two methods, *only it's a couple of strokes faster.* (We know, we know, we're unrepentant mouse-o-philes.)

Outside a VBA Module

When you're cruising around outside a VBA module—it was gettin' a bit stuffy packed in there with all that straight-laced New Courier source code—you can always fall back on the faithful Tools / Macro / Run menu or the Visual Basic toolbar's Run Macro button. For the latter to work, the Visual Basic toolbar must be visible. If it's not, then View / Toolbars / select the Visual Basic check box / OK.

Other objects can invoke macros. Objects as in … objects floating around in Excel's graphic layer—lines, arrows, rectangles, text boxes, command buttons, spinner controls, etc. (For a whirlwind tour of these objects, activate Excel's Drawing toolbar and click on each button with the Help Tool. Ditto for the Forms toolbar. Note: Forms controls can be used on worksheets as well as VBA dialog sheets.) Plus OLE objects and pictures. The trick in coupling an object, picture, toolbar button, dialog box control, or menu command and a macro is the handy-dandy facility called Assign Macro. Here are the steps for assigning a macro to a Drawing command button in Excel. (In a moment we cover the notable exceptions to these basic steps.)

1. Create a new worksheet—Insert / Worksheet. (These techniques work equally well on worksheet sheets, chart sheets, and Excel 4.0 macro sheets.)

2. Activate the Drawing toolbar if it's hidden—View / Toolbars / select the Drawing check box / OK.

3. Click on the Create Button button, then drag the drawing cursor to form the shape and size button you want.

Create Button button

4. In the case of a command button drawing object, the Assign Macro dialog pops up automatically, so select the macro you want to assign to this object—for example, select `sHelloDownThere`—then click OK. (The slightly different steps for a non-command button drawing object are reviewed shortly.)

5. At this point the command button is in a selected-for-editing state so you can't click on it to run the macro yet. (Notice the dotted line bordering the object and the presence of sizing handles; for an example of this display state, see Figure 5.14). Edit the button label text to your taste, or leave it as the default "Button 1." (To change the text, type in what you want to appear on the button. Use the arrow, Backspace, and Delete keys to make edits.) To un-select the object, click anywhere outside the object or press the Escape key. Then, as you pass the mouse pointer over the command button, you'll notice that the pointer changes into a Pointing Index Finger™ (see Figure 5.13.) Left-click once and `sHelloDownThere` is off and running.

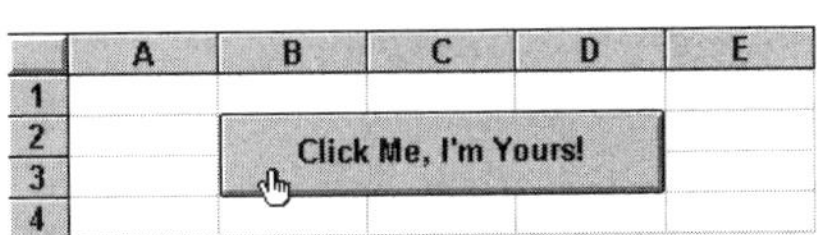

Figure 5.13 A Drawing Command Button Assigned to a Macro

For any other drawing object besides a command button—whose sole purpose in life is to run a macro, which is why it automatically pops up the Assign

Macro dialog—you have to manually invoke the Assign Macro dialog once you've created it. Here are the steps for assigning a macro to a text box.

1. Start out with a worksheet active.

2. Activate the Drawing toolbar if it's hidden.

Text Box button

3. Click on the Text Box button, then drag the drawing cursor to form the shape and size box you want.

4. Type in text and format the box however you like (we prefer the classic Post-it™ yellow, but you be the judge and jury). With the box in the selected-for-editing state, select Tools / Assign Macro / pick the lucky macro / OK.

5. Un-select the box. Henceforth, if you pass the mouse cursor over it you'll see the Pointing Index Finger™; if you click on the box, the macro ignites like Fourth of July fireworks. (Note that if you're using the Drawing Selection button to select objects, *and it's depressed,* you must click it off or you'll never see the Pointing Index Finger™.)

One last variation on the theme. You can assign macros to toolbar buttons. This works the same way whether you're adding a button to an existing toolbar (could be a ship-with toolbar or a custom toolbar you created previously) or creating a toolbar for the first time. In the following example you'll assign `sHelloDownThere` to a new button on the Standard toolbar.

1. View / Toolbars / select Standard if it isn't already selected / Customize / select Custom from the Categories list box (it's at the very bottom of the list) / pick a button face / drag-and-drop it to the Standard toolbar / pick a macro from the Assign Macro dialog that pops up here / OK / Close.

That's it for toolbar buttons and macro assignments. But that's not it for Assign Macro. The mystery is, how in tarnation do you edit or delete an object that's been assigned to a macro since whenever you try to click on it, the click causes the macro to run instead of placing the object into the selected-for-editing state? Good question, pilgrim. Here's the deal. Point at the object then *right-click instead of left-click.* You'll see the popup menu and the bottom command is just what Dr. Gooey ordered—Assign Macro. (See Figure 5.14.) Delete the macro name from the Macro Name/Reference text box (one push on the Delete key will do nicely), then click OK.

A quick way to delete all the objects on a particular sheet is Edit / Go To / Special / Objects / OK / all the current sheet's objects are now selected / press the Delete key. Au revoir en masse. Fair warning—*when we say all, we mean all the objects,* even the ones you can't see in the current window display. So use this method with the appropriate degree of reverence (or abandon).

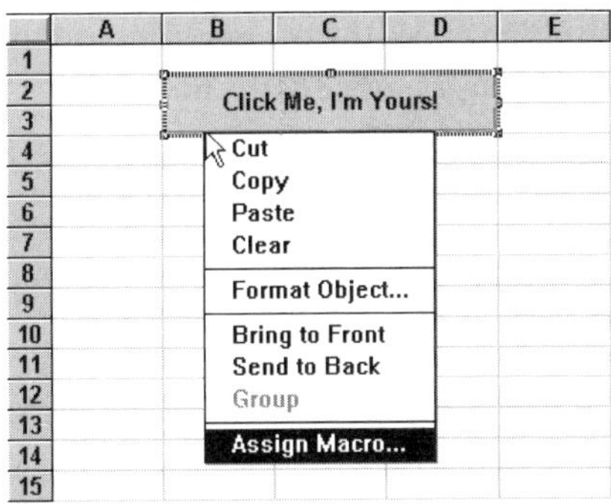

Figure 5.14 Right-click to the Rescue

Macro1 Calling Macro2, Come in Please, Over

At the risk of stating the obvious (we reckon that not taking that risk is how so many *User's Guides* go wrong), macros can certainly call each other. In point of fact, this is typically the case where a particular command button object on a worksheet might be connected to a `sFindOutWhatUserWants` subroutine that, guess what, finds out what the user wants (a dialog box or some other form of user interaction) then calls a particular procedure out of several possible procedures depending on the user's choice.

The caller and the callee

Events Can Invoke Macros

There are several categories of events that can trigger macros. This term *event* designates some tangible action that occurs in the Windows miasma (for example, the event of a particular workbook opening, a specific worksheet being activated, a dialog box being displayed, a control on a dialog box being clicked, and so on). Those of you familiar with Visual Basic 3.0 will recognize this as the "event-driven" part of "event-driven programming."

So, actually, in the preceding sections you've been dealing with events. Someone clicks on the "Click Me, I'm Yours!" button (the click is the event) and this fires off the assigned macro. The event categories supported by Excel follow.

- Automatic procedures (a.k.a. auto macros) apply to an entire workbook—Auto_Open and Auto_Close

- Automatic procedures customized at the worksheet level—Auto_Open..., Auto_Close..., Auto_Activate..., and Auto_Deactivate...

- OnEvent procedures—OnAction, OnCalculate, OnData, OnEntry, OnSheetActivate, OnSheetDeactivate, and OnWindow properties; OnKey, OnRepeat, OnTime, and OnUndo methods; and the On Error statement (note that "On Error" is a two-word VBA statement unlike the other OnSomething property and method key words that are melded together with no space in between)

ORIENTEERING 101

> One day Alice came to a fork in the road and saw a Cheshire cat in a tree. "Which road do I take?" she asked. His response was a question: "Where do you want to go?" "I don't know," Alice answered. "Then," said the cat, "it doesn't matter."
>
> Lewis Carroll
> *Alice in Wonderland*

At some time or another—like Real Soon Now—when you're controlling Excel via VBA you're going to need to get Excel to tell you what condition it's in. Off the cuff here's a list of intriguing questions for your consideration (yes, we do show you how to answer them one by one in this chapter).

- Are any workbooks open at all? If not, Excel is in a minimalist state called **null menu mode** where "null menu" refers to the primary menu bar that includes only the File and Help commands.

- Is an application (Excel or any other) already running on this computer?

- What kind of resources are available on this computer as of right now?

- If Excel is *not* in null menu mode, then how many workbooks are open?

- Does each workbook have a valid MS-DOS filename? If yes (they all do), then what is the fully qualified filename (path plus 8.3 filename) for each one? If no (not all of them do), then what are the temporary names of these temporary workbooks?

- Which workbook has the focus?

- What sheet is the active sheet within the current workbook; that is, what is the active sheet's position in the Sheets collection and what is the active sheet's name?

- Is the active sheet a worksheet, chart sheet, dialog sheet, module, Excel 4 macro sheet, or Excel 4 international macro sheet?

- List all the current workbook's sheet names in their positional or alphabetical order.

- Are there any hidden workbooks? If so, what are their names?

To successfully navigate around Excel with VBA, you need to become acquainted with Excel's object model and Excel's VBA command set. Together with OLE

Automation, VBA "knows" which property and method combinations are allowed for any particular object (or, as you'll see shortly, collection of objects). That's it. The end. Well, not really, you still have to put VBA statements into a logical context, deal with events that occur inside Excel, and so on. But the object model together with VBA itself give you all the referential (oh, we so love those sixty-four dollar words) firepower you're gonna need to *get things done, dammit*.

So in the following sections we explore frequently encountered objects, methods, and properties, all the while answering the questions raised at the beginning of this section.

Anybody Home?

- Are any workbooks open at all?

The custom function `fblnNullMenuState` returns a Boolean indicating whether or not Excel is in the null menu mode. Throughout this chapter we first provide the procedure code, followed immediately by a small block of code that demonstrates its use.

Excel's null menu mode

```
' ------------------------------------------------------------------
' Purpose:   Indicates whether Excel is in "null menu" state
'            (only File and Help in the active menu bar).
'
' Inputs:    None.
'
' Returns:   Boolean.
'
' Updated:   9/14/94
' ------------------------------------------------------------------
Function fblnNullMenuState() As Boolean
    Dim mnbActive As MenuBar
    Set mnbActive = Application.ActiveMenuBar
    If UCase(mnbActive.Caption) = UCase(NO_DOCS_OPEN) Then
        fblnNullMenuState = True
    Else
        fblnNullMenuState = False
    End If
End Function


' ------------------------------------------------------------------
' demo procedure
' ------------------------------------------------------------------
Sub sAnybodyHome()
    If fblnNullMenuState Then
        MsgBox "Excel is in null menu mode."
```

```
    Else
        MsgBox "Excel is not in null menu mode."
    End If
End Sub
```

This function demonstrates the following concepts.

- The `Dim mnbActive As MenuBar` statement is an example of declaring a variable as a specific type of OLE Automation object, in this case, as a MenuBar object.

- The `Set` statement assigns the `mnbActive` variable to point (or refer) to the active menu bar, represented by the expression `Application.ActiveMenuBar`.

- The user-defined constant `NO_DOCS_OPEN` has been declared and initialized globally outside this function procedure. By convention, user-defined constant names are in all capitals. The statement that provides this reads

```
Global Const NO_DOCS_OPEN = "No documents open"
```

- The `Global` key word, when used as a prefix to the `Const` statement, authorizes any procedure in any module in the current workbook (project) to use this constant. See Table 5.1 for a list of the globally declared constants and variables used in this chapter.

- `True` and `False` are two very popular restricted key words (where restricted means you cannot use them as names for your own variables or procedures). `True` represents the value -1 and `False` represents the value 0.

- The `If...Then...Else` statement (sometimes referred to as a construct) provides the switching logic by which different blocks of code are run depending on the evaluation of conditions.

- The object expression syntax is demonstrated twice in the function—`Application.ActiveMenuBar` and `mnbActive.Caption`.

- We use a structured procedure description block above each procedure.

- The trick, if it amounts to that, in writing this function was to first write a throw-away procedure that displayed `ActiveMenuBar.Caption` via a message box when Excel was in the null menu mode. This test message box revealed the "No documents open" string, which became the global constant `NO_DOCS_OPEN`.

Table 5.1 lists the global declarations you need for the code in this chapter to run properly. Our convention would be to create a separate module just for global constants and variables, name it modGlobals (remember, this is just a convention and you could name this module AnythingUnderTheSun if you wanted to), and key in each statement shown in Table 5.1.

Table 5.1 Global Declarations Used in Chapter 5

Global Constant and Variable Declarations

```
Global Const COLON = ":"
Global Const NO_DOCS_OPEN = "No documents open"
Global Const WORD6_MODULE_NAME = "WINWORD.EXE"
Global hModule As Integer
Global i As Integer
Global j As Integer
Global strModuleName As String
```

Is the Application Already Running?

- Is an application (Excel or any other) already running on this computer?

To determine if a particular application is running or not, no custom function is required. You can call the Windows API function GetModuleHandle which returns zero if the application is not running, and a non-zero value if it is running. GetModuleHandle's one argument is the application's module name. We provide a common list of these names in Table 5.2. You'll find the exact Windows API declaration statements appropriate for any dialect of Visual Basic in the help file `WIN31API.HLP` that ships with Visual Basic 3.0. Just copy-and-paste 'em!

Table 5.2 Office Applications' Module Names

Application	Module Name
Access 2	MSACCESS or MSACCESS.EXE
Excel 5	EXCEL or EXCEL.EXE
PowerPoint 4	POWERPNT.DLL only
Project 4	WINPROJ.EXE only
Word 6	WINWORD or WINWORD.EXE

```
Declare Function GetModuleHandle Lib "KERNEL" (ByVal lpModuleName As
String) As Integer

' put the following code into any procedure as needed
If GetModuleHandle(strModuleName) = 0 Then
    ' the app is *not* running
Else
    ' the app *is* running
End If
```

Resources to Boot?

- What kind of resources are available on this computer as of right now?

Generally, when you are concerned with system resources you are talking about the free space in either the USER or the GDI heap. Under Windows 3.x it boils down to the more you have the better, and the less you have the closer to a crash you are. The function here uses the Windows API function GetFreeSystemResources, which returns the available resources for either GDI or USER depending on what value you pass the function.

Here's an example of how you might use this API function.

```
Declare Function GetFreeSystemResources Lib "USER" (ByVal fuSysResource
As Integer) As Integer


' ------------------------------------------------------------------
' Purpose:   Provides USER and GDI free resource values.
'            GetFreeSystemResources takes a 1 to return GDI,
'            2 to return USER.
'
' Inputs:    None.
'
' Returns:   N/A.
'
' Updated:   10/24/94
' ------------------------------------------------------------------
Sub sResourcesToBoot()
    Dim intHowMuch As Integer
    Dim strTemp As String
    ' 1 for GDI
    intHowMuch = GetFreeSystemResources(1)
    strTemp = "GDI free resources are" & _
        Str(intHowMuch) & "%"
    strTemp = strTemp & Chr(13) & Chr(10)
    ' 2 for USER
    intHowMuch = GetFreeSystemResources(2)
    strTemp = strTemp & "USER free resources are" & _
        Str(intHowMuch) & "%"
    MsgBox strTemp
End Sub
```

How Many Little Piggies?

- If Excel is *not* in null menu mode, then how many workbooks are open?

Don't forget to count the workbooks in hidden windows. When you first count the number of workbooks with the expression `Workbooks.Count`, you might be surprised! If you have your `PERSONAL.XLS` hidden, as is the default, then even if only one workbook is visible in your

Window list, the expression returns 2. Rightly so! There's one hidden workbook and one unhidden workbook, for a total of two workbooks!

So, Little Fella, What's Your Name?

- Does each workbook have a valid MS-DOS filename? If they all do, then what is the fully qualified filename (path plus 8.3 filename) for each one? If no (not all of them do), then what are the temporary names of these temporary workbooks?

The custom function `fvntWorkbookNames` builds a list of the full names of all the currently open, unique workbook names. The list includes the names of hidden and unhidden workbooks. This function returns a Variant, which makes for an easy call to the function (you don't have to pass an explicit string array variable as an argument to the function). The disadvantage is that you can't refer to the Variant function itself inside the function body *as an array*. If you do, you get the error 450 "Wrong number of arguments."

If you try to sneak around this by dropping the element identifier—change the statement to `fvntWorkbookNames = wrkObject.FullName`—then you're assigning a simple, non-array string to the Variant, at which point it takes on that data type (String), which leaves you with code that iteratively overwrites `fvntWorkbookNames` with the current workbook name. So you have to build the list in a local holding string array, which is then assigned to the Variant in a single statement (this assignment statement is bolded in the example for emphasis).

```
' ------------------------------------------------------------------
' Purpose:   Provide an array of the full names (path plus 8.3 name)
'            of all open (hidden and unhidden) workbooks.
'
' Inputs:    None.
'
' Returns:   Variant.
'
' Updated:   9/18/94
' ------------------------------------------------------------------
Function fvntWorkbookNames() As Variant
    ' ----- Declarations
    Dim i As Integer
    Dim strTemp() As String
    Dim wrk As Workbook
    ' ----- Main body
    If Workbooks.Count <> 0 Then
        ReDim strTemp(Workbooks.Count - 1)
        i = 0
        For Each wrk In Workbooks
            strTemp(i) = wrk.FullName
```

```
                    i = i + 1
            Next wrk
        Else
            ' handle case where count is 0 (don't allow ReDim to -1)
            ReDim strTemp(0)
        End If
        fvntWorkbookNames = strTemp()
End Function


'   ------------------------------------------------------------------
'  demo procedure
'   ------------------------------------------------------------------
Sub sWhatsYourName()
    Dim intUBound As Integer
    Dim vntTemp As Variant
    vntTemp = fvntWorkbookNames
    intUBound = UBound(vntTemp)
    For i = 0 To intUBound
        MsgBox vntTemp(i)
    Next i
End Sub
```

In the case of zero workbooks, this function explicitly ReDims the string array
to 0, which results in a single empty string being stored in the array's 0th element.
An alternative would be to not initialize `fvntWorkbookNames` at all in the case
of zero workbooks. Then the caller would have to be prepared to deal with a
returned variable that is uninitialized. The `VarType()` built-in function returns 0
for an uninitialized variable. Using our approach the caller gets back a single-
element empty string array, which is decidedly different from the alternate of
getting back an uninitialized variable (less work for the caller, anyway).

This function demonstrates the following concepts.

- The `For Each…Next` statement (construct) allows you to systematically apply
  the statements inside the For and Next markers to each object in a collection.
  In this case, the statements apply to each Workbook in the Workbooks collection.

- How to assign an array to a Variant (as described above).

- How to use `ReDim` to dynamically redimension an array from some former
  dimension to a new one. This reduces overhead by initializing an array as
  compactly as possible and not allocating memory until needed.

- `Workbooks.Count` and `wrk.FullName` are examples of object expressions,
  with Workbooks serving as another collection example.

- How to synchronize a 0-based array's indices to a 1-based collection.

All Excel collections are 1-based, meaning that the index of the first object in the collection is 1. Many Basic and C programmers are accustomed to an indexing scheme called 0-based, where the index of the first object in the collection is 0. What to do about this quandary? Well, we weighed the pros and cons and recommend that you stick to 0-based array indexing in VBA primarily because (1) there's a large body of code floating around out there that's already 0-based and (2) the developers of VBA elected to make 0-based the default (see the help topic on `Option Base`).

So, synchronizing a 0-based array's indices to a 1-based collection involves (a) dimensioning the target array's upper bound to the absolute count minus one, (b) initializing the index counter i to 0 outside the loop, (c) assigning each array element i the value of the i + 1 item in the collection (the collection side of the operation is handled for you by the For Each...Next statement), and (d) incrementing the index counter by one inside the loop.

A Variant Fruit Salad

The Variant data type is convenient and powerful. However, it can be confusing at first because it's so incredibly flexible. Not only can a Variant variable contain any type of data, including arrays—*it can store individual elements each of which is a different type!* Perhaps some code is worth the proverbial thousand words. But be forewarned—using Variants too liberally can result in "code bloat" since Variants use far more storage than other data types.

```
Sub sVariantFruitSalad()
    ' ----- Declarations
    Dim blnTemp As Boolean
    Dim i As Integer
    Dim intTemp As Integer
    Dim strPrompt As String
    Dim strTemp As String
    Dim vntTemp(2) As Variant
    ' ----- Initializations
    intTemp = 99
    strTemp = "Agent Maxwell Smart"
    blnTemp = False
    vntTemp(0) = blnTemp       ' vbBoolean (11)
    vntTemp(1) = intTemp       ' vbInteger (2)
    vntTemp(2) = strTemp       ' vbString (8)
    ' ----- Main body
    For i = 0 To 2
        strPrompt = "Current vntTemp element is " & _
            vntTemp(i)
```

```
        strPrompt = strPrompt & Chr(13) & Chr(10) & _
            "VarType() of current vntTemp element is " & _
            VarType(vntTemp(i))
        MsgBox strPrompt
    Next i
End Sub
```

Hey You, Yeah, You with the Focus

- Which workbook has the focus?

8.3 or fully qualified, it's your choice. Here the real question is, "What is the name of the workbook with the focus (the active workbook), and I want you to give it to me either in its 8.3 format or its full name format." The custom function `fstrActiveWorkbookName()` does just that, by offering an argument to trigger which name format is returned (see the function's source code Inputs remarks). This function assumes the caller has already checked to determine if Excel is in null menu mode. If the active workbook doesn't have a valid filename yet (for example, is in the form "Book1"), then the function returns just that text in either case.

```
' ----------------------------------------------------------------
' Purpose:   Provide the active workbook's 8.3 or full name depending
'            on input.
'
' Inputs:    intPathName
'            =  0 indicates return 8.3 filename
'            <> 0 indicates return full filename (complete with path)
'
' Returns:   String.
'
' Updated:   10/6/94
' ----------------------------------------------------------------
Function fstrActiveWorkbookName(intPathName As Integer) As String
    If intPathName = 0 Then
        fstrActiveWorkbookName = ActiveWorkbook.Name
    Else
        fstrActiveWorkbookName = ActiveWorkbook.FullName
    End If
End Function


' ----------------------------------------------------------------
' demo procedure
' ----------------------------------------------------------------
Sub sHeyYouWithTheFocus()
    MsgBox fstrActiveWorkbookName(0)
    MsgBox fstrActiveWorkbookName(1)
End Sub
```

This function demonstrates the following concepts.

- The use of an argument in a custom function. The value of the `intPathName` argument tells the function how to behave. Are you curious as to why we choose an Integer type instead of a Boolean? After all, in its current form the If branch is binary—can go only one of two ways—so it seems a logical candidate for a Boolean switch. But you want to be able to expand the function later if needed, so a Boolean would be too restrictive. For example, if you want to get back the path minus the 8.3 filename, you'd have to retype the argument from Boolean to Integer anyway since you'd then have three conditions to deal with (0 could represent 8.3 only, 1 for fully qualified, and 2 for path only). Of course, there are some binary situations where you know you'll always be using a Boolean switch, but in this case we vote for a switch typed so that you can have the function jump more than two ways.

- The expressions `ActiveWorkbook.Name` and `ActiveWorkbook.FullName` serve as additional examples of object expressions.

My, You're an Active Little Sheet

- What sheet is the active sheet within the current workbook; that is, what is the active sheet's position in the Sheets collection and what is the active sheet's name?

To find out the active sheet's (unsorted) position in the Sheets collection, use the Index property—`ActiveSheet.Index`. To find out the active sheet's name, use the Name property—`ActiveSheet.Name`.

What Planet Did You Say You're From?

- Is the active sheet a worksheet, chart sheet, dialog sheet, module, Excel 4 macro sheet, or Excel 4 international macro sheet?

The Workbook object has four different "sheet" manifestations. In other words, four different and unique types of sheets that can belong to a workbook (or a Sheets collection).

The taxonomy of Sheets

- Worksheet object—of the "regular" worksheet flavor, Excel 4 macro sheet flavor, or the Excel 4 international macro sheet flavor

- Chart object

- DialogSheet object

- Module object

A discussion of this object taxonomy can be confusing either because of the terminology, the context, or both. For example, when you see or hear the word "chart," does that particular word refer to a Chart object (meaning, a Chart sheet object, as in what you get when you select Insert / Chart / As New Sheet) or an embedded Chart object (as in what you get when you select Insert / Chart / On This Sheet) that in turn belongs to a DrawingObjects collection that in turn lives in a Worksheet object or a DialogSheet object? See what we mean? Well, the solution is to try and be as clear as possible regarding the context of these objects when you're talking or writing about them. Then in your code the `ParentObject.ChildObject` chain typically keeps the context clear.

The custom function `fintActiveSheetType()` imposes our proprietary scheme to help answer the seemingly innocuous question "What kind of sheet is this?" There's no magic in our return code scheme, although we ordered the codes—starting with 1—in the order in which different sheet types appear in the real world. That is, worksheets pop up far more often than modules, so the former get assigned a return code of 1 and the latter get a 6. This function shields you from the headache of the overlapping values for some built-in Type property constants, and the fact that Worksheet and Chart sheets support the Type property but DialogSheet and Module sheets do not.

```
' ---------------------------------------------------------------------
' Purpose:    Positively identify the active sheet's type using a
'             proprietary return code scheme.
'             There's no special significance to these return values
'             other than they appear in order of most frequent
'             occurrence in the "real world."
'
' Inputs:     None.
'
' Returns:    Worksheet sheet:            1
'             embedded chart as window:   1 (NB: it's *embedded* chart)
'             "standard" Chart sheet:     2
'             empty Chart sheet           2
'             DialogSheet sheet           3
'             Excel 4 macro sheet         4
'             Excel 4 macro sheet (intl): 5
'             Module sheet:               6
'             Info window:                7
'             any error condition:        0
'
' Updated:    10/27/94
' ---------------------------------------------------------------------
Function fintActiveSheetType() As Integer
    ' ----- Declarations
    Dim strTypeName As String
```

```
    ' ----- Main body
    On Error GoTo ErrorTrap
    strTypeName = UCase(TypeName(ActiveSheet))
    If strTypeName = "WORKSHEET" Then
        Select Case ActiveSheet.Type
            Case xlWorksheet
                fintActiveSheetType = 1
            Case xlExcel4MacroSheet
                ' Warning: xlExcel4MacroSheet & xlColumn *both* = 3
                fintActiveSheetType = 4
            Case xlExcel4IntlMacroSheet
                ' Warning: xlExcel4IntlMacroSheet & xlLine *both* = 4
                fintActiveSheetType = 5
            Case Else
                ' should never happen
                fintActiveSheetType = 0
        End Select
    ElseIf strTypeName = "DIALOGSHEET" Then
        fintActiveSheetType = 3
    ElseIf strTypeName = "MODULE" Then
        fintActiveSheetType = 6
    Else
        Select Case ActiveSheet.Type
            Case xlArea, xlBar, xlColumn, xlLine, _
                xlPie, xlDoughnut, xlRadar, xlXYScatter, _
                xl3DArea, xl3DBar, xl3DColumn, xl3DLine, _
                xl3DPie, xl3DSurface
                fintActiveSheetType = 2
            Case Else
                ' should never happen
                fintActiveSheetType = 0
        End Select
    End If
    Exit Function
ErrorTrap:
    If Err = 1006 Then
        ' This happens when the active window is an Info window.
        If ActiveWindow.Type = xlInfo Then
            fintActiveSheetType = 7
        Else
            fintActiveSheetType = 0
        End If
    Else
        ' something completely unexpected happened
        fintActiveSheetType = 0
    End If
End Function
```

```
' ----------------------------------------------------------------
' demo procedure
' ----------------------------------------------------------------
Sub sWhatPlanetYouFrom()
    Dim sht As Object
    Dim strTemp As String
    For Each sht In Sheets
        sht.Select
        strTemp = "The sheet " & sht.Name
        strTemp = strTemp & " has a type of" & _
            Str(fintActiveSheetType)
        MsgBox strTemp
    Next sht
End Sub
```

This function demonstrates the following concepts.

- How to trap for errors using the `On Error` statement. In this procedure an error does an immediate branch to the block of code preceded by the label ErrorTrap (you could call the label anything, ErrorTrap is merely a loose convention). Note that the label itself must always be followed by a colon. The error processing code uses the key word `Err` to peek at the value of the error. In this procedure we want to trap for 1000, which technically means a particular object doesn't have a particular property—in this procedure it means that TypeName(ActiveSheet) blows up when it runs against a module. We also trap for 1006, which means that the current window is an Info window (which the error processing code subsequently verifies by comparing Type's value to `xlInfo`). Note the `Exit Function` statement immediately above the error processing code's label. This is important because it prevents the procedure from dropping down into the error processing code when there's not an error. Also, note that the error processing code includes an Else clause just in case an error value other than the expected 1000 or 1006 is encountered. Although this is a low-probability event, it's always best to trap for odd-ball stuff.

- The `Select Case` statement (construct) provides exactly the same sort of branching control as an `If...Then...Else` statement, but in a more readable fashion.

- Various built-in Excel constants are used in this function, like `xlWorksheet`, `xlChart`, `xlInfo`, etc.

My Kingdom for an Ordered Sheet List

- List all the current workbook's sheet names in their positional or alphabetical order.

The custom subroutine `sActiveWorkbookSheetNames()` takes a string array (0-based) you pass it, along with a parameter to indicate whether you want the list of sheet names back in positional (0) or alphabetical order (<>0), and returns the list sorted as you requested. Positional order means their appearance in the Sheets collection (reflected in the user interface inside the popup menu you see when you right-click on the tab bar's scrolling buttons). Note that the returned list commingles sheets of all types.

Also note that in this subroutine's statement `For Each sht In ActiveWorkbook.Sheets`, since any individual object in the collection could be any of four types—Chart, DialogSheet, Module, or Worksheet—you can't declare `Dim sht As Sheets`, you have to use the more generic `Dim sht As Object`. This avoids a run-time 13 "Type mismatch" error.

```
' -------------------------------------------------------------------
' Purpose:   Returns a list of all the active workbook's sheet names,
'            either in positional (collection) order, or sorted
'            alphabetically.
'
' Inputs:    strArray() - array to pack with the names
'            intOrder   - if = 0 then leave in positional order
'                         if <>0 then sort alphabetically
'
' Returns:   N/A.
'
' Updated:   9/21/94
' -------------------------------------------------------------------
Sub sActiveWorkbookSheetNames(strArray() As String, intOrder As
Integer)
    ' ----- Declarations
    Dim i As Integer
    Dim intSheetCount As Integer
    ' sht *must* be declared as a generic Object
    Dim sht As Object
    ' ----- Main body
    intSheetCount = ActiveWorkbook.Sheets.Count
    ReDim strArray(intSheetCount - 1)
    i = 0
    For Each sht In ActiveWorkbook.Sheets
        strArray(i) = sht.Name
        i = i + 1
    Next sht
    If intOrder <> 0 Then
        ' sort in alpha order, else do nothing
        sShellSort strArray()
    End If
End Sub
```

```
' --------------------------------------------------------------------
' Purpose:   Sort a string array. Ported w/ permission from WOPR 2's
'            ShellSort, © 1991-92 Pinecliffe International.
'
'            CRITICAL - Option Compare Text must be set in the current
'            module. This sub will not behave properly if the default
'            Option Compare Binary is used.
'
'            A fast, practical sort routine based on Donald L. Shell's
'            technique (CACM 2, July 1959, pp 30-32), as adapted by
'            Don Knuth ("The Art of Computer Programming, Vol 3,
'            Sorting and Searching", Addison-Wesley, 1975, pp 84-87);
'            see Knuth for a detailed description.
'
' Inputs:    strArray() - target string array (ASSUMED TO BE 0-BASED)
'
' Returns:   N/A
'
' Updated:   10/27/94
' --------------------------------------------------------------------
Sub sShellSort(strArray() As String)
    Dim i As Integer
    Dim j As Integer
    Dim n As Integer
    Dim s As Integer
    Dim strKey As String
    n = UBound(strArray)
    s = n
    While s > 1
        s = Int(s / 2)
        For j = s + 1 To n + 1
            i = j - s
            strKey = strArray(j - 1)
ShellNext:
            If strKey >= strArray(i - 1) Then GoTo SortNext
            strArray(i + s - 1) = strArray(i - 1)
            i = i - s
            If i > 0 Then GoTo ShellNext
SortNext:
            strArray(i + s - 1) = strKey
        Next
    Wend
End Sub


' --------------------------------------------------------------------
' demo procedure
' --------------------------------------------------------------------
Sub sMyKingdom()
    Dim strArray() As String
```

```
    sActiveWorkbookSheetNames strArray(), 1
    For i = 0 To UBound(strArray)
        MsgBox strArray(i)
    Next i
End Sub
```

This subroutine demonstrates the following concepts.

- Passing an array as an argument. Here `strArray()` is passed as the first of the procedure's two arguments. You should note that the argument's name is shown with trailing empty parentheses. Be careful because if you accidentally omit the trailing parentheses when you declare the subroutine, it will expect to see a non-array String variable instead of an array String variable and the subroutine won't work properly.

- The generic Object type is used for the variable `sht` because the Sheets collection may contain different types of sheets (Worksheet, Chart, Module, etc.). To avoid run-time errors, use the more abstract (higher level) Object variable type.

- This custom subroutine calls another custom subroutine in the statement `sShellSort strArray()`. The subroutine `sShellSort` has one argument, a string array, that is manipulated inside the subroutine so that all its elements are sorted in ascending alphabetical order (more on this shortly). Note that `fvntWorkbookNames` and `sShellSort` are similar in that they both provide the caller with an array of values. In `fvntWorkbookNames` the function itself returns a Variant array to the caller, whereas in `sShellSort` the subroutine manipulates an array passed to it as an argument. In both cases the caller ends up with an array as per its specifications. Recall that the Variant data type uses much more memory than other data types. On the other hand, the convenience of Variants is compelling. You'll have to decide which approach to use based on your project's specific requirements.

- To show you that we're fickle and don't always follow our own sage advice, you've probably already noticed that `sActiveWorkbookSheetNames()` violates our suggested naming conventions. (You did notice, didn't you?) Where the heck is this variable called `i` coming from? Some habits die real hard. `i` has been a commonly used counter variable name since before Hector was a pup writing FORTRAN, so we've stuck with it instead of something more, uhm, conventional like `intCount`. Like the global constants discussed earlier, we globally declared `i` like this, `Global i As Integer`, where `Global` replaces `Dim` to indicate a globally scoped variable.

Peek-a-boo

- Are there any hidden workbooks? If so, what are their names?

It's really the Window that's hidden, with a Workbook in the Window.

This particular assignment is a classic Excel brain-teaser. You can't just stand there and point to a Workbook object and ask it if it's hidden (coy little devils). In a way that's not surprising, is it? Because when you hide (or unhide) a workbook you select Window / Hide! That's right. It's a Window object, not a Workbook object, that is hidden! And of course a single workbook can be open in more than one window. Oh boy. So the challenge is to gather up a list of all the hidden window names, toss out the duplicates—count `FINDME.XLS:1` and `FINDME.XLS:2` as a single hidden workbook—then count up how many names are left when the dust settles. See how it's done in the custom function `fintWorkbookCountHidden()`. As an added feature, the function returns a passed array modified to include the hidden workbook names.

To find out how many open workbooks are *not* hidden, simply do the algebra using the `fintWordbookCount` function you've already built and the new `fintWorkbookCountHidden()` function.

```
fintWorkbookCount - fintWorkbookCountHidden()
```

This function uses ReDim's Preserve key word to cause the array's current contents to be preserved from its lower bound up to a new upper bound. This way, the array is initially dimensioned to be capable of storing the maximum possible number of hidden workbook names. When you end up with some number less than the maximum (say, because a couple of them were in ":2" type windows), then you strip out all dangling, empty array elements in one fell swoop with the Preserve key word.

```
' --------------------------------------------------------------------
' Purpose:   Count the number of open hidden workbooks (not necessarily
'            the same as the number of hidden windows).
'
' Inputs:    strHiddenWorkbookNames() - returns packed with any hidden
'            workbook names
'
' Returns:   Integer.
'
' Updated:   10/24/94
' --------------------------------------------------------------------
Function fintWorkbookCountHidden(strHiddenWorkbookNames() As String) As
Integer
    ' ----- Declarations
    Dim i As Integer
    Dim intPosition As Integer
```

```
    Dim wnd As Window
    ' ----- Main body
    i = 0
    ' this loop tells us if there any hidden windows at all
    For Each wnd In Windows
        If Not wnd.Visible Then
            i = i + 1
        End If
    Next wnd
    ' now deal with the hidden names if there are any
    If i <> 0 Then
        ' this is the *max* possible UBound
        ReDim strHiddenWorkbookNames(i - 1)
        j = 0
        ' stuff the array with only the "8.3" & "8.3:1"
        '   format hidden names,
        '   e.g., keep "UNIQUE.XLS" & "FINDME.XLS:1" but
        '   skip "FINDME.XLS:2"
        For Each wnd In Windows
            If Not wnd.Visible Then
                intPosition = InStr(wnd.Caption, COLON)
                If intPosition = 0 Then
                    ' it looks like this "FINDME.XLS" (no ":n" suffix)
                    strHiddenWorkbookNames(j) = wnd.Caption
                    j - j + 1
                ElseIf Right(wnd.Caption, 2) = ":1" Then
                    ' it looks like this "FINDME.XLS:1"
                    strHiddenWorkbookNames(j) = Left(wnd.Caption, _
                        Len(wnd.Caption) - 2)
                    j = j + 1
                End If
            End If
        Next wnd
        ' excise any dangling unassigned elements
        ReDim Preserve strHiddenWorkbookNames(j - 1)
        fintWorkbookCountHidden = j
    Else
        ' disallow redim to -1
        ReDim strHiddenWorkbookNames(0)
        fintWorkbookCountHidden = 0
    End If
End Function


' --------------------------------------------------------------------
' demo procedure
' --------------------------------------------------------------------
Sub sPeekABoo()
    Dim intCountHidden As Integer
    Dim strArray() As String
```

```
    Dim strPrompt As String
    intCountHidden = fintWorkbookCountHidden(strArray())
    strPrompt = "fintWorkbookCountHidden() returns " & _
        LTrim(Str(intCountHidden))
    MsgBox strPrompt
    For i = 0 To UBound(strArray)
        MsgBox strArray(i)
    Next i
End Sub
```

This function demonstrates the following concepts.

- Various string-manipulation functions like `InStr()`, `Right()`, `Left()`, and `Len()` that we encourage you to explore on your own.

- The `ReDim` statement's `Preserve` key word, explained earlier in this section.

HIP HIP ARRAY!

> I have convincing proof that I speak the truth: my poverty.
>
> Plato

Three cheers for the indefatigable array! In this section we address the most common questions asked by folks new to this wonderful creature.

- Can an array be passed as a by value argument?

  No. In VBA you must pass an array variable by reference.

- Can a single element of an array be passed as a by value argument?

  Yes.

- Can a function return an array data type that's not a Variant?

  No. It simply is not possible in VBA. To quote the *VBA User's Guide,* "You can return an array [from a user-defined function] only if you declare the data type of the return value as Variant." So it is possible to construct a function that returns a Variant data type which itself can *contain* an array. Note that the caller uses a Variant to receive the return value from the function `fvntArray()`, *that value being an array of strings.* Further proof comes by noting that once the function's return value has been assigned to `vntTemp`, `VarType(vntTemp)` returns 8200, which represents vbArray (8192) plus vbString (8). (Un-remark the MsgBox statement in `sTest_fvntArray` to see this on your screen.)

```
Function fvntArray() As Variant
    Dim strArray(3) As String
    strArray(0) = "Underground Guide to Excel"
```

```
    strArray(1) = "Underground Guide to Office"
    strArray(2) = "Underground Guide to Unix"
    strArray(3) = "Underground Guide to Word"
    fvntArray = strArray()
End Function


Sub sTest_fvntArray()
    Dim i As Integer
    Dim vntTemp As Variant
    vntTemp = fvntArray()
    ' MsgBox "VarType(vntTemp) is " & VarType(vntTemp)
    For i = LBound(vntTemp) To UBound(vntTemp)
        MsgBox vntTemp(i)
    Next i
End Sub
```

Note that a function like `fvntArray()` doesn't have to internally use an array of Strings. It could also manipulate an array of Variants, or an array of other primary data types—Boolean, Integer, Long, Single, Double, Currency, Date, and String. Like so.

```
Function fvntArray() As Variant
    Dim vntArray(3) As Variant
    vntArray(0) = "Underground Guide to Excel"
    vntArray(1) = "Underground Guide to Office"
    vntArray(2) = "Underground Guide to Unix"
    vntArray(3) = "Underground Guide to Word"
    fvntArray = vntArray()
End Function
```

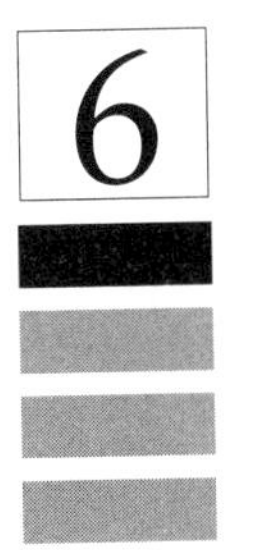

Visual Basic for Applications— Shake It All About

A man begins cutting his wisdom teeth the first time he bites off more than he can chew.

Herb Caen

In Chapter 5 we dealt with the mechanical aspects of VBA programming—stuff like constructing functions and subroutines, data typing, working with arrays, and such. In Chapter 6 we'll focus more on questions like "Hmmm, what's this gizmo here?" during which time we'll look at how to get at various components inside Excel itself. A mental downshift as it were—first you practice some orienteering to find the dig site, then you get down to the nitty gritty of sifting through the soil to see what treasures lie buried beneath.

Hmmm, what's this gizmo here?

THIS 'N THAT

All too many consultants, when asked "What is two and two?" respond, "What did you have in mind?"

Norman R. Augustine
American author and chairman, Martin Marietta Corporation

Assembled in this section you'll find a buffet of helpful VBA tidbits. And there'll be opportunities aplenty for their use in this chapter. Yes indeedy.

Cool Categorical Keywords by Task

... but I have a key that'll open any lock of this kind.

"Dynamite" Fletcher
The Green Hornet

As you delve deeper into VBA, you'll develop your own style of getting information quickly on a specific issue, whether with the Object Browser, on-line help, or even printed materials. Here's one helpful hint to consider adding to your own navigational tool kit.

The on-line help topic "Keywords by Task" provides a clear, concise categorical breakdown of VBA. Each category is handily set up as a jump topic. See Figure 6.1. To get to this topic from the Visual Basic Reference help file, select Search / type in "keywords" / Show Topics / select Keywords by Task / Goto.

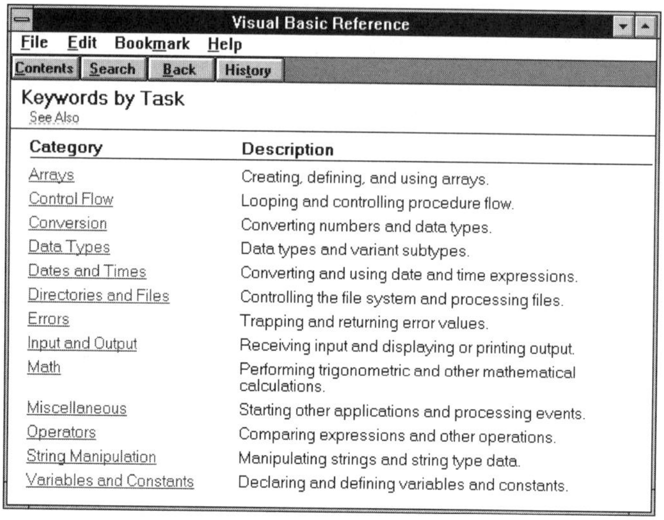

Figure 6.1 A Categorically Cool Listing

For an example of the convenient arrangement of the key words by action, once inside the topic "Keywords by Task" click Arrays. See Figure 6.2.

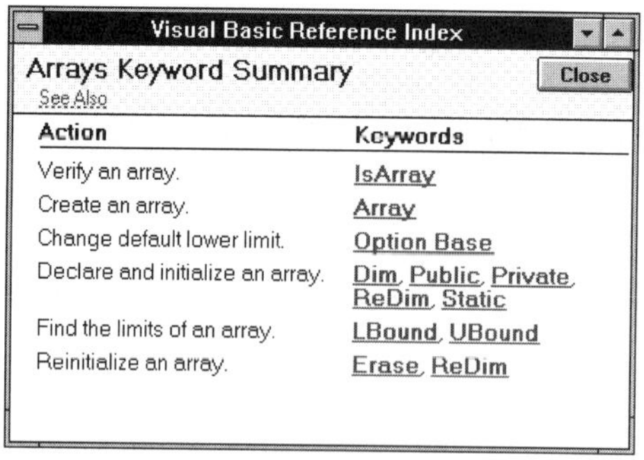

Figure 6.2 Ready for Action with Array Key Words

Also keep in mind that almost every function, method, property, and statement help topic contains an Example jump that pops up the Visual Basic Reference Example window. This window contains sample code for the key word of interest, and you can quickly copy that code to the clipboard for easy pasting into your own procedure. This is mind-bogglingly useful and should not be overlooked.

Active...Gizmos

> You go Uruguay and I'll go mine.
>
> Groucho Marx
> *Animal Crackers,* 1930

Excel VBA includes nine property key words with a prefix of "Active" that *return the currently active object*. That's right, these properties point to other objects. For example, the ActiveCell property "returns the active cell of the active window [where the] active cell is a Range object." These special and oft-used properties are listed below in alphabetical order. You would do well to study each of these in depth. (Project VBA has five such Active property key words.)

- ActiveCell
- ActiveChart
- ActiveDialog
- ActiveMenuBar
- ActivePane
- ActivePrinter
- ActiveSheet
- ActiveWindow
- ActiveWorkbook

You will ofttimes find yourself having to programmatically ponder "What's happening?", "What's currently selected?", "Where's that active cell?", "Is a range highlighted?", and so on. With these "Active..." property key words, you can answer these perplexities, and fast.

Collection Scrying

> The rule on staying alive as a forecaster is to give 'em a number or give 'em a date, but never give 'em both at once.
>
> Jane Bryant Quinn

There are two quick ways to call up a jump list of all collections. One is the Item Method help topic (see Figure 6.3) and the other is the Add Method help topic (see Figure 6.4). The former lists all collections as jump topics. The latter lists what happens when the Add method is applied to each collection, also with jump topics.

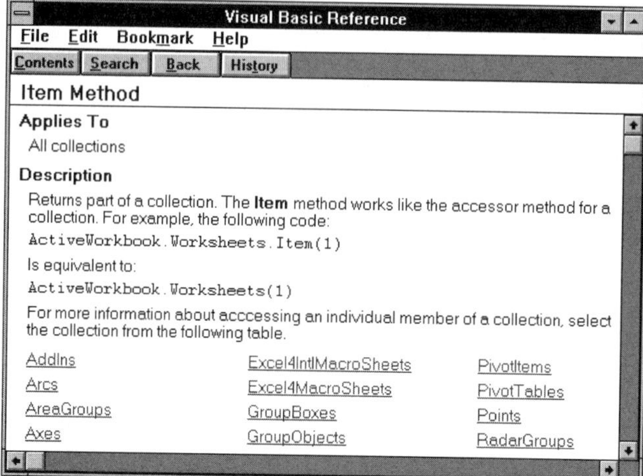

Figure 6.3 Item Method Help Topic—A Collection Help Trick

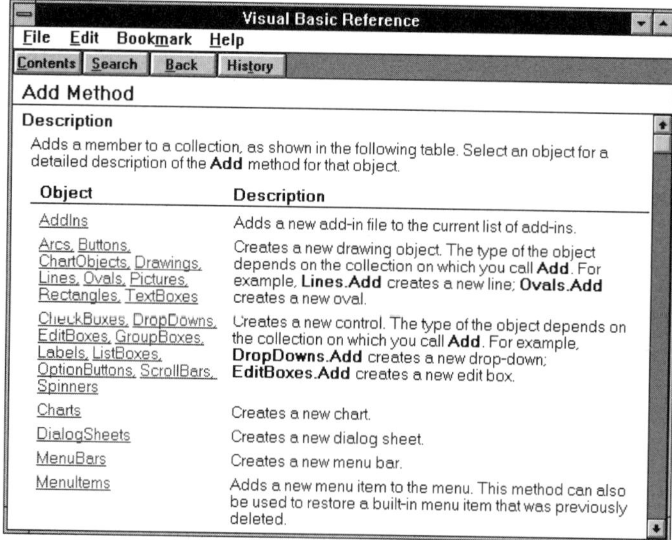

Figure 6.4 Add Method Help Topic—Another Collection Help Trick

To get to the Item Method help topic, you can search on Item Method / Show Topics / Go To or you can type "item" in a module sheet, leave the cursor at the end of the line, and hit the F1 key. For the Add Method, you can search for "Add Method" or just type "add" in a module sheet and hit F1.

Edit Find and Edit Replace

> You will see something new.
> Two things. And I call them
> Thing One and Thing Two.
>
> Dr. Seuss
> *The Cat in the Hat*, 1957

Muscle memory mania! Pilgrim, you may as well get accustomed to these two commands (if you aren't already) because you'll put them to good use, and often. Kudos for the module-specialized Edit Find (CTRL + F) and its side-kick Edit Replace (CTRL + H).

Select some text in a module, select Edit / Find or Edit / Replace, and the selected text is automatically placed in the Find What edit box. The module-specialized versions of these dialogs look for the target text in one of four ways: Procedure, Module, All Modules, or Selected Text. See Figure 6.5 for an example.

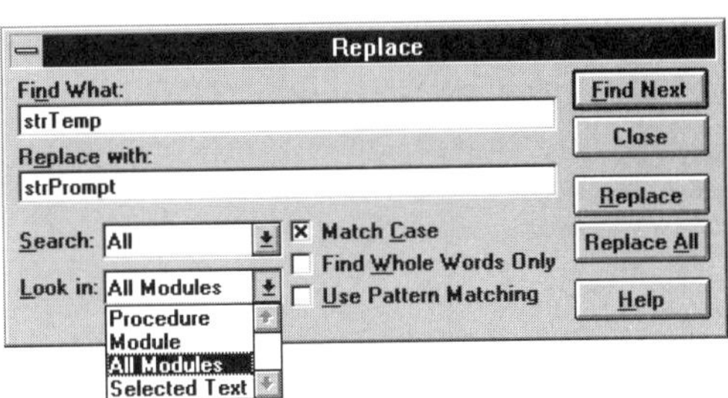

Figure 6.5 Doing that Edit Find and Replace Thing

Given the wide-open and often labyrinthine structure of even smallish VBA projects—"Hmmm, now doggone it, uhm, lessee, er, in what module and in which procedure in this project right over here, ahem, did I put that variable vntHideNSeek?"—you'll be thankful to have a robust text search engine.

Our Fave Range Methods and Properties

I'm not bald, I'm a person of scalp.

Unknown

Since you'll be putting the Range object's myriad methods and profuse properties to use over and over again, here's a list of our favorites.

Crucial Range object *methods*:

- Activate (see also Select)
- Address
- Cells
- Characters
- Columns
- Item
- Range
- Rows
- Select (see also Activate)
- Show

Crucial Range object *properties*:

- Column
- CurrentRegion
- Formula
- FormulaR1C1
- HasFormula
- Name
- Row
- Text
- Value

SOME MORE QUESTIONS

Where is everybody?
(Replying to the question, "What was it the last man on earth said?")

Carl Sandburg

Let's pose some more questions, then answer them in the ensuing sections.

- What is the current *content* of a particular, single cell? Note that this particular, single cell doesn't have to be the active cell.

- What is the current *result* of a particular, single cell? Note that this particular, single cell doesn't have to be the active cell.

- What is the current selection's address either in A1 or R1C1 notation, or both?

- What is a particular named range's address either in A1 or R1C1 notation, or both? This is different from the preceding question. In this case you (the caller) provide a range name as the key, and in the previous case you provide a range address as the key. Note that this particular named range doesn't have to be currently selected.

- Activate and/or select a particular sheet. Activate and/or select a range (single cell or multi-cell) via both address notation and a range name.

- Place some information into a particular range. Information here refers to the classic spreadsheet hat trick—a label, a number, or a formula that results in a label or a number.

Genie in a Bottle

> All the power of the universe, in a tiny little living space.
>
> The Genie
> *Aladdin,* 1992

- What is the current *content* of a particular, single cell?

The objective here is to snoop around inside a given cell and see what's inside. We want to examine its contents (appearance in the formula bar), not its result (appearance on the sheet). You, the caller, must provide the cell's address either in A1 or R1C1 notation. Let's use the trusty ol' cell A1 for this exercise, and for simplicity's sake, impose the restrictions that the cell address must be in A1 notation and that we're dealing with a standard Sheet1 in a standard workbook.

The first question for the genie is—to activate or not to activate. Meaning, do you need to explicitly apply the `Activate` method to Sheet1 in order to reveal A1's innards? The answer is, of course, yes and no.

```
MsgBox Range("A1").Formula
```

If you run this code (inside a subroutine procedure, natch) with the focus on the module itself, you'll get an immediate "Run-time error '1004': Range method of Application class failed" which translates as ... the object reference wasn't detailed enough, so VBA tacked the default object qualifier Application onto the short-hand object expression, ended up with `Application.Range("A1").Formula`, which failed because Range is an object that belongs to a sheet object of some sort, not the Application object. So one solution is to activate a sheet before examining a short-hand Range object, like this.

```
' technique #1
Sheets("Sheet1").Activate
MsgBox Range("A1").Formula
```

If you provide a legitimate object qualifier, as shown next in technique #2 with `Sheets("Sheet1")`, then you can run this code with the focus anywhere in the active workbook—in a module, another sheet, a chart sheet, and so on—and get a meaningful answer. Technique #2 does not activate the sheet so there is no focus change at all. Very neat.

```
' technique #2
MsgBox Sheets("Sheet1").Range("A1").Formula
```

Alternately, you could set an object variable to point to the entire object expression. In the following code, `objRange` points to the cell represented by `Sheets("Sheet1").Range("A1")` thereby making the Formula property call short and sweet—`objRange.Formula`. The advantages here are (1) brevity (a very short object expression) and (2) the ability to pass the variable `objRange` as an argument. Keep in mind that when you use the Range method in this way (referred to as "Syntax 1" in the help topic), the address must be either in the form of A1 notation or a range name.

```
' technique #3
Dim objRange As Range
Set objRange = Sheets("Sheet1").Range("A1")
MsgBox objRange.Formula
```

Table 6.1 shows the differences in return values between the three Range properties Formula, Text, and Value.

Table 6.2 takes the material in Table 6.1 one step further by providing examples of actual cell contents and each property's return values. Assumptions in Table 6.2's results are as follows: cell A4 contains the number (constant) 999; the cell containing the number 7000.545 is formatted with the Currency format code $#,##0.00_);($#,##0.00); a caret (^) represents a literal space character where it might be unclear that it's there; and we only explore a single-cell Range object here (for information on multi-cell Range objects or cells containing array formulas, see the *User's Guide* for

Table 6.1 The Return Values of Formula, Text, and Value Properties of the Range Object Depend on the Range's Contents

	Contents is Formula	Contents is Number	Contents is Text	Contents is Blank
Formula Property	formula as a string (formatting NMF)	number as an unformatted string	text as an unformatted string	empty string
Text Property	formula result as a string (formatting NMF)	number as a string *including format-related characters*	text as an unformatted string	empty string
Value Property	formula result in the appropriate data type	number as a number	text as an unformatted string	test via `IsEmpty()`

Table 6.2 Examples of Exactly What the Formula, Text, and Value Properties Return

	Contents is Formula	Contents is Number	Contents is Text	Contents is Blank
Contents	="Total "&A4	7000.545	SALES REVENUE	
Formula Property	="Total "&A4	7000.545	SALES REVENUE	empty string
Text Property	Total 999	$7,000.55^	SALES REVENUE	empty string
Value Property	Total 999	7000.545	SALES REVENUE	depends on assignee's data type

more information). Note that `VarType()` reports the following about what the Value property returns—the formula's type is String (8), the number's type is Currency (6), the text's type is String (8), and the blank cell's type is Empty (0). If you change the formula to =98/13, then its Value's type would be Double (5), so you can see that *the type returned by a formula's Value property is entirely dependent on that formula's result*. Also, if you change the number in this example to a non-currency formatting, the type changes accordingly. This is as it should be.

The custom function `fstrGetCellContents()` gives the caller the option of passing either a valid A1-style cell address (which includes a valid range name) or a variable that represents a cell object. When using an A1-style cell address, *the caller has the responsibility of guaranteeing that the A1-style cell address, if it's not a range name, include the target worksheet's sheet name and a bang prefix*. For example, Sheet1!H13 is correct but the function will fail on an address of H13 if the active sheet isn't a worksheet sheet. In no case does the parent worksheet need to be active.

```
' ------------------------------------------------------------------
' Purpose:   Provide a cell's contents in string (viewable) format.
'
' Inputs:    vntRange - either a vbl reference to a cell or just a
'            plain A1-style cell address. Note that in the case of
'            something like Sheets("Sheet1").Range("H3"), the Range
'            method's Syntax 1 dictates that the address must be in A1
'            notation. If vntRange is just a plain A1-style cell
'            address, the function assumes caller passes the address
'            in the format sheet_name!A1_address, i.e., the sheet's
'            name and the bang are required.
'
' Returns:   String.
'
' Updated:   11/17/94
' ------------------------------------------------------------------
Function fstrGetCellContents(vntRange As Variant) As String
    If IsObject(vntRange) Then
        ' vntRange is an object
        fstrGetCellContents = vntRange.Formula
    Else
        ' vntRange is a plain A1-style cell address
        ' fstrGetCellContents = ActiveSheet.Range(vntRange).Formula
        fstrGetCellContents = Range(vntRange).Formula
    End If
End Function


' ------------------------------------------------------------------
' demo procedure
' ------------------------------------------------------------------
Sub sGenieInABottle()
    Dim objRange As Range
    Dim strA1Address As String
    strA1Address = "Sheet1!H13"
    Set objRange = Sheets("Sheet1").Range("H13")
    MsgBox "Passing objRange returns " & _
        fstrGetCellContents(objRange)
    MsgBox "Passing an A1 notation address returns " & _
        fstrGetCellContents(strA1Address)
End Sub
```

This function demonstrates the following concepts.

- The use of a Variant argument so that a function can deal with a variety of different incoming data types.

- How to use the `IsObject()` function.

A Cellular Meisterstück

> First the hunt, then the revels!
>
> Leslie Banks
> *The Most Dangerous Game*, 1932

- What is the current *result* of a particular, single cell?

Now that you've explored a cell's innards, how about seeing what its result (value) is? The Value property of a Range object answers this question. The custom function `fvntGetCellResults()` uses an If...Then...Else construct much the same way as `fstrGetCellContents()` does. The exceptional cases the caller needs to deal with are (a) an empty cell and (b) an error value in the cell.

And the result is...

When a cell is empty, `fvntGetCellResults()` behaves properly and returns an empty Variant—with a VarType() of 0. The caller can do what it pleases with this situation; in our demo procedure `sACellularMeisterstuck` we opted to trap for this with `IsError()` and display a message box. It would be equally valid to use the function's return value in a string or numeric expression. (Remember, an uninitialized (empty) variable equals either 0 or a zero-length string depending on the data type context.)

When a cell contains an error value (see Figure 6.6), `fvntGetCellResults()` returns an Error Variant. You can trap for an Error Variant with `VarType()`. `VarType()` returns vbError or 10 for an error type. Then the challenge is figuring out which of Excel's seven (or possibly a user-defined) error values the variable represents. The only way to do this is with a brute-force Select Case construct. A good example of this technique is shown in Figure 6.7; this is the example code associated with the help topic "Cell Error Values."

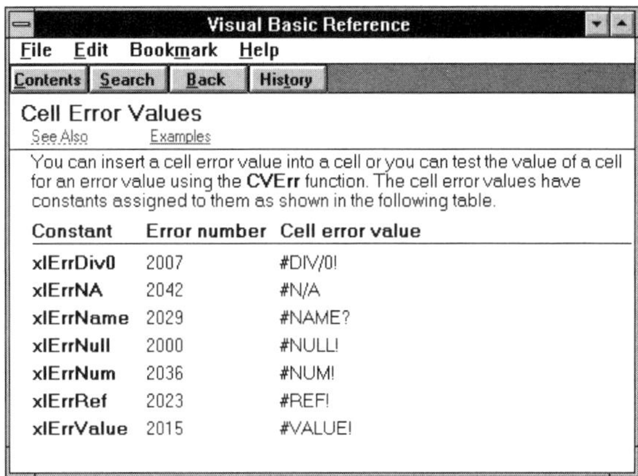

Constant	Error number	Cell error value
xlErrDiv0	2007	#DIV/0!
xlErrNA	2042	#N/A
xlErrName	2029	#NAME?
xlErrNull	2000	#NULL!
xlErrNum	2036	#NUM!
xlErrRef	2023	#REF!
xlErrValue	2015	#VALUE!

Figure 6.6 Cell Error Values, Cell Error Constants, and Error Numbers

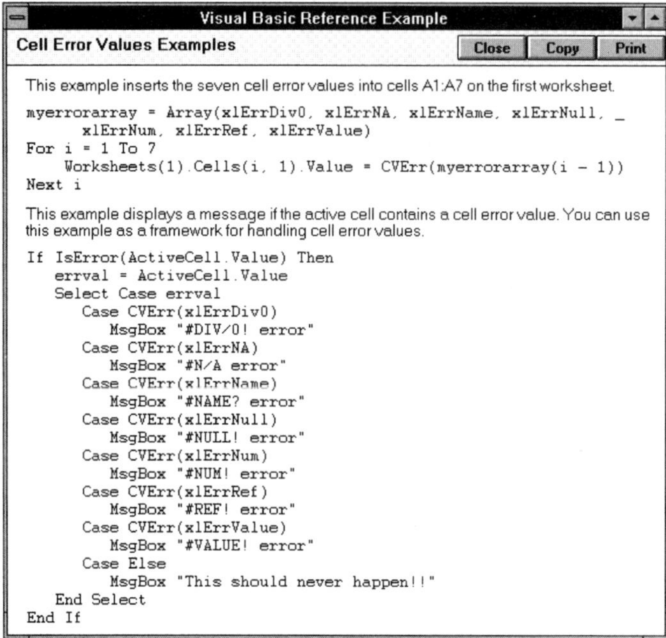

Figure 6.7 Dealing with Cell Error Values

Note that the function's second argument `blnFormatting` gives the caller the ability to specify whether or not to return formatting characters (if there are any). A typical example of this would be contents of 7000.545 with currency formatting. See Table 6.2 for more examples.

When using an A1-style cell address, *the caller has the responsibility of guaranteeing that the A1-style cell address, if it's not a range name, includes the target worksheet's sheet name and a bang prefix.* For example, Sheet1!H13 is correct but the function will fail on an address of H13 if the active sheet isn't a worksheet sheet. In no case does the parent worksheet need to be active.

```
' -------------------------------------------------------------------
' Purpose:   Provide a cell's results.
'
' Inputs:    vntRange - Either a pointer to a cell object or just a
'            plain A1-style cell address. Note that in the case of
'            something like Sheets("Sheet1").Range("H3"), the Range
'            method's Syntax 1 dictates that the address must be in A1
'            notation. If vntRange is just a plain A1-style cell
'            address, the function assumes caller passes the address
'            in the format sheet_name!A1_address, i.e., the sheet's
'            name and the bang are required.
'
```

```
'          blnFormatting - If True then return formatting characters,
'          e.g., "$7,000.55 " (string type) for a constant of
'          7000.545 with the format code of $#,##0.00_);($#,##0.00);
'          else don't return formatting characters.
'
' Returns:  Variant. Caller is responsible for handling the case where
'          fvntGetCellResults is returned as an error type (VarType()
'          returns vbError or 10).
'
' Updated:  11/17/94
' ------------------------------------------------------------------
Function fvntGetCellResults(vntRange As Variant, blnFormatting As
Boolean) As Variant
    Dim vntResults As Variant
    If IsObject(vntRange) Then
        ' vntRange is an object
        If blnFormatting Then
            ' use Text property to get back formatting chars
            vntResults = vntRange.Text
        Else
            ' use Value property to get back no formatting chars
            vntResults = vntRange.Value
        End If
    Else
        ' vntRange is a plain A1-style cell address
        If blnFormatting Then
            ' use Text property to get back formatting chars
            vntResults = Range(vntRange).Text
        Else
            ' use Value property to get back no formatting chars
            vntResults = Range(vntRange).Value
        End If
    End If
    fvntGetCellResults = vntResults
End Function


' ------------------------------------------------------------------
' demo procedure
' ------------------------------------------------------------------
Sub sACellularMeisterstuck()
    Dim blnFormatting As Boolean
    Dim intAnswer As Integer
    Dim objRange As Range
    Dim strA1Address As String
    Dim vntResults As Variant
    strA1Address = "Sheet1!H14"
    Set objRange = Sheets("Sheet1").Range("H14")
    intAnswer = MsgBox("Do you want to see formatting characters " & _
        "(if any)?", vbYesNo + vbQuestion)
```

```
    If intAnswer = vbYes Then
        blnFormatting = True
    Else
        blnFormatting = False
    End If
    vntResults = fvntGetCellResults(objRange, blnFormatting)
    If IsError(vntResults) Then
        MsgBox "The cell contains an error value."
    ElseIf IsEmpty(vntResults) Then
        MsgBox "The cell is empty."
    Else
        MsgBox "Passing objRange returns " & _
            fvntGetCellResults(objRange, blnFormatting)
        MsgBox "Passing an A1 notation address returns " & _
            fvntGetCellResults(strA1Address, blnFormatting)
    End If
End Sub
```

This function demonstrates the following concepts.

- Like its sibling `fstrGetCellContents()`, this function can deal with a variety of different incoming data types.

- How to successfully return an Error Variant.

- How to use the Value and Text properties as opposed to the Formula property to determine a cell's contents.

Hearth and Home

> There just isn't room for two doctors and two vampires in one small town.
>
> Max Adrian
> *Dr. Terror's House of Horrors,* 1967

- What is the current selection's address either in A1 or R1C1 notation, or both?

No custom function is needed to get the current selection's address. Use the Selection property to return a range object, then use the Address method with its various arguments to dictate what form the address takes. (See the "Address Method" help topic for more information.)

The following two statements show how to request A1 notation and R1C1 notation respectively.

```
Selection.Address(ReferenceStyle:=xlA1)
Selection.Address(ReferenceStyle:=xlR1C1)
```

Notice that if you apply this object expression to a multiple selection, VBA returns the address in the appropriate range-operator format. For example, if A1:B1 and C2:D2 are multi-selected, `Selection.Address` returns $A$1:$B$1,$C$2:$D$2 (the comma is Excel's union operator). To drop the absolute references use the statement

```
Selection.Address(RowAbsolute:=False, ColumnAbsolute:=False)
```

which returns, following our example, A1:B1,C2:D2.

Give Me a Range Where the Buffalo Roam

> A neighborhood is where, when you go out of it, you get beat up.
>
> Murray Kempton

- What is a particular named range's address either in A1 or R1C1 notation, or both?

To figure out a specific range name's address, first you need to make sure that the caller has provided a valid range name. If it's valid, then the RefersTo and RefersToR1C1 properties can reveal the formula behind the range name. The custom function `fstrGetRangeAddress()` returns a range name's address either in A1 or R1C1 notation, depending on the value of the function's second argument. Before the function takes the time to work its way through the current workbook's Names collection (which might take a relatively long time if there are lots of names), if it detects that the range name is an empty string it assigns an empty string to the function and gracefully exits. Otherwise it proceeds to loop through the Names collection one Name object at a time until it either finds the target range name or reaches the end of the collection, whichever comes first.

VBA's With statement makes this walk through the collection a simple process. The With statement is a study in elegant simplicity. It reduces clutter, period. Instead of having to use a bulky object reference like `ActiveWorkbook.Names.Count`, you just code `.Names.Count` inside the With...End With construct. *Note: the leading period operator before the Names object reference is very important*. Omit it and you'll get a run-time error faster than Office can outsell SmartSuite.

```
' ------------------------------------------------------------------
' Purpose:   Determine a range name's address in A1 or R1C1 notation.
'            Return an empty string if the range name is invalid.
'
' Inputs:    strRangeName - the range name
'            intNotation  - the notation desired (0 for A1, <> 0 for
'                           R1C1)
'
' Returns:   String.
'
' Updated:   11/18/94
' ------------------------------------------------------------------
Function fstrGetRangeAddress(strRangeName As String, intNotation As
Integer) As String
    ' ----- Declarations
    Dim blnFound As Boolean
    Dim intCounter As Integer
    Dim intNameCount As Integer
    ' ----- Main body
    If strRangeName = "" Then
        ' a quick test for an empty argument
        fstrGetRangeAddress = ""
        Exit Function
    End If
    blnFound = False
    intCounter = 1
    ' walk the active workbook's Names collection
    With ActiveWorkbook
        intNameCount = .Names.Count
        Do While (Not blnFound) And (intCounter <= intNameCount)
            If InStr(.Names(intCounter).Name, strRangeName) > 0 Then
                blnFound = True
            End If
            intCounter = intCounter + 1
        Loop
        If blnFound Then
            ' strRangeName *is* in the Names collection
            If intNotation = 0 Then
                ' 0 means A1 notation
                fstrGetRangeAddress = .Names(strRangeName).RefersTo
            Else
                ' <> 0 means R1C1 notation
                fstrGetRangeAddress = .Names(strRangeName).RefersToR1C1
            End If
        Else
            ' strRangeName is *not* in the Names collection
            fstrGetRangeAddress = ""
        End If
```

```
    End With
End Function


' -----------------------------------------------------------------
' demo procedure
' -----------------------------------------------------------------
Sub sGiveMeARange()
    Dim i As Integer
    Dim objName As Object
    Dim strTemp As String
    For i = 0 To 1
        With ActiveWorkbook
            ' walk through the active workbook's Names collection
            For Each objName In .Names
                strTemp = objName.Name
                If i = 0 Then
                    ' A1 notation request
                    strTemp = strTemp & " A1 address is "
                Else
                    ' R1C1 notation request
                    strTemp = strTemp & " R1C1 address is "
                End If
                strTemp = strTemp & _
                    fstrGetRangeAddress(objName.Name, i)
                MsgBox strTemp
            Next objName
        End With
        ' pass a bogus range name
        strTemp = "Smoky" & " A1 address is " & _
            fstrGetRangeAddress("Smoky", i)
        MsgBox strTemp
    Next i
End Sub
```

This function demonstrates the following concepts.

- The With statement (as described earlier in this section).

- How to test arguments for disallowed values early in a procedure and gracefully exit.

- The Count property of the Names collection.

- The Name, RefersTo, and RefersToR1C1 properties of the Name object.

- How to use the For Each statement to walk through a collection.

Sheet Surfin' and Range Rovin'

> It happened on a day in November 1964. There were six to eight waves in each set. The sun hit the face of these long walls that faded out towards Waimea Bay and made them breathtakingly beautiful. It was a surreal day. I was so mesmerized I'd stop paddling just to watch one of those beautiful waves move through. They were like pure, liquid energy. Then I'd jerk myself back into reality and say, "You'd better wake up, Pal. If this thing breaks on you, you might end up sucking suds."
>
> Greg Noll and Andrea Gabbard
> *Da Bull: Life Over the Edge*

- Activate and/or select a particular sheet or sheets. Activate and/or select a range (single cell or multi-cell) via both address notation and a range name.

Select this and activate that. Let's tackle these activate/select activities one by one. You can activate a specific sheet with a reference to an item in the Sheets collection, as in `Sheets("Sheet1").Activate` or `Sheets(1).Activate`. A sheet sub-type reference is okay too, as in `Worksheets(1).Activate` or `DialogSheets(1).Activate`.

If you want to select just one sheet (any type), simply call the Select method. Note that in this case you don't have to Activate first and then Select. But if you want to select multiple sheets (any type), then you must issue a series of Select calls, the second and all subsequent calls must use the Replace argument set to False (which extends the current selection to include any previously selected objects and this newly specified object), and the last statement should be an Activate call to land the focus on the desired sheet in the selected group. The rule here is that if you omit an explicit Activate call, the very first sheet in the group is the one on top when the dust settles. Here's a multiple sheet selection example.

```
Sub sSelectSeveralSheets()
    Sheets("Sheet1").Select
    Sheets("Sheet2").Select Replace:=False
    ' Without the following Activate call, *Sheet1* is on top!
    Sheets("Sheet2").Activate
End Sub
```

You can select a range using the Range object or the Cells method (this method returns a Range object). If you want to select (which concurrently activates) a lone cell, simply call the Activate method on that cell. But if you want to select multiple cells, first call Select on the range of cells, then call Activate *on the cell inside the selection* that you want to be active. (In Excel, only one cell can be the "active cell" at any given time.) If you don't explicitly call Activate, by default Excel activates the cell in the range's upper-left corner. In the first version of `sSelectSeveralCells` the active cell is in the upper-left corner by default. In the second version of `sSelectSeveralCells`, the active cell is the lower-right corner. The trick here is to count how many rows and columns are in the current selection and then use those values as relative offsets. (For more information on offsets, see the Remarks section of the "Cells Method" help topic.)

```
Sub sSelectSeveralCells()
    Sheets("Sheet1").Select
    Range("A1:D4").Select
    ' A1 is now the active cell (selection's upper left corner)
End Sub

Sub sSelectSeveralCells()
    Dim intColOffset As Integer
    Dim intRowOffset As Integer
    Sheets("Sheet1").Select
    Range("A1:D4").Select
    intRowOffset = Selection.Rows.Count
    intColOffset = Selection.Columns.Count
    Selection.Cells(intRowOffset, intColOffset).Activate
    ' D4 is now the active cell (selection's lower right corner)
End Sub
```

There are eleven objects to which the Activate method applies (the eleven count doesn't include these objects' corresponding collections). There are forty-nine objects that the Select method selects (again, not counting these objects' related collections). You are well advised to strap yourself back into your Jolt Cola chair of stimulation whilst perusing these combinations in detail. See Table 6.3 for a comparison of Activate-able objects and the related Select method. MenuBar, Pane, Window, and Workbook objects can be activated but can't be selected.

Activate versus Select, the Methods of champions

Table 6.3 Not All Activate-able Objects Can Be Selected

Activate-able Objects	Can This Object Be Selected?
Chart	Yes
ChartObject	Yes
DialogSheet	Yes
MenuBar	No
Module	Yes
OLEObject	Yes
Pane	No
Range	Yes
Window	No
Workbook	No
Worksheet	Yes

Please Allow Me to Introduce Myself

I am your father. I brought you into this world and I can take you out.

Bill Cosby
The Cosby Show

- Place some information into a particular range. Information here refers to the classic spreadsheet hat trick—a label, a number, or a formula that results in a label or a number.

Value and Formula properties comin' at ya

The following procedure shows how to pour information of all kinds into a cell by setting the Value and Formula properties. The last three statements in the procedure autofit the column and activate the last cell in the data entry stream for cosmetics only.

```
Sub sEnterData()
    Sheets("Sheet1").Select
    ' enter a label
    Cells(1, 1).Value = "Maxwell Smart"
    ' enter a number
    Cells(2, 1).Value = 99
    ' enter a formula
    Cells(3, 1).Formula = "=NOW()"
    Columns("A:A").Select
    Selection.Columns.AutoFit
    Cells(3, 1).Select
End Sub
```

DIALOG DEVELOPMENT

The man with the best job in the country is the vice president. All he has to do is get up every morning and say, "How's the President?"

Will Rogers

Dialog box, dbox, form, it's all the same to me.

Now that you're getting the hang of interacting with workbooks, worksheets, ranges, and so forth, what about interacting with the user? After all, what would all this stuff be without a customer at the keyboard, eh? Well, the dialog box is the supreme vehicle for interacting with your users. Your job as the developer is to help focus the user's attention on the task at hand. You can provide as much or as little default data and data validation as appropriate given the machine's state at the time the user fires up the dialog. Although this may seem like a daunting task at first blush, fear not. There's an entire and substantive body of knowledge surrounding graphical user interface design, much of which involves dialog box design. As a starter we recommend you get a copy of *The Windows Interface: An*

Application Design Guide (Microsoft Press). By studying this reference and using its recommended design tactics, your dialogs will have the look and feel of the dialogs produced by Microsoft and other ISVs.

The Dialog Sheet as a Development Environment

> Whoever said money can't buy happiness didn't know where to shop.
>
> Anonymous

Dialog boxes, unfortunately, don't grow on trees. Yet. But today's typical dialog development environment makes the process of constructing a dialog a relatively easy, painless task (heck, we'll even go out on a limb and say "it's fun!"). In Excel you create a dialog (also referred to as a form) in a special sheet called a dialog sheet.

The dialog sheet comes with the Forms toolbar shown in Figure 6.8.

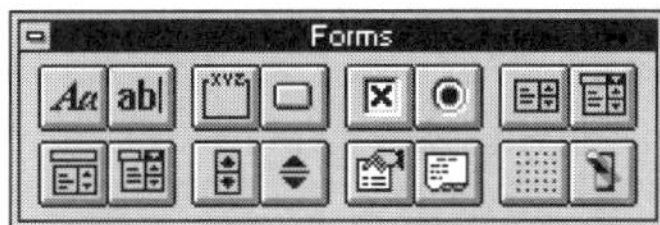

Figure 6.8 The Forms Toolbar

The dialog sheet also has a specialized set of Tools menu commands including Options, Tab Order, and Run Dialog. You'll see how to use the toolbar and menu commands in a from-scratch exercise coming up shortly.

Your First Custom Dialog, S'il Vous Plait

> All experience is an arch, to build upon.
>
> Henry Brooks Adams
> *The Education of Henry Adams,* 1907

In the mood to plot a course through the Möbius Continuum? Well, granted that's a bit off course given the nature of this tome, so let's build a custom dialog box, from scratch, instead. It's going to be a blast!

Here's an overview of what will happen in the following sections.

1. Build the Name Manager utility's dialog box.

2. Key in the required macro source code.

3. Connect the dialog box controls to various macros.

4. Test the utility to see how it lists all the names in the current workbook, along with the associated range and some other statistics. Observe that it allows you to jump to or delete any name in the current workbook.

Laying the Dialog Box Foundation

In this section you concentrate on building the dialog box itself. In a later section you'll hook it up to some event procedures. Naming conventions for dialog box controls are located in the ODK.

1. Create a new workbook and save it as NAMELIST.XLS.

2. Insert a dialog sheet and rename the sheet as dlgNameManager.

3. Change the name of the dialog frame from its default of "Dialog Frame 1" to dlgFrame—click anywhere on the dialog frame's border, highlight the name box text, type in dlgFrame, and press Enter.

Label button

4. Add a label control in the upper-left corner of the dialog box—click the Label button and then draw the control. For details on how to draw dialog box controls, see the *Excel Visual Basic User's Guide*.

5. Change the name of this label control from its default (might be something like "Label 4") to lblNames. Note that the first character in this control's name is the letter "l" ("l" as in "label") not the numeral one "1" (yes, they look deceptively similar, don't they?).

6. Change this label's text—click anywhere inside the control, highlight the text already there, type in Names: (note the trailing colon), then click anywhere outside the control. (If you press Enter when you're done entering a control's text it starts a new line of text; to exit the control either click outside the control or press Esc.)

List Box button

7. Add a list box control below the label control.

8. Change the name of this list box to lstNames.

9. Add a group box control below the list box.

Group Box button

10. Change this group box's text to Statistics.

11. Change the name of this group box to fraStatistics. (Note: you may be wondering why a control called a "group box" has a prefix of "fra." The answer is that the control was called "frame" in Visual Basic 3, so the convention remains even though the control is called "group box" in VBA. C'est la vie. If you prefer "grp," go for it!)

12. Add a label control in the lower-left corner of the group box.

13. Change the name of this label to lblRefersTo. You can leave whatever text appears inside the control as you'll change this programmatically later.

14. Add a label control a tad below lblRefersTo but still inside the group box.

15. Change the name of this label to lblVisible. You can leave whatever text appears inside the control as you'll change this programmatically later.

16. Delete the default OK command button—click the button then press `Del`.

17. Drag the default Cancel command button down a little more than its own height to make room for a new command button above it.

18. Change the name of this command button to cmdCancel.

19. Add a command button in the upper-right corner of the dialog box—click the Create Button button and then draw the control.

Create Button button

20. Change the name of this command button to cmdGoTo.

21. Change the text of this command button to Go To.

22. Add a command button below the cmdGoTo button.

23. Change the name of this command button to cmdDelete.

24. Change the text of this command button to Delete.

25. Save the workbook.

26. Test the dialog now by clicking the Run Dialog button. See Figure 6.9 for a sample of what the dialog box should look like.

Run Dialog button

27. When you're done testing it, click Cancel.

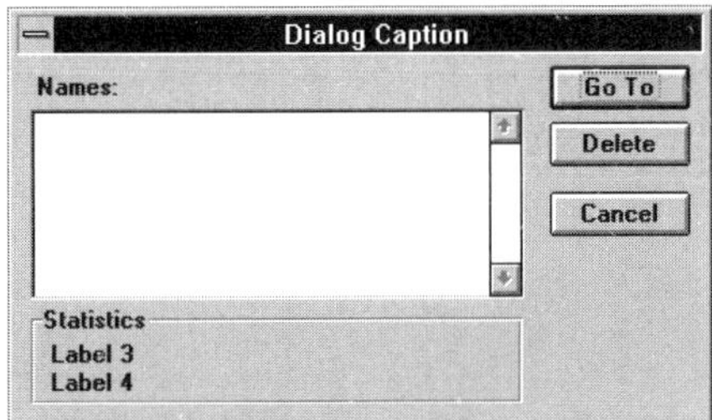

Figure 6.9 Name Manager in Its Infancy

Congratulations! You did it! While you're playing around with your custom dialog box, notice that if you use the Tab key to move from control to control, the order of the jumps may seem random. This property, called "tab focus order," can be cleaned up. In fact, that's exactly what you'll be doing in the next section.

Tweaking the Tab Focus Order

Follow these steps to set the appropriate tab focus order for your controls.

1. Select Tools / Tab Order (or right-click on the dialog frame or any open space inside the dialog frame and select Tab Order from the shortcut menu).

And the judge insisted, "I will have order in my dialog."

2. Use the Move up and Move down arrow buttons to arrange the controls in the following order—lblNames, lstNames, cmdGoTo, cmdDelete, cmdCancel, fraStatistics, lblRefersTo, lblVisible—then click OK.

3. Test the dialog now by clicking the Run Dialog button. As you tab through the controls, the selection indicator should start out in the lstNames list box, then jump to the Go To command button, the Delete command button, the Cancel button, and finally circle back to land on the lstNames list box.

4. When you're done testing it, click Cancel.

5. Save the workbook.

In step 2 the tab order of the controls fraStatistics, lblRefersTo, and lblVisible is irrelevant. If a control cannot receive focus, then it can be anywhere in the Tab Order list because Excel simply ignores it. We grouped these no-focus controls together at the end of the list in their order of appearance in the dialog only to be meticulous. This is by no means required, but you never know when you might get extra credit for neatness.

The exception (alas, isn't there always one?) is a label that's associated with a control that can receive focus, like lblNames and the list box lstNames. In this case, lblNames can be assigned an accelerator key and the list box lstNames can't. *So always be sure to put the label control in the right place in the Tab Order list— immediately before its associated focus control.*

Accelerator Adjustments, Among Others

So far the controls are mapped out nicely, the tab focus order is set, but you should add accelerator keys for each control.

1. Click on the lblNames control (this is the Names label) then select Format / Object / select the Control filecard / type N in the Accelerator Key field / click OK. You can also format a control by right-clicking on it and choosing the Format Object option from the shortcut menu.

2. Repeat the process and assign G to cmdGoTo. When you enter the accelerator key for this command button, select the Default check box (so this command button will be the one that responds when the user presses the Enter key) and make sure the Cancel, Dismiss, and Help check boxes are cleared.

3. Repeat the process and assign D to cmdDelete. When you enter the accelerator key for this command button, make sure the Default, Cancel, Dismiss, and Help check boxes are all cleared.

4. To force the Cancel button (and the Esc key) to dismiss the dialog, click on the Cancel button, select Format / Object / make sure the Cancel check box is

checked and that the Default, Dismiss, and Help check boxes are cleared / click OK.

5. Test the dialog as needed.

6. Save the workbook.

Da List Box Bone Is Connected to Da Procedure Bone....

For the purpose of this exercise we provide all the code you need to make the utility work. Your task is to connect each event procedure to the appropriate dialog box control. Table 6.4 shows which controls have an event procedure. Controls not listed aren't assigned to an event procedure.

Close connections of an event kind

Table 6.4 Name Manager Dialog Controls Assigned to Event Procedures

Dialog Control Name	Assigned Event Procedure
dlgFrame	sdlgFrame_Show
lstNames	slstNames_Click
cmdGoTo	scmdGoTo_Click
cmdDelete	scmdDelete_Click

First things first. You may be wondering if there's any special significance to the naming convention applied to event procedures. Although the underscore and the trailing verb are not required, this is a convention that we endorse. The convention is as follows: our standard "s" for subroutine prefix plus the control name, an underscore character, and then "Show" or "Click" as appropriate given the specific event being responded to. Let's assign each control in turn.

1. Create a new module and rename it as modNameManager.

2. Key in the code for the following local procedures (provided throughout the remainder of this chapter)—sNameManager, sLoadNames, sLoadNameStatistics, sdlgFrame_Show, slstNames_Click, scmdGoTo_Click, and scmdDelete_Click.

3. Key in the code for the following general-purpose procedures (store them outside the current module in modules named modFunctions and modSubroutines respectively, where you're accumulating all your general-purpose procedures)—fstrReplaceMarker() and sActiveWorkbookNames(). *It's very important that you use the same module and procedure names as we do throughout the course of this example.* See Table 6.5 for a map of Name Manager's modules and procedures.

Table 6.5 Name Manager's Module and Procedure Map

Module Name	Procedure Name
modFunctions	fblnNullMenuState fstrReplaceMarker
modGlobals	global constant and variable declarations (no procedure code)
modNameManager	scmdDelete_Click scmdGoTo_Click sdlgFrame_Show sLoadNames sLoadNameStatistics slstNames_Click sNameManager
modSubroutines	sActiveWorkbookNames

4. If you were typing along with us in Chapter 5 when we built the custom function procedure `fblnNullMenuState`, then just copy that procedure into this utility's modFunctions module. Otherwise, flip back to Chapter 5 and key in the code for `fblnNullMenuState` as appropriate.

5. From the dlgNameManager dialog sheet, click the dialog frame then select Tools / Assign Macro / type in (or scroll and select) sdlgFrame_Show / OK.

6. Click the Names list box then select Tools / Assign Macro / type in (or scroll and select) slstNames_Click / OK.

7. Click the Go To command button then select Tools / Assign Macro / type in (or scroll and select) scmdGoTo_Click / OK.

8. Click the Delete command button then select Tools / Assign Macro / type in (or scroll and select) scmdDelete_Click / OK.

9. Save the workbook.

10. At this point in the book you'll undoubtedly be flipping forward one page at a time, keying in the code and exploring each procedure that comprises Name Manager. When you get to the end of the upcoming sections that house the procedure code, we'll show you how to put Name Manager through its paces.

Global and Module-level Declarations, and the sNameManager Procedure

An object variable naming convention
The code in this section includes the project's global declarations as well as the module's declarations. Note the introduction of an object variable naming convention in the module declaration section. For example, the name of the variable that points to the utility's dialog sheet is `dlg`, taking the first three consonants

from the object name DialogSheet. The variables that point to two of the three label controls are named `lblRefersTo` and `lblVisible` respectively. The "lbl" part makes sense, right? But where in tarnation, you may ask, do the "RefersTo" and "Visible" suffixes come from? Fair question.

The second part of this convention is that when there's only one object of a particular class—say, DialogSheet—then the programmer has the discretion to provide no suffix. After all, since there's only one DialogSheet in this utility, what's the benefit of naming the associated variable `dlgDialogSheet` or some such as opposed to simply `dlg`? But in the case of more than one object of a particular class—say, Label—then the programmer should further qualify the names with a meaningful suffix. In the case of variables pointing to dialog controls, *preferably the variable name should be exactly the same as the actual name of the control itself* (over in the dialog sheet). This yields the two object variable names `lblRefersTo` and `lblVisible`.

The main body of `sNameManager` first checks for null menu state and exits gracefully if need be. Following some additional initializations, the procedure checks to see if there are no defined names in the active workbook. If there are none, it gracefully exits, otherwise it displays the dialog box. Note that some of the control references—like `dlg.Buttons("cmdGoTo")`—are handled with literal strings and some—like lblRefersTo—are handled as object variables. We show it both ways for demonstration purposes. Also, in some cases the control names are initialized by constants and in other cases by literals, again just for demonstration purposes. (However, if you're going to be distributing applications internationally, you'll want to use constants wherever possible, thereby keeping all your assignments in one central location; this minimizes the amount of work required to translate strings.)

```
Option Explicit

' ----- Global Declarations
Global Const BANG = "!"
Global Const BLANK = " "
Global Const MSG_HIDDEN = "Hidden (not visible)"
Global Const MSG_NAME_MGR_3D = "Cannot go to a 3-D range."
Global Const MSG_NAME_MGR_DELETE = "You are about to " & _
    "delete name <<>>. Are you sure?"
Global Const MSG_NAME_MGR_GATHER = "Gathering information " & _
    "about the available names. Please wait ..."
Global Const MSG_NAME_MGR_NO_NAMES = "This workbook contains no names."
Global Const MSG_NAME_MGR_NO_MORE_NAMES = "This workbook now contains
no names."
Global Const MSG_NO_RUN_FROM_NULLMENU = "Sorry, " & _
    "this procedure cannot be run when no workbooks are open. " & _
    "Please open at least one workbook and try again."
```

```
Global Const MSG_VISIBLE = "Visible"
Global i As Integer
Global strDboxTitle As String
Global strPrompt As String

'----- Module Declarations
Const DIALOG_NAME = "dlgNameManager"
Const MACRO_TITLE = "Underground Name Manager"
Const VERSION_NUMBER_LOCAL = "1.0"
Dim blnNoMoreNames As Boolean
Dim intNameIndex As Integer
Dim strNames() As String
Dim dlg As DialogSheet
Dim lblRefersTo As Label
Dim lblVisible As Label
Dim lst As ListBox


' -------------------------------------------------------------------
' Purpose:  Main subroutine.
'
' Updated:  11/2/94
' -------------------------------------------------------------------
Sub sNameManager()
    ' ----- Initializations
    strDboxTitle = MACRO_TITLE & BLANK & VERSION_NUMBER_LOCAL
    ' before doing anything else, bail if in null menu mode
    If fblnNullMenuState Then
        MsgBox MSG_NO_RUN_FROM_NULLMENU, vbOKOnly + vbExclamation, _
            strDboxTitle
        Exit Sub
    End If
    ' continue with initializations
    blnNoMoreNames = False
    Set dlg = ThisWorkbook.DialogSheets(DIALOG_NAME)
    Set lblRefersTo = dlg.Labels("lblRefersTo")
    Set lblVisible = dlg.Labels("lblVisible")
    Set lst = dlg.ListBoxes("lstNames")
    dlg.DialogFrame.Text = strDboxTitle
    dlg.Buttons("cmdGoTo").Enabled = True     ' reset cuz might've been
    dlg.Buttons("cmdDelete").Enabled = True   '   set False on prior run
    ' ----- Main body
    sActiveWorkbookNames strNames()
    If ActiveWorkbook.Names.Count = 0 Then
        ' inform user and don't show the dialog
        MsgBox MSG_NAME_MGR_NO_NAMES, vbExclamation, strDboxTitle
    Else
        dlg.Show
    End If
End Sub
```

If you try to run the utility now, without having completed all the numbered steps at the beginning of the section *Da List Box Bone Is Connected to Da Procedure Bone*, the utility will fail because you haven't typed in all the procedures yet.

The sLoadNames Procedure

This procedure's primary responsibility is to load the active workbook's names into a global string array and subsequently into the list box itself. This procedure also plays a critical role in detecting the case where the last name has been deleted. When this happens, the procedure sets the module-level Boolean flag `blnNoMoreNames` to True so that subsequent procedures can respond accordingly. The logic here is to report that there are no more names—first in a message box and subsequently in one of the statistics labels—and deaden any controls except the Cancel button.

Handle the exceptions gracefully.

```
' ----------------------------------------------------------------
' Purpose:  Load up strNames() array used by the "lstNames" control.
'
' Updated:  11/2/94
' ----------------------------------------------------------------
Sub sLoadNames()
    sActiveWorkbookNames strNames()
    If strNames(0) = "" Then
        blnNoMoreNames = True    ' used by subsequent procedures!
        ' inform user immediately that there are no more names
        MsgBox MSG_NAME_MGR_NO_MORE_NAMES, vbExclamation, strDboxTitle
    End If
    lst.List = strNames()
    If blnNoMoreNames Then
        ' ListIndex of 0 results in no reverse video selection
        '    in the list box
        lst.ListIndex = 0
        '  disable the two non-Cancel command buttons
        dlg.Buttons("cmdGoTo").Enabled = False
        dlg.Buttons("cmdDelete").Enabled = False
    Else
        lst.ListIndex = 1
    End If
End Sub
```

The sLoadNameStatistics Procedure

This procedure's primary responsibility is to initialize the statistics labels with information germane to the current name.

```
' -----------------------------------------------------------------
' Purpose:   Initialize controls related to name statistics.
'
' Updated:   11/2/94
' -----------------------------------------------------------------
Sub sLoadNameStatistics()
    intNameIndex = lst.ListIndex
    If blnNoMoreNames Then
        ' set statistics label to report the condition, then bail
        lblRefersTo.Text = MSG_NAME_MGR_NO_MORE_NAMES
        lblVisible.Text = ""
        Exit Sub
    End If
    With ActiveWorkbook
        ' Following stmt seems to fail because lst.ListIndex is
        '   a variant!?
        ' lblRefersTo.Text = .Names(lst.ListIndex).RefersTo
        lblRefersTo.Text = .Names(intNameIndex).RefersTo
        If .Names(intNameIndex).Visible Then
            lblVisible.Text = MSG_VISIBLE
        Else
            lblVisible.Text = MSG_HIDDEN
        End If
    End With
End Sub
```

The sdlgFrame_Show Event Procedure

This procedure is an event procedure that you assigned to the control sdlgFrame
earlier in this chapter. Its sole purpose is to load up the names and set the statistics
for the first name in the list. It gets called whenever the dialog is displayed via the
Show method.

```
' -----------------------------------------------------------------
' Purpose:   Initialization (dbox).
'            dlgNameManager's "dlgFrame" control is assigned to this
'            subroutine.
'
' Updated:   10/27/94
' -----------------------------------------------------------------
Sub sdlgFrame_Show()
    strPrompt = MSG_NAME_MGR_GATHER
    Application.StatusBar = strPrompt
    ' get the names list
    sLoadNames
    ' get statistics for the first name in the list
    sLoadNameStatistics
```

```
    Application.StatusBar = ""
End Sub
```

The slstNames_Click Event Procedure

This event procedure handles clicks on the Names list box. All it has to do is reinitialize the statistics controls to reflect the newly selected name.

```
' ------------------------------------------------------------------
' Purpose:   dlgNameManager's "lstNames" control is assigned to this
'            subroutine.
'
'
' Updated:   11/2/94
' ------------------------------------------------------------------
Sub slstNames_Click()
    If blnNoMoreNames Then
        ' no more names so do nothing
    Else
        sLoadNameStatistics
    End If
End Sub
```

The scmdGoTo_Click Event Procedure

This event procedure reacts to clicks on the GoTo command button. It uses the Activate and Select methods to pop up the appropriate sheet and select the appropriate range. Note that this procedure traps for 3-D range names using a brute-force error handler.

```
' ------------------------------------------------------------------
' Purpose:   dlgNameManager's "cmdGoTo" control is assigned to this
'            subroutine.
'
'
' Updated:   11/18/94
' ------------------------------------------------------------------
Sub scmdGoTo_Click()
    On Error GoTo ErrorTrap
    ' ----- Declarations
    Dim strName As String
    Dim strRefersTo As String
    Dim strSheet As String
    ' ----- Main body
    strName = strNames(lst.ListIndex - 1)
    strRefersTo = lblRefersTo.Text
    ' parse the sheet reference so we can activate it first
    strSheet = Mid(strRefersTo, 2, InStr(strRefersTo, BANG) - 2)
    Sheets(strSheet).Activate
```

```
    ' now select the desired range
    Range(strName).Select
    Exit Sub
ErrorTrap:
    ' attempting to go to a 3-D range results in 1004 error
    MsgBox MSG_NAME_MGR_3D, vbOKOnly + vbExclamation, _
            strDboxTitle
End Sub
```

The scmdDelete_Click Event Procedure

Assume "No" when proposing a deletion. This event procedure responds to clicks on the Delete command button. First it prompts the user, with a default focus on the No button as a cautionary measure (never assume Yes in response to a user's request to delete anything!), to verify that the user indeed wants to delete this name. If the user confirms the request, the procedure deletes it.

```
' ------------------------------------------------------------------
' Purpose:   dlgNameManager's "cmdDelete" control is assigned to this
'            subroutine.
'
' Updated:   11/2/94
' ------------------------------------------------------------------
Sub scmdDelete_Click()
    ' ----- Declarations
    Dim intAnswer As Integer
    ' ----- Main body
    strPrompt = fstrReplaceMarker(MSG_NAME_MGR_DELETE, _
        strNames(lst.ListIndex - 1))
    intAnswer = MsgBox(strPrompt, _
        vbYesNo + vbDefaultButton2 + vbQuestion, strDboxTitle)
    If intAnswer = vbYes Then
        Names(strNames(lst.ListIndex - 1)).Delete
        sdlgFrame_Show
    End If
End Sub
```

The sActiveWorkbookNames() General Purpose Procedure

This general purpose procedure loads an array argument with all the names in the active workbook, including hidden (not visible) names. If there are no names, then the array is dimensioned to a single zero-length element.

```
' ------------------------------------------------------------------
' Purpose:   Load an array argument with the active workbook's names.
'            Caller is responsible for making sure there *is* an active
'            workbook.
'
```

```
' Inputs:    strNames() - string array to be filled with the names
'
' Returns:  N/A.
'
' Updated:   10/22/94
' --------------------------------------------------------------------
Sub sActiveWorkbookNames(strNames() As String)
    ' ----- Declarations
    Dim i As Integer
    Dim intNameCount As Integer
    ' ----- Main body
    With ActiveWorkbook
        intNameCount = .Names.Count
        If intNameCount = 0 Then
            ReDim strNames(0)
            Exit Sub
        End If
        ReDim strNames(intNameCount - 1)
        For i = 0 To intNameCount - 1
            strNames(i) = .Names(i + 1).Name
        Next i
    End With
End Sub
```

The fstrReplaceMarker() General Purpose Procedure

The trick to this function procedure is to take a predetermined marker (here we use the characters "<<>>") from one argument and replace it with whatever is in the second argument. In this case we're replacing the marker with the current name's name. This makes it very easy to manage global strings, maintain their integrity, and localize them ("localize" is development jargon meaning to translate to some language other than the language of origin).

```
Global Const MARKER = "<<>>"


' --------------------------------------------------------------------
' Purpose:   Provide a simple way to replace a marker in global
'            constant message strings with context-relevant, current
'            information.
'            If the marker isn't found, function returns "".
'
' Inputs:    strMsg           - message string (*must* contain
'                                 the marker)
'            strReplacement - string to replace the marker with
'
' Returns:  String.
'
' Updated:   12/12/94
' --------------------------------------------------------------------
```

```
Public Function fstrReplaceMarker(strMsg As String, strReplacement As
String) As String
    ' ----- Declarations
    Dim intPos As Integer
    Dim strTemp As String
    ' ----- Main body
    intPos = InStr(strMsg, MARKER)
    If intPos = 0 Then
        fstrReplaceMarker = ""
        Exit Function
    End If
    strTemp = Left(strMsg, intPos - 1)
    strTemp = strTemp & strReplacement & _
        Right(strMsg, Len(strMsg) - (intPos + Len(MARKER) - 1))
    fstrReplaceMarker = strTemp
End Function
```

The Race Is On

> In a few generations you can breed a racehorse. The recipe for making a
> man like Delacroix is less well known.
>
> Pierre Auguste Renoir
> *Jean Renoir, Renoir My Father,* 1958

Yo! It's testing time! First add some range names to the current workbook, then run the sNameManager macro. See Figure 6.10 for a sample of what the dialog box should look like.

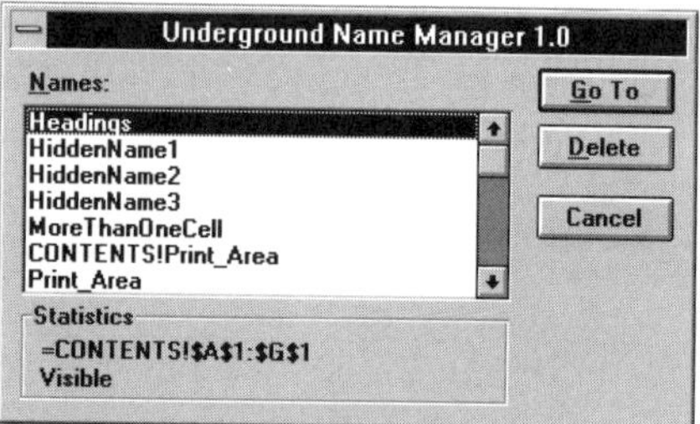

Figure 6.10 Name Manager Has a
Coming Out Party

The Edit Code button is an often overlooked but extraordinarily handy little button. To use it, first select any dialog control then click the button. This takes you immediately to the control's associated event procedure. If there's no event procedure, the button simply beeps and does nothing. Excellent!

You can throw some curve balls of your own at this utility, but here's a list of various ranges you might consider running through the gauntlet at this point. Test each of the utility's features on each type of range name. (Note that Name Manager traps for 3-D range names using a brute-force error handler. Later in the chapter we offer some suggestions for aspects of Name Manager you might consider embellishing on your own. One of these embellishments is to trap for 3-D range names without using an error trap.)

- A single-cell range name.

- A multi-cell range name.

- A sheet-level range name.

- A hidden range name. To hide a range name, run a throw-away subroutine containing a statement like this, replacing `RangeNameToHide` with your target range name—`Names("RangeNameToHide").Visible = False`.

Fit and Finish

Keep in mind that this is not necessarily the end of the road for a multi-purpose name utility. Here are some embellishments we encourage you to develop on your own.

Embellishments for you to ponder

- Add a command button labeled "Paste Names" that pastes all names and their references. But wait, you say, Excel already has this feature. True. By design, *none of Excel's name management features reveal hidden names*. So you'll be reinventing the wheel but to *your* specifications. And that's what customizable applications are all about!

- Add a command button labeled "Delete All" that deletes all the names in the list in one fell swoop.

- Add a command button labeled "Toggle Visible" that toggles the selected name between visible and hidden.

- Add a command button labeled "Help" that invokes a custom help file.

- Provide additional text labels to report even more statistics.

- Switch the Names list box logic from single select to multi-select.

- Handle Go To requests for 3-D range names without using an error trap.

- You get the idea. Happy hackin'.

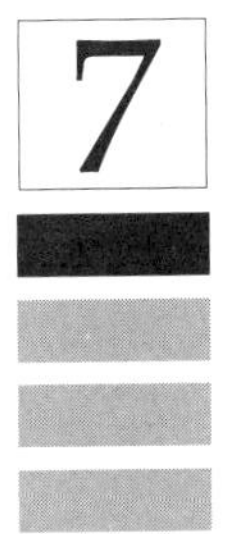

OLE Automation for Pragmatists

No particular results then, so far, but only an attitude of orientation, is what the pragmatic method means. The attitude of looking away from first things, principles, "categories," supposed necessities; and of looking toward last things, fruits, consequences, facts.

William James
Pragmatism, 1907

We have seen the future and it is OLE Automation. Like it, hate it, scream at it with vituperative vehemence, scratch your head and wonder at it, do what you will, it is the future. However you feel about it, you'll be dealing with OLE Automation if you want to control one Office application using another.

It's new and it's still in its infancy. It spits up now and then. It refuses to cooperate with you from time to time. It just plain doesn't work right in places, but where it does work it's amazing. And we think Microsoft will ram it down, er, ah, we think Microsoft will improve, yeah, that's it—Microsoft will improve it and make it better.

Love it or hate it, it's here to stay.

No matter, it's here and this is the straight dope on it.

USING OLE AUTOMATION TO CONTROL OTHER APPLICATIONS—OVERVIEW

Behind every successful man is a surprised woman.

Maryon Pearson

OLE Automation's raison d'être is to allow you to control one application from within another application's programming language. That's it, end of report. Now "control" covers a lot of territory. Say you build an application in Excel that at some point needs to get some data from a project in Project. OLE Automation, or OLEAuto for short, is the way to go. Start an application up, have it open a file, get some data, format some data, pass some data, save a file, close a file, shut down an application. You name it, OLEAuto can *control* it.

It'll tax your object.object syntax skills and probably make you just a little crazy, but it is worth the necessary skull sweat, rest assured. In this chapter you'll treat entire applications as objects and manipulate their methods and properties to no end. So grab a cup of java and we'll take it step by step.

Opening Statement Salvo

> Let him not boast who puts his armor on
> As he who puts it off, the battle done.
>
> Henry Wadsworth Longfellow
> *Morituri Salutamus, 1875*

Distilling it down to the essentials

If you distill OLE Automation coding down to the bare essentials, you're left with the following five steps.

1. Declare an OLE Automation object variable.

   You create an OLE Automation object variable using the key words As Object. This gives you a way to refer to the programmable object (which may be an application) you want to manipulate.

2. Set the OLE Automation object variable to a specific OLE object class.

   This is a scary way to say you conjure up, invoke, whatever, an object of an OLE class of the application you want to control. (For C++ devotees out there, "You conjure up an OLE class object of the application you want to control.") You'll usually use the GetObject or CreateObject functions to do this. This will **instantiate** (attach to an already running instance or create an instance of) the application that owns the OLE object class, that is, the server application, and assign to the object variable the OLE class object that is a child of the application instance.

3. Interact with the OLE Automation object through the variable, using the object's methods and properties.

   This is where you have your way with the server application, make it jump through some hoops, roll over, beg, whatever.

4. Close the running instance of the application's top-level Application object *if and only if your code explicitly started this specific instance of the Application object.* Whew, is this headshrinking stuff or what? The phrase "the application's top-level Application object" refers to the object at the top of the server's object model, and whether you find this bewildering or enlightening, that object's name is typically "Application" (note the capital "A"). In other words, if you

started Project via OLEAuto, you should shut Project down (close it) when you are done with it.

5. Set the OLE Automation object variable to Nothing.

The variable that you declared in step one should be explicitly set to Nothing, which disassociates the variable with the specific object. This releases all the *resources* associated with this specific instance of that object (you should never miss a chance to liberate some resources).

Keep in mind that you must explicitly quit the server application *and* then set the object variable to Nothing. Just setting the object variable to Nothing disassociates the object from the variable but leaves the server running (often in a cloaked window!).

Mind you, these five innocuous steps sport some sharp teeth and talons. Tread softly and carry a big stick when in the OLE Automation jungle, yes indeedy. We'll literally spend the remainder of this chapter slogging through the myriad idiosyncrasies that stem from the following variables in the OLE Automation equation.

Walkabout in the OLE Automation jungle

- Which application is the controller?
- Which application is the server?
- Does the server provide an object library?
- Is the server already running?
- If the server isn't already running, do you want to start it as a visible or a hidden application?
- What server startup behaviors can you live without?
- What server startup behaviors can you *not* live without?

If you need to refer to an OLE Automation object once and only once, you can compress these steps down to one single VBA statement. Yes, there are "some issues" (as we say in ConsultantSpeak) with this direct reference process, but it is possible. In this one statement you refer directly to the OLE Automation object in question. For example, issuing the statement

```
Excel.Application.DisplayFullScreen = True
```

from inside Project VBA would switch Excel to its full-screen mode, starting Excel if it wasn't already running (more on this direct reference technique in a later section). If your intent is to leave Excel running, you can call it a day after issuing this statement.

OLE Automation Object Variable Types and Naming Conventions

If your parents never had any children, chances are you won't, either.

Dick Cavett

In Chapter 1 we introduced the following simple procedure in which Excel communicates with Word using OLE Automation.

```
Sub ShowAndTell()
    Dim wordbas As Object
    Set wordbas = CreateObject("Word.Basic")
    wordbas.FileNewDefault
    wordbas.Insert "Hello Underground!"
    wordbas.StartOfDocument 1
    wordbas.FormatFont "36", _
        , , , , , , , , , , , , , , 1, 1
    wordbas.FilePrint 1
End Sub
```

"f" is for function as "s" is for subroutine. In the Chapter 1 example we briefly introduced the power of OLE Automation without getting into the nitty gritty. Now that you've worked your way through two chapters of VBA code, it's appropriate to apply the naming conventions we've been suggesting. One simple change is to the procedure name—since it's a subroutine procedure you need to add the "s" prefix to the procedure's name. The other naming convention change required here concerns OLEAuto object variable names, something we haven't mentioned until now.

Interestingly, and frustratingly, *you can't use an OLEAuto server's native object type names from within the controlling application.* Nosireebob. For example, if Excel is controlling Project and requires access to a Project object (a Project object is below the **top-level** Application object, MSProject), the following VBA code is illegal.

```
' This is an Excel VBA statement declaring an object variable.
' Illegal in VBA 1.0.
Dim prjPaintMyHouse As MSProject.Project
```

Instead, Excel the controlling application must refer to the generic Object type, like this.

```
' This is an Excel VBA statement declaring an object variable.
' Legal in VBA 1.0.
Dim prjPaintMyHouse As Object
Set prjPaintMyHouse = MSProject.Project
```

---

*This is a limitation of VBA 1.0 (Excel and Project). *In a future version of VBA this limitation may be abolished.* In such a future version of VBA the statement `Dim prjPaintMyHouse As MSProject.Project` would be perfectly legal.

The ODK proposes this convention—*if and only if you're writing code in a multi-application OLEAuto environment,* you create a prefix of one letter representing the server ("e" for Excel, "p" for Project, "v" for Visual Basic, "w" for Word), plus "ob" ("ob" being the first two letters of the "obj" prefix prescribed by the general variable naming convention), plus a specific object type reference, plus a discretionary name. Whew. So you'd end up with a declaration statement like this.

```
' This is an Excel VBA statement declaring an object variable
'    expressed the "ODK way."
' Legal in VBA 1.0.
Dim pobProjectPaintMyHouse As Object
```

Now take a deep breath, friend. We abide by the one-letter convention to distinguish between various server applications. Done deal. Beyond that, however, we have two problems with the ODK's multi-application convention. One, all of a sudden the "obj" constellation we've all grown accustomed to is missing, replaced by the truncated "ob." We don't know about you, but our eyes and brains get used to something and since we strive for maximum efficiency through consistency, we're going to stick with the unadulterated "obj." Two, the notion of using the complete spelling of the server's object type strikes us as contrary to the "three-consonant" convention that applies in a single-application project (like dlg for a DialogSheet object), and also results in veeeeccrrrrrry long variable names. Our convention continues to use the three-consonant abbreviations except we capitalize the first letter thereof to improve the prefix's readability. Like this.

The Underground naming convention (cont'd)

```
' This is an Excel VBA statement declaring an object variable
'    expressed "our way."
' Legal in VBA 1.0.
Dim pobjPrjPaintMyHouse As Object
```

In summary, here are the components of our multi-application object variable naming convention.

1. A one-letter abbreviation designating the OLEAuto server application—"e" for Excel, "p" for Project, "v" for Visual Basic, and "w" for Word (all in lower-case).

2. The characters "obj" to designate this is a generic object type variable (all in lower-case).

3. The three-consonant abbreviation of the OLEAuto server's object type (normal capitalization*), for example, "Dlg" for a DialogSheet object.

---

*First letter upper case, all subsequent letters lower case.

4. A discretionary name (normal capitalization), for example, "ConfRoom101" to refer to the resource known around the water cooler as Conference Room 101.

5. The exception to the three-consonant abbreviation rule is our use of "App" for the ubiquitous Application object, instead of the rather awkward "Ppl" mandated by strictest adherence to the letter of the law. ("Ppl" represents the first three consonants of the word "Application" with the first letter capitalized for distinction.)

Always declare OLEAuto variables globally.   The third and final change you should make, even in the case of such a simple procedure, is to declare the Application object (in Word's case, literally the Basic object) globally instead of at the procedure or module level. This is because when an OLEAuto object variable goes out of scope or is explicitly set to Nothing, the object variable is released from memory. In most cases (but not all cases, as you'll see shortly) the referenced object ceases to exist; meaning, in the case of Application and even some lower-level objects, *poof … suddenly the server application ain't running.* Bon voyage. Up ahead we walk you through all the ramifications of starting and exiting applications via OLE Automation, but the overriding rule is to always declare OLE Automation object variables globally.

```
Global wobjApp As Object
Sub sShowAndTell()
    Set wobjApp = CreateObject("Word.Basic")
    wobjApp.FileNewDefault
    wobjApp.Insert "Hello Underground!"
    wobjApp.StartOfDocument 1
    wobjApp.FormatFont "36", _
        , , , , , , , , , , , , , , 1, 1
    wobjApp.FilePrint 1
End Sub
```

This is the same code shown earlier, now conformed to our recommended naming conventions and with the OLE Automation object variable declared globally.

The Direct Reference Technique

> You know, I think you and I have some of the same people working for each other.
>
> Nikita Khrushchev
> Speaking to Central Intelligence Agency director Allen Dulles

The direct reference technique lets you grab another application's objects with no preamble whatsoever. No CreateObject or GetObject, just wham, bam, and launch.

The point of direct references is the existence of a direct reference to an OLB (type library) thereby eliminating the need for these two function calls.

First things first, however. Before any of the following examples will work, you must set the controlling application's reference settings. For example, before you can have Excel start snapping the whip and making Project do its bidding, you have to check a box in the Tools / References dialog box. Note that you must be in a module sheet in Excel to get access to Tools / References. See Figure 7.1.

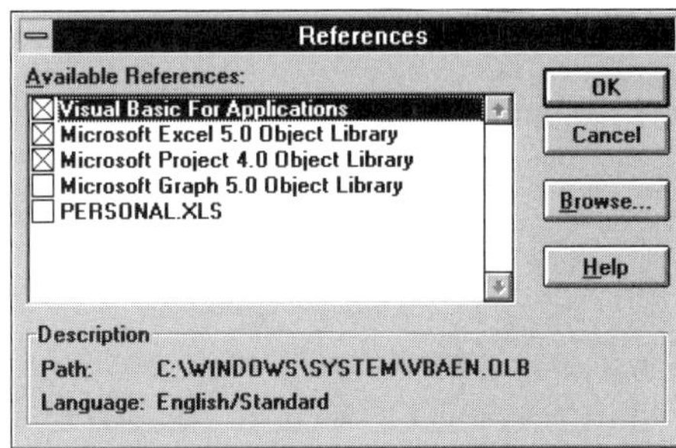

Figure 7.1 Excel's References Dialog Box

Notice that the box "Microsoft Project 4.0 Object Library" is checked. This lets you use the direct reference technique without getting an awkward error message. Should you fail to reference the server, an attempt to access it using this technique wins you the error message in Figure 7.2. **Check the proper box.**

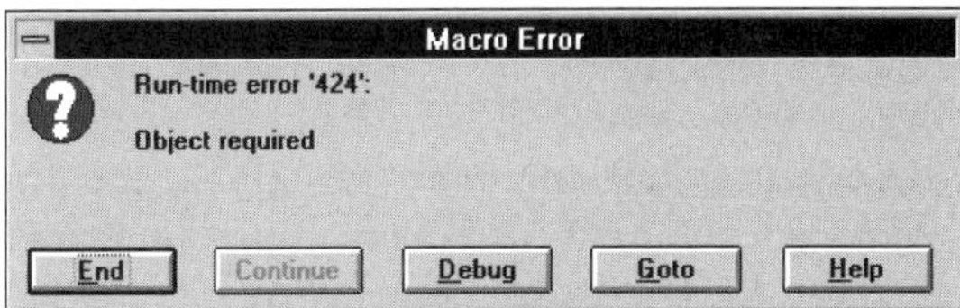

Figure 7.2 Error When Server is Not Referenced

Not too informative, is it? So make sure you are properly referenced (we talk about referencing again at the end of this chapter when we discuss the Object Browser) and then try the following examples.

Table 7.1 OLEAuto Direct References (No Variable Required)

OLEAuto Controller	OLEAuto Server	Sample Statement
Excel	Project	`MsgBox MSProject.Application.Visible` `MSProject.Application.WindowState = pjNormal`
Excel	Word	Not possible (no object library)
Project	Excel	`MsgBox Excel.Application.Visible` `Excel.Application.WindowState = xlNormal`

Let's take the first example in Table 7.1 and walk through what is happening. We'll assume that Project is not running.

```
MsgBox MSProject.Application.Visible
```

Testing for a property value   This statement causes Project to be loaded in a hidden window ("cloaked" is the term we used earlier, but since the ODK uses "hidden" we can live with that) and gets from Project the True or False value of Project's `Visible` property. Since Project is loaded hidden, the property is False and you get the message box in Figure 7.3.

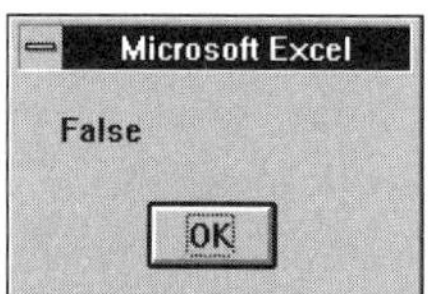

Figure 7.3 Project's Visible Property Returns False.

In the case of a direct reference containing no variable, the Application object reference is not required in Excel VBA but is required in Project VBA. In other words, in Excel VBA the statement `MSProject.Application.WindowState` `=pjNormal` is perfectly legal and so is the statement `MSProject.WindowState` `= pjNormal`. But in Project VBA the statement `Excel.WindowState =` `xlNormal` causes a "Member not defined" error. The only way to get Project VBA to process this statement is with `Excel.Application.WindowState` `= xlNormal`. Go figure. This is the first of many VBA/OLEAuto implementation hiccups you'll swallow from this point on in the Underground tour.

```
MSProject.Application.WindowState = pjNormal
```

This statement sets Project's WindowState property to normal (that is, a restored window on your Windows desktop) and has the side effect of making

Project itself visible. You can switch over to Project and you'll see that Project is indeed running and that it has been opened in the null menu mode (no projects loaded). Now, Project knows it has been started via OLE Automation. The proof of this is displayed when you try to close Project (see Figure 7.4).

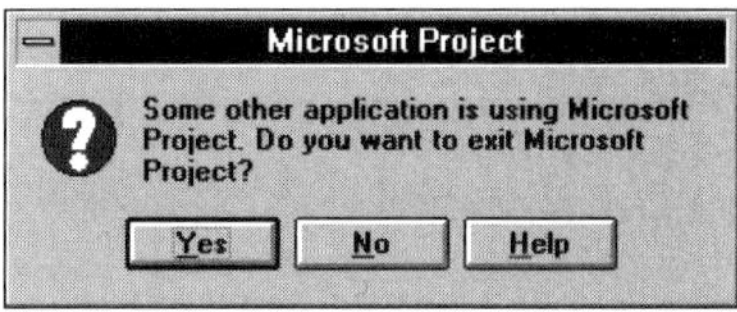

Figure 7.4 Project Keeps Track of Who Called It.

You are warned that another application has started Project and you must confirm that it's okay to shut it down. We'll talk about shutting down a server programmatically a little later. Just to make things interesting, Excel doesn't behave this way. This message box is unique to Project.

Table 7.2 shows you how to accomplish the same thing using a variable to point to the object. This is still direct referencing, make no mistake. The use of the variable allows you to write shorter statements and lets you pass the object variable to functions and subroutines.

Table 7.2 OLEAuto Direct References (*Using a Variable*)

OLEAuto Controller	OLEAuto Server	Sample Statement

Excel	Project	`Dim pobjApp As Object`
		`Set pobjApp = MSProject.Application`
		`MsgBox pobjApp.Visible`
		`pobjApp.WindowState = pjNormal`
		`pobjApp.Quit`
		`Set pobjApp = Nothing`

Excel	Word	Not possible (no object library)

Project	Excel	`Dim eobjApp As Object`
		`Set eobjApp = Excel.Application`
		`MsgBox eobjApp.Visible`
		`eobjApp.WindowState = xlNormal`
		`eobjApp.Quit`
		`Set eobjApp = Nothing`

Direct referencing, as you've seen, can cause the server application to be loaded. What's interesting is when the server application is already running as you can see in Table 7.3.

Table 7.3 Direct Reference Gyrations with OLEAuto Servers

OLEAuto Controller	OLEAuto Server	OLEAuto Server App Already Running	OLEAuto Server App Not Running
Excel	Project	Uses the running instance	*Loads Project hidden* then uses that instance
Project	Excel	*Loads a new instance of Excel hidden* then uses that instance	*Loads Excel hidden* then uses that instance

Multiple instances + limited resources = crash and burn.

Notice that Project ignores any currently running instances of Excel and loads another instance in a hidden window. Another anomaly is this—run the Project-as-controller code once when Excel isn't loaded at all and everything seems peachy, but when you try to run the code a second time you'll slam into the "Run-time error 440" brick wall and have to restart either Project, or maybe even Windows, to reset. Go figure. Project is the newest of the VBA-capable applications and we hope that this odd behavior is due to an oversight and is not a harbinger of things to come for VBA applications in general. Hmmm, maybe Microsoft is getting into the RAM business.

Another anomaly between Project and Excel is the result of maximizing the server's application window. A direct reference like

```
MSProject.Application.WindowState = pjMaximized
```

does two things: (1) starts Project hidden, then (2) the WindowState property reference automatically toggles Application's Visible property to True which, in effect, makes Project visible on the screen. *But it was initially loaded hidden.* Excel is just the opposite. The statement

```
Excel.Application.WindowState = xlMaximized
```

will not, we repeat, *will not* reveal Excel on screen. Gaak.

Direct Reference Disadvantages

I've always liked the direct approach.

> Wrong-Way Corrigan
> *attributed*

The process of guaranteeing that the controlling application's References* (select Tools / References on the VBA module's menu) are set up exactly right for the

---

*We capitalize "Reference" (an item in the Reference dialog) to distinguish this term from the more generic "reference."

ensuing code-based references is, well, there really is no way to guarantee anything regarding these References unless you're standing right there next to the user watching her/him play around with the References dialog. Ouch.

We're talking about two distinct but related problems with references. First, making sure the right options are selected in the Available References list box (see Figure 7.1). Second, making sure the selected references are in the right priority order. The controlling application's code environment resolves object, method, and property name conflicts based on the order of references in the Available References list box (in top-to-bottom order). This crucial but altogether fragile dependence on the References dialog settings renders it an undesirable technique.

As if that wasn't enough, if you use direct references in Project (acting as the client) it *completely ignores running instances of Excel as the target server application.* You end up with a needless incremental instance of Excel on your desktop, which typically is a recipe for a disaster of the resource kind. That's another Big Thumbs Down for direct references.

THE GREAT CREATEOBJECT AND GETOBJECT GORDIAN KNOT

Some days you're a bug, some days you're a windshield.

Price Cobb, after winning a car race in 1988

If the direct approach is out, what's a VBA commando to do? Ah, CreateObject and GetObject to the rescue! We'll be laying the foundation for what comes in Chapter 8 and it may seem a bit, well, involved. Despair not! The best way to approach this subject matter is by starting simple and working your way up to more complex scenarios, which is just what we're going to do. We'll show the complete steps necessary for successful execution so that good habits will start early.

Object, object, who's got the object?

We define the simplest case as when the controlling application is completely responsible for the server's behavior; this means that the controller explicitly starts the server. In such a case, the basic steps are the same as the ones with which we started this chapter.

1. Declare an OLE Automation object variable.

2. Set the OLE Automation object variable to a specific OLE object class.

3. Interact with the OLE Automation object through the variable, using the object's methods and properties. This includes explicitly changing the Application object's Visible property to True if you want to see the server on screen. (*Changing Visible to True is by no means mandatory; it's your choice based on your specific development needs.*)

4. Close the running instance of the application's top-level Application object.

5. Set the OLE Automation object variable to Nothing.

To keep it simple, throughout the following section(s) we ignore the issue of saving documents or other objects to disk from within the server (we cavalierly throw away changes for the time being). Remember that the server application does not need to be selected in the controlling application's References list when you use `CreateObject()` and `GetObject()`. This lets us avoid one of the major problems with the direct reference technique as seen in the previous section.

The `CreateObject()` function creates a reference to an OLE Automation object. An OLE Automation-capable application contains at least a single object type.

The `GetObject()` function lets you establish (get) a reference to an existing OLE Automation object. Makes sense, no? You can pass this function a fully qualified path to an existing filename to get the objects therein, and/or you can pass it a class name. See Table 7.4. Confusingly, both functions are capable of doing the opposite of what their names imply—CreateObject can connect to a running instance and GetObject can start a new instance. More on that a bit later in the chapter.

Table 7.4 A List of Class Names

Application	Object type	Class type
Microsoft Excel, version 5.0	Application Worksheet Chart	Excel.Application Excel.Sheet Excel.Chart
Microsoft Project, version 4.0	Application Project	MSProject.Application MSProject.Project
Microsoft Word, version 6.0	WordBasic	Word.Basic

In the following sections you'll work with each of Excel's classes using Project as the client. Onward!

Project Accessing Excel's Application Object via Excel.Application

In this section you'll see a simple example of Project initiating Excel, making it visible, and then quitting Excel. You'll make it a little trickier by clearing the Excel check box in Project's Reference dialog box.

When a server's object library is not available via a Reference, the controlling application can still quite easily interact with it and its objects as long as you explicitly declare any of the server's built-in constants as global constants. For example, in the demo procedure that follows, Excel's built-in constant xlNormal is declared as `Global Const xlNormal = -4143`.

You can get your hands on global constant declarations for all Excel and Project constants in the ODK. Look for P4JCONST.BAS and XLCONST.BAS in the \MSODK\CONST directory. As described in Chapter 5, another source for Excel constant information is XLCONST.XLS.

First, create a module in Project. Select Tools / References / clear the server's object library (in this case Microsoft Excel) from the Available References list / click OK. Enter the code shown here in the module and run it. All the code samples are heavily commented.

```
Global eobjApp As Object
Global Const xlNormal = -4143
' -------------------------------------------------------------------
' demo procedure
' -------------------------------------------------------------------
Sub sTest_ExcelApplicationCreate()
    ' ----- Have you globally declared all OLEAuto object variables?
    ' ----- Establish a reference to the object
    Set eobjApp = CreateObject("Excel.Application")
    ' ----- Check the server's visibility and set True if hidden
    If Not eobjApp.Visible Then
        eobjApp.Visible = True
    End If
    ' ----- Put code here to interact with the object
    eobjApp.WindowState = xlNormal
    ' ----- Shut down the server using the appropriate method
    eobjApp.Quit
    ' ----- Clear *all* references to the server and its objects
    Set eobjApp = Nothing
End Sub
```

Again, the constant declaration is required because we don't want to rely on Excel being properly referenced. Should you not declare the server constants that you intend to use *and* the server application is not checked in the client's Reference dialog box, you get an error. Try this experiment yourself. Comment out the `Global Const xlNormal = -4143` statement and rerun this procedure.

"Referencing"— don't count on it.

You'll get a "Run-time error" message box on the first offending constant. See Figure 7.5.

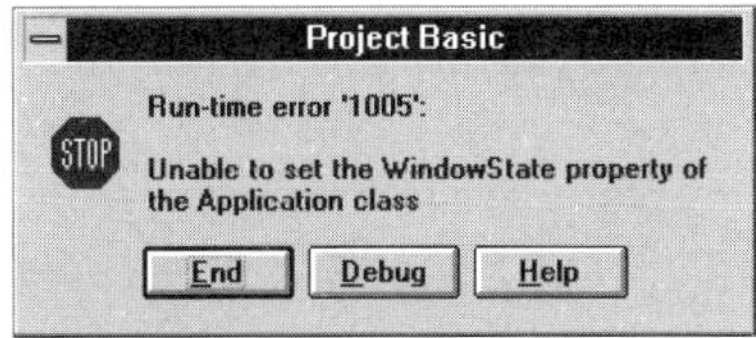

Figure 7.5 For the Want of a Constant, a Run-time Error Occurred.

Project Accessing a New Excel Workbook Sheet via Excel.Sheet

There is only one step from the sublime to the ridiculous.

Napoleon Bonaparte

In this example Project initiates Excel and manipulates a newly created workbook. Remember that Excel is starting via OLE Automation in null menu mode. The CreateObject function uses the Excel.Sheet class type to create a workbook and hence a sheet is available for the subroutine to tweak some of its properties.

You'll use this same subroutine in several of the remaining examples in this section. Again, note the declaration of the server constants so that there is no reliance on having the server application referenced in the controlling application.

```
Global eobjSht As Object
Global Const xlAutomatic = -4105
Global Const xlMaximized = -4137
Global Const xlNormal = -4143
Global Const xlSolid = 1
' --------------------------------------------------------------------
' demo procedure
' --------------------------------------------------------------------
Sub sTest_ExcelNewSheetCreate()
    ' ----- Have you globally declared all OLEAuto object variables?
    ' ----- Establish a reference to the object
    Set eobjSht = CreateObject("Excel.Sheet")
    ' ----- Check the server's visibility and set True if hidden
    If Not eobjSht.Application.Visible Then
       eobjSht.Application.Visible = True
    End If
    ' ----- Put code here to interact with the object
    eobjSht.Application.WindowState = xlNormal
    eobjSht.Application.ActiveWindow.WindowState = xlMaximized
    ' just for the visual effect, set all the sheet's cells blue
    sSetAllCellsBlue eobjSht
    ' ----- Shut down the server using the appropriate method
    eobjSht.Application.Quit
    ' ----- Clear *all* references to the server and its objects
    Set eobjSht = Nothing
End Sub


' --------------------------------------------------------------------
' demo procedure - VBA generic (callable from Excel or Project)
' --------------------------------------------------------------------
Sub sSetAllCellsBlue(wrkSomeSheet As Object)
    wrkSomeSheet.Cells.Select
    With wrkSomeSheet.Application.Selection.Interior
        .ColorIndex = 5
```

```
        .Pattern = xlSolid
        .PatternColorIndex = xlAutomatic
    End With
    wrkSomeSheet.Range("A1").Select
End Sub
```

Figure 7.6 shows what Excel looks like immediately after Visible has been set True.

Now you don't see it, and now you do.

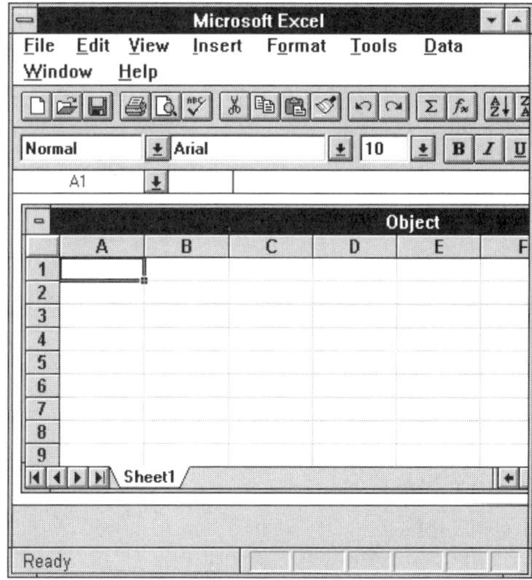

Figure 7.6 Excel Looks Like This After a CreateObject("Excel.Sheet").

Project Accessing a New Excel Workbook Chart via Excel.Chart

> If we do not find anything pleasant, at least we shall find something new.
>
> Voltaire

By changing the class type passed to the CreateObject function (in this example "Excel.Chart"), you can make Excel create a new workbook containing a chart sheet.

```
Global eobjChr As Object
Global Const xl3DColumn = -4100
Global Const xlNormal = -4143
' -----------------------------------------------------------------
' demo procedure
' -----------------------------------------------------------------
Sub sTest_ExcelNewChartCreate()
    ' ----- Have you globally declared all OLEAuto object variables?
```

```
     ' ----- Establish a reference to the object
     Set eobjChr = CreateObject("Excel.Chart")
     ' ----- Check the server's visibility and set True if hidden
     If Not eobjChr.Application.Visible Then
         eobjChr.Application.Visible = True
     End If
     ' ----- Put code here to interact with the object
     eobjChr.Application.WindowState = xlNormal
     ' just for visual effect, change the chart type to 3-D column
     eobjChr.Type = xl3DColumn
     ' ----- Shut down the server using the appropriate method
     eobjChr.Application.Quit
     ' ----- Clear *all* references to the server and its objects
     Set eobjChr = Nothing
End Sub
```

This procedure may shoot by so fast that you won't see Excel jumping through the hoops. You can remark the Quit and Set statements at the end of the procedure so that Excel remains visible with the chart sheet displayed if you like.

Project Accessing an Existing Excel Workbook Sheet via Excel.Sheet

> People don't ever seem to realize that doing what's right is no guarantee against misfortune.
>
> William McFee
> *Casuals of the Sea,* 1916

Building on the previous examples, this next code sample shows you how to get Excel to open a specific sheet. If you want to run this procedure yourself, make sure you change the `strPathName` setting to a valid path/filename on your system. The sample file (in our case `CH07SRCE.XLS`) must contain at least one worksheet.

Beware the GPF that rears its ugly head.

When the subroutine `sSetAllCellsBlue` is run, the current sheet's properties are modified. This subroutine is listed in an earlier example. If you don't happen to have a worksheet as the default sheet when your file opens, and you don't explicitly activate a worksheet before you try to manipulate it, you'll crash with a GPF in **EXCEL.EXE**. Every time. Is it a bug, is it by design? Who knows? As you'll see in the next section, doing this same type of procedure using the Excel.Chart class type does not cause a GPF no matter what the default sheet is. The real issue is that using any class type other than the highest level, Excel.Application, is fraught with peril. (Remember, this is a result of poor implementation by the individual application developers and not with the actual OLE Automation specifications or concept.) So why are we showing you all these examples using other class types? Because you'll see it time and again in the documentation. In the ODK, in sample files, white papers, what have you. It's not wrong to do it this way, but it's tricky as you'll see.

Anyway, it's simple to avoid this GPF by explicitly activating a given worksheet. Notice the line in the following procedure that reads

```
eobjSht.Application.Sheets("Sheet1").Select
```

This statement selects a given sheet, "Sheet1". Be sure that the name string is valid for your file if you're trying this yourself.

```
Global eobjSht As Object
Global Const xlMaximized = -4137
Global Const xlNormal = -4143
' -------------------------------------------------------------------
' demo procedure
' -------------------------------------------------------------------
Sub sTest_ExcelExistSheetGet()
    Dim strPathName As String
    ' Make sure the path and filename are correct for your system
    strPathName = "D:\DATA\TUGOLE\EXAMPLES\CH07SRCE.XLS"
    ' ----- Have you globally declared all OLEAuto object variables?
    ' ----- Establish a reference to the object
    Set eobjSht = GetObject(strPathName, "Excel.Sheet")
    ' ----- Check the server's visibility and set True if hidden
    If Not eobjSht.Application.Visible Then
        eobjSht.Application.Visible = True
    End If
    ' ----- Put code here to interact with the object
    eobjSht.Application.WindowState = xlNormal
    ' the workbook gets opened in a hidden window, so use the
    '    8.3 filename as a caption with which to reference
    '    (and subsequently unhide) this window
    eobjSht.Application.Windows("CH07SRCE.XLS").Visible = True
    eobjSht.Application.ActiveWindow.WindowState = xlMaximized
    ' Critical that a sheet in the target file be selected or GPF!
    ' Make sure the sheet name is valid for your target workbook
    eobjSht.Application.Sheets("Sheet1").Select
    ' just for visual effect, set all the sheet's cells blue
    sSetAllCellsBlue eobjSht
    ' ----- Shut down the server using the appropriate method
    ' a Sheet object's parent is a Workbook object
    eobjSht.Parent.Saved = True
    eobjSht.Application.Quit
    ' ----- Clear *all* references to the server and its objects
    Set eobjSht = Nothing
End Sub
```

Again, you can remark the Quit and Set statements at the end of the procedure so that Excel remains visible with the sheet displayed if you'd like.

Project Accessing an Existing Excel Workbook Chart via Excel.Chart

> This recipe is certainly silly. It says to separate the eggs, but it doesn't say how far to separate them.
>
> Gracie Allen
> *The George Burns and Gracie Allen Show,* 1950

Clang clang clang ... MIND-BENDING ALERT—Unlike the previous procedure `sTest_ExcelExistSheetGet` that GPFs if the current sheet selected isn't a worksheet, this procedure could care less whether a chart is currently selected or not. Because of the class type being used to instantiate Excel, as long as there is at least one chart sheet in the existing workbook it's no worries, mate, the first chart sheet in the workbook is the default for all further actions. If there is no chart in the specified workbook, you get the error in Figure 7.7.

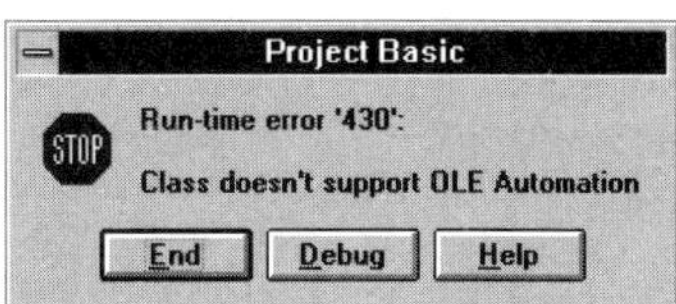

Figure 7.7 If There's No Charts,
Then Charts Got No Class.

In our test workbook `CH07SRCE.XLS` there is only a single chart, so the statement in the procedure

```
eobjChr.Type = xl3DColumn
```

works just peachy for the purpose of showing how to manipulate the properties of a chart. Ah, but to manipulate the properties of a given chart where there are several possibilities requires a more convoluted approach. If in `CH07SRCE.XLS` you have several sheets and want to tweak a chart named "Snark," use a statement like this

```
eobjChr.Parent.Sheets("Snark").Type = xl3DColumn
```

Gnarly, huh? From the current object up to the parent (in this case, the workbook), then down through the properties, methods, and collections to the proper chart sheet, finally setting the property for the chart to be a 3-D chart. Whew!

One other interesting twist involves quitting the server application. We stated earlier that you'd not be saving any files in these examples (you'll do battle with that dragon in Chapter 8). Most programs do not look kindly on your making changes to a document (dirtying it in ProgrammerSpeak) and then discarding those changes. You have to explicitly tell Excel that it doesn't have to save changes. If you use the `CreateObject()` function, you just pass the `Close` method the proper parameter and then quit. Like this

```
eobjChr.Parent.Close SaveChanges:=False
eobjChr.Application.Quit
```

This works like a charm! But, try to use these statements after initializing with the `GetObject()` function and it's another kettle of fish. Won't work. When you use the `GetObject()` function you have to set the Saved property of the workbook to True. Huh, what? Well, if a book's Saved property is True, Excel *thinks* that the workbook has no unsaved changes and that it can close it without worrying about saving it. If the property is False, then Excel is going to try to save it. You have to use the following statements.

Tricking Excel

```
eobjChr.Parent.Saved = True
eobjChr.Application.Quit
```

Remember, you're working with a chart and its parent is the workbook that it's in. Now the big question (drum roll, please), why do you have to do it differently depending on what function you use? Dunno.

Anyway, make sure the path, filename, and chart names are valid for your system and then—please, kids—*do* try this at home.

```
Global eobjChr As Object
Global Const xl3DColumn = -4100
Global Const xlMaximized = -4137
Global Const xlNormal = -4143
' ------------------------------------------------------------------
' demo procedure
' ------------------------------------------------------------------
Sub sTest_ExcelExistChartGet()
    Dim strPathName As String
    strPathName = "D:\DATA\TUGOLE\EXAMPLES\CH07SRCE.XLS"
    ' ----- Have you globally declared all OLEAuto object variables?
    ' ----- Establish a reference to the object
    Set eobjChr = GetObject(strPathName, "Excel.Chart")
    ' ----- Check the server's visibility and set True if hidden
    If Not eobjChr.Application.Visible Then
        eobjChr.Application.Visible = True
```

```
End If
' ----- Put code here to interact with the object
eobjChr.Application.WindowState = xlNormal
' the workbook gets opened in a hidden window, so use the
'    8.3 filename as a caption with which to reference
'    (and subsequently unhide) this window
eobjChr.Application.Windows("CH07SRCE.XLS").Visible = True
eobjChr.Application.ActiveWindow.WindowState = xlMaximized
' just for visual effect, change the chart type to 3-D column
eobjChr.Type = xl3DColumn
' ----- Shut down the server using the appropriate method
' a Chart sheet object's parent is a Workbook object
eobjChr.Parent.Saved = True
eobjChr.Application.Quit
' ----- Clear *all* references to the server and its objects
Set eobjChr = Nothing
End Sub
```

Project Accessing an Existing Excel Worksheet or Chart via Excel.Application

This is what we've been working up to, by golly! You've come full circle, cycling through the different class types in Excel and are finally back to the highest level, good old Excel.Application.

Twists, turns, and hiccups on the OLE Automation highway *Thaaaaaank goodness!* Believe it or not, finally we have some procedures that work with no bizarre twists, turns, hiccups, or other flatulent disruptions. It's about time, eh? Yessireebob, these procedures work. Period. Commands are straightforward and no long compound statements are necessary.

Go ahead. Pound on it. Kick the tires. Stick a sharp knife into the heart of it puh-leez, and it keeps on tickin'. What sheet was last active doesn't matter. It's got legs. Okay, okay, so it doesn't handle the case where `CH07SRCE.XLS` doesn't exist, or is password-protected, or has no chart or worksheets, and so on. We know all that. We'll get to that stuff in the next chapter. We're just stoked that something finally works as you'd expect it to, common sense-wise, you know?

The Right Way to Work with an Existing Workbook Sheet

Here 'tis. You start with the Application object and drill down from there.

```
Global eobjApp As Object
Global Const xlMaximized = -4137
Global Const xlNormal = -4143

' ----------------------------------------------------------------
' demo procedure
' ----------------------------------------------------------------
Sub sTest_ExcelExistSheetViaAppCreate()
    Dim strPathName As String
```

```
    strPathName = "D:\DATA\TUGOLE\EXAMPLES\CH07SRCE.XLS"
    ' ----- Have you globally declared all OLEAuto object variables?
    ' ----- Establish a reference to the object
    Set eobjApp = CreateObject("Excel.Application")
    ' ----- Check the server's visibility and set True if hidden
    If Not eobjApp.Visible Then
        eobjApp.Visible = True
    End If
    ' ----- Put code here to interact with the object
    eobjApp.WindowState = xlNormal
    eobjApp.Workbooks.Open Filename:=strPathName
    eobjApp.Sheets("Sheet1").Select
    eobjApp.ActiveWindow.WindowState = xlMaximized
    ' just for visual effect, set all the sheet's cells blue
    sSetAllCellsBlue eobjApp.ActiveSheet
    ' ----- Shut down the server using the appropriate method
    eobjApp.ActiveWorkbook.Close SaveChanges:=False
    eobjApp.Quit
    ' ----- Clear *all* references to the server and its objects
    Set eobjApp = Nothing
End Sub
```

The Right Way to Work with an Existing Workbook Chart

Make sure the path, filename, and chart names are valid for your system and as
Captain Picard would say—*engage!*

```
Global eobjApp As Object
Global Const xl3DColumn = -4100
Global Const xlMaximized = -4137
Global Const xlNormal = -4143
' --------------------------------------------------------------------
' demo procedure
' --------------------------------------------------------------------
Sub sTest_ExcelExistChartViaAppCreate()
    Dim strPathName As String
    strPathName = "D:\DATA\TUGOLE\EXAMPLES\CH07SRCE.XLS"
    ' ----- Have you globally declared all OLEAuto object variables?
    ' ----- Establish a reference to the object
    Set eobjApp = CreateObject("Excel.Application")
    ' ----- Check the server's visibility and set True if hidden
    If Not eobjApp.Visible Then
        eobjApp.Visible = True
    End If
    ' ----- Put code here to interact with the object
    eobjApp.WindowState = xlNormal
    eobjApp.Workbooks.Open Filename:=strPathName
    eobjApp.Sheets("Chart1").Select
```

```
      eobjApp.ActiveWindow.WindowState = xlMaximized
      ' just for visual effect, change the chart type to 3-D column
      eobjApp.ActiveSheet.Type = xl3DColumn
      ' ----- Shut down the server using the appropriate method
      eobjApp.ActiveWorkbook.Close SaveChanges:=False
      eobjApp.Quit
      ' ----- Clear *all* references to the server and its objects
      Set eobjApp = Nothing
End Sub
```

Project Accessing Excel—Miscellaneous Permutations

> Oh...calamity and woe!
>
> Android First Class Blinky
> *Bucky O'Hare,* Comics

Let's pull off at the rest area up ahead and take a breather. Man, our respective heads are killin' us. Definitely time to pop the tops on a couple of *really* cold ones. You know, where ice crystals form just in the neck of the bottle when the cap comes off. Gulp. Glug glug. Ahhhhhh, much better.

Now let's rerun all the previous experimental procedures with the server application *already running.* Masochists, aren't we? That's what they pay us for. *Heh, heh, heh.* See the results displayed in Table 7.5.

Table 7.5 A Permutational Assessment

Project VBA Procedure	Result When Server Excel Is Already Running
sTest_ExcelApplicationCreate	Starts new instance and uses it then closes only the new instance
sTest_ExcelNewSheetCreate	Uses running instance then closes it
sTest_ExcelNewChartCreate	Uses running instance then closes it
sTest_ExcelExistSheetGet	Uses running instance then closes it
sTest_ExcelExistChartGet	Uses running instance then closes it
sTest_ExcelExistSheetViaAppCreate	Starts new instance and uses it then closes only the new instance
sTest_ExcelExistChartViaAppCreate	Starts new instance and uses it then closes only the new instance

Friend, the upshot here is that it would—we repeat in the affirmative...would—be possible to build a table that describes all possible permutations of `CreateObject()` and `GetObject()` depending on what class type object you initially instantiate (top-level Application or some lower-level object like Chart or

Sheet), whether the server's already running or not, whether the particular object instantiated (if not top-level) was last on top within the Application object's screen-visible hierarchy of explicit user interface-based objects, et cetera et cetera et cetera. *Possible, yes, but…our enthusiasm would wane long before the list was complete.* And for what? What we're saying is—forget it! It's not worth the trouble. Now listen up. Here's the Big Secret. You won't read about it in the Microsoft documentation, either.

Instead of fiddling around with objects other than the top-level Application, the Big Secret is simply this—*establish a reference to the Application object only when you do the Set.* Start at the top and work your way down the server's object hierarchy. Trust us on this. By doing so you'll save yourself from an early retirement, sanitarium-style. Heck, this one tip will probably pay you back five, ten, golly, one hundred times the price of this book. No kidding.

> **Always start at the top level.**

DON'T UNTIE THE KNOT, JUST USE OCCAM'S RAZOR

> On the few occasions he was sober, Batu's mind was as sharp as his axe
> and he could cut straight to the point or right to the bone with equal
> facility.
>
> Amok Shing, Mongol
> *My Years in the Horde* (from the modern translation by K. Tibet, 1972)

Let's compress everything we've observed about the two functions CreateObject() and GetObject() into two tables—Table 7.6 for the case where the server is not already running and Table 7.7 for the case where the server is already running. Then let's carve 'em up by each syntax format of each function across each Office application that can act as an OLEAuto server. (Yes, this is going to make it easier, trust us.)

> **When it's hot and when it's not**

Table 7.6 Server Is Not Already Running

	Excel	Project	Word
CreateObject ("_.Application")	Starts hidden in null menu mode then uses that instance	Starts hidden in null menu mode then uses that instance	Starts visible in null menu mode; state inquiries leave focus stuck in Word
GetObject ("", "_.Application")	Starts hidden in null menu mode then uses that instance	Starts hidden in null menu mode then uses that instance	Starts visible in null menu mode; state inquiries leave focus stuck in Word
GetObject (, "_.Application")	OLEAuto error 440	OLEAuto error 440	OLEAuto error 440
GetObject ("_.Application")	OLEAuto error 440	OLEAuto error 440	OLEAuto error 440

Table 7.7 Server Is Already Running

	Excel	Project	Word
CreateObject ("_.Application")	Starts new hidden instance in null menu mode, then uses that instance	Uses running instance	Uses running instance; state inquiries do *not* leave focus stuck in Word
GetObject ("", "_.Application")	Starts new hidden instance in null menu mode, then uses that instance	Uses running instance	Uses running instance; state inquiries do *not* leave focus stuck in Word
GetObject (, "_.Application")	Uses running instance	Uses running instance	OLEAuto error 440
GetObject ("_.Application")	OLEAuto error 440	OLEAuto error 440	OLEAuto error 440

Remember that Word, as the wayward OLEAuto child of the Office family, calls its top-level object Basic instead of the standard Application. In the columns of these two tables that relate to Word, the CreateObject and GetObject arguments would read "_.Basic" instead of "_.Application."

So what does this tell you? For one thing it's pretty clear that Word is somewhat problematic at best (are we diplomatic or what?) with focus problems if it's not already running. Project and Excel behave in an opposite manner when the server is already running, except for one form of GetObject.

What this all means is that you have to be careful as hell and check this, trap that, watch out for falling rocks, stay behind the yellow line, and beware of the dog. You have to deal with these possibilities by choosing the syntax carefully and programmatically working around the pitfalls. You'll see how in Chapter 8.

NAMED ARGUMENTS WITH OLE AUTOMATION

No you didn't. You came here for an argument.

John Cleese
Monty Python's Flying Circus

At this point if you don't know what an argument is, programmatically speaking, then we're all in a lot of trouble. Well, maybe not. How many of you know the difference between an argument and a parameter? Let's see a show of hands. Be honest now. Ah ha.

Let's use an example. Consider the following purposefully simplified code snippet.

```
Sub TestMacro()
    Dim intVariable1 As Integer
    Dim intVariable2 As Integer
    intVariable1 = 10
    intVariable2 = 20
    MsgBox Str(fintMultiply(intVariable1, intVariable2))
End Sub

Function fintMultiply(A As Integer, B As Integer) As Integer
    fintMultiply = A * B
End Function
```

Here you have a function fintMultiply with two *arguments,* A and B. The *parameters* are 10 and 20 represented by the values in the variables intVariable1 and intVariable2 respectively. So the *parameter* is the value of the *argument* the function gets. Got it? Good. Now that you know the correct usage you can go back to using the terms interchangeably as is common practice.

Arguments, parameters, what's the diff?

Then what the heck is a named argument? Let's look at a WordBasic statement whose intent is to change the point size of some text, set the bold and italic attributes on, and set all other attributes off.

```
FormatFont .Points = "36", .Underline = 0, .Color = 0, .Strikethrough =
0, .Superscript = 0, .Subscript = 0, .Hidden = 0, .SmallCaps = 0,
.AllCaps = 0, .Spacing = "0 pt", .Position = "0 pt", .Kerning = 0,
.KerningMin = "", .Tab = "0", .Font = "Times New Roman", .Bold = 1,
.Italic = 1
```

The FormatFont statement can accept eighteen arguments. Each argument is named, that is, you set the point size by setting the .Point argument to some value. What makes named arguments cool is that you can omit arguments you are not interested in. For example, this statement achieves the same goal, leaves all other parameter values alone, and is easier to read.

```
FormatFont .Points = "36", .Bold = 1, .Italic = 1
```

Without named arguments you'd have to keep track of the argument order using commas as place holders. This manner of listing arguments is called "positional." Like this.

```
FormatFont "36", , , , , , , , , , , , , , , , 1, 1
```

Want to count those commas and make sure we didn't make a mistake? Pretty gruesome, huh? Good thing VBA utilizes named arguments, wot? For example, the Add method of the Sheets object accepts three arguments named After, Type, and Count.

```
ActiveWorkbook.Sheets.Add After:=ActiveWorkbook.Sheets("Module1"),
Type:=xlDialogSheet, Count:=2
```

Because the arguments are *named* you don't have to list them in any particular order or include any arguments that are not required.

So the good news is that WordBasic *and* VBA support named arguments. The bad news is that when you use OLE Automation to control Word *you have to use comma place holders* (meaning positional arguments) with VB3. On the other hand, VBA *can* use Word's named arguments. Earlier you saw the sShowAndTell procedure.

```
Global wobjApp As Object
Sub sShowAndTell()
    Set wobjApp = CreateObject("Word.Basic")
    wobjApp.FileNewDefault
    wobjApp.Insert "Hello Underground!"
    wobjApp.StartOfDocument 1
    wobjApp.FormatFont "36", _
        , , , , , , , , , , , , , , 1, 1
    wobjApp.FilePrint 1
End Sub
```

In this example, because Word is the OLEAuto server, FormatFont is passed the appropriate values using positional arguments. Keep in mind that, as you saw earlier, WordBasic itself uses named arguments. You just can't use them with Word via OLE Automation with VB3. Blecccch.

Visual Basic version 3 does not support a server's named arguments when acting as an OLE Automation client, so you have to use comma place holders (meaning positional arguments). We hope that the next version of Visual Basic will support named arguments when controlling OLEAuto servers.

THE MIGHTY OBJECT BROWSER

> Your Honor, I *object*!
>
> Robert Shapiro, Attorney

With a property here, a method there, here an object, there an object, everywhere an object.object, Old MacRedmond had a module, eeigh, eeigh, ooooh. Wheeee, is this fun stuff or what? Oh. Well, let's see how the handy dandy Object Browser can help you sort out and find object libraries, objects, methods, and properties.

Excel's Object Browser

> What we have here is a failure to communicate.
>
> Strother Martin
> *Cool Hand Luke,* 1967

In Figure 7.8 you see the Object Browser in Excel. We opened a workbook called
`PERSONAL.XLS`, which consists of several modules. A quick click on the Object
Browser button on the Visual Basic toolbar and the Browser dialog box is displayed.

**Object Browser
Button**

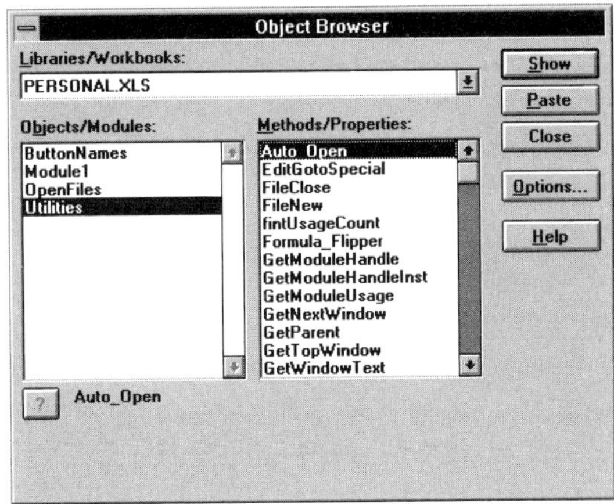

Figure 7.8 Excel's Flavor of Object Browser

In Excel you can browse not only *type libraries* but workbooks as well. You'll
note in the Libraries/Workbooks drop down list that `PERSONAL.XLS` is currently
selected. Let's take a closer look at the drop down list (see Figure 7.9).

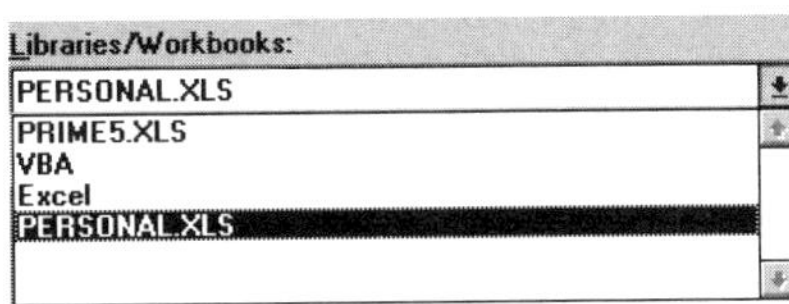

Figure 7.9 Excel's Libraries/
Workbooks Drop Down List

Workbooks

In Figure 7.9 you can see that sorting between the type libraries, VBA and Excel,
and the Workbooks `PRIME5.XLS` and `PERSONAL.XLS` is pretty straightforward.

Only workbooks with module sheets appear in the list. Select a workbook in the drop down list and the module sheets in that workbook appear in the Objects/Modules list box.

Here's what this means to you. Say you're writing a procedure in PRIME5.XLS and you want to drop in a call to a subroutine or function in one of the other module sheets in PERSONAL.XLS. You put the cursor on the line in the module sheet in PRIME5.XLS where you want the call, whistle up the Object Browser via the appropriate toolbar button, choose PERSONAL.XLS from the drop down list, click on the appropriate module name in the left-hand list box, click on the procedure/method you want in the right-hand list box, and finally click on the Paste button. Bang! The method name is pasted into the module you were working in like magic, along with any named arguments (if any).

Type Libraries

Okay, the workbook stuff makes sense, but what about the type libraries? According-ing to the *OLE Programmer's Reference, Volume 2,* "A type library contains descriptions of a collection of objects." Pure and simple. These objects can have methods and properties and the browser's job is to help you find the one you're looking for.

Browsing through the type library VBA appears as a library and you can browse the objects, properties, and methods contained in VBA. Excel has a collection of objects unique to Excel, so you have an Excel type library. For example, select the Excel library in the Library/Workbook drop down list. Excel has workbooks and an Excel workbook is an object, so you can scroll down the Objects/Modules list to Workbook and select it. In the list box on the right, you see listed all the methods and properties that pertain to the Workbook object in Excel.

Change the library type to VBA and you'll not find Workbook in the Object/Module list box. VBA's type library doesn't know beans about workbooks. As you can see, when Microsoft wanted to implement a global macro language they had to have one part that is truly global (the VBA type library) and another part that is unique to each application. In Excel that requires a set of unique Excel objects in a separate type library. Excel has workbooks but other applications do not. You see this split again in Project since Project needs a collection of unique objects for itself.

At Your Command

As mentioned in the previous section, you can select a method/property name and click the Paste button and get that name (plus its arguments, if any) pasted into your current module.

If you select a user-created procedure, the Show command button becomes available. Clicking on Show takes you to the module sheet that contains the selected procedure and puts the cursor at the beginning of the first line of code in that procedure.

Down in the lower-left corner of the Browser dialog box is a small button with a question mark on it. If you select a method or property that has a specific help topic associated with it, the button becomes available. See Figure 7.10.

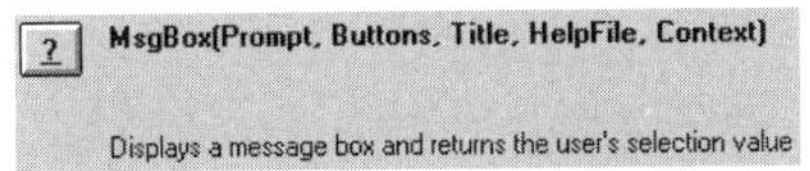

Figure 7.10 Help for a Given Method or Property

You'll notice that the name of the method or property appears next to the button along with any syntax for arguments. Finally, a brief description appears at the bottom of the dialog box. For user-created procedures, you can provide a description for each macro you create via Tools / Macros / Options or you can access the Macro Options dialog box directly from within Object Browser via the Options command button. Clicking on the Question mark button pops up the VBA help file with the appropriate topic displayed.

Referring to References

You can use a given application's Object Browser (Excel and Project have Object Browsers as they support the VBA macro language) to browse objects in other applications. Howzat? Okay, if you look on the Tools menu in Excel (or Project) when a module sheet is active, you'll notice an option called References, which displays the References dialog box. See Figure 7.11.

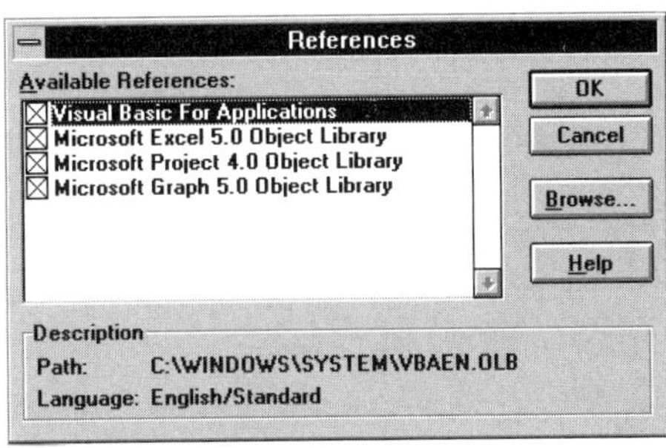

Figure 7.11 Excel's Reference Dialog Box

The References dialog box lists the object libraries installed on your system. Checking the check box adds that type library to the drop down Libraries list in the Object Browser.

Adding libraries to the Object Browser

You've got to exercise some caution if you enable type libraries for objects outside of the application you're working in. You wouldn't want to use a method that appears in the Object Browser that is not available in the application you're coding in.

Project's Object Browser

Project's Object Browser is nearly identical to Excel's in form and function with just two cosmetic exceptions. Project does not have "workbooks;" it has "projects," which can contain code modules. The label for the drop down list reflects this. See Figure 7.12.

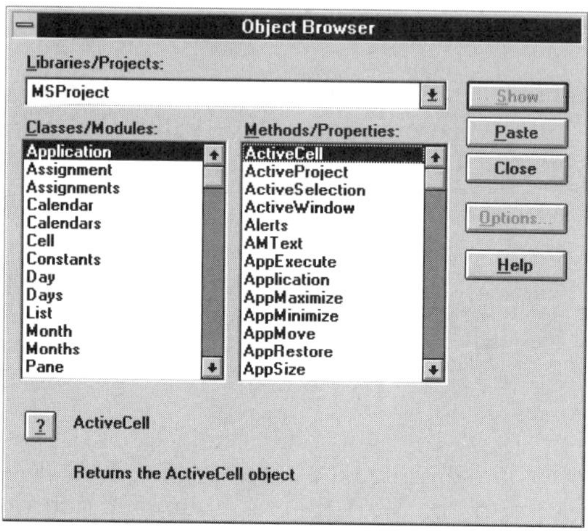

Figure 7.12 For Slicing and Dicing Objects in Project

The list box on the left is labeled Classes/Modules. DON'T PANIC! Without opening a whole can of lexical worms, just pretend that it says "Objects/Modules" as it should and let it go at that. To give you comfort and succor, take a peek at the ODK Browser in Figure 7.13. You'll see the same list of items for the MSProject type library and the good ol' ODK uses the label "Objects," which is consistent with the Excel browser. Just chalk this up to an unfortunate choice of labels made by an overworked Project developer.

The ODK's Object Browser

> What will be, has been.
>
> Igor Vlady
> Brian Lumley, *Necroscope*

The Office Developers Kit CD-ROM contains a generic Object Browser, ODKOB.EXE. See Figure 7.13.

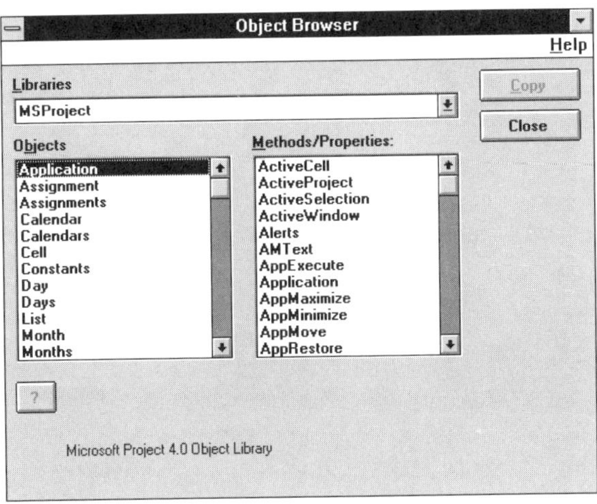

Figure 7.13 The ODK's Object Viewer

When you run it you get a list of all the installed type libraries on your system in the Libraries drop down list. You can browse the objects contained within each library and see the methods and properties of each.

Once you have selected a method or property, you can click on the Copy button to put that method or property on the clipboard.

 8   OLE Automation— Prince or Frog?

> The power of accurate observation is commonly called cynicism by those who have not got it.
>
> George Bernard Shaw

OLE Automation, on its own, is a virtuoso performance. A masterpiece. But it is ultimately just a specification, and as good as the specification may be, it is human beings (Microsoft product development team programmers, analysts, and managers) who, like alchemists, transmute that specification into a particular Office application's implementation of OLEAuto. This is where the, uh, fun begins. The Excel team takes a left turn on a particular aspect of OLEAuto, the Project team takes a right turn, and the Word team takes off in another direction still. Their paths all cross again shortly, but in the meantime some aspect of OLEAuto's implementation invariably ends up being different in appearance or behavior or both. That's when common folk like us start to get really ticked off. Rightly so.

Microsoft may apply the number suffix 2.0 to OLE and subsume under that both (a) the user interface features we talked about in the first half of this book and (b) OLE Automation, but in the end OLE Automation itself is absolutely, undeniably, definitely a 1.0 release. The application integration veteran, DDE, has been around for a while. This workhorse will serve as our comparison norm throughout this chapter as we examine how each of these two inter-application communication protocols hold up under scrutiny of our classic test *"hey, we just want to get things done, dammit."* **OLEAuto is 1.0 while OLE is 2.0.**

A chapter road map follows.

- Design some experiments that compare the speed of OLE Automation and DDE, the two reigning inter-application communication protocols.

- Run the experiments and note the results and implications.

- Detail the differences between OLEAuto and DDE on the issue of server startup behavior.

- Provide all the procedures and orchestration you need to get our "Underground OLE Automation Routine 1.0" to do your bidding.

- Do a brain-dump of the miscellaneous vexatious OLEAuto and DDE bugs we encountered.

OLE VERSUS DDE, BATTLE OF THE TLAs*

> O! the blood more stirs
> To rouse a lion than to start a hare!
>
> William Shakespeare
> *King Henry IV*

Microsoft supports DDE for "backward compatibility" only. Since OLE Automation and DDE, two vastly different inter-application communication protocols, are being supported by Microsoft simultaneously, it's important to compare them across a set of fundamental application integration dimensions. Although Microsoft says that DDE will continue to be supported in a "backward compatibility" mode only, and that OLE Automation is the now-and-into-the-future-amen vehicle for application integration, the truth is that each protocol has its pros and cons and you'll find yourself hopping from one to the other depending on your integration needs for any given development project. In Table 8.1 we call 'em as we see 'em. (If you need to brush up on DDE terminology and coding techniques, see Chapter 9.)

The following bulleted list provides more details about each of the rows in Table 8.1.

- Works with Project as server? Both protocols can interact with this application as a server. Sure, each protocol accomplishes this task differently, but at the bottom line both protocols can do it.

- Works with Word as server? Ditto.

- Works with Excel as server? Ditto.

- Office applications control non-Office applications as servers? If you've got to rap with the competition from within an Office application, DDE wins and OLE Automation loses. The notable exception is an application like Shapeware's Visio, which was specifically designed to fit into Office as an OLEAuto-controllable application. As of this writing, the number of other non-Microsoft applications that are OLEAuto-controllable is burgeoning exponentially, but mostly in the "componentware" arena. The jury is still out as to whether or not Microsoft's major competitors—Lotus, Novell, Borland, and

---

*TLA = Three-Letter Acronyms.

Table 8.1 OLE Automation and DDE Score Card

	OLE Automation	**DDE**
Works with Project as server?	Yes	Yes
Works with Word as server?	Yes	Yes
Works with Excel as server?	Yes	Yes
Office applications control non-Office applications as servers?	No	Yes
Non-Office applications control Office applications as servers?	No	Yes
Maximum directly accessible object size (in the server)	Effectively unlimited (except for Word's 255 character string limit)	Limited only by available clipboard formats negotiated by client and server
Time to complete our test on a 486DX2/66 (see Table 8.2 and Table 8.3)	81 seconds	127 seconds
Resource leakage (after versus before server activation)	0% User, 2–5% GDI	0% User, 2–4% GDI
Resource usage (during versus before server activation)	5–13% User, 10–16% GDI	11–13% User, 10–15% GDI
Can Word act as client (controller)?	No	Yes
Maximum string length returned from Word as server	255 characters	32,768+ characters
Does Word as server support its own, native FileExit method?	No	Yes

so on—will conform to OLE and OLEAuto or proffer a separate compound document and integration technology, or both. Only Jeanne Dixon knows for sure.

- Non-Office applications control Office applications as servers? If you've got to rap with Office applications from within a non-Office application (other than VB), DDE wins and OLE Automation loses.

- Maximum directly accessible object size (in the server). In DDE's case the degree to which an object is accessible boils down to the limits of the clipboard intermediary. In contrast, OLEAuto's architecture places no effective limits on how big (or how much of) an object you can grasp. Ahem, the notable exception being Word's 255 character string limit, which we rave about later in this chapter. Even given this ridiculous practical shortcoming, it's not OLEAuto's fault. The fault lies in the way in which the Word developers coded Word's feature set in regards to this particular OLE Automation mechanism, by limiting the return buffer to 255 characters. This oversight doesn't taint OLE Automation itself, rather Word's implementation thereof.

- Time to complete same task. See Table 8.2 and Table 8.3 for more details. The executive summary is that OLE never lags behind DDE on timing comparisons and typically runs about 50% faster.

- Resource leakage (after versus before server activation). Depending on (1) your interpretation of what's nominal in the context of Windows 3.1 resources and (2) your PC configuration, resource leakage caused by both protocols as a result of server activation is inconsequential. We cover this dimension in more detail in a subsequent section.

- Resource usage (during versus before server activation). Based on the caveats we just expressed, neither protocol produces any alarming results. We cover this dimension in more detail in a subsequent section.

- Can Word act as client (controller)? Not with OLE Automation (as implemented by Word). This really reeks. DDE's way out in front on this point, as in light-years. (Remember, the blame here lies squarely on the shoulders of the folks who developed Word, not OLE Automation.)

- Maximum string length returned from Word as server. Oops. OLEAuto (as implemented by Word) fumbles the football again.

- Does Word as server support its own, native FileExit method? This is a particularly offensive omission. Again, DDE eats OLEAuto (as implemented by Word) for lunch.

All We Want Is 256 Characters from Word

> Cross a termite with a praying mantis and you get a bug that says grace before eating your house.
>
> Unknown

Word is the wayward OLEAuto child. *Soapbox on.* Word is a wayward OLE Automation child in every way imaginable (and we're being diplomatic here). Time and time again you'll see that using Word as an OLE Automation server requires as much DDE programming savvy as it does OLEAuto savvy. Tsk tsk. We often find ourselves wondering, "Hell, why didn't Microsoft save everyone a lot of heartache and simply not include OLE Automation in Word 6, or include it only once they worked out the client-side kinks? DDE works fine with Word 6, thank you very much." Seriously. Then we all wouldn't have to break our backs learning new tricks just for Word 6 when surely a "pure" implementation—as opposed to the extant Word 6 wayward OLEAuto-bolted-onto-the-side catastrophe—will be forthcoming in Word 7, or Word 95, or Word 96, or Word Whatever. *Soapbox off.*

So, how bad is it? Real bad. The bug we're about to spew on should give you an idea of how bad "real bad" is.

When Word's acting as a DDE server you can get back the current contents of a particular bookmark (including the current selection), which can be at least 32,768 or so characters of text. Here's a quick and easy empirical proof. In Visual Basic a text box control can contain somewhat less than 32,768 (32K) characters when its MultiLine property is True as opposed to 2,048 bytes or so when MultiLine is False. The limiting factor here is probably VB3, and perhaps a future version of VB will up the ante, which simply means the 32K ceiling is the limit of the client's (VB3's) control set, *not a limit of DDE itself*. When Word's acting as an OLEAuto server you can get back the current contents of a particular bookmark (including the current selection) which can be up to, ahem, 255 characters of text. Hold on there, we're kidding, right? Wrong. We're serious. And we're mad as hell about this. So are lots of other folks, and you should be too. For whatever reason, the 'Softies in a position to fix this problem haven't. Don't hold your breath. Hmmm, let's see now ... they missed this one by a meager two orders of magnitude.

Let's work through an experiment that viscerally reveals this bug's insidious nature. First create and run the following throw-away WordBasic macro to create a saved file containing 256 characters (not including the paragraph mark at the end of the document). Of course, you may want or need to change the filename to suit your system's configuration.

```
Sub MAIN
    StringCount = 256
    FileNewDefault
    Insert String$(StringCount, "*")
    FileSaveAs .Name = "D:\DATA\WINWORD\DOCS\SMALLDOC.DOC"
End Sub
```

Next fire up Excel, and create the following macro sAskWordFor256Chars(). Be sure to synchronize whatever test filename you're using on your system to match the one you used in the scratch WordBasic macro.

```
Sub sAskWordFor256Chars()
    Dim wobjApp As Object
    Dim strTemp As String
    Set wobjApp = CreateObject("Word.Basic")
    wobjApp.FileOpen "D:\DATA\WINWORD\DOCS\SMALLDOC.DOC"
    strTemp = wobjApp.[GetBookmark$]("\Doc")
    MsgBox "Length of strTemp is " & LTrim(Len(strTemp))
    Set wobjApp = Nothing
End Sub
```

One of Word's sixteen predefined bookmarks, \Doc, retrieves the entire document contents minus the paragraph mark at the end of the document. When you run `sAskWordFor256Chars()` you'll get the nasty error message displayed in Figure 8.1.

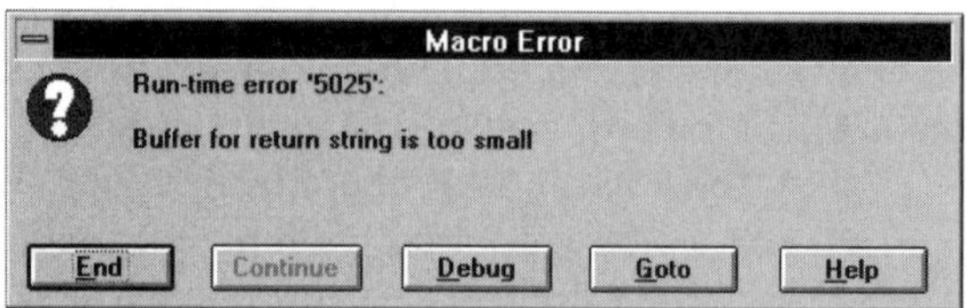

Figure 8.1 How Small Is Small? 255 Characters To Be Exact!

Guess what happens when you click the Help button for this enigmatic run-time error 5025? Well, you don't get any help, that's for sure, because the help topic doesn't exist (see Figure 8.2). Go figure. To find out what Word's 5000 series error messages mean, you have to root around on the TechNet CD (search on "Word API Errors") or scan the file WDERROR.H, which is supplied with the Word Developer's Kit.

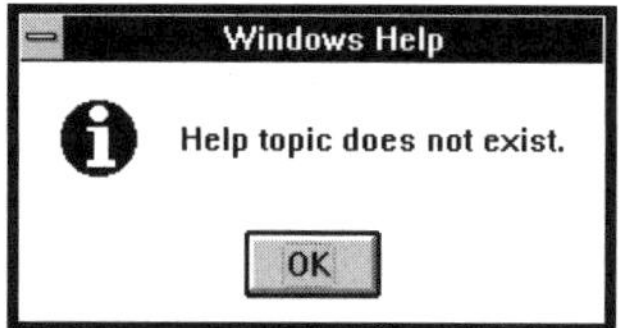

Figure 8.2 Thank You Very Much Error 5025 (Not)

Go back to `SMALLDOC.DOC` and manually delete one (and only one) asterisk. To verify the exact character count, select Tools / Word Count and make sure you see 255. Back in Excel, run `sAskWordFor256Chars()` and you'll get no error, instead you'll see the anticipated message box with the prompt "Length of strTemp is 255."

This bug is not specific to the Excel/Word permutation. Repeat this experiment with Project/Word and VB3/Word. It's 255 characters maximum all the way around. Bummer.

Timing Is Everything

> The trouble with being punctual is that nobody's there to appreciate it.
>
> Franklin P. Jones

Question: Which is faster, DDE or OLE Automation?
Answer: OLE Automation.

In this section we conduct two experiments. In the first we simply fire up and shut down a server *n* times and see how long it takes each protocol to do its civic duty. In the second, once the server is up and running we have it jump through some disk-and-file activity hoops, then go away. When the dust clears, OLE Automation clocks in at between 0% (at worst) and 56% (at best) faster than its elder sibling.

To set the proper scientific method mood, here are the experimental machine conditions.

Applying the scientific method

1. 486DX2/66 CPU with 16 MB of RAM running MS-DOS 6.20, Windows for Workgroups 3.1, and Office Professional 4.3.

2. ATI Graphics Ultra Pro VLB mach32 video card running the ATI mach32 driver at 800x600x256.

3. Reasonably normal `AUTOEXEC.BAT` and `CONFIG.SYS` settings (no esoteric third-party memory managers or other such beasts loaded).

4. Clean load= and run= keys in `WIN.INI`.

5. Program Manager as the Windows shell.

6. Nothing in the StartUp program group.

7. Resource sharing disabled in Control Panel (Network / clear the Enable Sharing check box and allow Windows to reboot itself).

8. An average number of program groups and items within those groups.

9. All applications running as close as possible to stock, out-of-the-box, as delivered by Office Setup. For example, no Word add-ins loaded but some Excel add-ins loaded (exactly as they were set up by Office Setup).

10. Suppress any AutoExec, AutoOpen, and AutoClose macros in Word's `NORMAL.DOT` and any other global templates. You can do this by renaming them, like this, AutoExec to AutoExecXXX and so on.

See Table 8.2 and Table 8.3 for the experimental results, with a detailed discussion in the following sections. Table 8.2 shows performance when simply loading, connecting to, and unloading a server.

Table 8.2 Results of the "Crank It Up" Experiment

Number of Iterations	OLE Automation (seconds)	DDE (seconds)	OLE Speed Benefit over DDE
1	7	7	0%
10	32	65	51%
100	284	642	56%

Table 8.3 shows performance when the server has some assignments to perform while it's active.

Table 8.3 Results of the "Let's Get Busy" Experiment

Number of Iterations	OLE Automation (seconds)	DDE (seconds)	OLE Speed Benefit over DDE
1	13	14	7%
10	81	127	36%
100	746	1261	41%

Crank It Up!

This experiment entails the following steps. *Before starting the experiment in all cases, you should manually verify that Word is not already running.* (Yes, we could have handled this with code, but for simplicity's sake opted to make this experimental condition a manual step.)

1. Start the server.

   In the DDE case, we use a `Shell` statement followed by a call to `DDEInitiate()`. Shell expects the server's shell (executable) file to be in a directory that is set in your DOS Path environmental variable. A second alternative is to pass Shell the fully qualified executable filename.

   In the OLEAuto case, we use `CreateObject()` and then include a clause to minimize Word in order to more closely mimic Word's display state in the DDE experiment. In OLEAuto, the process of instantiating the server automatically "connects" the client and server so there's no explicit equivalent of DDE's DDEInitiate command in OLEAuto.

2. Shut down the server.

   In the DDE case, due to the asynchronous nature of DDE messaging, the client has to sit tight and let the server's former instance go away before firing up the next instance. For this we use the `Do Loop` with a `DoEvents` statement inside it. In the OLEAuto case this is not necessary. Note that shutting down Word with DDE is trivial, while with OLEAuto it's a chore. This is because Word's Basic (remember, Basic, not Application, is the name of Word's top-level OLEAuto object) object doesn't support its own FileExit method, so we use the inelegant AppClose method instead. (The two-level, nested If...End If clauses figure out what Word's title bar is.) If you're worried that someone might have changed Word's title bar on you, for a totally bomb-proof solution look inside Chapter 9's `fAppLoad()` procedure. Contained therein is a title bar sniffing routine concocted by Vince Chen, this tome's technical editor and all-around wizard par excellence. For the time being, however, and to keep things simple, we assume Word's title bar is unsullied by malicious demons lurking in the Windows ether.

3. Repeat all preceding steps *n* times and note the elapsed seconds.

   We chose 1, 10, and 100 iterations respectively, using the variable intEnd. We restarted Windows after each of the three trials. Note that we used Excel as the client for all these experiments.

We used the macro `sCrankItUp_DDE()` for the DDE case and the macro `sCrankItUp_OLEAuto()` for the OLEAuto case. Code for these two macros follows. Note that in the OLEAuto macro we use a generic variable name of `objOAServer` instead of the Word-specific `wobjApp` because we want to be able to substitute any server's class name when instantiating the server.

Although the primary focus of this section is to report and assess the test results, we present the following code so you can conduct your own experiments.

```
Declare Function GetModuleHandle Lib "KERNEL" (ByVal lpModuleName As
String) As Integer
' -----------------------------------------------------------------
' demo procedure
' -----------------------------------------------------------------
Sub sCrankItUp_DDE()
    ' ----- Declarations
    Dim i As Integer
    Dim intEnd As Integer
    Dim intSysChanNum As Integer
    Dim lngElapsed As Long
    Dim lngStart As Long
    Dim strCommand As String
    Dim strModuleName As String
    Dim strShellName As String
    ' ----- Main body
    strModuleName = "WINWORD.EXE"
```

```
    strShellName = "WINWORD"
    intEnd = 1
    ' start the timer
    lngStart = Timer
    For i = 1 To intEnd
        Application.StatusBar = "Working through iteration " & _
            LTrim(Str(i)) & " of " & LTrim(Str(intEnd)) & " ..."
        ' Shell the server minimized without focus
        Shell strShellName, 6
        ' establish a DDE conversation with the server
        intSysChanNum = DDEInitiate(strShellName, "SYSTEM")
        ' shut down the server
        strCommand = "[FileExit]"
        DDEExecute intSysChanNum, strCommand
        DDETerminate intSysChanNum
        ' wait for server to go away completely before proceeding
        Do
            DoEvents
        Loop While GetModuleHandle(strModuleName) <> 0
    Next i
    Application.StatusBar = ""
    ' stop the timer
    lngElapsed = Timer - lngStart
    ' report the elapsed time in seconds
    MsgBox "Elapsed seconds is " & LTrim(Str(lngElapsed))
End Sub


' ----------------------------------------------------------------------
' demo procedure
' ----------------------------------------------------------------------
Sub sCrankItUp_OLEAuto()
    ' ----- Declarations
    Dim i As Integer
    Dim intEnd As Integer
    Dim lngElapsed As Long
    Dim lngStart As Long
    Dim objOAServer As Object
    Dim strOAServerName As String
    Dim strPrompt As String
    Dim strTitleBar As String
    ' ----- Main body
    strOAServerName = "Word.Basic"
    intEnd = 1
    ' start the timer
    lngStart = Timer
    For i = 1 To intEnd
        Application.StatusBar = "Working through iteration " & _
            LTrim(Str(i)) & " of " & LTrim(Str(intEnd)) & " ..."
```

```
      ' start the server
      Set objOAServer = CreateObject(strOAServerName)
      ' mimic Word's display state in the DDE experiment
      If objOAServer.AppMinimize() <> -1 Then
          objOAServer.AppMinimize
      End If
      ' shut down the server
      If objOAServer.CountWindows() <> 0 Then
          If objOAServer.DocMaximize() = -1 Then
              strTitleBar = "Microsoft Word - " & _
                  objOAServer.[WindowName$]()
          Else
              strTitleBar = "Microsoft Word"
          End If
      Else
          strTitleBar = "Microsoft Word"
      End If
      objOAServer.AppClose strTitleBar
      Set objOAServer = Nothing
  Next i
  Application.StatusBar = ""
  ' stop the timer
  lngElapsed = Timer - lngStart
  ' report the elapsed time in seconds
  MsgBox "Elapsed seconds is " & LTrim(Str(lngElapsed))
End Sub
```

Let's Get Busy

This experiment entails the following steps. *As in the last experiment, you should manually verify that Word is not already running.* Instructions for setting up the five test documents and modifying the test code to reflect your PC configuration are provided in the following steps where appropriate.

1. Start the server.

   No change from the previous experiment.

2. Open five preexisting test files from the local disk.

   This step involves a straightforward series of requests for Word to open five files. To create these files before running the experiment do the following: create a new file based on NORMAL.DOT; save the first file as DUMMY1.DOC (the second as DUMMY2.DOC, etc.); select Insert / Field / select Document Information in the Categories list / select FileName in the Field Names list / click Options / select the Field Specific Switches filecard / select the "\p" switch if it isn't already selected / click Add to Field / click OK / click OK; repeat until you've got DUMMY1.DOC through DUMMY5.DOC. Make a note of the path for these files and set `strPathOnly` in both macros to reflect this path. Be sure to include a trailing backslash. Finally, perform these steps on `DUMMY1.DOC` only: make sure field codes are turned off; select the fully qualified filename that's now the only text in the document (don't select the trailing paragraph mark); select Edit / Bookmark / type in Bookmark1 / click Add; save the file.

3. Get a list of all available files (topics).

   DDE provides such a list pro bono through its special "Topics" item argument in the `DDERequest()` function call. When Word is the server, the caller gets back a list of all open files and any other available non-file topics ("System" typically being the only one). There is no native function to provide the OLEAuto equivalent of this Topics inquiry, so we wrote one. It's called `sOAGetOpenFiles()` where "OA" stands for OLE Automation.

4. Put the list components into a range of cells starting at A3 (R3C1).

   Since a message box would interfere with the timer, we write the open files list to a range of cells so that we can verify the experiment's success (see Figure 8.3 and Figure 8.4). Make sure you've got a worksheet named Sheet1 in the workbook containing your test macros.

   The DDE list includes any global templates (for example, `NORMAL.DOT`) along with the special System topic. The OLEAuto list does not include any global templates, just those files that are explicitly open in Word's child windows. You could, of course, write another function or modify `sOAGetOpenFiles()` to include global templates.

5. Get the contents of Bookmark1 from `DUMMY1.DOC`.

   With DDE you have to use `DDERequest()` to get back the bookmark's contents. With OLEAuto you use Word's own native `GetBookmark$()` method to do this. Any `DDERequest()` returns a one-based Variant array type in VBA *regardless of the source item's data type*, whereas in OLEAuto the value returned by the call to Word's native method matches that method's native data type. In this case, `GetBookmark$()` returns a string so that's what comes back to VBA. (We use a Variant variable as the assignee just for expedience; if you do a `TypeName()` on vntData right after the `GetBookmark$()` call, you'll see that it's a string.)

   Also note that with DDE you establish a new channel with the source filename as the topic followed by the bookmark name as the item, whereas in OLEAuto you explicitly change focus to the source file then call `GetBookmark$()`.

6. Put Bookmark1's contents into the cell A1 (R1C1).

Here we avoid interrupting the timer with a message box and instead write the contents into a cell so that we can verify the experiment's success. Figure 8.3 shows the filename and bookmark contents listing produced by DDE.

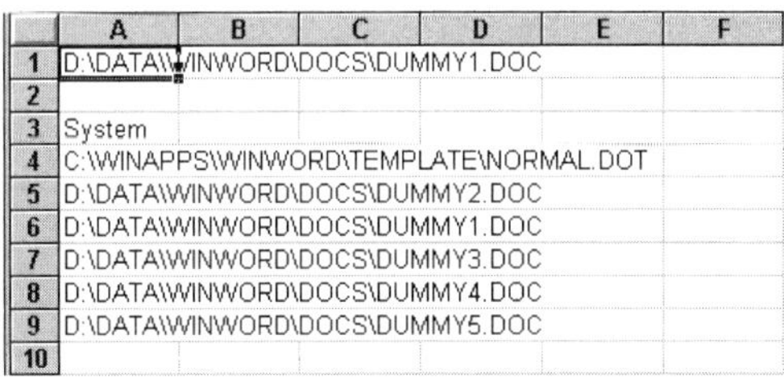

Figure 8.3 DDE Produces This List of Available Files (Topics); Bookmark1 Contents Is in A1

Figure 8.4 shows the corresponding listing produced by OLEAuto.

Figure 8.4 OLEAuto Produces This List of Available Files; Bookmark1 Contents Is in A1

7. Close all open files (no save).

   `FileCloseAll` with an argument value of 2 (meaning close all documents without saving changed documents) puts away all open files.

8. Shut down the server.

   No change from the previous experiment.

9. Repeat all preceding steps *n* times and note the elapsed seconds.
   We chose 1, 10, and 100 iterations respectively, using the variable intEnd. We restarted Windows after each of the three trials.

We used the macro `sLetsGetBusy_DDE()` for the DDE case and the macro `sLetsGetBusy_OLEAuto()` for the OLEAuto case. Code for these two macros follows.

Although the primary focus of this section is to report and assess the test results, we present the following code so that you can conduct your own experiments.

```
Declare Function GetModuleHandle Lib "KERNEL" (ByVal lpModuleName As
String) As Integer
' -------------------------------------------------------------------
' demo procedure
' -------------------------------------------------------------------
Sub sLetsGetBusy_DDE()
    ' ----- Declarations
    Dim i As Integer
    Dim intChanNum As Integer
    Dim intEnd As Integer
    Dim intSysChanNum As Integer
    Dim j As Integer
    Dim lngElapsed As Long
    Dim lngStart As Long
    Dim strCommand As String
    Dim strModuleName As String
    Dim strPathOnly As String
    Dim strQuote As String
    Dim strShellName As String
    Dim vntData As Variant
    ' ----- Main body
    strModuleName = "WINWORD.EXE"
    strPathOnly = "D:\DATA\WINWORD\DOCS\"
    strQuote = Chr(34)
    strShellName = "WINWORD"
    intEnd = 1
    ' start the timer
    lngStart = Timer
    For i = 1 To intEnd
        Application.StatusBar = "Working through iteration " & _
            LTrim(Str(i)) & " of " & LTrim(Str(intEnd)) & " ..."
        ' Shell the server minimized without focus
        Shell strShellName, 6
        ' establish a DDE conversation with the server
        intSysChanNum = DDEInitiate(strShellName, "SYSTEM")
        ' ----- START experiment #2 incremental code
        ' open the five test files
        For j = 1 To 5
            strCommand = "[FileOpen " & _
                strQuote & strPathOnly & _
                "DUMMY" & LTrim(Str(j)) & ".DOC" & strQuote & "]"
            DDEExecute intSysChanNum, strCommand
        Next j
        ' get a list of all available files (topics)
        vntData = DDERequest(intSysChanNum, "TOPICS")
```

```
        ' put the list components into a range of cells
        For j = LBound(vntData) To UBound(vntData)
            Sheets("Sheet2").Cells(j + 2, 1).Formula = vntData(j)
        Next j
        ' get the contents of Bookmark1 from DUMMY1.DOC
        intChanNum = DDEInitiate(strShellName, _
            strPathOnly & "DUMMY1.DOC")
        vntData = DDERequest(intChanNum, "Bookmark1")
        DDETerminate intChanNum
        ' put Bookmark1's contents into a cell
        Sheets("Sheet2").Range("A1").Formula = vntData(LBound(vntData))
        ' close all open files (no save)
        strCommand = "[FileCloseAll 2]"
        DDEExecute intSysChanNum, strCommand
        ' ----- END   experiment #2 incremental code
        ' shut down the server
        strCommand = "[FileExit]"
        DDEExecute intSysChanNum, strCommand
        DDETerminate intSysChanNum
        ' wait for server to go away completely before proceeding
        Do
            DoEvents
        Loop While GetModuleHandle(strModuleName) <> 0
    Next i
    Application.StatusBar = ""
    ' stop the timer
    lngElapsed = Timer - lngStart
    ' report the elapsed time in seconds
    MsgBox "Elapsed seconds is " & LTrim(Str(lngElapsed))
End Sub


' ------------------------------------------------------------------
' demo procedure
' ------------------------------------------------------------------
Sub sLetsGetBusy_OLEAuto()
    ' ----- Declarations
    Dim i As Integer
    Dim intEnd As Integer
    Dim j As Integer
    Dim lngElapsed As Long
    Dim lngStart As Long
    Dim objOAServer As Object
    Dim strFileNames() As String
    Dim strOAServerName As String
    Dim strPathOnly As String
    Dim strPrompt As String
    Dim StrShellName As String
    Dim strStartWindow As String
```

```
Dim strTitleBar As String
Dim vntData As Variant
' ----- Main body
strOAServerName = "Word.Basic"
strPathOnly = "D:\DATA\WINWORD\DOCS\"
strShellName = "WINWORD"
intEnd = 1
' start the timer
lngStart = Timer
For i = 1 To intEnd
    Application.StatusBar = "Working through iteration " & _
        LTrim(Str(i)) & " of " & LTrim(Str(intEnd)) & " ..."
    ' start the server
    Set objOAServer = CreatcObject(strOAServerName)
    ' mimic Word's display state in the DDE experiment
    If objOAServer.AppMinimize() <> -1 Then
        objOAServer.AppMinimize
    End If
    ' ----- START experiment #2 incremental code
    ' open the five test files
    For j = 1 To 5
        objOAServer.FileOpen _
            strPathOnly & "DUMMY" & LTrim(Str(j)) & ".DOC"
        If j = 1 Then
            ' capture DUMMY1.DOC's child window title
            strStartWindow = objOAServer.[WindowName$]()
        End If
    Next j
    ' get a list of all available files (topics)
    sOAGetOpenFiles objOAServer, strShellName, strFileNames()
    ' put the list components into a range of cells
    For j = LBound(strFileNames) To UBound(strFileNames)
        Sheets("Sheet2").Cells(j + 3, 1).Formula = strFileNames(j)
    Next j
    ' get the contents of Bookmark1 from DUMMY1.DOC
    objOAServer.Activate strStartWindow
    vntData = objOAServer.[GetBookmark$]("Bookmark1")
    ' put Bookmark1's contents into a cell
    Sheets("Sheet2").Range("A1").Formula = vntData
    ' close all open files (no save)
    objOAServer.FileCloseAll 2
    ' ----- END   experiment #2 incremental code
    ' shut down the server
    If objOAServer.CountWindows() <> 0 Then
        If objOAServer.DocMaximize() = -1 Then
            strTitleBar = "Microsoft Word - " & _
                objOAServer.[WindowName$]()
```

```
        Else
            strTitleBar = "Microsoft Word"
        End If
    Else
        strTitleBar = "Microsoft Word"
    End If
    objOAServer.AppClose strTitleBar
    Set objOAServer = Nothing
Next i
Application.StatusBar = ""
' stop the timer
lngElapsed = Timer - lngStart
' report the elapsed time in seconds
MsgBox "Elapsed seconds is " & LTrim(Str(lngElapsed))
End Sub
```

Here is the code for `sOAGetOpenFiles()` that stuffs a passed array argument
with the fully qualified names of all open files in any Office OLEAuto-compliant
server.

```
' ----- Global Declarations
Global Const EXCEL5_SHELL_NAME = "EXCEL"
Global Const PROJECT4_SHELL_NAME = "WINPROJ"
Global Const WORD6_SHELL_NAME = "WINWORD"


' ------------------------------------------------------------------
' Purpose:   Stuffs strFileNames with fully qualified
'            path-and-filename of each child window.
'
' Inputs:    objOAServer - pointer to the current OLEAuto server
'            strShellName - used as a unique hook to each server
'            strFileNames() - array to be stuffed
'
' Updated:   12/20/94
' ------------------------------------------------------------------
Public Sub sOAGetOpenFiles(objOAServer As Object, strShellName As
String, strFileNames() As String)
    ' ----- Declarations
    Dim i As Integer
    Dim intFWN As Integer        ' FWN = file window names
    Dim intWindowCount As Integer
    Dim strStartWindow As String
    Dim vntOpenFiles As Variant
    ' ----- Main body
    ' react differently depending on the OLEAuto server
    Select Case strShellName
        Case EXCEL5_SHELL_NAME
            vntOpenFiles = fvntOAFileNames(objOAServer.Workbooks)
```

```
            ReDim strFileNames(UBound(vntOpenFiles))
            For i = LBound(vntOpenFiles) To UBound(vntOpenFiles)
                strFileNames(i) = vntOpenFiles(i)
            Next i
        Case PROJECT4_SHELL_NAME
            vntOpenFiles = fvntOAFileNames(objOAServer.Projects)
            ReDim strFileNames(UBound(vntOpenFiles))
            For i = LBound(vntOpenFiles) To UBound(vntOpenFiles)
                strFileNames(i) = vntOpenFiles(i)
            Next i
        Case WORD6_SHELL_NAME
            intWindowCount = objOAServer.CountWindows()
            If intWindowCount = 0 Then
                ' there are no open files
                ReDim strFileNames(0)
                strFileNames(0) = ""
                Exit Sub
            End If
            ReDim strFileNames(intWindowCount - 1)
            ' first capture current child window title
            strStartWindow = objOAServer.[WindowName$]()
            For i = 1 To intWindowCount
                strFileNames(i - 1) = _
                    objOAServer.[FileNameFromWindow$](i)
            Next i
            ' now return focus to original child window
            objOAServer.Activate strStartWindow
        Case Else
    End Select
End Sub
```

Leaky Resources Yea or Nay?

> But then they danced down the street like dingledodies, and I shambled
> after as I've been doing all my life after people who interest me, because
> the only people for me are the mad ones, the ones who are mad to live,
> mad to talk, mad to be saved, desirous of everything at the same time, the
> ones who never yawn or say a commonplace thing, but burn, burn, burn
> like fabulous yellow roman candles exploding like spiders across the stars
> and in the middle you see the blue centerlight pop and everybody goes
> "Awww!"
>
> Jack Kerouac
> *On the Road,* 1957

Resource drain proves nominal for both protocols. *Both OLE Automation and DDE leak resources* (from the perspective of before and *after* the server's activation). The leakage doesn't seem to grow in proportion to the number of iterative calls or the complexity of the tasks being performed.

When the protocols are simply loading and unloading the server, it's a tie. When we sandwich some tasks in between, OLEAuto sucks up an additional 2% GDI relative to DDE.

What about resource usage before and *during* the server's activation? (We're talking about usage here, not leakage; the comparison is between the point in time before the server loads and the point in time when it is loaded and producing the maximum drain on resources.) When the protocols are simply loading and unloading the server, the differential between pre-loaded and loaded is less with OLEAuto than DDE. In a ten-iteration test case, DDE server activation consumes 11% and 10% (User and GDI percent free resources respectively) while OLEAuto server activation consumes 5% and 10%. So the OLEAuto server consumes six absolute percentage points less of User's heap space. This six-point reduction is almost a 50% reduction in the load relative to DDE (six points down from 11% is a difference of 45%).

On the other hand, in a ten-iteration test case when we sandwich some tasks in between, OLEAuto consumes one more point of the GDI heap than DDE. Practically speaking, it's far more likely in a real-world scenario that the server will have some tasks to perform, so the bottom line seems to be that OLEAuto consumes nominally (1%) more GDI resources than DDE.

Your mileage may vary, of course.

START ME UP

> I am that which began;
> Out of me the years roll;
> Out of me God and man;
> I am equal and whole;
> God changes, and man, and the form of them bodily; I am the soul.
>
> Algernon Charles Swinburne
> *Hertha*, 1871

In this section we explore what happens when various Office applications are **You started it.** loaded as both OLE Automation and DDE servers. Bits and pieces of this puzzle with respect to OLE Automation were revealed earlier in Chapter 7 when we ran through the `CreateObject()` and `GetObject()` gauntlet. But our objective here is to show the differences between OLE Automation and DDE in one fell swoop.

Table 8.4 reveals that whereas DDE starts servers visible, OLEAuto starts servers hidden except for Word, which starts visible. *Excel and Project's initial hidden state is by design* and prevents the user of an OLEAuto custom application from being able to manually switch to the server and interact with it.

You can force Word to be hidden by issuing the AppHide command right after the `CreateObject()` or `GetObject()` call; but Word will still be visible very briefly between the time that it is loaded and the issuance of AppHide.

Table 8.4 OLE Automation vs. DDE—Server Visibility When Started

	OLE Automation	**DDE**
Excel	Not visible	Visible
Project	Not visible	Visible
Word	Visible	Visible

We noticed nothing unusual about OLE Automation servers in terms of add-ins (also referred to as "globals") being available when started, ahem, except in the case of Excel. *Oh brother*. See Table 8.5.

When OLEAuto starts Excel and you create a new file (either programmatically or by setting Excel visible and creating a new file manually), that file will not be based on any of your custom templates in your XLSTART directory. For example, if you have a custom `BOOK.XLT` template it will *not* be used as the basis for new books during an OLEAuto session. As you saw back in Chapter 3, Word allows you to specify a template to be used when new documents are created with OLEAuto by setting OLEDot=template.ext in the `WINWORD6.INI` file, but there is no equivalent trick for Excel.

Table 8.5 OLE Automation vs. DDE—Global Template/Add-in Availability and Behavior When Started

	OLE Automation	**DDE**
Excel	Add-ins are "as usual" except ignores a loaded add-in's Auto_Open macro; File / New ignores Excel templates (like `BOOK.XLT`).	Add-ins are "as usual" (a loaded add-in's Auto_Open macro works as usual); File / New uses Excel templates (like `BOOK.XLT`).
Project	No equivalent to Excel or Word's global/add-in feature (`GLOBAL.MPT` is "as usual" if you open any file).	No equivalent to Excel or Word's global/add-in feature (`GLOBAL.MPT` is "as usual" if you open any file).
Word	Add-ins are "as usual"; global AutoExec macro works as usual.	Add-ins are "as usual"; global AutoExec macro works as usual.

When OLEAuto starts Excel, if a loaded add-in (one that's been previously selected in the Tools / Add-Ins list) contains an Auto_Open macro, *Excel ignores it*, whereas a DDE session runs the Auto_Open normally. With OLEAuto and Excel, loaded add-ins are still available, mind you, but Auto_Open is ignored. Go figure.

OLE Automation and DDE are precisely the opposite in regard to whether or not the server is started with a default document present. OLEAuto consistently provides no default document, that is, starts the server in null menu mode. DDE consistently starts the server with a default document open. See Table 8.6.

Opposites don't always attract.

Table 8.6 OLE Automation vs. DDE—Traditional Default Document Status When Started

	OLE Automation	DDE
Excel	Starts in null menu mode (no default document).	Book1 as usual.
Project	Starts in null menu mode (no default document).	Project1 as usual.
Word	Starts in null menu mode (no default document).	Document1 as usual.

MISCELLANEOUS VEXATIOUS OLE AUTOMATION AND DDE INSECTOIDS

> There is freedom in getting completely screwed up because you know things can't get any worse.
>
> *The Freshman* (1990 movie)

This section includes a hodgepodge of bugs we discovered along the grueling OLE Automation and DDE circuit. We present them here in no particular order.

1. Project VBA is missing the `DDERequest()` and the `DDEPoke()` methods. Excel VBA has both. Go figure.

2. It's too easy to get lost in the VBA inter-dialect miasma. All VBA help file topics should be flagged somehow to indicate the parent application's name. It is possible to establish a Reference in one dialect of VBA (say, Project as the host with a Reference to Excel), type in a statement that includes a method that is valid in Excel but not Project (say, `DDERequest()`), and wind up looking at a perfectly valid help topic on that method. *But you're really looking at Excel's help file, not Project's, and there's no way to tell the difference unless you click the Contents button and leave the topic you wanted in the first place.* Nuts. This demon ran us right down a piddling rabbit trail. Don't let it happen to you!

3. As a matter of general principle and merchantability, it's inexcusable that Project's VBA coding environment is different from Excel's. But it is, in numerous ways that you'll see after about the first 60 seconds of browsing around in a Project module.

4. One very annoying problem with Project's module sheet is this: when you press F1 for context-sensitive help on a VBA key word, if you have multiple References (say, Project and Excel), then the resulting list box items can't be double-clicked for expedient selection. Instead you have to select a list box item then click the OK button. Ditto this glitch for Project's Object Browser. *This is contrary to all published Windows application development guidelines.* Go figure.

5. An Excel 5 workbook module sheet cannot act as a source for a DDE conversation. Whether you consider this to be obvious or not, this point sure isn't documented anywhere.

6. The *Excel Visual Basic User's Guide* is dead wrong in its claim that, "Unlike CreateObject, however, GetObject does not start Word if it is not already running." This is so completely wrong that we assume someone made a typesetting error. Whatever the cause, the truth is that both CreateObject and GetObject, when used in the syntactically correct way, do start Word if it is not already running.

7. Excel's Application object supports the StatusBar property, a mechanism by which hundreds of thousands of developers the world over write messages to the status bar to keep their users informed about an application's progress. This is a good thing, so Excel gets a gold star. On the other hand, Project's Application object does *not* support the StatusBar property, thereby placing itself squarely on Santa's bad child list this year. This means (1) you can't write to Project's status bar with VBA, and (2) you have to remark out any Application.StatusBar statements in code you port from Excel to Project. Portability schmortability. If Microsoft's stock price were to reflect bumps in the glory road to a "common macro language," today would be a down day on the market for ol' MSFT, yes indeedy.

ONE BIG, FAT, AND SASSY OLE AUTOMATION ROUTINE

> When you come to a fork in the road, take it.
>
> Yogi Berra

The remainder of this chapter is devoted to providing you with a set of general-purpose OLE Automation procedures to make the process of inter-application communication, OLEAuto-style, as easy as possible. Along the way you'll see how we orchestrate these procedures and pick up some ideas about how you can use them to do your own bidding.

Keep in mind that these procedures work whether the client application is Excel, Project, or Visual Basic. To the degree that OLE Automation and the various server applications' object models are amenable, this sassy collection of procedures is plug-and-play. Let's get hackin'. **We give you plug and play OLEAuto.**

Global and Module-level Declarations and the sOLEAutoRoutine Procedure

> How is it possible to find meaning in a finite world, given my waist and shirt size?
>
> Woody Allen

Here are the steps for creating your own version of this utility.

1. Create a new module and rename it as modOLEAutoRoutine. (We assume you're still working in the project from Chapter 6 in which you created the modules modFunctions, modGlobals, and modSubroutines respectively. If not, then create them now.)

2. Key in the code for the procedures listed by name in Table 8.7. Source code for these procedures is located in the following sections.

3. Save the workbook.

4. At this point in the book you'll undoubtedly be flipping forward one page at a time, keying in the code and exploring each procedure. When you get to the end of the upcoming sections that house the procedure code, we'll show you how to put this OLE Automation routine through its paces.

Table 8.7 OLE Automation Routine's Module and Procedure Map

Module Name	Procedure Name
modFunctions	fintOAAppLoad fintOAFileStatus fvntOAProjectNames fstrGetHostTitleBar
modGlobals	global constant and variable declarations (no procedure code)
modOLEAutoRoutine	sOLEAutoRoutine
modSubroutines	sOAGetOpenFiles sOAShutDownApp

The code in this section includes the project's global declarations as well as the module's declarations.

This procedure is the orchestra leader.

The `sOLEAutoRoutine` procedure is simply one example of how you might stitch together your own OLEAuto quilt. *It orchestrates all the general-purpose functions and subroutines you'll need to put an OLEAuto session together.* This is why you'll see an entire section of `sOLEAutoRoutine` commented like this: "Put your OLEAuto commands below (examples follow)." It (and the accompanying procedures) is written to work from within any OLEAuto-compatible client, which as of the date of this writing are Excel, Project, and Visual Basic 3. The specific code you see throughout this and following sections was taken directly from an Excel project. To port the code to run from inside Project, you'll have to make a relatively small number of changes. We discuss this port to Project later in this chapter. Porting to Visual Basic 3 is rendered a bit more tedious by the fact that VB3 doesn't support VBA named arguments, so for that port to work you have to convert all the VBA named arguments to positional arguments. Tedious? Yes, but nonetheless all the code herein is ready to be ported to any VBA dialect as well as VB3. *Three utilities for the price of one!*

Just add some elbow grease.

We're going to assume you're willing to put in a little elbow grease when experimenting with this utility. Specifically, we won't be spelling out all the granular steps for setting up Excel, Project, and Word test source files complete with the appropriately configured objects, and so on. We figure that at this point in the book you're comfortable with those housekeeping details and can infer from `sOLEAutoRoutine`'s source code comments how to calibrate these odds and ends. Rest assured that in our lab this utility ran swimmingly under all test conditions across all client/server permutations, so enjoy!

Here's a walk-through of the main sections of `sOLEAutoRoutine`.

- Determine app's loaded status and react accordingly. Figure out whether the server is already loaded and load it only if it isn't. If Word's the server we always hide it *but only if we loaded it.* If we get an error value from `fintOAAppLoad()`, then report it and hit the brakes.

- Determine file's loaded status and react accordingly. Throughout this exercise we assume the client is interested in some file-based data. Figure out whether the file of interest is already open and open it only if it isn't. If we get an error value from `fintOAFileStatus()` then report it and hit the brakes.

- Interact with the server and its objects. Here we use a Select Case statement to route the utility depending on who the server is. We use the server's shell name as the test expression because Excel, Project, and Word don't support one common naming "hook."

Microsoft documentation states that every top-level object in an OLEAuto server should be named "Application." Excel and Project comply but the wayward Word doesn't (it uses "Basic"). Microsoft documentation states that every top-level object in an OLEAuto server should support the Name property. Excel's Application object's Name property returns "Microsoft Excel." That's good. Project's Application object's Name property returns "Microsoft Project." That's fine. Alas, *Word's Basic object doesn't support the Name property at all*, so you can't use Name as a common hook.

We thought about using the `TypeName()` function but it returns values that are too generic to be of any use—"Application," "Object," and "wordbasic" for Excel, Project, and Word respectively. Although these strings are uniquely different for the time being, the day when other OLEAuto servers come along and also return "Application" is too close at hand. Our only recourse is to supply a module-level variable to uniquely identify the server throughout the lifetime of the utility. To do this we use the server's shell name assigned to the variable strShellName.

- Shut down the application if appropriate (and always remember to Set the OLEAuto object variable to Nothing). Remembering whether the server was already loaded before we came along or if we loaded it, when it's time to quit we leave it alone if it was already loaded or shut it down if we loaded it. We also remember whether the source file was open before we came along; if we in fact opened the file then we're going to close it before deciding what to do about the server itself.

Notice that we make the main procedure, not the `sOAShutDownApp()` procedure, responsible for closing a file. The syntax for closing a file is maddeningly different for each server (a truck-swallowing crater in Microsoft's "common programming language" road to glory). Excel's Workbook object uses the Close method. Project's Application object uses the FileClose method—that's right, a different object and a different method between Excel and Project. Word's Basic object uses FileClose. Need we point out that all the arguments are different? No surprise there, eh? Excel's SaveChanges argument, when True, saves the changes to the file. Project's Save argument, when pjSave (1), saves any changes to the file. Excel workbooks ignore any local Auto_Open and Auto_Close macros when opened and closed if they are opened by VBA, but Project is just the opposite. Project provides a NoAuto argument for both its FileOpen and FileClose methods that, when True, suppresses the execution of auto macros. Word's FileClose method only has one argument that, when 1, saves the document before closing it.

> **Syntax bumps in the road to a truly common macro language**

- General comments—We provide an error handler in `sOLEAutoRoutine` but it's not hooked up. By personal preference, we let any errors local to

sOLEAutoRoutine occur naturally. If you want to use the error handler, go
for it. Throughout these procedures you'll see the statement `AppActivate`
`strTitleBar` whose role is to return focus to the client. While experimenting
with various servers we noticed that occasionally, for no discernible reason,
the client wouldn't get the focus back after some activity in the server (this
was particularly true with Word). The simplest solution is to sandwich this
AppActivate statement wherever focus is likely to be held up by the server.

```
Option Explicit

Declare Function GetActiveWindow Lib "USER" () As Integer
Declare Function GetModuleHandle Lib "KERNEL" (ByVal lpModuleName As
String) As Integer
Declare Function GetWindowText Lib "USER" (ByVal hWnd As Integer, ByVal
lpString As String, ByVal aint As Integer) As Integer

' ----- Global Declarations
Global Const EXCEL5_MODULE_NAME = "EXCEL.EXE"
Global Const EXCEL5_OLEAUTO_NAME = "Excel.Application"
Global Const EXCEL5_SHELL_NAME = "EXCEL"
Global Const PROJECT4_MODULE_NAME = "WINPROJ.EXE"
Global Const PROJECT4_OLEAUTO_NAME = "MSProject.Application"
Global Const PROJECT4_SHELL_NAME = "WINPROJ"
Global Const WORD6_MODULE_NAME = "WINWORD.EXE"
Global Const WORD6_OLEAUTO_NAME = "Word.Basic"
Global Const WORD6_SHELL_NAME = "WINWORD"

Global hWnd As Integer
Global i As Integer
Global strDboxTitle As String
Global strModuleName As String
Global strPrompt As String
Global strShellName As String
Global strTitleBar As String

' ----- Module Declarations
Const MACRO_TITLE = "Underground Automation Routine"
Const pjSave = 1
Const VERSION_NUMBER_LOCAL = "1.0"


' ------------------------------------------------------------------
' Purpose:  Emulate our traditional "DDE routine" procedure using
'           OLE Automation.
'
' Updated: 12/5/94
' ------------------------------------------------------------------
```

```
Public Sub sOLEAutoRoutine()
    ' ----- Declarations
    Dim intAppStatus As Integer
    Dim intFileStatus As Integer
    ' "OA" for "OLE Automation"
    Dim objOAServer As Object
    Dim strOAServerName As String
    Dim strSourceFileName As String
    Dim vntData As Variant
    ' ----- Main body
    strDboxTitle = "Underground OLEAuto Routine 1.0"
    ' ----- Case where Excel is the server
    ' strModuleName = EXCEL5_MODULE_NAME
    ' strOAServerName = EXCEL5_OLEAUTO_NAME
    ' strShellName = EXCEL5_SHELL_NAME
    ' strSourceFileName = "C:\OLEDDE2\CUSTOM.XLS"
    ' ----- Case where Project is the server
    strModuleName = PROJECT4_MODULE_NAME
    strOAServerName = PROJECT4_OLEAUTO_NAME
    strShellName = PROJECT4_SHELL_NAME
    strSourceFileName = "D:\DATA\TUGOLE\EXAMPLES\CUSTOM.MPP"
    ' ----- Case where Word is the server
    ' strModuleName = WORD6_MODULE_NAME
    ' strOAServerName = WORD6_OLEAUTO_NAME
    ' strShellName = WORD6_SHELL_NAME
    ' strSourceFileName = "D:\DATA\WINWORD\DOCS\DUMMY1.DOC"
    ' get host's current title bar
    strTitleBar = fstrGetHostTitleBar()
    ' ----- Determine app's loaded status and react accordingly
    intAppStatus = fintOAAppLoad(objOAServer, strOAServerName, _
        strModuleName)
    If intAppStatus = 0 Then
        strPrompt = "Could not connect to " & strOAServerName & "."
        MsgBox strPrompt, vbInformation, strDboxTitle
        Exit Sub
    End If
    ' fintOAAppLoad() not responsible for app's display state
    If strOAServerName = WORD6_OLEAUTO_NAME And intAppStatus = 2 Then
        ' hide server only if it's Word 6 *and* only if we loaded it
        objOAServer.AppHide
    End If
    ' ----- Determine file's loaded status and react accordingly
    intFileStatus = fintOAFileStatus(objOAServer, strShellName, _
            strSourceFileName)
    If intFileStatus = 0 Then
        ' file open error, problem, or a bogus filename
        AppActivate strTitleBar
        strPrompt = "The file " & strSourceFileName & _
            " cannot be found."
```

```
        MsgBox strPrompt, vbInformation, strDboxTitle
        sOAShutDownApp objOAServer, strShellName, intAppStatus
        Exit Sub
End If
' no problems with the file, so continue
' ----- Interact with the server and its objects
' proceed differently depending on the OLEAuto server
' -----------------------------------------------------------------
' ----- Put your OLEAuto commands below (examples follow)
Select Case strShellName
    Case EXCEL5_SHELL_NAME
        strPrompt = "A1's formula is:  " & _
            Chr(13) & String(2, Chr(10))
        vntData = objOAServer.Sheets("CUSTOM").Range("A1").Formula
        AppActivate strTitleBar
        strPrompt = strPrompt & vntData
        MsgBox strPrompt, vbOKOnly, strDboxTitle
    Case PROJECT4_SHELL_NAME
        strPrompt = "Task 1's name is:  " & _
            Chr(13) & String(2, Chr(10))
        vntData = objOAServer.ActiveProject.Tasks(1).Name
        AppActivate strTitleBar
        strPrompt = strPrompt & vntData
        MsgBox strPrompt, vbOKOnly, strDboxTitle
    Case WORD6_SHELL_NAME
        strPrompt = "Bookmark contents is:  " & _
            Chr(13) & String(2, Chr(10))
        vntData = objOAServer.[GetBookmark$]("Bookmark1")
        AppActivate strTitleBar
        strPrompt = strPrompt & vntData
        MsgBox strPrompt, vbOKOnly, strDboxTitle
    Case Else
End Select
' ----- Put your own OLEAuto commands above
' -----------------------------------------------------------------
' ----- Shut down application if appropriate (always de-reference)
' close the file *only* if we opened it
If intFileStatus = 2 Then
    ' proceed differently depending on the OLEAuto server
    Select Case strShellName
        ' in *all* cases if we've opened >1 file,
        '    be sure to guarantee focus is on this specific one
        Case EXCEL5_SHELL_NAME
            objOAServer.ActiveWorkbook.Close SaveChanges:=True
        Case PROJECT4_SHELL_NAME
            ' pjSave = save then close
            objOAServer.FileClose Save:=pjSave, NoAuto:=True
```

```
        Case WORD6_SHELL_NAME
            ' 1 = save then close
            objOAServer.FileClose 1
        Case Else
    End Select
End If
sOAShutDownApp objOAServer, strShellName, intAppStatus
Exit Sub
ErrorTrap:
AppActivate strTitleBar
Select Case Err
    ' Case ... provide other Case statements here as you see fit
    Case Else
        strPrompt = "OLEAuto routine encountered " & _
            "error number" & Str(Err) & "."
End Select
MsgBox strPrompt, vbExclamation, strDboxTitle
End Sub
```

If you try to run the utility now, without having completed all the numbered steps at the beginning of this section, the utility will fail because you haven't typed in all the procedures yet.

The fintOAAppLoad() Procedure

> Opportunity knocked. My doorman threw him out.
>
> Adrienne E. Gusoff

This procedure's primary responsibility is to load an application if it isn't already running, connect to it if it is already running, and return a value indicating the final status either way. It uses the Windows API call GetModuleHandle to determine if the application's already running. If it is already running then `CreateObject()` is the function of choice; if it isn't already running then in the special case of Excel as a server we use `GetObject()` in a form where the pathname argument is omitted entirely but the comma argument separator is provided. We decided exactly which `CreateObject()` or `GetObject()` form to use based on the material presented in Chapter 7.

You might wonder why we provide separate Case blocks even when one or more of the potential servers use the same `CreateObject()` or `GetObject()` form. We figure Microsoft will eventually iron out the idiosyncrasies of these two functions, but until then we want to leave the architecture of this procedure open to provide for any fine-tuning that might be warranted until OLE Automation matures. This procedure's error checking makes sure the module name isn't null and that the server class name is not bogus. Finally, if there's any type of OLEAuto error when setting the object variable, this is also trapped.

Always be prepared.

```
' -------------------------------------------------------------------
' Purpose:   Uses OLE Automation to load an application if it isn't
'            already running, connect to it if it is already running,
'            and returns an integer indicating final status either way.
'
' Inputs:    objOAServer - pointer to the server
'            strOAServerName - the server's top-level class name, for
'            example, "Excel.Application" for Excel 5
'            strModuleName - the server's module name
'
' Returns:   An integer where ...
'            0 = error
'            1 = was already loaded
'            2 = was *not* already loaded
'
' Updated:   12/4/94
' -------------------------------------------------------------------
Public Function fintOAAppLoad(objOAServer As Object, strOAServerName As
String, strModuleName As String) As Integer
    ' ----- Main body
    If strModuleName = "" Then
        ' don't allow null to be processed
        fintOAAppLoad = 0
        Exit Function
    End If
    On Error Resume Next
    If GetModuleHandle(strModuleName) = 0 Then
        ' the Module name is not found (app is not already running)
        Select Case strOAServerName
            Case EXCEL5_OLEAUTO_NAME
                Set objOAServer = CreateObject(strOAServerName)
            Case PROJECT4_OLEAUTO_NAME
                Set objOAServer = CreateObject(strOAServerName)
            Case WORD6_OLEAUTO_NAME
                Set objOAServer = CreateObject(strOAServerName)
            Case Else
                ' reject any other server class name passed by caller
                fintOAAppLoad = 0
                Exit Function
        End Select
        ' make sure there were no OLEAuto errors
        If Err = 0 Then
            fintOAAppLoad = 2
        Else
            fintOAAppLoad = 0
        End If
    Else
        ' the Module name is found (app is already running)
```

```
    Select Case strOAServerName
        Case EXCEL5_OLEAUTO_NAME
            Set objOAServer = GetObject(, strOAServerName)
        Case PROJECT4_OLEAUTO_NAME
            Set objOAServer = CreateObject(strOAServerName)
        Case WORD6_OLEAUTO_NAME
            Set objOAServer = CreateObject(strOAServerName)
        Case Else
            ' reject any other server class name passed by caller
            fintOAAppLoad = 0
            Exit Function
    End Select
    ' make sure there were no OLEAuto errors
    If Err = 0 Then
        fintOAAppLoad = 1
    Else
        fintOAAppLoad = 0
    End If
    End If
End Function
```

The fintOAFileStatus() Procedure

> It's time to open your parachute when cars look as big as ants. If ants look
> as big as cars, you've waited too long.
>
> Ernst Luposchainsky III

This procedure determines whether or not the file of interest is open. It in turn
calls `sOAGetOpenFiles()` to get a list of all the server's open files. If the file of
interest isn't in the list, the procedure opens it. If the file is already open, this
procedure makes sure the file has the focus in preparation for any subsequent file
interaction in the OLEAuto session. If you prefer to segregate the process of
focusing a particular file as a separate procedure, that's fine with us.

When you try to brute-force activate a hidden window via VBA (without first
unhiding it), Excel and Project balk with a run-time error. Nonetheless, in this
function for simplicity we assume that the source file is not hidden. If you want to
roll your own version that handles this unusual circumstance, go for it!

Annoyingly, each OLEAuto server in our triumvirate has different syntax for
opening a file. Excel's Workbook object uses a method called Open. Project's
Application object uses a method called FileOpen, ditto for Word's Basic object,
but of course the arguments are all different, as we observed earlier when discussing opening files. Gaak.

Error checking includes trapping if the file doesn't exist where the caller says
it is and making sure that the server's file open process was successful.

Syntax potholes, again

```
' --------------------------------------------------------------------
' Purpose:   Determines if a file is already open. This function
'            assumes you've already Set a valid object variable.
'
' Inputs:    objOAServer - pointer to the server
'            strShellName - server's shell name
'            strSourceFileName - source filename (s/b fully qualified)
'
' Returns:   Integer where ...
'            0 = bogus filename
'            1 = already open
'            2 = we opened it successfully
'            3 = filename is OK but the file open method failed
'
' Updated: 12/20/94
' --------------------------------------------------------------------
Public Function fintOAFileStatus(objOAServer As Object, strShellName As
String, strSourceFileName As String) As Integer
    ' ----- Declarations
    Dim blnFileOpen As Boolean
    Dim i As Integer
    Dim strFileNames() As String
    Dim strTemp As String
    ' ----- Main body
    sOAGetOpenFiles objOAServer, strShellName, strFileNames()
    If strFileNames(0) <> "" Then
        For i = LBound(strFileNames) To UBound(strFileNames)
            If InStr(UCase(strFileNames(i)), _
                UCase(strSourceFileName)) <> 0 Then
                strPrompt = "The file " & _
                    strSourceFileName & " is already open."
                Application.StatusBar = strPrompt
                fintOAFileStatus = 1
                ' force focus to this specific file's window
                Select Case strShellName
                    Case EXCEL5_SHELL_NAME
                        strTemp = _
                            fstrFileNameFromPath(strSourceFileName)
                        objOAServer.Workbooks(strTemp).Activate
                    Case PROJECT4_SHELL_NAME
                        strTemp = _
                            fstrFileNameFromPath(strSourceFileName)
                        objOAServer.Projects(strTemp).Activate
                    Case WORD6_SHELL_NAME
                        ' for Word, strFileNames() is in window# order
                        '   (just add 1)
                        objOAServer.WindowList i + 1
                    Case Else
                End Select
```

```
                Application.StatusBar = ""
                Exit Function
            End If
        Next i
    End If
    ' target file is not currently open
    strPrompt = "I'm looking for the file " & _
        strSourceFileName & ", I'll be done shortly..."
    Application.StatusBar = strPrompt
    ' test if target file exists
    If Dir(strSourceFileName) = "" Then
        ' target file does not exist
        fintOAFileStatus = 0
        Application.StatusBar = ""
        Exit Function
    End If
    strPrompt = "I'm opening the file " & _
        strSourceFileName & ", I'll be done shortly..."
    Application.StatusBar = strPrompt
    ' proceed differently depending on the OLEAuto server
    Select Case strShellName
        Case EXCEL5_SHELL_NAME
            ' assignment form produces 440...
            objOAServer.Workbooks.Open Filename:=strSourceFileName, _
                Editable:=True
            blnFileOpen = True   ' ...so capriciously set the flag true
        Case PROJECT4_SHELL_NAME
            blnFileOpen = objOAServer.FileOpen(Name:= _
                strSourceFileName, NoAuto:=True)
        Case WORD6_SHELL_NAME
            ' can't directly capture failure/success of Word's method
            objOAServer.FileOpen strSourceFileName
            blnFileOpen = True
        Case Else
    End Select
    If Not blnFileOpen Then
        ' the file open process failed somehow
        fintOAFileStatus = 3
    Else
        ' the file open process succeeded
        fintOAFileStatus = 2
        strPrompt = strSourceFileName & " is now open."
        Application.StatusBar = strPrompt
    End If
    Application.StatusBar = ""
End Function
```

The sOAGetOpenFiles() Procedure

> If you're lost in the woods, start playing solitaire with a pack of cards.
> Someone is sure to show up and tell you to put the red jack on the black
> queen.
>
> Unknown

Roll your own open files list. This procedure emulates the form of DDE's `DDERequest()` function call that uses the Topics item key word. In DDE, the ability to get a list of the server's open files comes for free, but in OLE Automation you have to write it yourself; thus, this procedure was born.

The source code for this procedure was listed earlier in this chapter so it isn't repeated here.

The sOAShutDownApp() Procedure

> Life is pleasant. Death is peaceful. It's the transition that's troublesome.
>
> Isaac Asimov

This procedure assumes the server contains no open files or that if it does, they've all been saved. If the server was loaded before we came along, then it leaves it running. If we loaded the server, then we're going to shut it down. Excel and Project's Application objects both support the standard Quit method. Wayward Word doesn't (hell, it doesn't even support its own FileExit method), so the hoops we jump through are to trap Word's title bar then issue an AppClose on Word itself using that same title bar string. Hey, it works. (As we mentioned earlier in the book, in case Windows gremlins are wont to modify your parent application title bar strings—God forbid—you can use Vince Chen's API-based title bar sniffer solution instead. See Chapter 9.)

Always Set your OLEAuto object variables to Nothing on the way out. Notice that the server object variable is explicitly Set to Nothing on the way out of this procedure. Very important. Error checking handles any errors that occur as a result of Quit or AppClose.

You could convert this procedure from a subroutine to a function if you experience lots of shut-down errors. The function form could report these errors via an error sub-type return value.

```
' -----------------------------------------------------------------------
' Purpose:   Shut down the OLE Automation server.
'
' Inputs:    objOAServer - pointer to the server
'            strShellName - server's shell name
'            intAppStatus - app's loaded status (see fintOAAppLoad())
'
```

```
' Updated: 12/5/94
' -----------------------------------------------------------------
Public Sub sOAShutDownApp(objOAServer As Object, strShellName As
String, intAppStatus As Integer)
    If intAppStatus = 1 Then
        ' was already loaded so leave it alone
        Exit Sub
    End If
    ' trap any error caused by the Quit method
    On Error GoTo ErrorTrap
    strPrompt = "I am closing the application " & _
        strShellName & " now, I'll be done shortly..."
    Application.StatusBar = strPrompt
    ' proceed differently depending on the OLEAuto server
    Select Case strShellName
        Case EXCEL5_SHELL_NAME
            objOAServer.Quit
        Case PROJECT4_SHELL_NAME
            objOAServer.Quit
        Case WORD6_SHELL_NAME
            If objOAServer.CountWindows() <> 0 Then
                If objOAServer.DocMaximize() = -1 Then
                    strTitleBar = "Microsoft Word - " & _
                        objOAServer.[WindowName$]()
                Else
                    strTitleBar = "Microsoft Word"
                End If
            Else
                strTitleBar = "Microsoft Word"
            End If
            objOAServer.AppClose strTitleBar
        Case Else
    End Select
    Set objOAServer = Nothing
    Application.StatusBar = ""
    Exit Sub
ErrorTrap:
    AppActivate strTitleBar
    Application.StatusBar = ""
    Select Case Err
        ' Case ... provide other Case statements here as you see fit
        Case Else
            strPrompt = "sOAShutDownApp() encountered " & _
                "error number" & Str(Err) & "."
    End Select
    MsgBox strPrompt, vbExclamation, strDboxTitle
End Sub
```

The fvntOAFileNames() Procedure

> A self-made man may prefer a self-made name.
>
> Judge Learned Hand
> (On permitting Samuel Goldfish to change his name to Samuel Goldwyn)

Consistent object models make for reusable, common procedures.

This function works for either Excel or Project as the server. The function's one argument is an object variable that points to the collection that contains the server application's file objects. In Excel it's the Workbooks collection and in Project it's the Projects collection. Since both collections support the Count and FullName properties, the same function can be used. This is an example of how a well-structured, consistent object model can result in reusable, common procedures. We hate to point out the ants at the picnic, but this function's very elegance reveals how non-standard Word's object model is. We confess that this application-independent function effectively replaces the Excel-specific `fvntWorkbookNames()` function from Chapter 5.

```vb
' -------------------------------------------------------------------
' Purpose:   Provide an array of the full names (path plus 8.3 name)
'            of all open (hidden and unhidden) files in the server.
'
' Inputs:    objCollection - points to server's collection of "file"
'            objects (in Excel, it's the Workbooks collection; in
'            Project it's the Projects collection)
'
' Returns:   Variant.
'
' Updated: 12/11/94
' -------------------------------------------------------------------
Public Function fvntOAFileNames(objCollection As Object) As Variant
    ' ----- Declarations
    Dim i As Integer
    Dim strTemp() As String
    Dim file As Object
    ' ----- Main body
    If objCollection.Count <> 0 Then
        ReDim strTemp(objCollection.Count - 1)
        i = 0
        For Each file In objCollection
            strTemp(i) = file.FullName
            i = i + 1
        Next file
    Else
        ' handle case where count is 0 (don't allow ReDim to -1)
        ReDim strTemp(0)
    End If
    fvntOAFileNames = strTemp()
End Function
```

The fstrFileNameFromPath() General Purpose Procedure

> More than any other time in history, mankind faces a crossroads. One
> path leads to despair and utter hopelessness. The other, to total extinc-
> tion. Let us pray we have the wisdom to choose correctly.
>
> Woody Allen
> *Side Effects,* 1980

This general-purpose function strips the 8.3 filename portion out of a fully qualified filename.

```
Global Const DIR_SEP = "\"


' ----------------------------------------------------------------
' Purpose:   Strips the 8.3 filename from a fully qualifed filename.
'            Returns a zero-length string if no "\" is found.
'
' Inputs:    strSourceFileName - the fully qualified filename
'
' Returns:   String.
'
' Updated:   12/21/94
' ----------------------------------------------------------------
Public Function fstrFileNameFromPath(strSourceFileName As String) As
String
    Dim i As Integer
    For i = Len(strSourceFileName) To 1 Step -1
        If Mid(strSourceFileName, i, 1) = DIR_SEP Then
            Exit For
        End If
    Next i
    If i = 0 Then
        fstrFileNameFromPath = strSourceFileName
    Else
        fstrFileNameFromPath = Right(strSourceFileName, _
            Len(strSourceFileName) - i)
    End If
End Function
```

The fstrGetHostTitleBar() General Purpose Procedure

> Names are not always what they seem. The common Welsh name
> Bzjxxllwcp is pronounced Jackson.
>
> Mark Twain

This general-purpose function grabs the client application's current title bar
string.

```
Global intRC As Integer

' ----------------------------------------------------------------
' Purpose:  Get host application's current title bar.
'
' Inputs:   None.
'
' Returns:  String.
'
' Updated: 12/9/94
' ----------------------------------------------------------------
Public Function fstrGetHostTitleBar() As String
    Dim strTitleBar As String
    strTitleBar = String(255, 0)
    hWnd = GetActiveWindow
    intRC = GetWindowText(hWnd, strTitleBar, Len(strTitleBar))
    strTitleBar = Left(strTitleBar, intRC)
    fstrGetHostTitleBar = strTitleBar
End Function
```

Putting It to the Test

> What, sir, would you make a ship sail against the wind and currents by
> lighting a bonfire under her deck? I pray you excuse me. I have no time to
> listen to such nonsense.
>
> Napoleon Bonaparte
> (Speaking to Robert Fulton)

It's testing time!

1. Throughout `sOLEAutoRoutine`, comment out all initializations that refer to
   Excel in the "Case where Excel is the server" section, if they aren't already. We
   assume here that Excel is the client in your first test.

2. Throughout `sOLEAutoRoutine` in Excel, pick either Project or Word as the
   target server, un-remark all initializations that refer to the target application,
   and comment out all initializations that refer to the other application.

3. Calibrate your chosen server's target file. For example, make sure the filename
   variable for the target file points to a valid directory and filename, and so on.
   Of course, you may want to test these out-of-bounds, error-producing conditions. The baton's in your hands now, maestro. Play on.

4. Run `sOLEAutoRoutine`.

Now let's look at the steps for porting this utility from Excel VBA to Project VBA.

1. Use the clipboard to copy the contents of Excel's modules over to Project.

2. Throughout modOLEAutoRoutine in Project, comment out all Application.StatusBar references because Project doesn't support the StatusBar property. (Tip: use a module-wide Edit / Replace.)

3. Throughout sOLEAutoRoutine in Project, comment out all initializations that refer to Project in the "Case where Project is the server" section.

4. Throughout sOLEAutoRoutine in Project, pick either Excel or Word as the target server, un-remark all initializations that refer to the target application, and comment out all initializations that refer to the other application.

5. Run sOLEAutoRoutine.

Although having to comment out all references to StatusBar is annoying, it's encouraging to see how relatively painless it is to migrate code from one VBA client to another.

Cairo, we're waiting….

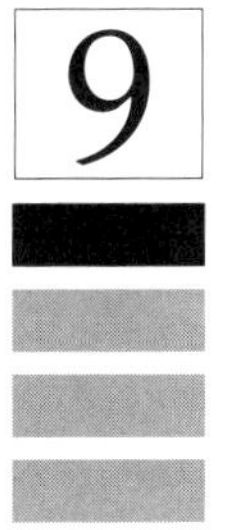

Dynamic Data Exchange— Microsoft's Redheaded Stepchild

> We did not know how to make the theory fit experiment. It was our judgment, however, that the beauty of the idea alone merited attention.
>
> Chen Ning Yang
> *The Second Creation: Makers of the Revolution in 20th Century Physics*, 1985

Dynamic Data Exchange, more commonly known as DDE, is the precursor to OLE. It provided the first communications protocol that allowed two applications to talk to each other under Windows. When this first came out it was like magic, really way cool stuff from the Redmond Wizards.

But alas, DDE has fallen from favor and is being subsumed into the OLE protocol, which provides not only linking but embedding as well. OLE Automation will eventually bring about DDE's complete and total demise as it provides a more structured way for one application to talk to and control another program.

DDE on hard times

Ah, but not all programs support OLE Automation yet. If you want to build something in Word, for example, that is going to manipulate Excel, you've got to use DDE. Say you have a name and address list in Excel and you want to search it from Word so you can plunk an address into a letter document. It's DDE or bust. Maybe the WordGods will give us VBA and all that it entails in Word 7, but until then it can't hurt to have some facts about DDE on hand. Since we sized up OLE Automation vis-à-vis DDE back in Chapter 8, you may find it helpful to flip back and forth as you work through this chapter.

DA FUNDAMENTALS

> Basic research is what I'm doing when I don't know what I'm doing.
>
> Wernher Von Braun
> A rocket scientist

In broad terms, here's what you'll probably be doing with DDE.

- Establishing permanent and intelligent links between two applications regarding one or more specific data items.

- Maintaining links between applications programmatically.

- Executing commands in a remote application where either the remote or supporting program doesn't support OLE Automation

Client-server: A Data Relationship

> —I came to Casablanca for the waters.
> —But we're in the middle of the desert!
> —I was misinformed.
>
> Humphrey Bogart and Claude Rains
> *Casablanca,* 1942

In the context of DDE, the terms "client" and "server" take on a specific meaning. A DDE client is the application that initiates and controls a DDE conversation with another application. Think of the client as the requester of some information. Like the guy on the late show in the black topcoat sneering, "Ve haff vays of making you talk."

Scotty, I want answers!   A DDE server is the application that sits there with the bright lights shining in its eyes being forced to respond to the DDE inquiries and instructions from the sinister DDE client. It's like the scene when Major Strasser converses with Rick. The Major asks the questions, Rick responds, the topic of conversation is who gets out of Casablanca, and the letters of transit are the item in question. Now that was drama.

Data Unit Hierarchy: Application, Topic, Item

> Up the airy mountain
> Down the rushy glen,
> We daren't go a-hunting
> For fear of little men.
>
> William Allingham (1824-1889)
> *The Fairies*

The data structure of a DDE conversation is technically represented by a three-level "data unit hierarchy." This somewhat unwieldy phrase is a technical way of describing the fact that a DDE conversation occurs between applications, is about a particular topic, and involves the exchange of specific data items. Thus the hierarchy—application, topic, and item.

The syntax of a reference to a specific data item is

```
Application|Topic!Item
```

Sounds simple enough right? Well, the issue (you knew that there'd be an issue, didn't you?) is that the way you put these three things together differs from application to application. The appropriate syntax for Word, Excel, and Visual Basic DDE commands is discussed a little later. This is the biggest failing of DDE. Every ISV that implemented DDE in an application did it a little differently. Ah, don't despair, just remember that no matter how weird it gets you really only have to deal with three things: the Application, the Topic, and the Item.

Application

An application, in this context, is a Windows application that supports DDE. For example, Microsoft Access, Excel, Project, Visual Basic, and Word all support DDE.

Topic

A topic is typically the file name of a specific document. For example, `C:\DATA\WINWORD\SALES.XLS` is a valid topic for an Excel workbook. In some applications a topic is an application-specific string. As in a conversation between two people, a topic is equivalent to the subject under discussion.

Item

An item is a specific data element. For example, an item could be a cell value, bookmark value, table, range, graphic object, picture, and so on contained within a document (the topic) of an application. Continuing with the human conversation analogy, an item is like a specific word, phrase, or idea exchanged between the two conversationalists.

System: A Special Topic

System is a topic used to allow the client to gather some critical information about what's going on with the server when the conversation is initiated.

Once a DDE conversation has begun on the System topic, several "items" are available to provide information about the server: SysItems, Topics, and Formats, among others. What's that? Did we just say "Topics" is an item you can converse about using the topic System. Yup, that's what we said all right. There is an *item* called Topics which is not a *topic* but an *item*. Oy, is it any wonder that something has to replace DDE? Anyway, Topics is a very useful item in that it generally

Who did you say was on first?

returns a tab-delimited list of the filenames of all currently open documents, enabling you to find out if the document you are interested in is already open or needs to be opened. We say "generally" because you are at the mercy of how the server application was programmed. As an example of a non-filename list, when you tickle Program Manager's DDE fancy it returns a list of all available Program Groups or all Program Items in a given Group. Fortunately the applications in Office Professional (with the exception of PowerPoint that does not support DDE) plus Project return the list of open files on the Topics item.

Application developers are encouraged to support the System topic as a convenient way for other applications to examine the status of their application as it is running. Some developers do and some do not. There is a lot of trial and error when you deal with DDE.

DDE Messages and Commands

MARTIANS BUILD TWO IMMENSE CANALS IN TWO YEARS.

New York Times, August 27, 1911

DDE, I command thee! A DDE conversation is an exchange of messages between "windows" in each participating application. We enclose the term "windows" in quotes to bring your attention to the fact that these DDE windows—unlike the application, document, and child windows you are accustomed to seeing on your screen—are hidden or cloaked windows used only for handling DDE messages. Lots of stuff happenin' behind the screens with DDE.

If you are interested in the C code nuts and bolts of the DDE messaging protocol, read Charles Petzold's definitive textbook *Programming Windows*. Our objective is to present material at an application level rather than at the C code level, so we will leave out references to messages like Acknowledge, Advise, and Unadvise. Onward!

INITIATE

An Initiate message is sent by a client to a server to indicate that the client wants to start a DDE conversation. It's like Word picking up the phone, calling Excel, and saying, "Hey, Excel, let's chat."

REQUEST

A Request message is sent by a client requesting a one-time data transfer from the server. The conversation has been previously established (via an Initiate message), the topic is now chosen, and an item of information is now requested.

POKE

A Poke message is unsolicited data sent by a client application to a server. Sorta like, "Here, take this!"

EXECUTE

An Execute message is a string sent by the client application representing commands to be executed by the server. This is what OLE Automation does (and in a much more straightforward manner). With DDE you enter a morass of quote marks within brackets, within parentheses, within literal quote marks, within ... you get the idea?

TERMINATE

A Terminate message is sent by either the client or the server to terminate a DDE conversation. Like in real life where either party can just slam down the phone thereby bringing the conversation to a screeching halt.

The Channel

> Good evening, Mr. and Mrs. America, and all the ships at sea.
>
> Walter Winchell

A DDE conversation between a specific client-server application pair is assigned a channel, represented by a numeric value. Assigning a unique channel value to each inter-application communication avoids the chaos that would occur if multiple conversations were to all take place simultaneously on the same channel. The channel number simply serves to identify a specific conversation. Imagine a nightmare where your old high school sweetheart is on line 1 and your spouse is on line 2. Now you wouldn't want to get *those* lines of communications crossed now, would you?

To demonstrate, here is a quick DDE programming exercise you can do in WordBasic where Word, as client, communicates and establishes a channel with Excel, as server.

1. In Word, select Tools Macro, type in WhatsMyNumber for the macro name, then choose the Create button.

2. Type in the following macro:

```
Sub Main
    SysChanNum = DDEInitiate("Excel", "System")
    MsgBox Str$(SysChanNum)
    DDETerminate SysChanNum
End Sub
```

3. Start the macro by clicking on the Start button.

**WordBasic
Start Button**

Whoa! Almost forgot to mention that this example assumes that you have Excel running *before* you try to initiate a conversation with it from Word. In a later example you'll see how to properly check to see if the application you want to chat with is running or not and how to start it, if necessary, using the Shell statement. Oh, and Excel lets you hang out a "do not disturb" sign which prevents *any* DDE conversations from taking place. If you keep getting a "cannot initiate link" message, check Excel's Tools / Options / General filecard, and make sure the Ignore Other Applications check box is not checked.

If the channel is established, you get back a non-zero value. If the channel is not established, you get back zero for the channel number. This sample code fires up a channel between Word and Excel, shows you the channel number in a message box, and once you clear the message box it terminates the channel. You need to get into the habit of terminating your conversations when you're done, otherwise the channel stays open sucking up system resources. You don't lay the phone down without hanging it up when you're done talking to someone, do you? If you want to see the channel number increment, just remark out the DDETerminate statement and run the macro a few times.

This is not to say that you can't have multiple conversations all going on at once. The DDE protocol can handle multiple simultaneous conversations just fine. Although there may be circumstances in which having, say, ten or more ongoing conversations would be desirable, these are probably few and far between. Each DDE conversation takes up memory and system resources. There are no hard and fast rules about this, but at some point you're going to go belly up, system-wise that is, if you get too much going on at one time.

Conclusion: be prudent in the number of DDE conversations you start; terminate any conversation as soon as the transaction is complete; always trap for errors; and be mindful of the system-level factors that could affect your application when it starts running (number of and type of applications already running, which effectively determine available memory and systems resources). The resource issue extends to automatic links you have established between applications via the paste-link methodologies discussed in earlier chapters. Each of these links maintain an open channel and depletes system resources.

DDE COMMAND SYNTAX

> Genghis was really pretty much misunderstood. He didn't have what you would call good people skills. Many's the time I told him, "Khan, it's not what you say, it's the bloody way you say it that gets you into these scrapes."
>
> Amok Shing, Mongol
> *My Years in the Horde* (from the modern translation by K. Tibet, 1972)

Using DDE in your macros can be a daunting task. Particularly confounding is the inconsistent command syntax across different applications. Let's examine the DDE command syntax using three of the most exemplary applications—Word, Excel, and Visual Basic.

How to say it in Word, Excel, and Visual Basic

The Word for Windows Way

> You've got to walk it like you talk it or you'll lose the beat.
>
> Anonymous

Word's implementation of DDE commands is straightforward. In WordBasic the suffix dollar sign ($) character denotes string variables and string functions. See Table 9.1.

Table 9.1 Word's DDE Command Syntax

Message	Description	WordBasic Syntax
INITIATE	Sent by a client to a server, indicating that the client wants to start a DDE conversation.	`Channel = DDEInitiate("App", "Topic")`
REQUEST	Sent by a client requesting a one-time data transfer from the server.	`A$ = DDERequest$(Channel, "Item")`
POKE	Unsolicited data sent by a client app to a server.	`DDEPoke Channel, "Item", "Data"`
EXECUTE	A string sent by client app representing commands to be executed by the server.	`DDEExecute Channel, "Command"`
TERMINATE	Sent by either client or server to terminate a DDE conversation. WordBasic's DDETerminateAll closes all open channels and should be used carefully.	`DDETerminate Channel` `DDETerminateAll`

In the Terminate row, notice that WordBasic has a command lacking in both Excel and Visual Basic—DDETerminateAll. Since this command closes all open

TerminateAll— handle with care.

channels in which Word is the client (it does *not* affect any link fields present, however), no matter what state any individual conversation is in, you should use it with caution.

The Two Faces of Excel

> This is the circus of Dr. Lao,
> he show you things that you don't know.
> He spare no feelings, he spare no dough,
> but man he sure gives you one hell of a show.
>
> Tony Randall
> *The Seven Faces of Dr. Lao*

Excel, at present, has a split personality. You can program in Excel using either the new wunderkind VBA or the older (but still has a following) XLM macro language. Tables 9.2 and 9.3 show you the syntax for both.

Table 9.2 Excel VBA's DDE Command Syntax

Message	Description	Excel VBA Syntax
INITIATE	Sent by a client to a server, indicating that the client wants to start a DDE conversation.	`object.DDEInitiate(app, topic)`
REQUEST	Sent by a client requesting a one-time data transfer from the server.	`object.DDERequest(channel, item)`
POKE	Unsolicited data sent by a client app to a server.	`object.DDEPoke(channel, item, data)`
EXECUTE	A string sent by client app representing commands to be executed by the server.	`object.DDEExecute(channel, string)`
TERMINATE	Sent by either client or server to terminate a DDE conversation.	`object.DDETerminate(channel)`

Table 9.3 Excel XLM's DDE Command Syntax

Message	Description	Excel XLM Syntax
INITIATE	Sent by a client to a server, indicating that the client wants to start a DDE conversation.	`=INITIATE("App","Topic")`
REQUEST	Sent by a client requesting a one-time data transfer from the server.	`=REQUEST(Channel,"Item")`
POKE	Unsolicited data sent by a client app to a server.	`=POKE(Channel,"Item","Data")`
EXECUTE	A string sent by client app representing commands to be executed by the server.	`=EXECUTE(Channel,"Command")`
TERMINATE	Sent by either client or server to terminate a DDE conversation.	`=TERMINATE(Channel)`

Visual Basic and DDE

> "Listen, three eyes," he said, "don't you try to out weird me, I get stranger things than you free with my breakfast cereal."
>
> Zaphod Beeblebrox
> Douglas Adams, *Restaurant at the End of the Universe*

Okay, so far we have resisted getting into any discussion of Visual Basic because after having to deal with OLE in myriad forms as well as the new implementation of VBA we figured you've suffered enough. But this was just too strange to pass up. For example, in Visual Basic you need three lines of code to initiate a DDE session. And like Word prefaces each DDE command with "DDE," Visual Basic prefaces each command with "Link." Wild. See Table 9.4.

The missing Link prefix

Visual Basic's command syntax differs significantly from that of various Office application's macro languages due to the nature of Visual Basic's form-based coding environment. For details refer to *Microsoft Visual Basic Programmer's Guide*.

Table 9.4 DDE Command and Visual Basic's Syntax

Message	Description	Visual Basic Syntax
INITIATE	Sent by a client to a server, indicating that the client wants to start a DDE conversation.	`[form.][control.]LinkTopic = "Application|Topic"` `[form.][control.]LinkItem = "Item"` `[form.][control.]LinkMode = Mode`
REQUEST	Sent by a client requesting a one-time data transfer from the server.	`control.LinkRequest`
POKE	Unsolicited data sent by a client app to a server.	`control.LinkPoke`
EXECUTE	A string sent by client app representing commands to be executed by the server.	`control.LinkExecute "Command"`
TERMINATE	Sent by either client or server to terminate a DDE conversation.	`[form.][control.]LinkMode = 0`

Passing Command Strings with DDE

> I never said I had no idea about most of the things you said I said I had
> no idea about.
>
> Elliott Abrams
> Iran-Contra hearings, June 3, 1987

Each application handles DDE command strings in a slightly different way. Which is a lot like saying that while cardiac catheterization and a three-cushion bank shot are both complicated procedures, they are performed "in slightly different ways." Oh yeah!

Typically command strings are sent across the channel enclosed in square brackets. Excel, for example, supports multiple commands within the same string, like this.

```
[OPEN("SALES1.XLS")] [SAVE()] [QUIT()]
```

The square
bracket's
connected to
the double-
quotes....

The preceding commands open the specified worksheet, save it, and close Excel. Other applications may not support sending multiple contiguous commands. You may have to make each command a separate DDE Execute statement. For example, the following code snippet in WordBasic starts a conversation with Excel, opens a specific file (notice the path and filename are provided), and then maximizes the workbook window.

```
Sub Main
    Q$ = Chr$(34)
    SysChanNum = DDEInitiate("Excel", "System")
    DDEExecute SysChanNum, "[OPEN(" + Q$ + "C:\PCG.XLS" + Q$ + ")]"
    DDEExecute SysChanNum, "[WINDOW.MAXIMIZE()]"
    DDETerminate SysChanNum
End Sub
```

Here's what'll make you crazy when working with DDE command strings. Notice the Open command inside the square brackets. The square brackets are themselves inside double quotes. Then the fully qualified filename is inside double quotes and is in turn nested inside what are called literal quote marks (the Q$ variable). Confused? Aren't we all. The literal double quote shows how a double quote is passed through the channel so that Excel gets it, literally. All the actual quotes get stripped out when Word processes the statement. You might also make a note that in WordBasic you use the "+" symbol to concatenate strings as opposed to the ampersand "&" symbol that you see in the VBA code examples throughout this book. Actually, VBA can use the "+" symbol to concatenate as well as the "&" symbol, but the VBA documentation says you should use the "&" to concatenate and the "+" to add two values together to "eliminate ambiguity and provide self-documenting code." Take it for what it's worth.

A DDE Routine for All Occasions

> Your client is a poor, rejected stepchild, whose best friends are dwarfs.
> Can you insure her against poisoned apples?
>
> Continental Insurance Company
> Advertisement

This code demonstrates all the inter-application communication techniques you'll need to use if you do anything serious with DDE. Again, we're using Word as the client and Excel as the server. It assumes you have a workbook, `CUSTOM.XLS`, in a specific directory, `C:\DEMO`.

Another thing you need to be aware of is that you'll have far fewer problems if you have the applications you want to talk to on the path. Shell can be used with a fully qualified path, but trust us and put the proper directory in your path statement.

You'll notice in the sample code that we go to a lot of trouble to keep track of the title bar text of both the server and client applications. The AppActivate command allows you to switch the focus between applications, but you have to know the title bar text of the application you are switching to. What makes that an issue is that you can't be sure that the title bar text has not been changed via the

SetWindowText API function. Will Excel's title bar read "Microsoft Excel" or "Big John Bootie's Amazing Spreadsheet"? So we jump through some hoops to capture the title bar text so that we can jump the focus back and forth as needed.

Why, you may ask, do you need to move the focus around? Good question. Executing commands or shelling an application leaves the focus in that application so you need to bring the focus back to Word. We have also found that in the "c" maintenance release of Word and Excel you need to place the focus on Excel before you DDEExecute a command like [OPEN()]or [QUIT()] to it. Why? Dunno. We've used this routine in our classes for years and never had to focus on a server before DDEExecuting to it then, bang, we upgrade to Word 6.0c and Excel 5.0c and everything falls apart. Doesn't inspire too much confidence, does it?

```
' ----------------------------------------------------------------
' Purpose:  A DDE session manager from Word using Excel as server.
'
' Located:   DDE.DOT:DDERoutine
'
' Updated:   11/19/94
' ----------------------------------------------------------------
Declare Function GetModuleHandle Lib "kernel"(name$) As Integer
Declare Function GetActiveWindow Lib "User" As Integer
Declare Function GetWindowText Lib "User"(hWnd As Integer,
CurrWindowText$, MaxChars As Integer) As Integer
Declare Function FindWindow Lib "User"(lpClassName As String,
lpWindowName As Long) As Integer

Dim Shared IconAttention    ' declare global variables
Dim Shared Q$
Dim Shared SysChanNum
Dim Shared ClientTitlebar$
Dim Shared ServerTitlebar$
Dim Shared ClassName$
Dim Shared MaxCharsToGet

Sub MAIN
    On Error Goto ErrorTrap
    Debug = - 1                ' initialize Debug = 0 for distribution
    IconInformation = 64       ' MsgBox icon constant
    IconAttention = 48
    IconStop = 16
    ModuleName$ = "EXCEL"      ' substitute server's module name here
    Q$ = Chr$(34)
    ShellName$ = "EXCEL"       ' substitute server's shell name here
    ClassName$ = "XLMAIN"      ' substitute server's class name here
    ShortTopic$ = "[CUSTOM.XLS]CUSTOM"
    SourceFileName$ = "C:\DATA\CUSTOM.XLS"' fully qualified filename
```

```
    TrimAmount = 1
    If Debug Then
        DDETerminateAll
    End If
    ' capture Word's title bar text to ClientTitlebar$
    hWnd = GetActiveWindow
    MaxCharsToGet = 255
    NumChars = GetWindowText(hWnd, ClientTitlebar$, MaxCharsToGet)
    AppStatus = fAppLoad(ModuleName$, ShellName$)
    If AppStatus <> 0 Then
        SysChanNum = DDEInitiate(ShellName$, "SYSTEM")
    Else
        MsgBox "Could not load application " + \
            ShellName$ + ".", IconInformation
        Goto EndMacro
    End If
    If fDDEFileStatus(ShellName$, SourceFileName$, ShortTopic$) Then
        ' PUT YOUR OWN DDE COMMANDS HERE, AN EXAMPLE FOLLOWS
        ChanNum = DDEInitiate(ShellName$, ShortTopic$)
        Data$ = DDERequest$(ChanNum, "R1C1") ' Get contents of cell A1
        Data$ = Left$(Data$, Len(Data$) - TrimAmount) ' Trim xtra chars
        MsgBox "Requested item is " + Q$ + Data$ + Q$
        DDETerminate ChanNum    ' terminate file-topic conversation
    Else
        MsgBox "The file " + SourceFileName$ + \
            " cannot be found.", IconInformation
    End If
    sShutDownApp(SysChanNum, ShellName$, AppStatus)
    Goto EndMacro
ErrorTrap:
    Select Case Err
     Case 500
      Temp$ = "Cannot initiate link to server " + ShellName$ + ". " + \
            "The server's EXE file may have been renamed or relocated."
     Case Else
      Temp$ = "Error number" + Str$(Err) + "."
    End Select
    MsgBox Temp$, IconStop
EndMacro:
End Sub


' -----------------------------------------------------------------
' Purpose:   Loads an application if it isn't already running, leaves
'            it alone if it is already running, and returns an integer
'            indicating final status either way.
'
' Inputs:    ModuleName$ - the target app's module name
'            ShellName$ - the target app's shell name
'
```

```
' Returns:   An integer where ...
'              0 = error
'              1 = was already loaded
'              2 = was *not* already loaded
'
' Updated:   11/19/94
' ------------------------------------------------------------------
Function fAppLoad(ModuleName$, ShellName$)
If ModuleName$ = ""  Or ShellName$ = "" Then
        fAppLoad = 0
    ElseIf GetModuleHandle(ModuleName$) = 0 Then'Module name not found
        Print "I'm loading the application " + ShellName$ + \
            ", I'll be done shortly..."
        Shell ShellName$, 0        ' shell the app minimized
        ' capture Excel's title text to ServerTitlebar$
        hWnd = GetActiveWindow
        sGetServerTitlebar(hWnd)
        AppActivate ClientTitlebar$, 1  ' put the focus back on Word
        fAppLoad = 2
        Print ""
    Else
        fAppLoad = 1   ' app is already loaded
        ' capture the running version of Excel's title text to
        ' ServerTitlebar$
        hWnd = FindWindow(ClassName$, 0)
        If hWnd <> 0 Then
            sGetServerTitlebar(hWnd)
        End If
        Print "The application " + ShellName$ + " is already loaded."
    End If
    Print ""
End Function


' ------------------------------------------------------------------
' Purpose:   Determine if a particular file is currently loaded in the
'            server app. This function assumes you've already started a
'            valid conversation on SysChanNum.
'
' Inputs:    ShellName$ - the target app's shell name
'            SourceFileName$ - the target app's source file
'            ShortTopic$ - special case for Excel 5
'
' Returns:   Boolcan (0 or -1).
'
' Updated:   11/19/94
' ------------------------------------------------------------------
Function fDDEFileStatus(ShellName$, SourceFileName$, ShortTopic$)
    Data$ = DDERequest$(SysChanNum, "TOPICS")
```

```
    If InStr(UCase$(Data$), UCase$(ShortTopic$)) = 0 Then
        Print "I'm looking for the file " + SourceFileName$ + \
            ", I'll be done shortly..."
        If Files$(SourceFileName$) = "" Then ' test topic file exists
            fDDEFileStatus = 0
            Goto EndFunction
        End If
        Print "I'm opening the file " + SourceFileName$ + \
            ", I'll be done shortly..."
        AppActivate ServerTitlebar$, 1
        DDEExecute SysChanNum, "[OPEN(" + Q$ + \
            SourceFileName$ + Q$ + ")]"
        ' update server titlebar as opened file may be maximized
        hWnd = GetActiveWindow
        sGetServerTitlebar(hWnd)
        AppActivate ClientTitlebar$, 1
        fDDEFileStatus = - 1
        Print SourceFileName$ + " is now open."
    Else
        fDDEFileStatus = - 1
        Print "The file " + SourceFileName$ + " is already open."
    End If
EndFunction:
Print ""
End Function


' -----------------------------------------------------------------
' Purpose:  Use DDEExecute commands to shut down a DDE-invoked app.
'           Assumes that Channel is valid.
'
' Inputs:   Channel - the channel # for DDEExecute commands
'           ShellName$ - the target app's shell name
'           AppStatus - see fAppLoad()
'
' Updated:  11/19/94
' -----------------------------------------------------------------
Sub sShutDownApp(Channel, ShellName$, AppStatus)
    ButtonDefaultTwo = 256    ' make No the default
    ButtonYesNo = 4
    IconQuestion = 32
    If AppStatus = 1 Then     ' was already loaded
        Answer = MsgBox("The application " + ShellName$ + \
            " was running prior to your request. " + \
            "Do you want to close it now?", \
            ButtonYesNo + IconQuestion + ButtonDefaultTwo)
        If Answer = 0 Then    ' user answered No
            Goto EndSub
        End If
    End If
```

```
        On Error Goto ErrorTrap  ' trap any error caused by QUIT
        Print "I am closing the application " + ShellName$ + \
            " now, I'll be done shortly..."
        AppActivate ServerTitlebar$, 1
        DDEExecute Channel, "[QUIT()]"
        AppActivate ClientTitlebar$, 1
        Goto EndSub
ErrorTrap:
    If Err = 502 Then       ' Err 502 is "Application does not respond"
        MsgBox "Word reports it has shut down " + \
            ShellName$, IconAttention
    Else
        MsgBox "Error number" + Str$(Err) + " has occurred.", \
            IconAttention
    End If
    ' at this point, things may have degraded beyond hope so forge
    ' ahead w/ normal error trapping
    On Error Goto 0
EndSub:
    Print "The DDERoutine utility is now complete."
End Sub


' --------------------------------------------------------------------
' Purpose:  Grab the server application's title bar as ServerTitlebar$.
'
' Inputs:   The hWnd to the server Window.
'
' Updated:  12/13/94
' --------------------------------------------------------------------
Sub sGetServerTitlebar(hWnd)
    NumChars = GetWindowText(hWnd, ServerTitlebar$, MaxCharsToGet)
End Sub
```

Assistance and Augmentation —OLÉ

> Captain, it is I—Ensign Pulver—and I just threw your stinking palm tree
> overboard. Now, what's all this crud about no movie tonight?
>
> Jack Lemmon
> *Mr. Roberts*, 1955

Tame the raging OLE bull.

"Toro, toro" you say as you're staring down that raging integration bull. Your fingers fly across the keyboard, the data appears as if by magic. The links update, application A jumps through the flaming hoop at the direction of application B, *the crowd jumps to its feet and yells, OLÉ, OLÉ!*

Nice fantasy, huh? Still, if you've made it this far, you have a pretty fair map of the shortcuts and pitfalls that await explorers of the powerful technologies we discuss in this tome. Your transformation into a full-fledged integration warrior is almost complete. Let's just kit you up with some additional ammunition. Oh, and keep in mind the universal rule of TANSTAAFL.* Most of this stuff costs money, but no pain, no gain.

DO IT YOURSELF REFERENCE STUFF

> The Library of Alexandria was fabulous. All the knowledge of the world
> at our fingertips. We sacked it.
>
> Amok Shing, Mongol
> *My Years in the Horde* (from the modern translation by K. Tibet, 1972)

We've mentioned some of the reference materials that we as developers and users of this cutting edge technology avail ourselves of, and here we'll tell you a little more about them and how you can make them your very own.

*There Ain't No Such Thing As A Free Lunch.

Microsoft TechNet and the Knowledge Base

> ...knowledge which produces not dogmatic certitude but diagnostic skill,
> not clairvoyance but insight.
>
> Arthur M. Schlesinger, Jr.
> *The Bitter Heritage: Vietnam and American Democracy, 1941–1966,* 1967

Pound for pound, one of the best values around

This is a Microsoft service you subscribe to. For an annual fee of $295 you receive a monthly CD-ROM disk replete with all kinds of stuff like Microsoft press releases, Tech*Ed presentations, information on other Microsoft programs, and some actually useful stuff like the Microsoft Knowledge Base.

The Knowledge Base is a very handy thing to have access to. Ever call Microsoft technical support and have the person on the other end say "hang on a minute while I check something"? The *something* that they are checking is the Knowledge Base. The very same as you get on the TechNet CD-ROM. Hey, you can look it up yourself (and you don't have to wait on hold listening to some wretched, pablum muzak).

The Knowledge Base is vast. Within its seemingly unlimited confines you'll find (broken down by product) application notes, bug lists, jillions of "how to" subject papers, lists of problems and corrected problems, and tons of what the Redmond Rangers call "related information" just to name a few. Megabytes of notes from Microsoft Product Support Services (PSS), those folks who answer the telephone when you call technical support. It is very, very neat. See Figure A.1.

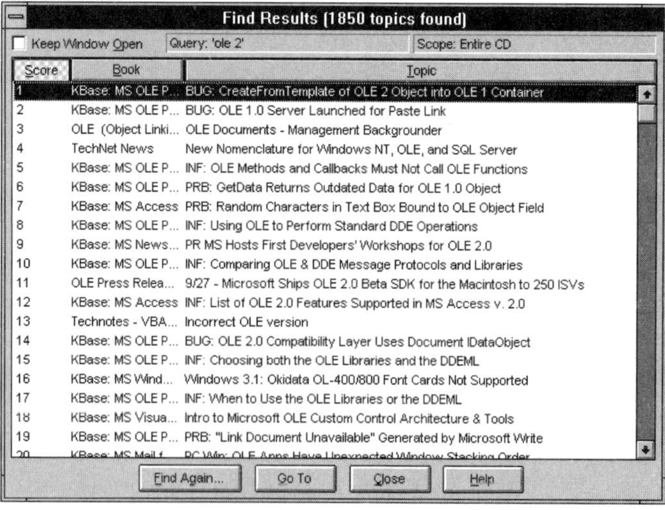

Figure A.1 'OLE 2' Search Yields 1850 Intriguing Hits on TechNet CD.

Oh, and every once in a while the kind folks at TechNet toss in a CD-ROM full of Supplemental Drivers and Patches. It's got drivers (bunches of 'em), patches, sample software, the latest maintenance releases, sample code, technical articles.... About the only thing lacking is a *good* latte mocha.

A grab bag of supplemental goodies

But wait, there's more! The technical resource kits for several Microsoft products are also provided. Whether you subscribe to TechNet or not you can still access the TechNet forum on CIS (GO TECHNET), so you can hob nob with other seekers of wisdom, TechNet subscribers, and Microsoft's own TechNet staff. Call 800-344-2121 and check it out.

The Knowledge Base Without TechNet

> Hey, Rocky! Watch me pull a rabbit out of the hat.
>
> Bullwinkle the Moose
> *The Adventures of Rocky and Bullwinkle*

Several times throughout this book we mention Microsoft Knowledge Base articles by their reference number. If you have TechNet you can look them up, but what if you don't have TechNet (which, after all, costs some bucks)?

Ah, it can be done. One method is to tap into the information superhighway. The Microsoft Network (code named Marvel) has the Knowledge Base on it. This on-line service is not available yet but should be by the time you read this.

Another on-line solution is the ever popular CompuServe Information System (or CI$ to its friends and detractors alike). To get to the Microsoft Knowledge Base articles on CIS, log on and type GO MSKB. From there it's menu driven. You can find the same information on the Internet at ftp.microsoft.com.

If you have neither TechNet nor modem yet know the article number of the Knowledge Base article you want, you can call one of the Microsoft Product Support Services (PSS) numbers (they differ from product to product so consult your documentation) and ask 'em real nice to fax it to you.

Microsoft Developer Network

> The *healthy*, the *strong* individual, is the one who asks for help when he needs it.
>
> Rona Barrett
> *Miss Rona: An Autobiography,* 1974

This is another CD-ROM subscription service available from Microsoft (call 800-759-5454). It has a two-level setup. You can subscribe to Level 1 for $195 a year or Level 2, which will cost you a whopping $495 per year. So what's the bang for the buck? Glad you asked.

Level 1

What you get is a quarterly updated CD-ROM, the *Microsoft Development Library,* which contains a comprehensive compendium of information on developing in the Windows environment.

We're talking the Developer Knowledge Base, technical articles, code samples for C/C++, Access Basic, Visual Basic, and so on, the documentation for the Windows and Win32 Software Development Kits (SDK), C/C++, Visual C, the *Microsoft Office Developer's Kit* (ODK), and more. And the "more" is killer stuff.

20% discount on all Microsoft Press books

Consider that you get the complete text of *Programming Windows 3.1* (Charles Petzold's authoritative work on Windows programming) as well as Kraig Brockschmidt's classic, *Inside OLE 2.0.* You also get tools (several of which we've discussed in earlier chapters), Tech*Ed and WinDev conference white papers, and a 20% discount on Microsoft Press books.

Level 2

If you pop for the big ticket, Level 2, subscription you get all the Level 1 benefits plus the *Microsoft Development Platform.* This is another quarterly updated CD-ROM collection that contains *all* Microsoft operating systems (like Windows, Windows for Workgroups, Windows NT, and so on), *all* SDKs, all DDKs (Device Driver Kits), and any pre-release software not covered by a non-disclosure agreement (yes, there actually is some software that falls into this category).

Office Developer's Kit

> Our blokes might well need all the help they can get. And I really don't think that in this case the standard kit is sufficient.
>
> Alec Kyle
> Brian Lumley—*Vamphyri!: Necroscope II*

The *Microsoft Office Developer's Kit* is a nifty resource. The ODK is comprised of a book for designing and programming integrated solutions, the Object Model Reference Chart (which is way cool), and a CD-ROM. On the CD you'll find the `PJ4CONST.BAS` and `XLCONST.BAS` Visual Basic 3 files that list all the constant declarations in Project and Excel, the Word 6.0 Developer's Kit, and much more. See Figure A.2.

You can get an ODK of your very own by calling 800-426-9400, extension 11771, and the nice Developer Services people will sell you a copy for 100 smackers or so.

Ah, but there are other ways to lay your mitts on the ODK. First, if you have Visual Basic 3 Professional *it comes with it!* Yep, if you have VB3-Pro you already

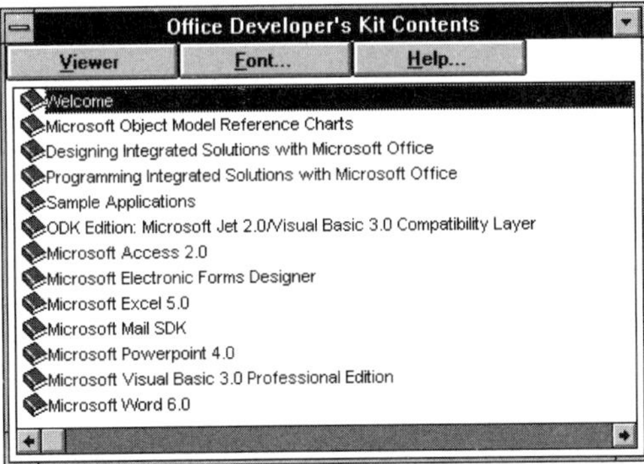

Figure A.2 Just Some of the Material Available on the ODK

have the ODK. If you have an older version of VB3-Pro that did not come with the ODK, just call the 800 number in the preceding paragraph and you can get the ODK for $50. And if you subscribe to MSDN, the ODK is on the MSDN CD-ROM (sheesh, this is acronym hell). You don't get the hard copy components (the book and the Reference Chart), but their components are on the CD.

Inside OLE 2 and *OLE 2 Programmer's Reference*, **Volumes 1 & 2**

> But need alone is not enough to set power free: there must be knowledge.
>
> Ursula K. Le Guin
> *A Wizard of Earthsea*

Now this is mind-bending stuff for hardcore programmer types, so if you don't fall into that category, move on! But if you want the nitty gritty on programming OLE-compliant applications in C or C++, these two books get you off to a solid start.

They are both available through Microsoft Press (and can be found in many bookstores at a discount). To order direct from Microsoft Press, call 800-677-7377. Full price will set you back about $50 for *Inside OLE 2* by Kraig Brockschmidt. The *OLE 2 Programmer's Reference* volumes cost $30 for Volume 1 and $25 for Volume 2.

If you subscribe to MSDN, you'll find Kraig's book on the CD-ROM. Very neat.

WHERE TO GET PROFESSIONAL HELP

> There are two kinds of talents, man-made talent and God-given talent. With man-made talent you have to work very hard. With God-given talent, you just touch it up once in a while.
>
> Pearl Bailey
> *Newsweek*, December 4, 1967

Maybe a CD-ROM doesn't sound like the perfect help source to you. Perhaps you want a real live human being to converse with and to help you with your integration problems. No problem.

PRIME Consulting Group, Inc. 310-318-5212

> When the going gets weird, the weird turn pro.
>
> Hunter S. Thompson
> *The Great American Shark Hunt*

Yep. That's us. We do consulting as a Microsoft Solution Provider, we're both Certified Professionals and Trainers (well, certifiable anyway), and we actually teach classes that focus on this stuff. Give us a call and let's talk about it. We've also written a pair of add-in utility sets for Word and Excel. See the ads in the back of the book.

Directory of Microsoft Solution Providers 800-227-4679

> The wheel of fortune goes 'round and 'round and where she stops nobody knows.
>
> Major Bowes
> *Major Bowes and His Original Amateur Hour*, 1934

This service is provided by Microsoft Corporation. It gives referrals to Microsoft Solution Providers around the world. You tell 'em what you want and where you are and they type in your zip code or some such geographical datum and out pops the lucky winner (or winners, depending on the density of consultants in your neighborhood).

Be prepared for what may well be the world's longest phone-voice menuing system announcement message. Have a cup of coffee on hand. Hey, if you have TechNet or MSDN, you actually get the Solution Provider database so you can save a phone call. Oh, joy of joys!

CompuServe Information Service

> Behind the white coats, the disarming jargon, the elaborate instrumentation, and at the core of what has often seemed an automatic process, one finds what Dorothy found in Oz: modern technology is human after all.
>
> David Noble

An on-ramp to that Information Superhighway If you don't want to pop for a hired gun to help you deal with OLE and OLE Automation in real time, you can go the cyberspace route on the CompuServe Information Service (CIS).

CIS is a great way to get answers to specific questions or to find out the latest news on bugs and workarounds. You can post a question and any of the best and brightest who hang out there may answer your question for free. Several Redmond Rangers monitor the forums discussed in this section, and they work hard at never letting a question go unanswered or a problem unresolved. You may have to wait a day or so, but you sure can't beat the price.

To sign up for a CIS membership, call 800-848-8990.

Go MSOFFICE

There is a forum dedicated to questions on Microsoft Office. Type GO MSOFFICE at any CompuServe prompt and warp (no pun intended) right to it. There are also forums on each Office component (except PowerPoint). You can GO MSEXCEL, GO MSWORD, GO MSACCESS, GO MSDESKTOP (for Project), or GO MSDTAPP to the Microsoft Desktop Applications menu. You can get into the individual application sections from there.

Go PROGMSA

This is the Programming Microsoft Applications forum. There are sections that deal with programming issues for various applications like Word and Excel.

Go MSKB

The Knowledge Base, manna from Redmond.

Go TECHNET

This is the TechNet forum. You do *not* need to be a TechNet subscriber to get access to this forum. Is that Information Superhighway great or what?

Go MSDN

This is the Microsoft Developers Network forum. You do *not* need to be a MSDN subscriber to get access to this forum. On this forum you can search the developer Knowledge Base (which is not the same as the Knowledge Base available on the TechNet CD-ROM and in the MSKB forum).

Go MSL

This is the Microsoft Software Library forum. The hot tip for VBA is to download a file called `WE0993.EXE`. This self-expanding file (you run it and it unzips itself, oh!) contains `XLCONST.XLS`, an Excel workbook that lists all the Excel built-in constants.

Go MSBASIC

This is the forum to go to for Visual Basic information. Lots of sample code and you can usually find someone with a kind word or cool fix when you hit that programming mental block in the wee small hours of the morning. Section 10 is "Using OLE/DDE"; check it out.

Go WINOBJ

Here's one for the C and C++ programming types among you. This is the Windows Objects forum and there are several sections dealing with the myrid aspects of OLE to be found here. Okay, you don't *have* to be a C programmer to find useful stuff on this forum, but it is geared towards the more advanced aspects of objects.

Glossary

Active   Having the focus. For example, if the application Word is running and you are typing text into a Word document, the Word application is the active application.

Adaptable Link   A link that can survive the moving of a directory structure to a new location.

Aggregation   The merging of menu options in a container application when an embedded object is activated for in-place editing.

API   See *Application Programming Interface.*

Application-centric   The current computing paradigm where each data file is "owned" and maintained by a specific application.

Application Programming Interface (API)   From *Microsoft Press Computer Dictionary,* "A set of routines that an application program uses to request and carry out lower-level services performed by a computer's operating system." By common usage, has come to generally refer to any related set of functions and subroutines callable from a procedure.

Bookmark   A Word feature whereby a location within a Word document can be referenced by name. Equivalent to an Excel range name.

Built-in Constant (see also **Constant**)   A constant that is native to the programming language.

Built-in Function   A function that is native to the programming language. The NOW() function is an example of a VBA built-in function.

Cairo   The code name for Microsoft's next generation object-oriented operating system. The holy grail of operating systems.

Chicago   The code name for Microsoft's top-secret attempt to break into the automobile manufacturing industry. Now referred to as Windows 95.

Class Name   The name of a given class of OLE object. For example, Excel.Sheet.5 is the class name for an Excel version 5 worksheet.

Client Application   Often used as a synonym for "destination application," but in this case is best used within the context of a DDE client/server conversation. Within the context of editing an embedded object, refers to the application that contains the object. Note that "client" and "controlling" are synonymous when used in this manner.

COM   See **Component Object Model**.

Component Object Model (COM)   According to the *OLE 2 Programmer's Reference*, "The Component Object Model specifies how objects interact within a single application or between applications."

Compound Document   A data file maintained by a container application and which contains one or more embedded objects.

Compound Files (see also **DocFiles**)   According to Kraig Brockschmidt in *Inside OLE 2*, "[OLE 2's *Structured Storage Model* is a] standard for exactly *where* individual data structures (those defined by the application) are stored *within* a particular file, regardless of the underlying file system. The implementation of this standard is provided in OLE 2 as *Compound Files*. Both will become incorporated into future versions of the Windows operating system…. Compound files implement storage and stream objects on top of the FAT file system under Windows 3.1 and on top of FAT and NTFS under Windows NT."

Constant   A named item the value of which remains unchanged while a given procedure is executed.

Container Application   An application used to create a file that contains links to data in other files or that contains another application's file or files embedded within it.

Controlling Application (a.k.a. Controller)   An application utilizing OLE Automation to control another application via that application's programmable object model.

Data Type   The characteristic of a variable that determines what kind of data it can hold.

Data Typing   Limiting a variable to a given kind of data (string, integer, boolean, and so on) throughout the code's execution.

Data Unit Hierarchy   The application, topic, item structure of a DDE conversation between two applications.

DDE   See **Dynamic Data Exchange**.

Destination Application   The application that presents the source data that belongs to an OLE link. See also **Client Application**.

DocFiles   See **Compound Files**.

Document-centric   A computing paradigm where a document is not created by a single program but by the operating system using various add-in toolsets providing application-like features. *Ka-ching!*

Drag-and-drop   A mouse method whereby the user clicks on an object or data in a document, and while holding down a mouse button drags the data (or a copy thereof) to a new location within the same document, or in a different document, and "drops" the data by releasing the mouse button.

Dynamic Data Exchange (DDE)   An inter-application communications protocol that allows Windows applications to exchange data and control one another remotely.

Editor   An application used to create or edit an embedded data object.

Embedded Object   An object (usually data created and maintained by another application) embedded or contained within the binary data structure of a compound document.

Function   A distinct, named block of source code that returns a value to whatever procedure called it.

Hatched Border   The border placed around an object that has been activated for in-place editing, consisting of short diagonal lines.

Instantiate   To start an *instance* of a program running on a system. Usually used to refer to the starting of an application using OLE Automation or DDE.

General Protection Fault (GPF)   You can think of this message that appears just before your application crashes as a malevolent ex-tooth fairy zapping your system and yelling "Gotcha!"

Global Template   A template in Word that has been loaded in Word's global context layer. Macros in a template loaded globally are available no matter which template or document has the focus.

GPF   See **General Protection Fault**.

In Situ Editing   See **In-place Activation**.

Information-centric   See **Document-centric**.

In-place Activation   Viewing or editing an embedded object using the source application's tools where those tools are made available inside the container application. The menus of the source application merge with the container application's menus. The toolbars for the source application appear, replacing the container application's toolbars.

In-place Editing   See **In-place Activation**.

Integration   The ability to share information and functionality between applications.

Linked Object   A pointer to data that is physically stored outside the document that contains the link.

Macro   Originally used to mean a pre-recorded series of keystrokes but now used to describe a procedure written in an application programming language.

MAPI   See **Messaging Application Program Interface**.

Messaging Application Program Interface (MAPI)   Allows mail-enabled Windows applications to interact with a variety of electronic mail services. Provides a number of APIs that can be accessed programmatically to add email features to various user-created applications.

Method   Capability to act or the result of that act, as performed by a particular object using some underlying code procedure.

Module   In Excel and Project, the storage sheet for user written procedures.

Nested Embedded Object   An object that has been embedded within an object that is itself embedded in a container document. Nested embedded objects can be an arbitrary number of layers deep.

Nested Linked Object   A link to an object that's inside the container document instead of outside of it.

Null Menu Mode   When an application has no open documents it is in "null menu mode"; the menu bar is generally reduced to only the File and Help options.

Object   Take your pick from among thousands of tedious definitions. Here's one of them: An object is a single element that encapsulates both properties (characteristics) and methods (behavior).

Object Linking and Embedding (OLE)   An application programming interface that provides a standard set of object services. See anywhere in Chapters 1 through 9 for more information. It's a big subject.

Object Type Name   A name that describes a programmable (OLE Automation) object within a specific application's object model. Gaak. For example, the object type name for Excel's workbook object is, you guessed it, Workbook. It's typically just that easy, but not always. For example, Excel's object model includes an object called DrawingObjects, a name you can't really guess as easily as something like Workbook. Fear not—all you need to do is look at the ODK's object model cheat sheet, browse around in the application's VBA help file, or use an Object Browser until you find the name of the object you're looking for. Whew.

ODBC   See **Open Database Connectivity**.

OLE   See **Object Linking and Embedding**.

OLE Automation   Programs that support OLE Automation expose their OLE objects thereby making it possible for other applications to control these objects.

Open Database Connectivity (ODBC)   From Microsoft's TechNet CD article *Understanding the ODBC Extensions*, "Open database connectivity (ODBC) is an application programming interface that uses structured query language (SQL) to access and manipulate data in database management systems such as dBASE, Paradox, and Microsoft Access." In other words, it's a transparent (doesn't get in your way too much) vehicle for you to use when trying to get your hands on data locked away in a database somewhere out there in the ether.

Procedure   A distinct, named block of source code, written in a programming language that performs some task.

Programmable Application   An application capable of being controlled by another application via OLE Automation.

Programmable Object   An object that is capable of being manipulated via another application's macro language via OLE Automation.

Programmability   The ability to create a program to perform some useful function, or the ability to control some operation in another program or data file via a program.

Property   A named attribute of an object, defining an object's characteristics (such as size, color, and screen location) or the object's behaviors (for example, whether it is enabled or disabled). A read-only property can be looked at programmatically but not changed, while a read-write property can be examined and changed.

Selected   Placing the focus on something, usually done via the mouse.

Server Application   Often used as a synonym for "source application," but in this case is best used within the context of a DDE client/server conversation. Within the context of editing an embedded or a linked object, refers to the application that created and can act on the object. Note that "server" and "source" are synonymous when used in this manner.

Sizing Handles   Small black squares located around the perimeter of a selected graphic object, used to resize the object via click and drag with the mouse.

Source Application   The application that physically contains and maintains the source data for an OLE link. See also **Server Application**.

System   A special DDE topic used to query an application for information about its current status.

Type Libraries   According to the *OLE Programmer's Reference, Volume 2*, "A type library contains descriptions of a collection of objects."

User-defined Constant (see also **Constant**)   A constant you create that remains static during the execution of a procedure.

User Interface   The on-screen and keyboard/mouse methods whereby an application's user operates a program.

VBA   See **Visual Basic for Applications**.

Visual Basic for Applications (VBA)   Microsoft's common macro language (currently only available in Excel 5 and Project 4). A robust programming language that Microsoft eventually will implement in all its desktop applications.

Visual Editing   See **In-place Activation**.

Index

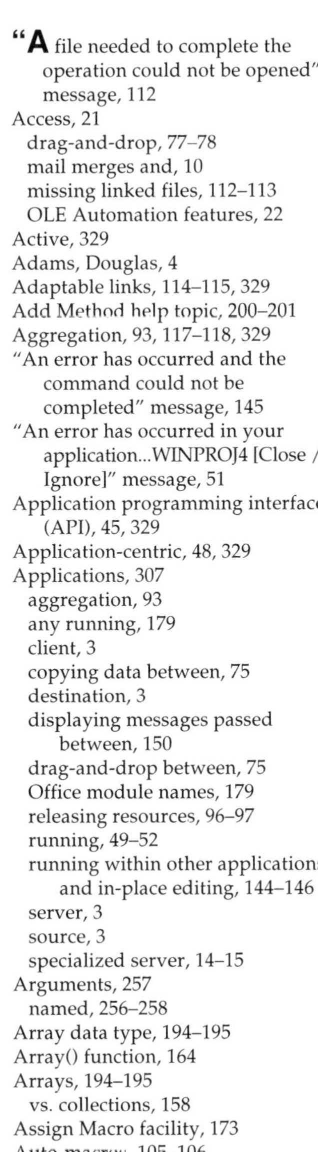

PRIME *Add-ins!*

PRIME 5 for Excel for Windows

Now that you are a member of the Underground, we'd like to tell you about an add-in for Microsoft Excel that you'll want to have. PRIME 5 contains custom toolbars and indispensable utilities, such as *Cell Protection Viewer,* for seeing which cells are locked or unlocked. *Window Assistant,* for one-stop window management. *Name Assistant,* for dealing with range names and named formulas (even hidden names!). *Toolbar Lister,* for inspecting toolbar elements and changing ToolTip text. *Zoomer,* the ultimate zoom control. *ProgMan Icon Generator,* for automatically creating icons in Program Manager for your Excel worksheets. Included with these utilities is the PRIME 5 *API,* more than 40 custom VBA subroutines and functions that you can call from your own Excel macros. (Call 314-965-5630 for information on additional VB3/VBA development spin-off products with a focus on OLE Automation.) List price is $19.95 (plus $4.50 shipping and handling in the USA and Canada; $9.50, all other countries).

PRIME 6 for Word for Windows

The perfect complement to Word 6 includes utilities such as *Fast Spell Checker,* for quicker spell checking with all misspelled words in a document available in a single list. *FileNew,* for complete template management. *AutoText Lister,* for viewing local and global AutoText contents and statistics side-by-side. *Window Manager,* for one-stop window management. *Document Variable Manager,* for adding, viewing, modifying, deleting or cataloging those pesky document variables. *Bookmark Manager,* the definitive utility for dealing with bookmarks. *Zoomer, Macro Manager, Toolbar Lister, ResetChar, ProgMan Icon Generator,* 36 custom WordBasic subroutines and functions, a list of Word and WordBasic bugs and workarounds, et cetera. List price is $39.95 (plus $4.50 shipping and handling in the USA and Canada; $9.50, all other countries).

SPECIAL $5 DISCOUNT FOR *UNDERGROUND* READERS

Place an order and mention that you're an Underground Guide reader to get $5.00 off the list price of either utility set. All our shareware add-in products come with an unlimited, lifetime, no-questions-asked, 100% money-back guarantee. If you don't like it, send it back, and we'll rush you a full refund. We promise. Hacker's honor.

PRIME Consulting Group, Inc.
c/o Advanced Support Group, Inc.
11900 Grant Place
Des Peres, Missouri USA 63131
Voice: 800-788-0787 (314-965-5630 outside North America)
Fax: 314-966-1833 • CompuServe: 70304,3642 or GO WOPR